"This book is excellent. It will be of great help to all those interested in learning more about the Latino market and the Latino population. I myself plan to use it in my classes."

Guillermo Gibens, Ph.D.
Massachusetts College of Liberal Arts
North Adams, MA

"A very good assortment of topics that should enable communication practitioners to better understand and address the U.S. Hispanic market...I am sure it will be useful. There is very little good and thoughtful information out there. This is a great compendium."

Felipe Korzenny, Ph.D.
Professor and Director of the Center
for the Study of Hispanic Marketing
Communication and Cheskin Co-Founder

"The book is written at an appropriate level of understanding for the novice as well as the seasoned practitioner who may not be familiar with this market. It is certainly a book that will offer much to those interested in reaching this growing market in the world."

Virginia Kreimeyer, APR
Major, USAF (Ret.)

"This book is comprehensive, authoritative and very readable. This will be a great reference book for any Hispanic marketer's bookshelf. A great combination of solid statistics and heartfelt essays from a wide variety of experts...a great resource, but also suitable for marketing execs needing a good primer."

Lisa Skriloff
President, Multicultural
Marketing Resources, Inc.

Hispanic Marketing & Public Relations

Understanding and Targeting America's Largest Minority

Edited by Elena del Valle

First Edition

Poyeen Publishing • Boca Raton, Florida

Hispanic Marketing & Public Relations

Understanding and Targeting America's Largest Minority

Edited by Elena del Valle

Published by:

Poyeen Publishing
2901 Clint Moore #265
Boca Raton, Florida 33496

http://www.poyeen.com

ISBN - 1-932534-08-3
LCCN - 2005903630

First Printing 2005
Cover Art by Catgraphix http://www.catgraphix.net

This publication is designed to provide accurate and authoritative information in regard to the subject matter covered. It is sold with the understanding the the publisher is not engaged in rendering legal, accounting, or other professional service. If legal advice or other expert assistance is required, the services of a competent professional person should be sought.

Printing Number
10 9 8 7 6 5 4 3 2

Acknowledgements

As of this writing, it has been more than two years since I began work on this book. From the beginning, dozens of people have encouraged and supported my efforts. Many of them sent letters of support for the project including Hispanic Public Relations Wire, National Multicultural Professional Interest Section of the Public Relations Society of America, Agatha Ogazon Ph.D., *Portada*, Ralph McElroy Translation Company, Valassis, Walters Media Group Inc., Camen's Cupones y Consejos.

I especially want to express my appreciation to all the authors who have given of their expert knowledge and time to contribute a chapter or more (Miguel Gomez Winebrenner wrote two chapters and Federico Subervi was co-author of two chapters) and to Carlos Santiago who wrote the Foreword.

I wish to thank Cristina Ascunce of Catgraphix for the cover design, Gary Cox for his invaluable assistance with charts, graphs and much more, Diana Luger in Chicago, Smilka Valenzuela and Geoscape for their assistance with statistical data and Richard Velez and MASS Promotions, Inc.

Our volunteer reviewers also deserve recognition for their time and input: Lori Billingsly, Senior Vice President, Porter Novelli; Guillermo Gibens, Ph.D. Massachusetts College of Liberal Arts; Felipe Korzenny, Ph.D. Professor and Director of the Center for the Study of Hispanic Marketing Communication and Cheskin Co-Founder; Virginia Kreimeyer, APR Major, USAF (Ret.); Carmen M. Rodriguez, Community Advocate in Northern New Mexico; Lisa Skriloff, President, Multicultural Marketing Resources, Inc., New York City; Mónica Talán, Senior Vice President Fleishman-Hillard.

Companion Website

Please visit the companion website to the book at:

http://www.HispanicMPR.com

Hispanicmpr.com serves as a forum for the exchange of information and ideas on Hispanic marketing and public relations. The web log format provides a way to communicate with the authors of *Hispanic Marketing & Public Relations* and others with an interest in the topic.

Table of Contents

Chapter 10 - Hispanic Public Relations and Its Emergence as an Industry · · · · · · · · · · · 233
Dora O. Tovar, M.P.Aff

Chapter 11 - Latino Media: A Cultural Connection 285
Federico Subervi, Ph.D.
Heidi Eusebio

Chapter 12 - Electronic Publicity and Broadcast Public Relations · 327
David Henry

Table of Figures

Chapter 1 - A Snapshot of the U.S. Hispanic Market

Chapter 2 - Latino Identity & Situational *Latinidad*

Chapter 3 - Beyond Skin Color

Chapter 4 - A Deeper Look into the U.S. Hispanic Market

Chapter 5 - Hispanic Projections

Chapter 6 - Qualitative and Quantitative Research Strategies

Chapter 7 - Segmentation by Level of Acculturation

Chapter 8 - Effective Translations

Chapter 9 - Marketing to U.S. Hispanics Online

Chapter 10 - Hispanic Public Relations and Its Emergence as an Industry

Chapter 11 - Latino Media: A Cultural Connection

Chapter 12 - Electronic Publicity and Broadcast Public Relations

Chapter 13 - Maximizing Public Relations Results with Entertainment

Chapter 14 - Hispanic Public Relations Return on Investment

Chapter 15 - Cultural Understanding Key to Effective Hispanic Media Training

XV

From the Editor

The nineteen authors of *Hispanic Marketing & Public Relations* are professors and practitioners dedicated to their particular specialties. For some, this book represents the first time their experiences are captured in a published work. Without exception, they have taken time from jobs, and sometimes family, to research and write their respective chapters. Many of the chapters are informal in their tone while others are more academically oriented. Each one provides useful, insightful and practical information based on the author(s) many years of experience.

Hispanic Marketing & Public Relations paints a picture in time. The essence of the book is the varied, perceptive and valuable lessons shared by the authors. These were gained through trial and error and years of experience, many of them in the field. Through the numerous graphics, charts and factual data we learn about this growing, often misunderstood and widely coveted market. Through the case studies and how-to snippets we explore the corners of the market and define our interests and needs.

There are academic, marketing, translation services, public relations, research, entertainment, and media experts from across the country. Each author developed his, her or their own chapter independently from the others. As a result there is some duplication of information and there are differences of opinion on objective issues, such as statistics, and subjective aspects of the market. There is at least one notable difference in definition: two separate chapters define and address *Latinidad* and they do so from different perspectives. That is a reflection of the wide-ranging opinions and fact interpretation that exist in the market. There are multiple possible right answers and interpretations, it is up to you, the reader, to identify the information that is relevant and construe it as you see fit.

The use of the terms Latino and Hispanic varies according to author preferences. There is much controversy around these terms, which have diverse connotations across the country. Although there are differences worth noting, there is no universal agreement on their use. For purposes of this book, assume they are interchangeable unless a particular author(s) indicates otherwise in his or her chapter.

My role was to identify and invite select Hispanic market experts to participate as contributing authors. Once the chapter submissions arrived, it was necessary to integrate the individual chapters into a book with a cohesive theme and a sense of unity. In terms of the writing, I only made slight changes to facilitate the reader's understanding. The writing style of each author(s) is their own as is the tone and message. Once the chapters were organized, a dedicated group of volunteers read through the manuscript and shared their comments and suggestions. These were then integrated and the book finalized.

I trust that Hispanic *Marketing & Public Relations* and its companion website http://www.hispanicMPR.com will support your efforts to understand and reach Americas's largest minority effectively.

Sincerely,
Elena del Valle
President
LNA World Communications

Foreword

It is surprising that despite the explosive growth of U.S. Hispanics in the American marketplace, many marketers still misunderstand, and do, so little to adapt their businesses to capture Hispanic loyalties. Indeed, Hispanic marketing has spread in most categories from a few visionary leading companies to a handful of players' intent in deciphering new growth formulas. Yet still, inertia or superficial repetitive theatrics towards correctly marketing to this increasingly sophisticated consumer base, abounds American businesses. Resistance to adapting products, deeply changing infrastructures, strategies and processes, inevitably end-up weakening brands for sustainable growth.

Long-standing self-fulfilling practices towards mining growth from the influential large urban centers are becoming harder and harder to hide under business rugs. Superficial and sub-standard actions towards real growth are now beginning to be scrutinized by CEOs, CMOs and senior decision makers. As cost-cutting or rationalizing that traditional brands consumers bases are disappearing does not cut it anymore, many growth hungry brands are showing that top-line growth can be surgically identified. More and more, industry analysts, investors and obviously Hispanic consumers, readily see through the plethora of "me-too" efforts which are often transparent, disjointed and ineffective "lip service" programs.

Fueling double-digit growth is within the reach of every size unit and region. Over the last twenty years, I have made a career out of leveraging trends and building strong multicultural business units in Fortune 50 organizations. Based on quantitative techniques, my consulting group has partnered with aggressive forward-looking companies, "General Market" strategic firms and ad agencies, to consult for clients determined to find high value sub-segments. Achieved when departments have moved away from silos to fully aligning consumer-centric strategies to create distinct products, culturally-relevant customer experiences and welcoming touch-points, it has proven to accelerate product adoption curves.

As some managers awaken their organizations, they are demonstrating others how to seize the only remaining window of new American consumers. In effect, these confident risk-takers are rapidly evolving businesses as quick as the dynamic Hispanic customer base is evolving. While sticking to fundamental business and marketing principles, Hispanic market leaders have upgraded their processes to reliably identify "low-hanging" to "long-term" opportunities while leveraging core cultural triggers. To attain enduring results, these successful Hispanic marketers are turning away from basic insights to scientific approaches across business disciplines.

My colleagues in this book have shed their "many lights" into the challenge of fully understanding the Hispanic market. In soft-handed ways through their data and case studies, these authors leave up to individual companies to figure out what to do about and how to develop their own corporate Hispanic business strategies to achieve greater success.

- From demonstrating demographic shifts to sub-segments consumer mind-sets
- From mass broadcast approaches to direct response
- From front-lines and brick and mortar channels to dedicated bilingual call centers to online and customer relationship management systems
- From Spanish-only to Bilingual to English only efforts
- From traditional Latin American to bicultural to 'mainstream' American appeals
- From targeting foreign-born recent arrivals all the way to third generation U.S. Born's
- From awareness and brand attributes gap closures to effective cost of new acquisitions
- From influencing purchase behaviors to delighting their experience to eliciting passionate word of mouth
- From California to Texas, New York, and Miami to Nevada and the Carolinas

The featured authors that you will get to know, openly share their vast experiences so that you can

- validate what you already knew
- be smart enough to accept where your organizations doesn't know enough yet
- prevent your cross functional groups from too quickly jumping to dangerous conclusions about what to do next

These selected experts present facts and best business practices from different angles and points of view, showcasing small to large competitors, from truly innovative in-market solutions, to 'tried and proven' formulas. Throughout each fascinating chapter, these Hispanic segment experts intend to disseminate key learnings with you to enlighten and leap-frog your own Hispanic market business disciplines experience curve. Yet, bringing it home, applying what makes best sense to your own role, organization reality and culture, as with every other equally promising strategic pathway, rests only on you. As in all key, but unconventional decisions, it is all up to you to validate, internalize, prioritize, sell bottom-up, secure funding, and pro-actively become a leading change agent. This will ensure that the required actions towards execution become deeply rooted. The tremendous task at hand is one of stepping outside of quarterly targets and committing to the challenges associated with seizing this tremendous opportunity in advance of your competitors.

Whether it is your own company, your career, or just an adventure, your investment on the line, your pension, or this year's performance target towards a cash bonus, the Hispanic market potential represents one common meaning to all readers of this book

- Creating overall incremental economic value and
- Effectively serving the needs of the changing face of the American marketplace and culture.

I hope the contributors of this book help you anticipate opportunities, revisit current tactics and question your organizations current "perceived" departmental solutions. That is, the authors may inspire your organizations' behaviors to move from merely being aware of growth markets to embarking on meaningful strategies for alternative business scenarios. Better yet, I hope their expert advice helps you in leading a paradigm shift for your healthy survival. Challenge your organization to rightfully re-set resource allocations and 360 degree strategies to win growth from the Hispanic consumer and enjoy the lifetime value opportunity they offer.

"Buena suerte" in your upcoming business endeavors!

Carlos Santiago
President
Santiago Solutions Group
January 18, 2005

Chapter One

A Snapshot of the U.S. Hispanic Market

Jonathan R. Ashton
Michele Valdovinos

In This Chapter

- An overview of the U.S. Hispanic market
- General demographics of the Hispanic population
- Key issues such as the role of language, acculturation, media consumption, bilingual packaging, brand loyalty and marketing to Hispanic children

Introduction

The growing Hispanic population in the United States, particularly over the last decade, has awakened a great interest in marketers. However, by no means should this vast group be viewed as homogenous. There are many unique characteristics among Hispanics. They vary depending on the person's country of origin. It is even important to understand the varied use of language. The purpose of this chapter is to paint a broad picture of this culturally diverse group, and help the marketer gain knowledge about some key demographic and behavioral elements and the various micro-cultures that compose the U.S. Hispanic market.

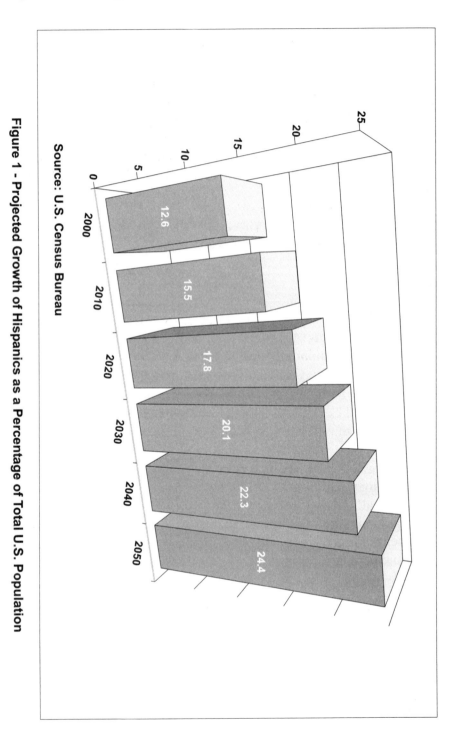

Source: U.S. Census Bureau

Figure 1 - Projected Growth of Hispanics as a Percentage of Total U.S. Population

Hispanic Population Growth

The U.S. Hispanic population is projected to sustain continued growth. Some 37.4 million Hispanics comprised 13.3 percent of the total U.S. population according to a Census population report in March 2002. It is estimated that, as early as 2002, Hispanics had already edged African-Americans as the single largest minority in the U.S. Figure 1 shows a projected estimate that one in five people in the U.S. will be Hispanic by 2030. Further Census estimates show that concurrent with the explosive growth of Hispanics in the U.S., African-Americans will have very slow growth while the non-Hispanic white majority gradually erodes over time. It is important to note that unlike other minorities, Hispanics can be white or black, prompting the Census to add a separate question about Hispanic origin. The vast majority of U.S. Hispanics trace their heritage to twenty countries. Those of Mexican origin comprise 67 percent of the total, followed distantly by Puerto Ricans (9 percent) and Cubans (4 percent). Hispanics tend to concentrate regionally. Mexican populations are often in the Southwest, Puerto Rican populations in New York and Chicago, and most Cubans have made southern Florida home.

Where They Live

Although Hispanics primarily reside in and around large metropolitan areas, they also live with increasing regularity in towns and communities of all sizes throughout the United States. The ten largest metropolitan areas of Hispanic population in descending order appear together in Figure 2 with the approximate percentage of the total U.S. Hispanic population which they comprise (U.S. Census 2000).

Note that these 10 metropolitan areas alone make up about two-thirds of the entire U.S. Hispanic population. Los Angeles is clearly the dominant market with one-fifth of all U.S. Hispanics. Despite Los Angeles' dominance in sheer population, the state of New Mexico has the highest percentage of Hispanics (42 percent) followed by California (32 percent) and Texas (32 percent). The largest concentration of His-

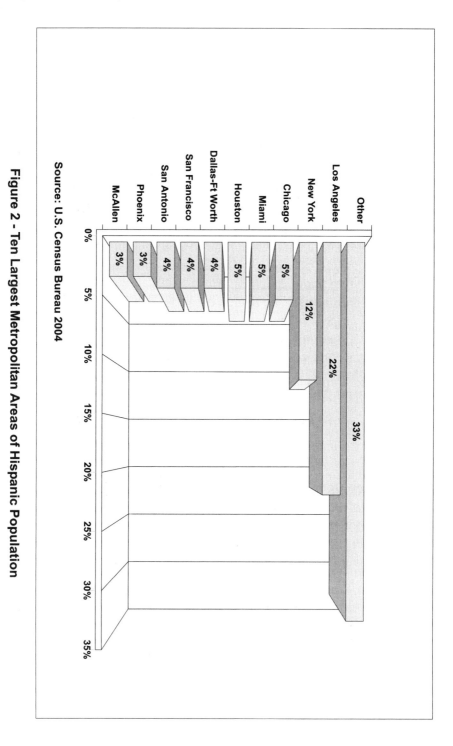

Figure 2 - Ten Largest Metropolitan Areas of Hispanic Population

Source: U.S. Census Bureau 2004

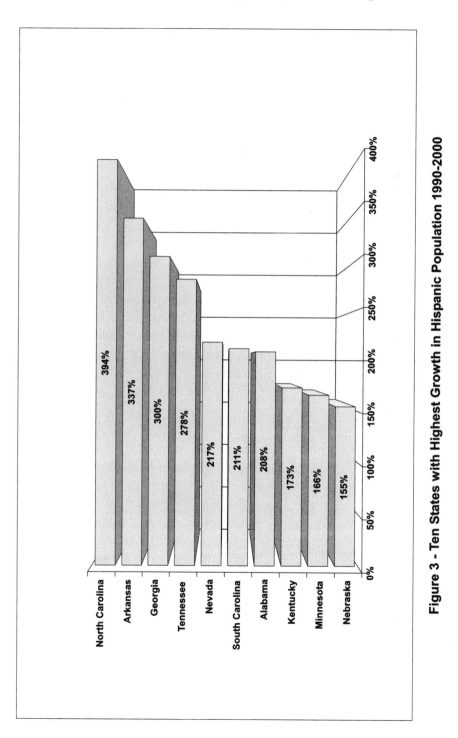

Figure 3 - Ten States with Highest Growth in Hispanic Population 1990-2000

North Carolina 394%
Arkansas 337%
Georgia 300%
Tennessee 278%
Nevada 217%
South Carolina 211%
Alabama 208%
Kentucky 173%
Minnesota 166%
Nebraska 155%

panic residents in a U.S. county is in Starr County, in Texas' Rio Grande Valley (98 percent).

However, Hispanics are no longer solely in large, metropolitan areas. Some of the fastest growing states include those not typically associated with having substantial Hispanic populations. Shown in Figure 3 are the top ten states with the highest rate of growth in the decade 1990-2000 according to the U.S. Census Bureau.

For the most part, the greatest rate of growth is occurring in the southern United States. All indications are that this trend will continue. Additionally, some have called this penetration more rapid than any "previous immigrant wave or internal migration" (Pew Hispanic Center). The Pew study reports that 54 percent of Hispanics now reside in U.S. suburbs. Georgia is particularly interesting because according to a report from the University of Georgia's Selig Center for Economic Growth, the state remains the nation's most attractive African-American consumer market, based on its size, growth rate and concentration. Look for Atlanta to have its own Latino micro-culture flourishing in coming years, just to name one of the newly expanding multi-ethnic markets.

Role of Language

Spanish has become the second most spoken language in the United States; an estimated 28 million people comfortably speak Spanish in this country. Unlike the many languages represented in the Asian American market, Spanish is the dominant language of the Hispanic. We must consider a number of colloquialisms and variations, strongly tied to the country of origin. The same word can have two or three different meanings, depending on the country where they speak it. For example, if you wanted to catch a bus, a Hispanic person might tell you where the nearest *camión, guagua, omnibus,* or *micro* passes by. Each of these alternatives comes from a different country of origin. In addition, to make things even more interesting, a *guagua* (bus in the Caribbean) is a common word for "baby" in Chile (where they use the term *micro* for a bus)!

The existence of large populations of Hispanics concentrated in specific geographies has created virtual countries within a country and helped to perpetuate the Spanish language. Facts on English and Spanish language ability among U.S. Hispanics are limited and often unclear. The U.S. Census 2000 reported that more than 28 million people in the United States spoke Spanish at home and just over half (14.2 million) of these claimed to speak English "very well." That leaves just under half that do not speak it "very well." An earlier study in Los Angeles among U.S.-born, second generation Mexican-Americans (clearly the largest Hispanic group) showed that 12 percent spoke only Spanish or were "Spanish Preferred." Another 26 percent considered themselves bilingual, 33 percent were "English Preferred," and 30 percent English only. In that same study, the vast majority (more than 90 percent) of U.S.-born Hispanics of Mexican origin spoke English fluently.

Hispanics tend to be more likely to emphasize the need for their children to retain Spanish, compared to other immigrant groups. The New Jersey-based Educational Testing Service found "a cultural difference between the Asian and Hispanic parents with respect to having their children maintain their native language." As stated earlier, the sheer size and establishment of mature Hispanic communities has helped to foster fluency of the Spanish language. Although second and third-generation Hispanics gain English skills, they tend to preserve proficiency in Spanish. In short, language is one of the few precious links to their origin that Hispanics desire to pass on to their children. If this is to occur, however, it generally must take place in the home. Once children enter the typically English-dominant public school system, Spanish tends to take a back seat unless diligent parents foster Spanish-language opportunities at home.

Acculturation Process Among U.S. Hispanics

In 2002, two-fifths of U.S. Hispanics were foreign-born. One of the key factors that make Hispanics different from other immigrant populations in U.S. history is their process of acculturation. Where previous waves of immigrants have assimilated into American culture over time, Hispanics experience a different process, one of acculturation.

Acculturation is the process of assimilation by which new immigrants adapt and assume behavioral or attitudinal characteristics from their immigrating country. This process helps them evolve and embrace new customs and traditions that dominate and define the culture of the population. Several factors (environmental or self contained) will help along the process: length of residency in new country, language(s) spoken, social network, place of birth, and where they lived their formative years. Cultural Access Group, a multi-cultural research firm, has developed the following model to help segment the main acculturation groups that exist within the U.S. Latino population:

- Unacculturated – Embrace their own culture and have probably not acquired any characteristics from the new culture
- Partially Unacculturated – Hold most characteristics from their own culture and have acquired a few characteristics from the new culture
- Bicultural – Have balanced their own traditions and customs with the new ones
- Partially Acculturated – Have acquired many characteristics from the new culture and still hold a few of their own culture
- Acculturated – Most resemble the characteristic of the new culture and less likely to resemble their own culture

The reasons Hispanics differ from other immigrants in this process include:

- In language, in-culture media base: for decades, the U.S. has had several television, radio, and print vehicles that provide news and entertainment for Hispanics. These professional organizations have created and sustained a sophisticated Hispanic media industry including a multi-million dollar advertising investment from major U.S. companies as well as local retailers.
- Sustained bi-nationalism: proximity to home countries means Hispanics in the U.S. can and do visit their native land regularly. This phenomenon was not an option for previous waves or even current immigrants originating from other parts of the world. The ability to maintain close, personal communication with their

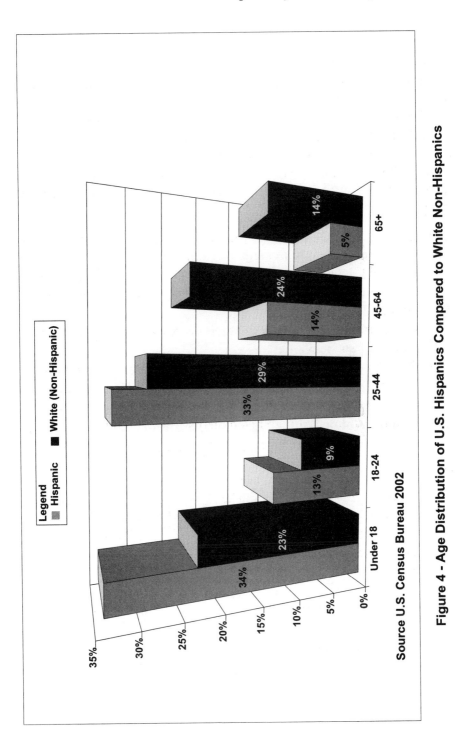

Figure 4 - Age Distribution of U.S. Hispanics Compared to White Non-Hispanics

Source U.S. Census Bureau 2002

Legend
Hispanic
White (Non-Hispanic)

Under 18: 34%, 23%
18-24: 13%, 9%
25-44: 33%, 29%
45-64: 14%, 24%
65+: 5%, 14%

home country means that Hispanics do not have to break their ties and can enjoy the best aspects of both cultures.

• Technology: the Internet connects U.S. Hispanics constantly and immediately with their countries of origin. Years ago, household telephone penetration was low. Now phones, including cellular phones pervade Hispanic households.

With sizeable populations across acculturation segments, marketers are finding there is an ideal target for their products and services within the Hispanic market. While an in-culture approach is always important, Hispanics at different acculturation levels have varying needs and values. Identifying the appropriate group within the population is critical and necessitates measures to analyze the total market with acculturation segmentation in mind.

Age and Gender

Hispanics in the United States are generally younger than the total population. Figure 4 shows the proportion of key age groups for Hispanics compared to white Non-Hispanics according to Census 2000 data. Note the dramatic differences in the youngest and oldest age groups. In terms of marketing, the U.S. Hispanic population is tantalizingly young and impressionable, and gaining in disposable income and buying power.

Overall, the Census shows that the Hispanic population is virtually even between males (51 percent) and females (49 percent). However, an interesting result of explosive growth in newly developing, suburban areas is that males outnumber females by as much as 17 percent (Pew Hispanic Center). This is attributed to men who migrate to developing areas in search of work and have temporarily left their families behind. Many of these men adapt to their new surroundings and then bring their families to these areas, thus contributing to the growth of previously non-Hispanic locales.

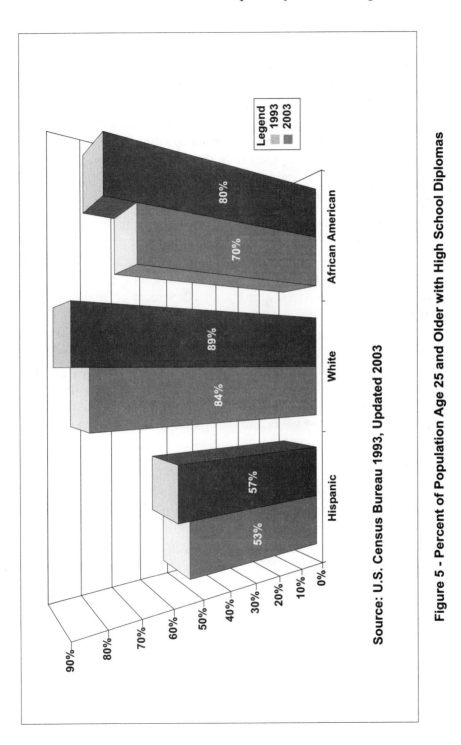

Legend
1993
2003

80%
70%
89%
84%
57%
53%

African American
White
Hispanic

90%
80%
70%
60%
50%
40%
30%
20%
10%
0%

Source: U.S. Census Bureau 1993, Updated 2003

Figure 5 - Percent of Population Age 25 and Older with High School Diplomas

Education

Hispanics currently lag behind both African-Americans and whites in attaining higher education. Hispanics who came to the U.S. from countries where educational opportunities do not abound face the challenge of catching up. They have not traditionally kept pace with their increasing growth and participation in the labor force. Part of the challenge is with language: establishing a foundation of English language ability facilitates most opportunities for education in this country.

It starts in high school, where more than 89 percent of whites age 25 and over had graduated, compared with 80 percent of Blacks and 57 percent of Hispanics, according to Census Bureau data in 2003, and shown in Figure 5. Compare this to 1993 when 84 percent of whites were high school graduates, along with 70 percent of Blacks and 53 percent of Latinos. The gap remains wide for Latinos, especially foreign-born and non-naturalized Hispanics who bypass education to enter the workforce. A product of the tremendous growth in places where researchers were not aware Hispanics had a significant population, as mentioned earlier, is that schools will have to prepare for the influx of Hispanic students and address their unique needs. Big city schools have adapted for years, but the challenge will soon lie in suburban and newly developing areas.

Among Hispanics age 25 or older, educational attainment of high school graduation varies greatly depending on country of origin. Mexican-Americans had the lowest rate in 2002 (51 percent) compared to Cubans (67 percent) and Puerto Ricans (71 percent), for example.

Hispanic Employment

During 2003, the nation's unemployment rate averaged 5.7 percent. The rate among Hispanics (7.7 percent) was higher than the average, but lower than for African-Americans (10.8 percent). Due to sparse educational opportunities in many of their countries of origin, Hispanics come to the U.S. somewhat insecure about their education and prefer a paycheck. They are eager to embrace the physical labor that brings steady income.

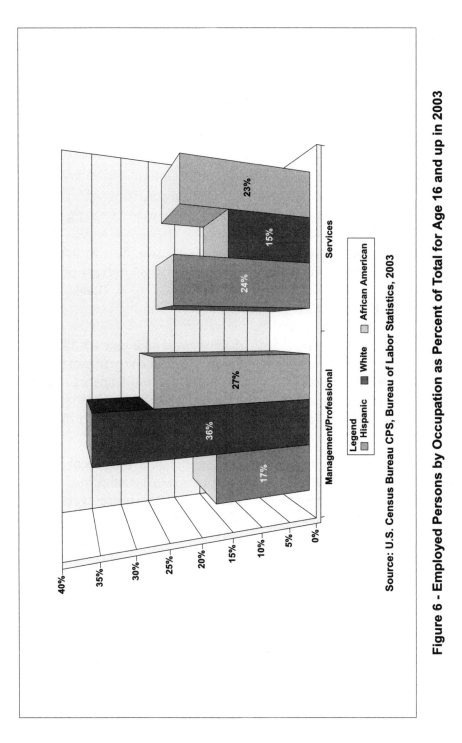

Figure 6 - Employed Persons by Occupation as Percent of Total for Age 16 and up in 2003

Source: U.S. Census Bureau CPS, Bureau of Labor Statistics, 2003

Many Hispanics take jobs in lower-paying, labor-intensive fields. Hispanics' willingness to work in low-wage jobs makes them attractive to industries like construction, agriculture, and services. As seen in Figure 6, Hispanics have significantly fewer managers and professionals compared to whites and African-Americans. There are many more Hispanics than whites in the services sector, but they are at parity with African-Americans.

The powerful combination of Hispanics' willingness to take a job and companies' zeal to hire them results in fewer Hispanics on unemployment rolls. This does not apply to all Hispanics, however. For the same 2003 year reported earlier, Puerto Rican men had a 10.1 percent jobless rate, nearly at par with African-American men, while Cuban men had a far lower jobless rate of 5.9 percent.

Income and Buying Power

Hispanics were more likely than whites and just as likely as African-Americans to be below the established poverty line in Census 2000 data. About one-fourth (26 percent) of Puerto Ricans and 24 percent of Mexicans were below poverty level, while a lower proportion of Central and South Americans and Cubans (17 percent each) lived below the poverty line.

Hispanics' median household income (3-year average 1998-2000) was $31,703, higher than the $28,679 for African-Americans, but far below the $45,514 for non-Hispanic whites. Hispanics' median income, while higher than that of African-Americans, has not seen substantial change between 2002 and 2003. According to Census data, median Hispanic income fell 2.6 percent in that period.

Hispanic households are larger and extended and most employable members of the household contribute income, which drives Hispanic household income. Researchers estimate that four-fifths of Hispanics live in family households compared to 69 percent of non-Hispanics (Census 2000). Over half (56 percent) of Hispanic family households had four or more people. They also estimate that half of Southern California households have at least three income-earners. The individual

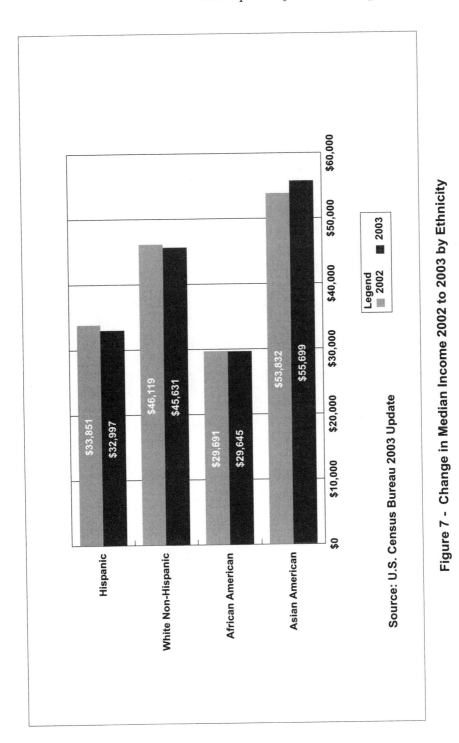

Figure 7 - **Change in Median Income 2002 to 2003 by Ethnicity**

Source: U.S. Census Bureau 2003 Update

Legend
2002
2003

Hispanic $33,851 $32,997

White Non-Hispanic $46,119 $45,631

African American $29,691 $29,645

Asian American $53,832 $55,699

wages may be lower, but these households function like a typical middle-class household with only two incomes.

Home mortgage lenders, for example, may begin to recognize Hispanic families who want to become homeowners and assist them to fix credit problems, examine their credit worthiness as renters, their tendency to be multi-income earning households, and help them move towards home ownership, creating a vast boon to the industry.

Increased buying power from this group derives from its sheer size and growth, as well as the development of Hispanic-owned businesses. Estimates vary, but some estimate U.S. Hispanic buying power now exceeds one-half trillion dollars, based on the Selig Center for Economic Growth at the University of Georgia's estimate of $452 billion as early as 2001. The number of Hispanic-owned companies in the U.S. has climbed steadily from around a half million businesses in 1987 to over 1.5 million currently. That is important because while many of these operations are small, they are growing larger and more numerous. A Hispanic-owned business tends to employ more Hispanics, over time prepares, and moves those workers into better jobs with better wages.

The Selig Center estimated that Hispanic buying power would increase 357 percent from 1990 to 2008 due to this growth and activity. Contrast this increase with the estimated 189 percent increase for African-American buying power in this same period and the major impact Hispanics will have on the economy becomes clear.

Social Life

Understanding Hispanic culture is essential to understanding Hispanics. High on the list of cultural influences are food, music, language, and family ties. Communal events among friends and family are central to their way of life. Birthdays, anniversaries, *quinceañeras* (a party for a 15 year girl), and family reunions are big productions. Unlike some other immigrant groups, Hispanics tend to hold their traditions and language in unusually high esteem and have a great desire to preserve them, even as they assimilate simultaneously into U.S. culture. Hispanics often adopt and adapt U.S. holidays and even "Hispanicize" them.

For example, Thanksgiving might include a turkey dinner embellished with rice and beans.

Politics

Hispanic voters have keen interest in policies ranging from education and health care to immigration and foreign policy. Hispanics, no longer considered an interest group, have begun to shape policy at all levels. According to the Census' 2002 CPS survey, 33 percent of Hispanics of voting age are registered voters. Female Hispanics are more likely to be registered voters than their male counterparts (36 percent versus 29 percent) are. In the 2000 election, the turnout of Hispanic voters (45 percent) was unchanged from the 1996 elections. However, the number of Hispanic voters increased by 20 percent, reflected by the growth in the voting-age and citizen population of Hispanics during that time. Registration rates of voting-age citizens were unchanged for eligible Hispanics.

Hispanics are also entering key political positions across the country and at all levels of politics from local to federal. Henry Cisneros was the first Hispanic mayor of a major U.S. city (San Antonio) and eventually served as Bill Clinton's secretary of Housing and Urban Development. Many more voters elected Hispanics into positions in towns of all sizes around the U.S. The current Democratic governor of New Mexico, Bill Richardson (the nation's only Hispanic governor), was born in Mexico.

In past years, Hispanics voted Democratic. Since 1976, Republican presidential candidates have earned no higher than 37 percent of the Hispanic vote, earned by Ronald Reagan in 1980 and 1984. In the 2000 election, George W. Bush won 35 percent of the Hispanic vote, while Democratic candidate Al Gore earned 62 percent. As Hispanics have continued to grow in number since the last election, this important voting bloc may have affected the 2004 presidential election, just concluded at this writing. According to two exit polls (Edison Media Research/Mitofsky International and CNN), George W. Bush earned between 42 and 44 percent of the Hispanic vote. Consider New Mexico for example; where the population grew by nearly 100,000 Hispanics since the 2000 election and registered Democrats now outnumber Republicans. In the 2000 election, Bush lost by a narrow margin in New Mexico and its five electoral votes went to Gore. In 2004, New Mexico went into Bush's electoral column by a 50 to 49 percent margin.

In a recent survey done by the Pew Hispanic Center in spring 2004 among 1,166 registered Latino voters, some interesting findings showed how active these voters could be in their communities. One-fourth (26 percent) of these registered voters reported having attended a public meeting or demonstration in the past year. Four-fifths are more concerned with U.S. politics than the politics in their countries of origin.

Media Consumption

While the general market struggles with the challenges of diminishing television audiences, the Hispanic television market has given new life to the medium. Spanish-language television has enjoyed increasing viewership to coincide with the growing U.S. Hispanic population. Spanish-language radio stations are the number one rated stations in several large U.S. markets including Los Angeles and Miami, and spreading to some of the smaller, but emerging Hispanic markets. Spanish-language print media is also growing, speared by launches of daily newspapers in several markets.

The Pew Hispanic Center conducted a media survey among 1,316 Hispanics in early 2004 and found that while 31 percent prefer to get news from any media source in English and 24 percent prefer Spanish, most (44 percent) consume a combination of news in both languages, dominated by a preference for television news by far over newspapers and radio.

Compared to their general market counterparts, Hispanics tend to report watching more television, on average. According to Nielsen Media Research, Hispanics watch just over 17 hours of prime-time television per week while the total U.S. household mark is just over 13 hours. Couple that with the explosive growth anticipated for U.S. Hispanics in the coming years, and you can quickly paint a rosy picture for Spanish-language media.

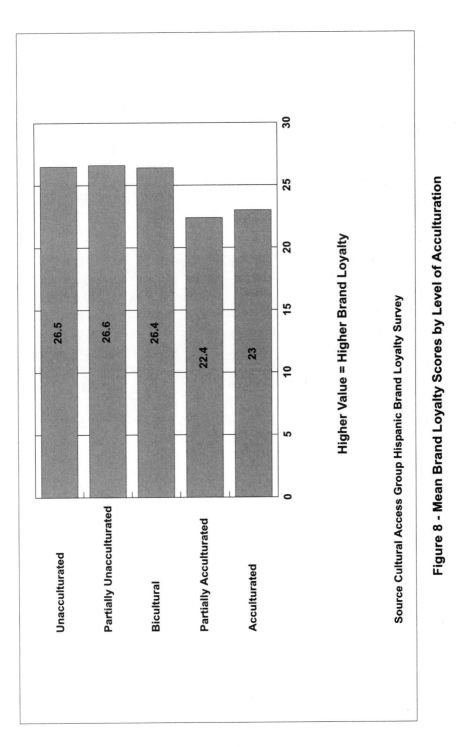

Figure 8 - Mean Brand Loyalty Scores by Level of Acculturation

Source Cultural Access Group Hispanic Brand Loyalty Survey

Higher Value = Higher Brand Loyalty

Unacculturated — 26.5
Partially Unacculturated — 26.6
Bicultural — 26.4
Partially Acculturated — 22.4
Acculturated — 23

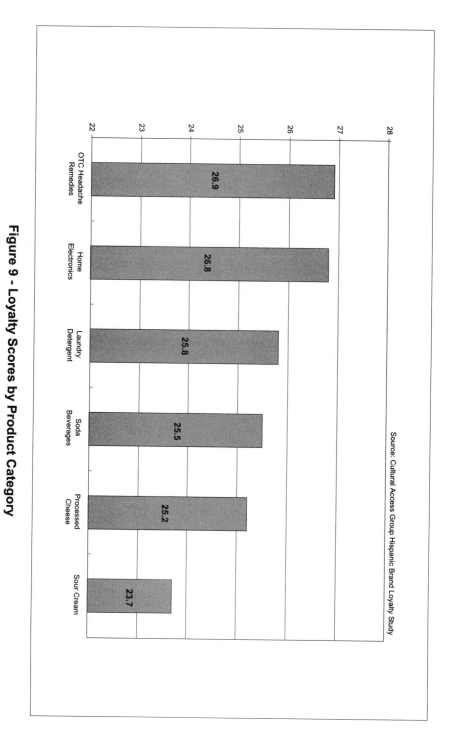

Figure 9 - Loyalty Scores by Product Category

Source: Cultural Access Group Hispanic Brand Loyalty Study

Bilingual Packaging

A Spanish-dominant Hispanic can generally call on a relative to help translate materials in English if needed. The importance of bilingual packaging, goods that are marketed with information in both Spanish and English on the label or package, goes beyond the need for a Hispanic consumer to understand the label or instructions; it makes a statement about the brand that is powerful. For this reason, Hispanics tend to have a positive perception of bilingual packaging. Anecdotally, Hispanics report that the presence of Spanish on a label or package indicates that the manufacturer is sincerely interested in attracting their business and has made a significant investment in products designed for them. It is an indicator of inclusiveness, even for bilingual Hispanics who are capable of reading English.

On another perspective, the presence of English on a label is an assurance that the product meets the important standards for quality regulated in the United States. Thus, packaging that presents both Spanish and English appeals to both the emotional (Spanish) as well as the rational (English) core of U.S. Hispanics. Research has shown the degree to which this holds true varies by product categories, in those that are medical, health-related or otherwise involve a more serious product, English is an important factor for the security and assurance it provides.

Brand Loyalty

One of the enduring myths of the U.S. Hispanic market is that these consumers are more brand loyal than others. Until recently, research to validate or disprove this myth was not readily available. In 2003, a study from Cultural Access Group explored this concept and resulted in some key insights about the different brand loyalty segments within the Hispanic population. The most important finding from the study reveals that brand loyalty among Hispanics is not an absolute; rather it varies by the consumer's acculturation level and varies by product category.

Within the five acculturation segments of the Hispanic population, brand loyalty is at its highest among the unacculturated. Interestingly, the level of affinity remains steady through the partially unacculturated and bicultural segments. It declines significantly in the partially acculturated before gaining somewhat among acculturated Hispanics, as seen in Figure 8. The primary lesson for marketers is that they need to capture the hearts and minds of Hispanic consumers in their early stages because once they begin to acculturate, loyalty drops and new trails begin in earnest. An acculturated Hispanic settles back into a more brand loyal mindset, a critical point of brand behavior.

In addition to the difference seen among acculturation segments, the study found that brand loyalty also varies by product category. Those products considered more serious or important tend to have stronger brand affinity for Hispanics; Hispanics are less willing to experiment in these categories, preferring to stick with the tried and trusted products they already use. Additionally, categories that have a higher price point or where the branded product carries a bit of prestige also see higher than average brand loyalty. Figure 9 shows results for several product categories. Over the counter headache remedies carry a significantly higher loyalty than sour cream, for example.

Marketing to Hispanic Children

Children in the U.S. are increasingly diverse. The U.S. Census reports that among children under age 15, there are more than 11 million children of Hispanic descent making up nearly 30 percent of the total Hispanic population. Among African-Americans, 27 percent of the population is under 15; and among Asians, 21 percent are under 15. In total, more than 40 percent of the overall population of children under age 15 in the U.S. is Asian, Hispanic, and African-American. Clearly, this is a large target market for anyone involved in products, messages, and services directed toward children and their parents.

The current generation of youth is the most diverse generation of any that has come before. Marketing to multicultural children requires a profound and relevant understanding of their lifestyles, attitudes, and behaviors, as well as an appreciation for the cultural differences at the heart of their family and environment. This complexity is at the core of

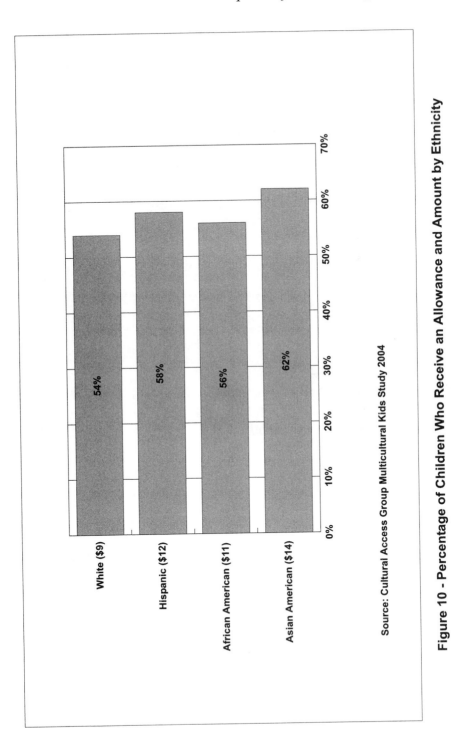

Figure 10 - Percentage of Children Who Receive an Allowance and Amount by Ethnicity

Source: Cultural Access Group Multicultural Kids Study 2004

White ($9) — 54%
Hispanic ($12) — 58%
African American ($11) — 56%
Asian American ($14) — 62%

children' self-perception, self-confidence and self-awareness, and manifests in many ways.

Cultural Access Group's U.S. Multicultural Kids Study 2004 found that one of the ways that cultural values affect children's lives is in their daily activities and roles within the house. For example, despite lower than average household income, Hispanic children received one of the highest amounts of allowance ($12 per week on average) versus children of other ethnicities, as seen in Figure 10. However, they also reported that this allowance was significantly more likely to be contingent upon doing chores in the home (80 percent), confirming the importance of fulfilling their family responsibilities. Hispanic children were also more likely to report that they did odd jobs, such as babysitting, to earn extra money indicating a strong work ethic.

Further to developing an understanding of children' lives, it is important to examine the current environment they may be experiencing in society. Given the greater diversity among children, we may theorize that children are also experiencing greater interaction with children of many different cultures. However, data from the U.S. Multicultural Kids Study shows that this interaction is limited, particularly for African-American and white children. Hispanic children have greater interaction in their neighborhoods than they do at their schools, where half of all Hispanic children attend with all or mostly Hispanic children.

Chapter Summary

- 37.4 million Hispanics comprise over 13 percent of the U.S. population.
- Hispanics have now edged African-Americans as the single, largest minority in the U.S.
- By some estimates, one in five Americans will be of Hispanic birth or descent by 2030.
- The greatest rate of growth is occurring in the southern United States.
- All indications are that this trend will continue.
- Substantial Hispanic communities are no longer confined to the largest metropolitan cities of the U.S.

- The size of mature Hispanic communities has helped to foster fluency of the Spanish language.
- Although second-generation and beyond Hispanics gain English skills, they tend to preserve proficiency in Spanish.
- Language is one of the few precious links to origin that Hispanics pass on to their children.
- Hispanics in the United States are generally younger than the total population.
- An interesting result of explosive growth in newly developing, suburban areas is that males outnumber females.
- We attribute this trend to men who migrate to developing areas in search of work and have temporarily left their families behind.
- Among children under age 15, there are more than 11 million Hispanic children making up nearly 30 percent of the total Hispanic population.
- Among African-Americans, 27 percent of their population is under 15; and among Asians, 21 percent are under 15.
- Hispanics lag behind both African-Americans and whites in attaining higher education.
- It starts in high school, where in 2003; more than 89 percent of whites age 25 and over had graduated, compared with 80 percent of African-Americans and 57 percent of Hispanics.
- During 2003, the unemployment rate among Hispanics (7.7 percent) was higher than the average (5.7 percent) but lower than among African-Americans (10.8 percent).
- Hispanics tend to take jobs in lower-paying, labor-intensive fields.
- Hispanics' willingness to work in low-wage jobs makes them attractive to industries like construction, agriculture, and services.
- Hispanics' median household income (3-year average 1998-2000) was $31,703, higher than the $28,679 for African-Americans, but far below the $45,514 for non-Hispanic whites.
- Growth in this population drives the numbers.
- One source estimates that Hispanic buying power will have increased 357 percent from 1990 to 2008.

- Total buying power may have already surpassed one-half trillion dollars.
- The Hispanic media industry has given new life to the market.
- Spanish-language television has enjoyed increasing viewer ship to coincide with the growing U.S. Hispanic population.
- Additionally, Hispanics consume more television and radio, on average.
- Birthdays, anniversaries, *quinceañeras* (15th birthday), and family reunions are big productions.
- Hispanics hold traditions in high esteem and have a greater desire to preserve them, even as they assimilate simultaneously into U.S. culture.
- Hispanics tend to favor the Democratic Party.
- Since 1976, Republican presidential candidates have earned no higher than 37 percent of the Hispanic vote, won by Ronald Reagan in 1980 and 1984.
- In the 2000 election, George W. Bush won 35 percent of the Hispanic vote, but Democratic candidate Al Gore earned 62 percent.
- The growing Hispanic voting bloc might have had significant impact on the 2004 election. Some exit polls indicate that George W. Bush received the highest proportion of the Latino vote for a Republican since Ronald Reagan.
- Hispanic brand loyalty is not an absolute; rather it varies by the consumer's acculturation level and varies by product category.

About the Authors

Jonathan R. Ashton, Vice President, Quantitative Research, Cultural Access Group

Jonathan Ashton, who has spent 14 years in market research, began his career as a telephone interviewer while attending college. He functions both as vice president of the Quantitative Group, and as project manager for complex projects, specializing in telecom and financial services. He graduated at Brigham Young University with a degree in Education, and then received his Master's in Business Administration at the University of Utah.

Michele Valdovinos, Vice President, Research and Marketing, Cultural Access Group

Michele Valdovinos is vice president of Research & Marketing at Cultural Access Group's offices in Los Angeles. She oversees the firm's marketing functions and leads the Senior Management Analysis and Review Team to provide actionable insights and recommendations for the company's clients. Michele brings more than twelve years of professional experience having worked in high-profile industries such as network television, entertainment, international marketing, and Hispanic market advertising. Michele obtained a Bachelor of Arts degree in Media Management from Pepperdine University. She is a graduate of the University of Southern California's Annenberg School of Communications with a master's degree in Communications Management.

Chapter Two

Latino Identity & Situational *Latinidad*

Federico Subervi, Ph.D.
Diana Rios, Ph.D.

In This Chapter

- Some complexities of Latino identity
- How that identity must be understood as situational

Introduction

Latino identity or *"identidad Latina"* is both a simple concept as well as complex one. At the most basic level, it is a state of mind that propels a person to state: "I am Latino" or "I am Latina" simply because he or she considers him or herself Latino or Latina. There may be one or many reasons for such sense of identification, which can be expressed internally (to self) or externally (to others). In essence, that identity is a personal declaration of being part of a group called Latino.

Furthermore, Latino identity is also an existence defined, established, guided, or pressured by self, family, neighborhood and society. It is most complex when specifics are taken into consideration regarding which internal and/or external factors are most important for the societal level recognition of that identity, and also how, where, and with whom that identity is expressed.

This chapter aims to explain some of the complexities of situational Latino identity. As we will discern from the pages that follow, there are many factors, elements and conditions under which a person can self-identify or under which others may identify the person as Latino. Understanding these issues is certain to enhance the way in which public relations practitioners and other media professionals relate to and work with Latinos across the country.

One of Many Identities

Latino identity is one of many ways people use to establish a connection with a large group. Social class, age, job, profession, body type, gender or gender orientation, and zodiac sign are among the infinite factors that individually or collectively can contribute to a person's sense of belonging or being part of a larger group. Latino identity is just one of the ethnic identities people use in the United States. Within the context of the principal "minority" groups of this nation, other ethnic identities are African American, Asian American, and American Indian. Of course, there are others as well.

Region, Race, Culture

Ethnic identities emerge from a combination of one or more of the following factors: region of origin of the individual or his/her family, the race (physical characteristics) of the person, and a number of cultural characteristics expressed individually or collectively by members of the group. We may evidence that expression of culture in terms of knowledge, attitudes, and behaviors exhibited in private or public settings. We will address each of these within the framework of Latinos.

Region

Aside from just making a statement such as "I am Latino," a person can claim to be Latino(a) if he or she, or if one or more of his or her parents or grandparents were born in the region that encompasses any of the Spanish-speaking countries from Mexico to Chile as well as the Caribbean. Sometimes, but not frequently, people whose national heritage is from Brazil or other non-Spanish-speaking countries in Latin America also claim to be Latino. People from Spain, Portugal and other countries; such as Italy and Romania that share a language rooted in Latin do not usually claim to be Latino in the United States. The typical regional identity of these people is either their national origin or "European."

Latino identity based on region of origin may also apply when the heritage, even though one or more generations past, is from the former Mexican territories such as California, Arizona, Colorado, Nevada, New Mexico, and Texas. Individuals whose ancestors were Mexicans from that region may self identify as Latino, or possibly as Chicano. This latter term carries cultural and political connotations in the sense that those who identify as such are prone to affirm their Mexican cultural roots regardless of their place of birth (i.e., U.S.), and their determination to struggle in political (as well as social, cultural, and educational) arenas to maintain and enhance the values of that heritage.

The choice of stating a Latino identity based on that regional origin heritage may be personal and may carry an emotional meaning. However, an entity external to the individual such as a government agency, (e.g. the U.S. Census Bureau, or a private or public organization that gives some value to the classifications) may establish an ethnic identity. These classifications are nominal because they imply that based on whatever defining rule, the individual either fits or does not fit into a particular category. For the defining agency or office, there is only a functional, not an emotional, value associated with the classification. These types of ethnic identifications are used for assessing population trends, analyzing patterns of selected subgroups, or promoting certain programs and activities (e.g., equal opportunity hiring assessments and plans) that, for whatever reason, should target particular ethnic groups, (e.g., Latinos in general, or subgroups such as Puerto Ricans as a Latino subgroup).

The situational component of a regionally based Latino identity is triggered in at least a couple of settings. First, others may use regional or generic identities when they serve as a contrast to other group identities. For example, Latino identity is widely employed in contrast to Anglo, Anglo Saxon, or white identity (although the latter category is a racial one). Some also use it in contrast to American Indian, African American, or Asian American even though some Latinos ancestors may have African, Asian, or Indigenous roots. When Latinos who have close ties to their respective Latin American countries gather among themselves, they may highlight the national origins and distinctive cultural characteristics of these origins. However, the same Latinos mingling in a setting that includes Anglo Saxons (whites), Asians, etc., may then turn to affirming a Latino identity as a way to distinguish them from others who are not from the same region.

Furthermore, research has consistently demonstrated that people whose background is from Spanish-speaking countries in Latin America and the Caribbean prefer to affirm an identity stemming from a specific country, not a generic Latino (or Hispanic) Latin American or Caribbean identity. If specific national origin categories were not an option, the situation would require the more generic Latino identity (or in this case identification).

At the more personal level, individuals who have parents or grandparents who are of both Latino and non-Latino heritage usually decide on their own whether to claim Latino identity. In some families, one child of mixed parental background may claim to be Latino while another may prefer not to claim that identity or even deny it completely. Which identity they claim will depend primarily on how strong one of the parents (grandparents or other relatives) promotes the cultural elements associated with his or her particular culture.

Identity based on regional heritage (or based on cultural elements such as those discussed later in this chapter) is also a product of the environment an individual faces at different times in his or her life. Friends, teachers, church and spiritual leaders, and co-workers all play a role in the expression or transfiguration of an identity. Mass media also disseminates images, sounds and impressions attributed to particular ethnicities. To the extent that a Latino identity is acceptable, and even valued by these external and environmental sources, then the greater the probabilities a Latino will embrace and express to self and others that he or she is Latino.

We can discuss much more about the environmental factors that contribute to *"identidad Latina."* For now, it should be clear that regional origin and perceptions of that origin are some of the factors in establishing Latino identity.

In the practice of public relations and marketing, always keep in mind that the context usually requires consideration. It can be appropriate to identify an individual or a group using the generic Latino term, or it can be best to use a more specific national or regionally based term. When in doubt, consider asking the person or a reliable representative of the group.

Race

Latinos are not a race. They encompass people of all types of races and combinations of these. For the most part, even people whose family heritage is from a particular country or region are not exclusively of one race. In fact, in some families, it is common to observe a wide range of racial features such as skin color, the shape of the nose, lips, eyes and other physical characteristics, among brothers and sisters of the same parents. If there were one "racial" pattern discernable among the majority of Latinos, it would be the mix, the combination, the fusion of various races.

At the same time, particular racial patterns are more prominent than others are among Latinos from selected countries. Most, but not all Latinos from Mexico, Puerto Rico, Cuba, Venezuela, Colombia, Peru, the Dominican Republic, the countries of Central America, etc., are brown-skinned and have a variety of shapes in other physical features. They reflect centuries of the mix of the Europeans, African Blacks, native Indian populations, and even Asians and Arabs who migrated to the Americas. Some people from these countries are Black because their primary heritage is from former African slaves. Others are white, the product of primarily European heritage.

Thus, the generic Latino identity or the specific national identities of Latinos are usually not racially based. In the U.S., Latinos whose regional identity is from Mexico would usually not claim their primary identity as being the "brown race of Mexico," even though a large percentage of the country's nationals are brown. Likewise, Latinos whose regional identity is from Argentina would usually not claim their primary identity as being the "white race of Argentina," even though a large percentage of the country's nationals are white of European heritage (i.e., not black, from Africa or India).

Nevertheless, Latinos do use racial terms to refer to themselves or others. Words that suggest different shades of brown, such as *trigueño, negro, mulato, and moreno*, are among the myriad of terms sprinkled in conversations about self and about others of the same or different heritage. Sometimes it is the mix of regional and racial identifiers such as *puertorriqueño moreno, cubano trigueño, dominicano negro* that are used.

The situational use of these racial terms for Latino identity once again depends on institutions, the individual or a social setting. At the institutional level for example, the U.S. Census Bureau asks respondents to first identify their race (e.g., white, black), and then their national heritage (Hispanic, etc.). During the year 2000 Census counts, most Latinos ended up indicating that their race was "white" because the forms did not offer the option to indicate brown, or shades of brown (e.g., *trigueño, moreno, café con leche*).

In addition, some organizations, such as the National Council of La Raza, NCLR, include the term "race" in their name. In the NCLR's case, the use of the term is not to establish a "racial" component of its individual or organizational members and affiliates. It is used figuratively and inclusively to denote the organization's broad-based services, activities, and mission.

A situational context at the individual and societal level is evident when a person uses or does not use a racial indicator when discussing his or her identity, depending on the place and the company at hand. In familiar settings with friends and family that are not negatively prejudiced against "brown" or its darker shades, they may mention racial terms positively. For example, the endearing *"mi negrita"* or *"mi negrito"* (my little black one) is frequently used among many Latinos of Caribbean heritage when referring to a loved partner or child. However, if they perceive the setting and company as potentially or actually prejudiced, they might omit or consciously deny that part of the Latino identity if possible.

With the diminishing of overt racism and racial intolerance in society (at least when contrasted to the reality of how things were a few decades ago), there may be fewer Latinos who refer to their identity by denying or trying to deny or hide their racial characteristics, especially if these are brown or darker shades of brown. However, "racialized" prejudice, sometimes direct, other times subtle is still present in American society. We use the term "racialized" here because although Latinos are not a race, they are collectively or individually perceived and/or (mis)treated as if they were. While some Latinos continue to react to that prejudice with personal shame, guilt and self-denial of their non-white racial features, others challenge the prejudice and express their particular racial heritage more prominently.

Unfortunately, the problem of racial prejudice does not stem exclusively from non-Latinos. Even among members of this group, there are people who individually or collectively (e.g., as may be reflected in the unwritten norms of their social club) express racial prejudice towards fellow Latinos. The targets of that prejudice are usually Latinos of darker skin and/or physical characteristics such as hair type, and size and form of lips, eyes, and nose.

For those who place a higher value on "whiteness," that part of the Latino identity may become regularly and prominently featured in his or her self-concept, behaviors, and/or conversations. For example, that person may develop a (false) sense of superiority due to their lighter skin. He or she may opt to straighten and color their hair (usually blond) not just for fun or fashion, but because it helps in the "appearance" of being white. That person's conversations could also stress the perceived "value" of being of fair skin, blond, etc., and in some settings exhibit, consciously or unconsciously, prejudicial behavior towards Latinos (and others) who are physically not like them.

In sum, being Latino or having *identidad Latina* is not dependent on a person's skin color or other physical characteristics. It also precludes personality traits related to prejudice or lack there of. Such prejudicial attitudes and behaviors are personal, not an indicator of being or not being Latino.

A key lesson here is to avoid assuming a person is or is not Latino based on the color of his or her skin or other physical characteristics. Even though there are certain racial patterns among some Latinos, it is also a fact that Latinos encompass all types of skin color, hair color and type, as well as every other imaginable physical characteristic. Thus, the phrase "you do not look Latino" (or Puerto Rican, Mexican, Cuban, etc.) should never be uttered by a public relations practitioner, or for that matter anybody else.

Culture

Culture is the most important factor that contributes to a person having an ethnic-based identity. Distinctive patterns with respect to language, religion, music, art, cuisine, celebrations, literature, history, myths, clothing styles, as well as individual, family and societal values and rituals are among the infinite elements that converge in the formation of local, national, or regional cultures. Members of society may consider an individual part of the ethnic group identified with the culture depending on the degree to which he or she (a) knows about the characteristics of the culture, (b) has positive values about or towards the culture, and (c) behaves in public and/or private settings in ways that are congruent with the culture.

The Spanish language is a key element in Latino identity, recognized as an important common bond or denominator for and among Latinos. Variations in the accents, intonations, and slang of the Spanish language reflect particular patterns that stem from home countries or regions of the countries and may contribute to Latino subgroup identities. A person may claim Latino identity because, among other reasons, the individual knows the Spanish language, has positive attitudes towards the language, and/or can speak or read it in public and private settings. The more a person's knowledge about the Spanish language, the higher that person's degree of language *Latinidad* is. Likewise, the greater the positive attitudes towards Spanish, and the greater the disposition to speak and read the language someone has, the higher that person's degree of language *Latinidad* is.

Of course, not all people who consider themselves Latino or whom others consider Latino speak and read Spanish fluently or at all. In addition, not everybody who speaks and reads the language merits being considered Latino just because he or she knows, likes, and practices the language.

The point here is that among people who can claim to be Latino (due to a regional heritage); there are variations in that *Latinidad*, based on command of the Spanish language. However, this affirmation need not be a value statement about the supremacy of the Spanish language for the Latino identity. It should simply show that there are different dimensions and degrees of *Latinidad* and language is one of them.

The Catholic religion, for centuries the most common religion among Latinos, is another element in Latino identity. However, Catholicism is obviously not even a requirement to be Latino. Increasingly more Latinos are of other religions. Latinos who learn about and practice their religion in settings (e.g., churches) attended primarily by other Latinos can be considered to have a higher degree of publicly visible and religious *Latinidad* than those who do not actively and publicly practice their religion or do so in settings where there are few other Latinos. However, people who practice their religion privately, in a way that includes liturgy, rituals, chants or other patterns primarily identified or associated with Latinos, can also claim religious-based Latinidad.

Certain types of music also help define Latino identity, albeit the patterns vary widely across Latinos of different national and even regional backgrounds. For example, *salsa* and *merengue* distinguish Latinos of the Caribbean islands. People who know about this music, like it and dance to its rhythms can claim this type of musical *Latinidad*. Even so, some Latinos with heritage from that region may still be Latino regardless of whether they know much about the music, like it or dance it. The Latino identity could be related to other elements.

Another important set of elements that can help define a culture is the sources used for information, news, and entertainment. Books, newspapers, magazines, radio, television, videos, theaters and the Internet are among the sources that feature, promote, and sustain cultures. We can certainly find an enhanced sense of *Latinidad* among Latinos who know more about such Latino-oriented sources, value and like those sources, and attend to them on a regular basis.

Yet as with any other indicator of identity, use of Latino sources for information or entertainment is not a necessary condition of *Latinidad*. A Latino may claim a Latino identity regardless of the type of sources (radio, television, etc.) used on a regular basis or even just occasionally. In some locations, there is limited access to one or another of these sources, or the material (content) offered in them is not of particular interest to some Latinos.

For example, daily Spanish-language Latino-oriented newspapers are published only in a dozen cities in the U.S. Therefore, it would be incorrect to assume that a Latino would have a lower sense of *Latinidad* because he or she does not read Spanish-language newspapers on a daily basis. There are full-time or part-time Spanish-language radio stations in most major cities with Latino populations. However, in some cities the music played by one or all of those stations may be of a particular type that is not appealing to some Latino listeners. Similar limitations apply with respect to watching Spanish-language television. For example, Latinos who are fans of science fiction and whose main reason for watching television is such content, would most likely not tune into the current major Spanish-language networks in the U.S. since those networks do not offer that kind of programming.

Thus, a sole reflection of a person's *Latinidad* should not be whether a Latino reads Spanish-language press on a daily basis, listens to Spanish-language radio regularly, or watches Spanish-language television. Here we should recall that some Latinos do not speak Spanish. For them, exposure to Spanish-language media is not an option even though they may still identify as and consider themselves Latino because of parental regional heritage or based on some other cultural elements.

We could go on discussing similar examples about *Latinidad* based on many other elements such as family and social values. In the interest of space and time, we will emphasize the key point: we can discern the degree of *Latinidad* with respect to Latino culture from a person's knowledge, attitudes, and/or behaviors related to one or more of those cultural indicators. We must add here that the attitudes, positive, neutral or negative, toward one or more cultural elements or specific parts of those elements is what carries the emotional charge that then leads to the internal and external identity of *Latinidad*.

Another important point to keep in mind is that it is not always easy to agree upon all the elements that distinguish the Latino culture or the various regional subcultures. Individuals and groups may vary in their assessments of what is required to claim *Latinidad* in general or *Latinidad* related to a regional component (Puerto Rican in the U.S., Mexican American, etc.). Of course, there are identifiable elements and patterns stemming from, and related to, different regional heritages. What we do not always agree upon is how, where and when an individual should express those particular and defining cultural patterns for us to consider them part of the group.

In these modern times, reaching an agreement about those elements and patterns to define a particular culture can be challenging. More than ever before, cultures are flexible, dynamic, and under pressure to change and adapt. Some cultural arenas are fusing with others to create new variations even as the old ones thrive. Such is the case at least with respect to music (e.g., Latin Jazz fusion) and cuisine (Latin fusion cuisine) now available in many major cities across the U.S., Latin America and Europe.

It is in these complex contexts that *Latinidad*, especially based on cultural elements, is even more situational. A Latino by birth or family heritage can express some cultural elements commonly recognized as being Latino, for example the preference for the Spanish language and Latino music. That same person, however, may dislike other elements, such as spicy food. Moreover, the expression of some of the Latino elements may be visible in private spheres, as would be the case of listening to Spanish-language radio at home, but not in public arenas, especially if there is concern about negative public reaction to the expression of that cultural element. Latino identity is thus very situational, not an all or nothing state of mind or being.

Opening the Doors to the Expression of Latinidad

Starting in the 1960s and gradually more so during the last few years, a number of factors have contributed to the increased expression of *Latinidad*. The Civil Rights movement of the 1960s and 1970s marked the beginning of what has continued to be an ongoing struggle to incorporate Latinos to their rightful place, center stage, in practically every social, cultural, economic, and political arena of the United States. The exponential increase of the Latino population in this country is another major factor especially after the year 2000 Census count showed how quickly Latinos would become (and now already are) the largest ethnic minority in the country. A complementary population factor is that a large number of Latinos reside in states that have played prominent roles in political campaigns for both state and national electoral affairs (e.g., California, Texas, Florida, Arizona, and New Mexico). Yet another factor is the growth of Latinos' purchasing power, which at this writing surpasses $700 billion per year.

Tying all of these together has been the growth of Latino-oriented media, which constantly feature Latinos in news, advertisements, and entertainment shows. The combination of these factors has brought Latinos to the forefront of major corporations and organizations seeking to capitalize on this "niche" population and "commodify" (turn into and exploit the commercial value of) selected elements of the Latino culture. The same applies with respect to political parties and candidates seeking to win Latino votes.

In their efforts to sell their products, be it consumer goods or political candidates, the advertising and marketing industries have increased the participation and presence of Latinos in all types of images from television advertisements to posters to other types of promotional materials. While we still observe stereotyped representations, there is also a large number and more diverse presence of Latino people and Latino-oriented images in mainstream commercials and political promotions as well as in Latino-oriented media.

A related arena where Latinos are also increasingly visible is in the entertainment industry. For example, promoters support Latino music and artists in all types of media and venues. That is especially the case for those performers who exemplify the fusion of the best attributes of their respective Latino heritage along with the rhythms and styles of the modern global youth cultures; however, one may wish to define these. For those performers that entrepreneurs see as potentially bringing mega-dollars in profits, no efforts are too small to sell them, with glowing images and hype, to the Latino and non-Latino consumers all over the U.S. and the world. Among the most prominent of these, we can mention Ricky Martin, Julio and Enrique Iglesias, Jennifer Lopez, Cristina Aguilera, Salma Hayak, and Antonio Banderas. Some are indeed Latinos from the U.S., others have moved to the U.S. and thus been perceived as Latinos, while others are natives of their respective countries but still promoted as "Latin" stars. In either case, the "commodification" of their music, images, and presence in the U.S. and global markets was accomplished building on their attraction to Latinos of different regional backgrounds, language skills, racial characteristics, etc.

One of the consequences of the enhanced attention to and presence of Latinos in advertising, marketing, and popular culture has been the diminishing of the "stigma" of being Latino, and therefore the enhanced expression of *Latinidad* in some form or fashion. Thus, as the media feature Latino super stars and other prominent political and civic figures (Governor Bill Richardson, congresswomen Loretta and Linda Sanchez, Henry Cisneros, and Raúl Yzaguirre), and make them more acceptable among non-Latinos; a sense of validation, self-worth, and self-esteem among Latinos themselves increases; even as they increasingly adapt to and participate in social, political, economic, and cultural arenas in which Latinos are not the dominant players.

Acculturation Issues

Latinos do not assimilate. They acculturate, as do most other people who partake in a setting in which they are not the majority numerically, with respect to political and economic power, or in terms of perceived social standing. For the most part Latinos are pluralistic as they are selectively situational in terms of which cultural characteristics (Latino and/or non-Latino) they embrace and express.

41

Assimilation implies fully taking on all the characteristics of another culture and society, that the dominant society accepts the assimilated, while he or she also abandons (forgets, neglects, denies) his or her original culture and society. Acculturation also implies change, but mostly in terms of learning and adapting to new or different cultural elements without necessarily having to abandon the original culture in all of its manifestations. It also does not require that the dominant society accept the acculturating individual. On the other hand, being pluralistic means concurrently expressing in some settings the cultural characteristics of the dominant group, but simultaneously retaining and expressing in other settings the cultural traits inherited from another group.

If we look at the full spectrum of Latinos in the United States, we should easily conclude that a lot of acculturation is taking place, especially among Latinos who have migrated from other countries. It will be easy to find Latinos who may have acculturated very well in terms of learning the English language. A rapid and high degree of acculturation is also evident as Latinos abandon the more restrictive traditional family ties and embrace modern interpersonal relations, especially in the arena of dating and pre-marital sexual norms.

At the same time, a pluralistic Latino identity is still widely reflected in many ways. Examples include the art and decoration Latinos display in their homes, the music they buy and play privately or in parties they host, the social clubs they go to for dancing, and the continued embracing of selected family values and ties that show reverence for parents and elders. That Latino identity is also alive and well with respect to the food they prefer, especially during family gatherings.

Are Latinos who primarily watch English-language television "assimilated"? Are Latinos who do not dance *salsa* or *merengue* "assimilated"? What about Latinos who no longer like fatty foods, which are probably prominent during many family fiestas, especially with the Latino grandparents? Answer to each of these questions: no, unless we define assimilation only in terms of television watched, type of music danced to, or food liked. Taken collectively, these may give an indication of some degree of identity on one or more arenas (language, musical, culinary). However, there are many more indicators and arenas in which Latino identity may be expressed.

Could we apply the term "assimilated" or even "acculturated" to Latinos who pursue a college education, gain high-paying professional jobs, and move to the suburbs? Again, no. These are socio-economic indicators common in, and the norm for, thousands of Latino families, be they well established in the U.S. or recent migrants. In addition, in and of themselves these achievements preclude the expression of a whole gamut of other cultural characteristics that could show a person's *Latinidad* in different ways.

Assimilation cannot be defined only in terms of the language. Moreover, to the extent that such a Latino speaks English and Spanish fluently, choosing which one circumstantially, and displays other cultural characteristics of two (or more) cultures, that person is pluralistic. For example, even for a Latino who is fluent in Spanish, his or her limited exposure to Spanish-language television may simply be due to the limited availability of Spanish-language broadcast or cable options. Alternatively, it could reflect that person's preference for science fiction, a genre hardly found on Spanish-language television in the U.S.

The same precaution must be kept in mind when assessing the degree and type of acculturation as well as pluralistic expressions with respect to other elements that define a culture, and to what degree a person is (or a whole group of people) part of that culture. As mentioned previously, when dislikes or threats to the Latino culture are perceived or feared, then Latinos will be less likely to express their *Latinidad*. However, the self-acknowledgment or external expression of one aspect or many elements of *Latinidad* will ultimately depend on the extent to which Latinos perceive that their cultural heritage and traits are acceptable by the "others" who are not Latinos.

Lastly, retro-acculturation is the process of learning (or re-learning) about the cultural elements that characterize a group about which one is part of, but had, at an earlier age, little or no opportunity to learn about such culture. For Latinos, this may imply learning (or re-learning) the Spanish-language or about other elements of the Latino culture such as music, literature, cuisine, etc. Which cultural traits are (re)learned depends on the person's contexts of perceived validation of the traits, environment of support for (re)learning the traits, and personal interests and lifestyle.

The Challenge

The challenge for public relations practitioners, media professionals and others working with and relating to the expanding Latino communities across the country is to recognize both the simplicity of Latino identity, its complexity, and how situational the expression of that identity can be. There is no set rule to classify Latinos based on racial elements. While we delineate more the rules for defining who is Latino based on regional factors, such is not the case for culturally based classifications of Latinos.

The complexity of *Latinidad* was made even more evident in the discussion about acculturation issues, including assimilation, acculturation, pluralism and retro-acculturation. Each of these processes, related to adaptation, is dynamic and multidimensional. A person is not simply "assimilated" or "not assimilated," "acculturated" or "not acculturated." It is all a matter of degrees of adaptation, and specific areas in which the transformation may occur.

In essence, *Latinidad* is contextual and situational. The best way to understand it calls for regular immersion into the particular individual, family, community and social settings that shed light on Latino identity and *Latinidad*. The basic rule to follow when dealing with Latinos in professional or personal settings is: when in doubt, ask cordially about the labels or terms to use to refer to the individual or group. Most importantly, engage in open-minded conversations that will help you learn about the cultural patterns that best define them, and how to relate to them to meet common goals.

Chapter Summary

- Latino identity or *"identidad* Latina" is a state of mind.
- It is also an existence defined, sculpted, guided, or pressured by self, family, neighborhood and society.
- Latinos, or Hispanics, are a heterogeneous population.
- They claim roots that are Mexican, Puerto Rican, Cuban or other roots from Central and South America.

- Latinos are defined by scholars, government officials, and others by the region of origin and by a common ethnic mother tongue, Spanish, which they do not all have command over.
- There are strong interpersonal support systems and other support mechanisms for the Spanish language that will keep Spanish alive for U.S. Latinos.
- Latinos live a pluralistic existence.
- Being pluralistic means concurrently expressing in some settings the cultural characteristics of the dominant group, while simultaneously retaining and expressing the cultural traits inherited from another group in other settings.
- Latinos have gradations of ethnic group consciousness and differing degrees of acculturation.
- Latino identity is best understood as an evolving and ever-changing matrix of human possibilities.
- It is a phenomenon of ethnic connection that necessitates self-reflection, self-claiming and self-affirmation.
- The situational use of racial terms for Latino identity depends on institutions, the individual or a social setting.
- The problem of racial prejudice does not stem exclusively from non-Latinos.
- Latinos themselves can direct unhealthy biases within the group based on skin color and other features.
- Certain types of music help define Latino identity, albeit the patterns vary widely across Latinos of different national and even regional backgrounds.
- It would be incorrect to assume that a Latino would have a lower sense of *Latinidad* because he or she does not use Spanish-language newspapers or other Spanish-language or Latino-oriented media on a daily basis.
- When in doubt, public relations professionals should ask cordially about the labels to use when referring to an individual or a group.

About the Authors

Federico Subervi, Ph.D., Professor, School of Journalism and Mass Communication Texas State University, San Marcos Director, The Latinos and Media Project

Frederico Subervi directs the Latinos and Media Project, an emerging non-profit organization dedicated to the gathering and dissemination of research and resources pertaining to Latinos and the media. For over twenty years, he has been teaching, conducting research, and publishing on issues pertaining to the mass media and ethnic groups, especially Latinos in the United States. He is currently finishing a book on mass media and Latino politics and teaching at Texas State University, San Marcos.

Diana Rios, Ph.D., Associate Professor, Department of Communication Sciences and Puerto Rican/Latino Studies Institute (PRLS), University of Connecticut

Diana Rios is associate professor in the Department of Communication Sciences and the Puerto Rican/Latino Studies Institute (PRLS) at the University of Connecticut. Her research and teaching include minorities, women and media, media effects, and cross-cultural communication. She earned her Ph.D. at the University of Texas at Austin.

46

Chapter Three

Beyond Skin Color
Unveiling the Screen of Prejudice and Misconceptions

Deborah Vallejo

In This Chapter

- The key to success is proper research, planning and understanding of your target audience

Introduction

Students of Advertising 101 frequently learn to be careful about what a word or image may mean in another language. The classic examples include the Chevy car called Nova (Spanish for "doesn't go") and an airline blunder promoting its leather seats inferred passengers fly "bare-skinned." A more recent translation faux pas is the "Got Milk?" campaign, which marketers initially translated as "¿Tienes Leche?" which can mean, "Are you lactating?"

Relying on a Spanish-English dictionary does not suffice. Forget about the fact that a name for a common food product in one Latin American country may mean a four-letter word to someone across the border. Alternatively, what a standard English/Spanish dictionary uses to describe a woman of Chinese origin means "orange" in Puerto Rico yet "curly-haired" to a Mexican. Although words are extremely important to the public relations professional, this discipline goes well beyond the obvious.

Public relations delve into the psyche and the heart of the consumer and reach out to the influencers, families, trendsetters and community of the desired public. Just as most North American public relations practitioners would be wary about going to work in North Korea or the former Yugoslavia, novice public relations people need to be attuned to the minority markets here in the United States. If the white-haired, white men in navy suits running Congress are no longer a representation of the average American, neither is the stereotypical blonde, blue-eyed 20-something public relations novice going to have the insights to represent the average American.

An "Average American" in the 21st century is a somewhat overweight, Hispanic female 18-34 with several children. In downtown Houston, Chicago, New York, Miami, Los Angeles and San Antonio, the skinny-white-girl is not too easy to find among throngs of Hispanic, African-American and Asian women. In the next 20 years, the white "majority" will be an even smaller minority. In the year 2000, 21 percent of births were to a Hispanic mom and more than half of all deliveries in Los Angeles were Hispanic babies. While the Hispanic population surge makes the headlines from time to time, rarely is the Asian-American growth rate discussed, which is zooming forward at a much higher speed than that of Latinos in the United States. Maybe this land of ours is returning to its roots; a land comprised of tribes of people of color. What would the outcome have been if the European settlers had conducted advance market research to identify hot spots among the public, learned the languages and cultures of the tribes, and devised a strategic public awareness and public affairs campaign designed to encourage the natives to support "the new regime?"

According to lore, in Mexico, the Spanish conquistadors were welcomed with open-arms, thanks in part to a long-time legend that a bearded man with light eyes would be the peoples' messiah. According to Mexican journalist, Juan Miralles, in his biography, "Hernan Cortes, Inventor of Mexico," when the Spanish ships landed in Mexico, the natives believed the newcomers were Quetzalcoatl and his court. After surviving on primitive diets in the Caribbean, the natives treated the conquistadors with great respect and served them hearty meals fit for a king. While they feasted, artists traced Cortes, his troop, their horses, dogs, cannons and ships. The natives were in awe; they had never before seen a tall white bearded man, nor the animals or armaments they brought from Europe. The natives viewed even the African slaves that accompanied the conquistadors with wonder and treated them with great respect.

As legend recounts, Cortes took advantage of their misperceptions to convert the natives to Christianity and took their gold back to Spain. His fame spread rapidly to different parts of the land, easing his way to rule the entire territory. However, in reality, there was a royal ordinance, or *Requerimiento*, including a sketchy marketing communications edict to take over the new land. "Discoveries are not to be called conquests. Since we wish them to be carried out peacefully and charitably, we do not want the use of the term 'conquest' to offer any excuse for the employment of force or the causing of injury to the Indian. They should be persuaded to give up of their own free will those things that are contrary to our Holy Catholic Faith and the evangelical doctrine." According to Mexican anthropologist Miguel Leon Portilla, the Indians' chronicles are very different from those of the Spanish. "The Spaniards began to wage war against us. They attacked all. A vast number of our warriors were killed by their metal darts." Given the realities, it seems many believed the Spaniards' "spin" for the next 500 years.

Leading public relations agencies understand the value of research. It is essential to delve into consumer insights prior to developing a strategic campaign. If the public relations team is not able to understand the diverse marketplace of today, they need to hire a multicultural marketing specialist or ignore the fastest growing consumer segments and miss a major portion of the marketplace. In a similar fashion, the executive boardroom cannot rely on the token Hispanic to tell them if they are on track. That would be almost analogous to the white-haired senator asking O.J. Simpson how to conduct an African-American public affairs campaign in Mississippi. To better address the multicultural arena, one needs to look at how history has shaped today's society, to gain an improved understanding that stereotypes are not based on reality.

From Carmen Miranda to Carmen Electra

Today's parents are bombarded with messages about the influence of television on their children's lives: how violence on television contributes to the creation of violent youth. If the Marlboro man exudes a desirable image that leads to increased smoking, then it is safe to assume that stereotypes on television or in the movies lead to further prejudice. A step back in time reveals a smattering of odd characters, which may have forged today's modern day unbalanced perception of Hispanics. Early images of Hispanics on the silver screen were limited to Carmen Miranda. A Brazilian femme fatale, Carmen danced and sang while balancing a large hat filled with fruit atop her head. That image is so commonplace, that even the 2003 release of Dr. Seuss' "The Cat in the Hat" featured a scene in which the oversized cat danced while dressed in Miranda-garb, complete with the fruit. In some countries, people do carry food home from the market on their head and Brazil is a country with rich African inspired music beats. Yet this equation does not add up to the MGM role for Carmen who made approximately 20 movies in the 1930s.

Older baby boomers may remember the television show "El Zorro," which was based on a silent film, produced in 1920 with Douglas Fairbanks, and a second film in 1940 that starred Tyrone Power. Back in the early days of the black and white television set, Zorro was a masked hero who brandished a sword and tore a big letter Z with the tip of his weapon to mark his territory. Created by Walt Disney in 1957, Zorro, personified by Guy Williams, was dressed in dark colors with high boots and strode atop a dark horse.

Years later, Antonio Banderas would recreate the more hip Zorro image. Banderas, born in Spain, has personified many Western heroes on film including "*El Mariachi*" and "Desperado." While there are horsemen in many parts of Latin America and cutting tools such as machetes are frequently used for agricultural purposes, the traditional use of both the horse and the machetes do not add up to the Zorro equation.

The next swashbuckling Latino screen legend led a more traditional urban life, filled with routine ups and downs. "I Love Lucy," syndicated in at least 80 countries, first aired in 1951. Although the show would go on to be one of the most successful television shows in history, when Lucille Ball and her real-life husband, Desi Arnaz, set out to create the show, no one would finance or produce it. By 1951, Lucille Ball and Desi Arnaz had each built themselves a solid history in the entertainment industry. Lucy had appeared in approximately 60 movies while Desi had appeared in movies and led his orchestra in concerts across the country. The production companies would not place their faith, or financial backing, in a mixed-marriage household in which the husband had an accent and played the bongos.

Without the cameras and the studio's support, Lucy and Desi tested their concept of "I Love Lucy" in Vaudeville. Audiences responded. Convinced they could succeed; the couple took $5,000 in savings to form Desilu Studios, and ultimately, became one of the country's favorite screen couples and ran a production company that owned 16 television series. Desi's on-screen character, Ricky Ricardo, was prominently featured singing traditional tropical music at his Tropicana nightclub in New York. His real-life Cuban roots were a part of the story line. Desi's adaptation to life in the U.S., and learning to live with a fiery stage-struck American wife, was also an important element of the show's plot. Desi was prone to blurt out diatribes in Spanish, and, there were no subtitles. The viewer comprehended the messages, rather than the words. The Lucy/Desi marriage showcased spats along with the cultural differences of the pair, with which nearly everyone in the 1950s, and still today, could identify.

Jorge Moreno, a Latin Grammy winner, made his television debut singing *"Babalu"* on a 2001 CBS tribute to "I Love Lucy."

"It is truly amazing that 'I Love Lucy' still holds up as one of the funniest sitcoms to light up the small screen," Jorge says. "The show and the characters have been a staple throughout my life. Not only did I grow up watching the show, which is kind of amazing on its own, being that it was made in the early 50s, but I would sing along with 'Babalu' and beat on any flat surface in my perimeter. As a film and television major at the University of Miami, I remember studying a whole chapter on 'I Love Lucy' and how Desilu set new standards in the business and creative sense. Desi introduced new ways of shooting a sitcom using more cameras and ultimately changing television history."

Another love story between the cultures was the modernized Romeo and Juliet plot of "West Side Story." The movie glorified day-to-day conflicts between the Puerto Rican and white gangs of New York with the help of Leonard Bernstein's award-winning musical score and top-of-the-line choreography. The star of the 1961 movie, "Maria," was in fact played by Russian-American Natalie Wood wearing a darker than natural shade of pancake base. Her on-screen brother was personified by a Greek-American actor and dancer, George Chakaris.

A young dancer, Rita Moreno, was one of the few Hispanics cast in this award-winning film. Born in Puerto Rico, but raised in the States, Rita faked a thick accent in "West Side Story." Among her early roles, she had a guest appearance on the television set of "Father Knows Best" in which she played a foreign exchange student from India. She also was cast as one of the women of Siam in the 1956 movie "The King and I." More than 50 years later, Rita has proven she is more than a dancer. At the age of 72, she is featured prominently on HBO's "Oz," has had recurring appearances on Showtime's "Resurrection Boulevard" and is a leading character in the 2003 John Sayles release, "*Casa de los Babys.*"

In the Broadway version of "West Side Story," one of the actors who played the Puerto Rican leading lady was dancer and choreographer Debbie Allen. The African-American dancer/choreographer, and sister of "The Cosby Show" mom, Phylicia Rashad, won her first Tony nomination for her role as Maria. She later went on to direct, produce, choreograph and star in the 1980s television version of "Fame."

"West Side Story" explored prejudices in a violent, albeit stylized, sense. The next decade, however, was during the Black is Beautiful and Chicano Pride era that led to today's politically correct, PC, standards. Producer Norman Lear shocked audiences with Archie Bunker, a traditional middle-aged white Anglo-Saxon protestant who was openly racist and prejudiced. Although still in syndication today, and viewed as a traditional sit-com, Lear's venture with this program brought about such indignation and outrage, that in its initial year, advertisers were prompted to boycott the show.

Despite the rough edges and no-holds-barred style of "All in the Family's" patriarch, 60 percent of television viewers tuned in to the show that ran from 1971 to 1979. By the end of its run, the show had garnered 49 Emmy award nominations. Archie represented what many privately believed, but were not able to express openly. Before Lear's brave personification of changing cultural mores, these issues were swept under the carpet; though they were not visible, they were lumpy enough for viewers to trip on them. Perhaps the openness of prejudice enabled society to address the issue and move forward. This sit-com may have done more to promote minorities on television than any other show in history. It sparked a series of spin-offs including "Maude," "The Jeffersons" and "Good Times," thereby introducing a bevy of Black and Hispanic sideline actors to mainstream television.

The success of "All in the Family" led to a show, which in 1974 made Freddie Prinze an instant celebrity in "Chico and the Man." By 1976, Prinze was nominated for a Golden Globe, along with longtime celebrities Sammy Davis, Jr., Tony Randall, Alan Alda and Hal Linden for Actor in a Leading Role. The show was ranked number three, behind "All in the Family" and "Sanford and Son." Playing a hopeful young businessman in East Los Angeles pitted against a cranky cynic, viewers saw that the bigger "man" facing day-to-day prejudices was "Chico." Its theme song, written and performed by Jose Feliciano, directed Chico to "don't be discouraged; things will be better." The young Puerto Rican star became one of the first Hispanics to break through as a leading character on mainstream television. He showed Hispanic youth that they, too, could have dreams and fight stereotypes. Freddie was the leading man in this short-lived television show, and he supplemented his stardom with a hectic stand-up road show schedule. Prinze, who committed suicide at the age of 22, while on prime time television, countered many stereotypes and was well spoken on behalf of the Hispanic community. Even his name, Prinze, forced people to reckon with the fact that many Hispanics are not Spanish surnamed. Today, his son, Freddie Prinze, Jr., is a well-known actor who has never played a "Hispanic" role.

Where is the Mustache?

Aside from his mustache and affected accent, Freddie Prinze did not fit the Hispanic stereotype. They could easily have typecast him as a Greek fisherman, just as they typecast George Chakaris as the Puerto Rican lead in "West Side Story," and Mexican-American Anthony Quinn was best known as "Zorba the Greek."

Oftentimes, the people in power mold the "Hispanic look" according to their own images. Ask almost any Hispanic actor about casting calls, and you will hear complaints about "the right look." All the English-language stations turned down a Cuban-American television personality in Chicago purportedly because she "did not look Hispanic." Would an Italian-American be denied a job because they did not "look Italian?" Somehow, equal employment opportunity has its glitches.

At a women's seminar, actress Diana-Maria Riva, joked with the audience about her real-life experiences that made her thick-skinned, and ultimately successful, to survive in a society rife with prejudice and stereotypes. A master in fine arts and a long list of credits is not always what is required. Riva enjoyed supporting roles in "What Women Want" and "Chasing Papi," and was a regular on "Philly," "Common Law," the pilot for "Sabrina, the Teenage Witch" and "Miss Miami." She also had recurring appearances on "Everybody Loves Raymond," "NYPD Blue," "The Hughleys," "Family Law" and "City of Angels." Yet, the curly-haired Dominican was turned down repeatedly for not having "the right look."

> "I've been told I was too tall, and not tall enough; too short, and not short enough; too plump, and not plump enough. Most often, it was 'We're not going ethnic for this role,' or I just 'didn't have the look.' Whoever came up with the definition of 'the look,' I can assure you of two certain facts: a) It was a man and b) He was not Latino. But I never let that stand in my way. No matter what you look like when you are going in for an audition, nine times out of ten you are not exactly what they

visualized. You have to show them what you can bring out of this character."

Diana-Maria has shown the casting directors her character. In 2003, she won a principal role in Fox television's sit-com, "Luis."

Belita Moreno, of "The George Lopez Show," has been acting for 30 years. She told one group of Latinas about her experiences with stereotypes and typecasting. At one casting call, although she arrived early, she was asked to wait. After being there for two hours, she started to notice that the women that they were seeing had more stereotypical Mexican features. When she asked when she would be called to audition, they asked her if she was Mexican-American. She replied, "Yes. Spanish is my first language." They said, "You don't look it..." They told her they were not interested because "we don't need for you to audition because you're not the right type." She did not look Hispanic.

In Chicago, a Puerto Rican with solid English-language radio experience lost the chance to work at a top 40 radio station because he was white. The station was looking for diversity in its employees. However, the African-American interviewer did not recognize his Spanish surname, nor could she look past his light hair and skin to see what many Hispanics would recognize as Caribbean features.

As a child, I always looked at a family portrait of our relatives in Brazil. A group photo of about ten in the extended family, they looked more Brazilian than Carmen Miranda. All the men had dark mustaches, and the women had dark wavy hair. They all had a serious pose in circa 1950s garb. Fast forward to the 1990s and the Brazilian immigration wave to South Florida. My Gen X and Y Brazilian clan were a bunch of suntanned, sun-bleached blond California surfer types riding motorcycles down the causeways.

Follow the Roots

A Hispanic "look," is what we choose to see, because Hispanics are of all races and ethnicities. Manuel Portuondo, editor of South Florida's *El Colusa* newspaper explains the diversity of the Hispanic "race" in a Hispanic Heritage Month editorial.

"*Hispanidad* is something that surrounds us and hits us from all sides, constantly. It is a social-historical reality composed of a group of peoples spread across diverse territories. It is a formal community that shows a series of unique features that unite Spaniards with Filipinos and Iberoamericans. *Hispanidad* means Spain. But, it also means *guarapo, chicha, arepa, ajiaco, poncho, ayacas, pru, mulatas, trigueñas, bolero, son, guayaba, mangos* and all that which defines the mix that our Spanish forefathers over the centuries have not been able to, nor will be able to, free ourselves from the hidden past. Our roots. The Berbers. The Arabs. The Jews. The Gypsies. The amalgam that is us."

The tie that binds, as weak as it may be, is the motherland, Spain. Most Hispanics can trace some ancestry to Spain, and Spain is a European nation, albeit "colored" by the Moors and Sephardic Jews. The Moors invaded Spain in 711 and gained control of part of the Iberian Peninsula for the next 700 years. During the tenth century, there were 800 mosques in what was then called al-Andalus. Modern-day Spanish relies on more than 4,000 words of Arabic origin for everyday expressions, such as *almohada, alcachofa*, and *ojalá*. The early poetry of Spain was written in Castilian, Galician, Arabic and Hebrew, with Spain being the center of Jewish learning for the new civilization. Gerona, just north of Barcelona, was one of the early centers for Cabbalistic studies, an ancient form of interpreting Judaic law, currently in vogue and practiced by Madonna. Interestingly enough, 500 years after the inquisition, most every town of considerable size in Spain has its *judería, alhama* or *call*, the respective Castilian, Arabic and Catalan names for "Jewish quarter."

However, as Portuondo indicates, the history of Spain goes far beyond the Moors and the Jews. Over the centuries, there was a rich blend that included Celts, Visigoths, Romans, Britons and Bourbons, among others. For example, the roots of Spanish Flamenco music are unknown. Some suggest it is Flemish. Others claim it is Hindi. Still others steer the roots of the traditional Spanish music and dance to the Gypsies, Byzantines or Jews. Due to this richness in ethnic diversity in

Spain, skin colors and features vary greatly. This abundant cultural and ethnic diversity changes from region to region.

The Mexican *mestizaje* (blending of races) is rich. Most notable are the many Indian groups, along with French, Arabic and Chinese adding to diversity in the bloodlines. Additionally, there are pockets in Mexico with large concentrations of Jews and Amish. While the Mexican culture is very vivid, French, Poles and Germans all gave rise to what we now consider *Mexicanismo*. Maximillian and Carlota ruled in Mexico from the 1830s to the 1860s, bringing about new forms of music, including polka and mariachi. Among today's Mexican superstars, singer Ana Gabriel is of Chinese descent. Salma Hayek's father is Lebanese and Luis Miguel is the son of a Spanish father and Italian mother. Frida Kahlo, a Mexican icon, was the daughter of a German Jewish immigrant, and her famous husband, Diego Rivera, was of Jewish ancestry.

In Southern Cone countries, due to the annihilation of the natives and heavy proliferation of German and Italian immigrants, the *mestizaje* is different from that of Mexico. For example, approximately 50 percent of all Argentines are of Italian descent, because of an influx of three million Italians prior to 1950. This immigration influenced the language, culture and traditional foods of this region where residents eat homemade pasta while they play tango music in the background and people chatter with a singsong attributed to the Italian influence. The Italians bolster even the Argentine soccer fever. Among the players of River Plate, Argentina's famed soccer team, are Costanzo, Saccone, Cavenaghi, Tuccio and Ameli. As an example of the Southern Cone ethnic diversity, look at Argentina's recent president, Carlos Menem, son of Syrian immigrants, and his current wife, former Miss Universe Cecilia Bolocco, a Chilean of Italian descent. Although the European influence may be widespread in the South Cone, 10 percent of Argentina's inhabitants can claim Arabic ancestry.

Italians are commonplace in Peru, as well. However, the Asian influence is more conspicuous. The influx of Chinese and Japanese was crucial to the development of Peru, Brazil and Chile, in particular. Japanese flocked to Peru as early as 1899, mostly from Okinawa. By 1930, more than 20,000 Japanese were living in Peru. Peru elected a president of Japanese descent, and because of economic turmoil, many

57

Peruvians immigrated to Japan in the 1990s. Alertanet.org, a portal dedicated to law and society, in an article by Rodrigo Montoya Rojas gives an overview of today's Peru.

"A launching pad to analyze the Peruvian reality is its multicultural character. In the year 2001, in Peru, there were 50 cultures or languages. Two were based in the Andes, 42 in the Amazon, five that are a result of the Japanese, Chinese, Italian, Jewish and Arabic colonies and, finally, the western Creole culture. If we superimpose the languages with population data, I maintain that in 2,000 with 25 million Peruvians, 19,614,000 (78.4 percent) are Spanish-speakers; 4,500,000 (18 percent) speak Quechua; 500,000 (0.2 percent) speak Aymara; and 350,000 (01.2 percent) and 86,000 (00.3 percent) each speak Chinese, Japanese, Italian, Hebrew and Arabic."

The Asian Diaspora reached the Caribbean islands, too. Havana's pre-Castro *Barrio Chino* (Chinatown) was the largest in Latin America. The Chinese arrived in Cuba as early as 1847 to work on the sugar plantations. One estimate is that nearly 130,000 went to Cuba as indentured workers. By 1960, most had sought asylum in the United States or other countries. Although the majority of Cubans on the island are of African descent, Cuban-Americans are predominantly white. Adding to the diversity of Cuban-Americans is the significant number of Cuban Jews and Spanish Cubans. No wonder traditional Spanish food is integral to Cuban cuisine, just as Italian food is to the Argentine diet.

The African influence in Cuba and other Latin American and Caribbean countries has given rise to rich Afro-Caribbean music as well as *Santería* (a belief system or religion). Although we understand the African impact in the Caribbean and Brazil, where half the population has African roots, we are less able to acknowledge, the equally important Andean countries such as Colombia and Ecuador. Racial data is not well defined in parts of Latin America, due in part to interracial marriages. For example, figures for Afro-Venezuelans range from nine to 60 percent of the population, depending on the criteria used. In Colombia, one in five is considered black or black-mixed race, and, in Ecuador, the figure is 10 percent. Typically, those of African ancestry live in coastal zones, but people are more mobile now and are not destined to remain in their hometown for life. Afro-Latinos are visible everywhere, from the market to the television screen, even in countries with a relatively small number of African descended residents.

Taís Araújo starred in one of the hottest *telenovelas* (soap operas), based on the life of a slave in Brazil, Xica da Silva. This was the first leading role for a black woman, and became a rage throughout the Americas. The next television screen sensation was Colombian-produced *"Betty la Fea"* which in Miami, generated a 7.4 Nielsen rating. In Colombia, 70 percent of the viewing public tuned in, and worldwide, there were an estimated 80 million Betty fans. The title character in *"Betty la Fea"* was a meek, but smart, employee supported by her league of co-workers, one of which was portrayed by Maria Eugenia Arboleda, an Afro-Latina.

When the reality show mania hit the U.S. Hispanic world, Telemundo network was the place to go for Spanish language reality shows. *"Protagonistas de la Música"* was similar to "American Idol" and "Real World" mixed into one. Viewers voted for the male and female performers they wanted to win. Of the finalists, two were Afro-Latinos, one of whom went on to win the show.

Se Habla Castellano

Iron-fisted ruler, Francisco Franco attempted to unify Spain during his 40-year regime that ended in 1975. He used repression against separatists and cultural groups. He outlawed speaking any of the non-Castilian languages in public, and ordered all children's names to be Castilian (a.k.a. Spanish). His slogan was "Spain, one, large and free." In 1960, Jordi Pujol was imprisoned for spearheading a public singing of a Catalan anthem. Today, he is president of the Catalan government. Franco's dictatorial unification scheme apparently backfired. Linguistic differences survived.

Spain has always been a multilingual, multicultural country in which there are four basic languages, and seven dialects. The separatists in Northern Spain live in the province called "Basque Country."

Basque, spoken in both Spain and France, bears no semblance to French or Spanish. In fact, it has no connection with any of the romance languages. It is not even an Indo-European language. Whereas July is *Julio* in Spanish and *Juillet* in French, in Basque, the name for the seventh month is *Uztaila*. Even the name for "Basque Country," *Euzkadi*, sounds nothing like the Romance root, *País Vasco*.

Just east of the Basque Country is the Generalitat d' Catalunya or Catalan Government. Catalan, and its derivatives, is spoken in the eastern parts of Spain and throughout the Balearic Islands. Approximately ten million people live in the lands where Catalan is spoken. Nearly one-third of television broadcasts are in Catalan. Visitors to Barcelona immediately notice the prominent use of Catalan everywhere. Names such as Güell, Gaudí, Milà, Batlló and Miró, sound nothing like Spanish. Books, movies and public performances are typically in Catalan, though Spanish versions are available on a less frequent basis.

Because of Spain's multilingual roots, a significant number of Spaniards are multilingual, and in Spain and Latin America, many refer to the Spanish language as *castellano*, not *español*. Due to the language differentiation in Spain, Rocha, Ros, Roche, Roig, Ross and Rosa are all common "Spanish" surnames. Add to that the influx of immigrants from outside Ibero-America to western Americas, and it is impossible to classify ethnicity by surname, alone. Surprisingly, in this country, people are identified by their looks and their name, and marketers frequently rely on surname to identify the target audiences.

While increasingly, we find Hispanics without Spanish names, there are more and more non-Hispanics with Spanish names. Filipinos have traditional Spanish surnames due to the era in which Spain colonized the islands. Filipinos are the second largest Asian sub-group in the United States, with 400,000 in California, alone, and 2.4 million nationwide. Few would consider East Indians Hispanic. After Vasco de Gama conquered India, there was a time when the Portuguese were prevalent in many parts of the land. Today, a large number of people in Goa, India, have a clear connection to their Portuguese ancestry and maintain Portuguese surnames, which sound more Spanish than those of Basque or Catalan origin do. Consider people such as Madonna's first-born,

Lourdes. Her father is Cuban-American, but will she self identify as Hispanic or speak Spanish?

Spanglish Rules

After surnames, the second most common way to classify Hispanics is by language. While this is effective to identify segmented groups, it shuts out a huge number of Latinos who prefer English. Language preference is not defined easily.

Nowadays, the average Hispanic American juggles time split between both English and Spanish. The vast majority of Latinos in the country have some degree of fluency in both languages. Nonetheless, there are some that speak Spanish primarily, and a significant number do not understand any Spanish. Approximately twice as many people say they speak Spanish at home than English. Of U.S. born Hispanics, 61 percent are English dominant and only 4 percent Spanish dominant. The 4 percent figure repeats itself among first generation Spanish dominant Hispanics. Second generation Hispanics are 47 percent bilingual and 47 percent English dominant. By the next generation, those numbers shift to 78 percent English dominant, 22 percent bilingual and zero percent Spanish dominant.

Terra.com is the leading portal in the Spanish-speaking world. In the United States, it attracts the largest percentage of English dominant Hispanics. Researchers and Terra.com executives attribute this to the cultural content offerings not found on traditional English language portals.

According to Terra.com's Chief Executive Officer Manuel Bellod, English dominant users seek Latino oriented topics and are willing to read them in Spanish if that is the language in which the information is available. He emphasizes that content and relevance are what is important. They are willing to consult sites in the U.S. and in their country of origin. Online behavior research indicates that more than half of U.S. Hispanics who are online visit sites from their country of origin.

According to Terra's research department, 28 percent of Hispanics online are bilingual and visit sites in Spanish. However, a much larger market segment is the English-preferred Hispanic. This accounts for 52 percent, or 6.5 million users who visit Spanish-language sites. Altogether, almost 10 million or 80 percent of U.S. Hispanic Internet users are either bilingual or English-preferred. This leaves a much smaller percentage of Spanish dominant people.

In 2001 a Latina journalist covering the Hispanic community for publications including *The Washington Post, People,* and *U.S.A. Today,* created a national magazine, *CATALINA,* to serve the nation's English-dominant Hispanic women, a segment long ignored by general and Hispanic market publications. The magazine's aim was to provide culturally appropriate content for women living in two cultures.

> "Unfortunately, the perception of many non-Hispanics is that all or most Hispanics are Spanish dominant. Some believe that the magazine is not Hispanic because it's not in Spanish," says *CATALINA* Publisher Cathy Areu Jones. "Being and feeling Latino is so much more than a language. Hispanic American women are complex and not easily labeled, and they are not defined by a language."

Countering Stereotypes

The February 2003 issue of *Vanity Fair* caused an outburst of responses from irate readers. In the very issue that featured Salma Hayek on its cover, Dame Edna in a tongue-in-cheek style displayed blatant racism and ignorance about the largest minority group and fastest growing population segment in the U.S. In response to a reader's question about the Spanish language, Dame Edna replied that there is no reason for (white America) to know Spanish, unless you want to speak with "leaf blowers."

Ernest Bromley, chief executive officer of Bromley Communications, a leading Hispanic marketing agency founded in 1981, was one of many who blasted *Vanity Fair* for its insensitivity, albeit draped in humor.

"To be bilingual in Spanish and English is truly an American experience, ever since Christopher Columbus discovered America in 1492; a venture funded by a Spanish woman, Queen Isabella of Spain. I respect that your reader may want to learn French or Italian, which is great. However, her friends have a greater understanding of the American landscape than Dame Edna does. For Dame Edna to refer to the Hispanic community as solely full of unskilled workers like 'the help' or 'leaf blowers' displays a total lack of understanding of the U.S. Hispanic community.

Furthermore, it is a total insult to U.S. Hispanic *campesinos*. While they may be unskilled, they have a fire in their eyes for the 'American Dream.' These people have taken great risk, leaving all that is familiar to them in their mother country, to carve out a new life for their family, both here in the U.S., and in their mother country. They bring the same work ethics, family values, and entrepreneurial drive that previous waves of immigrants have brought to this country. These people are truly heroes as they embrace the American Dream to earn good money, have comfortable homes, a car or two, and perhaps purchase a lifestyle magazine like *Vanity Fair*."

Apparently, the publishers of *Vanity Fair* did not realize Hispanics read English, and read their magazine, or at least used to read it. Hispanics watch all the mainstream media and movies. Hollywood's blockbuster power is worldwide and its titles are tops everywhere. Christmas 2003 DVD movie releases were selling in Mexico black markets just one week after the stateside big screen premieres.

The studio's marketing muscle is responsible for the success of Hollywood releases, according to Calixto Chinchilla, founder and executive director of the New York International Latino Film Festival. The Festival, along with several other similar entities in the country, attempts to "improve the images of Latinos in the media and present a more complete picture of this diverse nation." Although independent American film makers are producing high quality, culturally relevant and on-target material, they do not get the viewings of the powerhouse studio releases. This is not because of the quality or the content, but because of a lack of marketing. Well-acclaimed films such as "Girlfight," which was not commercially successful, unfortunately are relegated to the aisles of the movie rentals rather than the movie theaters. Actress Michelle Rodriguez cut her teeth in "Girlfight" and as a result was then cast in back-to-back leading roles in "The Fast and the Furious," "Resident Evil," "Blue Crush" and "SWAT."

Star power, rather than good acting, affects ticket sales. According to Chinchilla, who was an ethnic marketing consultant for major movie studios prior to founding the Festival in 1999, "Girlfight" missed the boat. Though the critics liked the film, it was a marketing issue and the studios do not have the funds. "Chasing Papi" on the other hand, was everywhere. The studios promoted the film well. It is often difficult to secure that kind of support and the funds for it.

Frito Bandito, Talking Chihuahuas and The Fantanas

The advertising community has tried its best to portray Hispanics in an accurate and non-stereotypical light. Back in the early days of Hispanic advertising, voice overs and translations were the norm. They did not necessarily hire professional talent or translators to do the work. Anyone who could pinch-hit in Spanish was involved in the "creative" executive. The early Spanish television stations routinely panned, for thirty seconds, what looked like a business card in lieu of an actual advertisement with messaging, visuals and strategy. Frequently, the audience heard one or two voices on nearly all television commercials, and chances are that voice was also a radio DJ (disk jockey) heard throughout much of the day.

At one production shoot in the 1980s, the talent, a well-known, handsome television personality with impeccable Spanish, proved that looks and language are not all that count. Despite his years of on-camera experience, his attempt with a script was embarrassing. After numerous takes, it was obvious he could not move about on the set, while saying his lines, all within thirty seconds. Yet the spot aired.

Despite the fact that Hispanics are the minority majority, Hispanic marketing is still in its growing stages. The evolution of Hispanic marketing prompted an education process between the agencies, the clients and the media. Because of the push and pulls, at times, Spanish advertising was leaking common stereotypes. If it is *Cinco de Mayo*, then there must be big *sombreros* (hats). As the market matured and ratings systems improved in Spanish media, we saw an increase in the interest from corporate America.

By the time the 2000 Census numbers came out, advertisers realized they needed to merge on to the express lane. Finally, there was a validation of what Hispanic marketers had been touting for a decade or two. Hispanics have large families. Hispanics live beyond New York City and Texas. Hispanics are younger. Hispanics speak English, and, Hispanics have money.

"Our purchasing power cannot be denied," says Catarino Lopez, creative director of Bromley Communications. "This justifiable interest has led to a creative revolution within Hispanic advertising. Now, companies are getting serious about reaching the Hispanic consumer." Budgets are increasing. Competition for business is high. Hispanic agencies try to differentiate themselves from their peers to win new business and retain current clients. Consequently, Hispanic ads are changing for the better.

"At Bromley, we strive to create insightful communications to win the hearts and minds of consumers," adds Lopez. "Being creative for creative sake might win you awards, but it's not going to change consumer behavior. Finding insights that connect and bring the brand to life is what motivates. For Crest, we introduced the insight of the *Bechito*. Latinos have a different sense of personal space. We hug people freely when we meet as opposed to shaking hands. We kiss on the cheek when we say hello. Consequently, we needed toothpaste that whitened our teeth and freshened our breath. The commercial we created shows a husband returning time and time again for a goodbye kiss after his wife uses the product." Another execution shows a grandmother and her grandson who asks for more kisses.

"For Coors, we needed an idea that would appeal to traditional and contemporary Mexicans. Billboards were going up in areas where both segments would see them. The least common denominator was language. Both segments used many of the same slang terms. Coors Light was an American beer that had no right to use the slang so we did a funny literal translation so bilingual guys could identify."

Bromley Communications also created television spots for Coors Light, appealing to Southwestern lifestyles. The agency assembled an "A-list" Hispanic creative and production team to produce the edgy concepts, including world-renowned director Angel Gracia and members of Oscar-nominated films "Frida" and "Amores Perros."

Another beer company, Miller, pulled off top-of-the-line Spanish-language television commercials in the early 1990s with the help of Emmanuel Lubezki. Lubezki is better known as director of photography for films such as "A Walk in the Clouds," "Sleepy Hollow," "Great Expectations," "Like Water for Chocolate," "*Y Tu Mamá Tambien,*" "The Little Princess" and "The Cat in the Hat." Born and raised in Mexico, Lubezki has won numerous awards, including an Academy Award and three Ariels, Mexico's equivalent of the U.S. film honors.

While Enrique Iglesias, Marc Anthony, Shakira and other pop stars lent their names, images and music to advertisements, the return on investment, ROI, is based on the celebrity power, rather than the actual notes and score. Most television ads use original melodies from independent musicians as the background music. When a reporter from a major general market national publication asked an advertising exec if the music used in a new Spanish-language commercial was "Hispanic," it sounded out of left field. A musical score is a musical score. Background music may have different instrumentation that sounds more jazzy, pop, classical or middle-of-the-road, but modern day television commercials do not insert *mariachi,* tango or *cumbia* scores without strategic rationale.

Where are Waldo and Juan?

Although advertisers have made astronomical strides in the last twenty years, some say the television industry has been working in a vacuum. For several years in a row, the National Council of La Raza (NCLR) led a "brownout," designed to create a call-to-action to the television industry to ensure adequate representation of Hispanics on screen. In 2001, a study released by NCLR and the National Association of Hispanic Journalists (NAHJ) found gross misrepresentation of Hispanics, in particular by the English-language broadcast news media. While magazine covers and radio stations were running a blitz of Ricky Martin, J. Lo (Jennifer Lopez) and Cristina Aguilera to tout the Latino crossover mania, television programming in the year 2000 was still operating in a vacuum. For example, out of 16,000 network news stories analyzed in the study, only 0.53 percent were about Latinos. For the year 2002, the coverage expanded to 0.75 percent. Additionally, stereotypes proliferated in the news media. An inappropriate use of salsa or mariachi music accompanied news stories and the media depicted a "ghettoization of Latinos" via B-roll footage. Finally, although the majority of U.S. Hispanics speaks English, ABC, NBC, CBS and CNN primarily portrayed Hispanics as Spanish-only speakers. George W. Bush's attempt to speak Spanish to potential voters, for example, was one of the most remembered stories.

"There's no question that the last place you'd know Latinos are the largest minority is by watching television," commented Lisa Navarrete, a spokesperson for NCLR. Finally, in January of 2002, the Public Broadcasting Service (PBS) premiered "American Family," a star-studded production filmed in East Los Angeles about an average, everyday Mexican-American family. Originally produced by Fox Studios and designed to be telecast on one of the major networks, syndication fell through. The Public Broadcasting Service picked up the series in a rare venture in which original prime time dramatic programming aired on PBS.

"Never in the history of broadcast television has there been a Latino-themed dramatic show in prime time, and we commend PBS for this breakthrough. It is critical for the Latino community to help show the entertainment industry that there is an audience and a hunger for this kind of programming and that the stories that the Latinos have to tell are compelling and appealing to everyone. It is darned good television," stated Raul Yzaguirre, former NCLR president.

Gregory Nava produces "American Family." His credits also double as suggested viewing for students interested in seeing movies that depict Latinos in a realistic and sensitive light: *"El Norte,"* "Frida," "Lean on Me," "Selena" and "Why Do Fools Fall in Love?" The television series strives to deliver what the title relays, portraits and scenes from a typical American family. Only this family's surname is Gonzalez. Raquel Welch is "Aunt Dora," Edward James Olmos is the patriarch, and AJ Lamas is the grandson. In 2004, the series continued with original programming. The Public Broadcasting Service PBS supported it with teacher and community guides and promotional tours.

In an attempt to provide viewers with what was missing from mainstream television, Jeff Valdez founded Sí TV in 1997, as an English-language, culturally relevant production company targeting younger, urban America. In 1999, Sí TV hit it big with "The Brothers Garcia," the first English-language sit-com with an all-Latino cast and creative team. Set in San Antonio, Texas, the show made it to its fourth season with a nationwide audience on Nickelodeon. When the show first aired, it boosted the cable network's ratings 260 percent from the same time in the prior year. According to Sí TV, it consistently reaches nearly five million viewers, including approximately two million viewers weekly in each of the 9-14 and 6-11 age categories. To reflect the realities of the multicultural urban setting typical of most Hispanic youth, John Leguizamo narrated the show's fourth season. The show features guest appearances by hip-hop artist Shaggy, singer Solange Knowles (Beyonce's sister) and the Jaguars. Other guest stars in 2004 included Cheech Marin and Roseanne Barr. The series has won a bevy of awards including the NCLR's ALMA Award.

Taking the simple concept of providing good quality entertainment designed for a younger audience in which the main characters happen to be Hispanic was not a simple task for Sí TV. Advertisers and programming executives and networks could not accept that Hispanic programming could be in English, or, that good English-language programming could feature Hispanic casts.

"It's been a massive challenge. We were told, 'you already have Univision and Telemundo'. Yet, they are as different from us as night and day. It's bizarre that you have to tell people that it's a show for everyone. It's like saying J. Lo (Jennifer Lopez) can only sell her CDs to Puerto Ricans in New York. We have shown that our productions, 'The Brothers Garcia,' 'Funny is Funny' and the 'Latino Laugh Festival' are equally successful in both the general and Latino markets," comments Sí TV's Valdez.

"People think we have equality, but you turn on the news and you see hate. As programmers, we have a responsibility. I hope this cable channel will help. I refused to be defeated. We intend to consolidate this success into one network which can serve as a platform for the talent that has not had access thus far."

Sí TV is launching its cable network with eight million viewing households, one of the largest cable launches in history. The National Council of La Raza also applauded "The George Lopez Show." "ABC gave 'The George Lopez Show' what no other Latino-themed show on network television had in three decades, a chance," said Yzaguirre. "A chance to air more than a handful of times in order to allow it to gain the audience and the popularity this delightful, family-friendly show deserves."

Although Lopez had admirable support from executive producer, Sandra Bullock, he still had his mountains to climb. Originally, the concept for the show included stereotypical images, which Lopez had to fight against in an attempt to portray an accurate image of today's Hispanic family.

Further endorsing a reform in on-screen representation of Hispanics, was the League of United Latin American Citizens (LULAC), the oldest and largest Latino civil rights organization in the country. One of the key issues facing LULAC in the new millennium was to encourage broadcasters and regulators to increase Hispanic-oriented programming in all facets of the media. "Programs should provide a positive and accurate portrayal of the cultural breadth of Latinos in the United States," stated Hector Flores, LULAC president. "As part of their public service obligations, we encourage the FCC (Federal Communications Commission) to require broadcasters to provide better Latino programming and representation in prime-time slots throughout the day. Overt discrimination is now something of the past, but there are still serious issues inherent in our society."

Understanding that it is important to countering stereotypes and presenting role models early on, Scholastic Entertainment, a division of Scholastic Inc., is producing its own new television series scheduled to premiere for release on PBS KIDS in the fall of 2004. "The Misadventures of Maya and Miguel" is an animated series that features a multicultural voice-over cast including Carlos Alazraqui (voice of the Taco Bell Chihuahua and Sponge Bob), Erik Estrada ("CHIPS" and "The Bold and the Beautiful"), Lupe Ontiveros ("Selena" and "Real Women Have Curves"), Lucy Liu ("Charlie's Angels" and "Kill Bill"), singer and actor Carlos Ponce, Elizabeth Pena ("Tortilla Soup" and "Rush Hour"). The lead characters are ten-year-old Hispanic twins living in a multicultural neighborhood.

Project Director Arminda Figueroa explains why Scholastic set out on this venture.

> "At Scholastic, we are convinced that this initiative will not only be important for it is not only important for a child's development but it is also reflective of part of our country's reality. 'Maya and Miguel' attempts to respond to the social transformation in the U.S. resulting from shifting, due to our changing demographics and the needs of second language learners, a society in which minority groups constitute the majority. Our new animated series, attempts to respond to the social transformation in the U.S. resulting from our shifting demographics and research regarding the needs of second language learners."

Scholastic's objectives are two fold: "To promote the value of a culturally diverse society by supporting, respecting and validating the variety of perspectives, traditions, languages and experiences that populate today's world and to support English language acquisition and usage in personal, social and cultural interactions, with a special emphasis on vocabulary." To ensure that the series accurately reflects our country's diverse culture-appropriate representation of the diverse characters, Scholastic Entertainment formed an advisory board of community leaders, educators and experts in diversity and multiculturalism.

A Tortilla Chicken Noodle Soup

Marketing to Hispanics in the 2000s requires going deeper than the surface. Communications professionals can wave three wands and connect to Mexicans in Los Angeles, Puerto Ricans in New York and Cubans in Miami. Or can they? The landscape of the American public is changing, and even the government recognizes that.

Unsure about who Hispanics were, and many years before the term "Hispanic" was bolstered by the Census Bureau, in the 1920 Census, Mexicans were considered whites. In 1930, a new category popped up for Mexicans. Two decades later, they reclassified Mexicans as white. By 1950, the U.S. Census counted four million Hispanics. Immigrant populations, traditionally fearing the Census as a branch of the government connected to immigration authorities, were severely undercounted. For the 2000 Census, the government launched an all-out public relations campaign in early 1999 to sensitize the Hispanic community to the benefits of responding to the Census; and to eliminate the fear that had persisted in the past among Hispanics not wanting to give government workers information about their families.

In addition to the heavy public relations campaign, for the first time ever, the Census Bureau coordinated a paid publicity campaign designed to "reach all adults living in the United States (including Puerto Rico and the island areas.)" They tweaked the messaging strategy for each of the major ethnic groups. The overriding communication points informed people about the benefits in responding to the census mailings and surveyors. In all, they spent one hundred million dollars on more than 130,000 announcements played on 3,000 media outlets in 17 languages. AdTrack, a *USA Today* consumer poll named the ad blitz, planned and executed by five advertising agencies, including Young &

Rubicam's Hispanic arm, The Bravo Group, the second most effective campaign.

The government also deemed it necessary to make operational changes for the Census 2000. For the first time, respondents had more options with which to self-identify their race and ethnicity. During the prior census survey, in the year 1990, ten million people did not list their race. Census officials, understanding that race was no longer a black/white issue, redesigned the 2000 survey to allow for multiple racial listings. Nearly seven million respondents chose two or more race categories. Approximately half were teens. In that same year, 53 percent of all "multiethnic" births were to a Hispanic parent. Not surprisingly, *The New York Times* in 2001 reported that two-thirds of intermarriages in California were with a Latino partner. Some estimates report that half of Latinos today marry outside the Hispanic box.

In addition to the rise in people of "mixed-race," there is a meshing of Hispanic groups within the United States. No longer can you neatly divide Mexicans, Puerto Ricans and Cubans. Aside from the fact that South and Central Americans have been immigrating in large numbers to this country in the last decade due to economic and political woes, there is "inter-marriage" within the Hispanic segment. Take "Girlfight's" Michelle Rodriguez: born in Mexican-dominant San Antonio, she is of Puerto Rican and Dominican descent. She grew up in Puerto Rico, the Dominican Republic, and New Jersey.

Just as Cubans have long been eating turkey along with *lechon asado* (roast pork) and rice and beans for Thanksgiving dinners, nowadays, Mexican *migas* and *tortilla* soup, Colombian *arepas* (corn flower bread) and Cuban *mojitos* (a drink made with spearmint and rum) are consumed by people of all ethnicities in high density Hispanic markets like Miami, San Antonio and Houston. Häagen-Dazs offers new flavors like *Tres Leches*, a traditional Nicaraguan dessert, and caramel flavored *dulce de leche*, which has its origins in Argentina. *Tortillas* were a four billion dollar business in 2000. *Salsa* (a sauce), a seven million dollar business, has been outselling catsup since the mid-90s. *Salsa* music is outselling traditional genres in the record stores where music is crossing cultural boundaries as well.

To sell that much *salsa* and *tortillas*, you have to go beyond the *barrios* (neighborhoods). Interestingly, the areas with the greatest surge in Hispanic density are not the usual suspects. Drawn by job opportunities, the emerging Hispanic markets are sprouting up in places where the twang is no longer Texan or *Nuyorican*. As a result, Lowes Foods and Super K-Mart introduced Latin American food products in Wilkesboro, NC. Shoppers in small towns like Sleepy Hollow, New Jersey can purchase Ecuadorian *cuyes* (roasted guinea pig) and *humitas* (sweet tamales). To help target the new consumers, Hispanic marketing companies are now operating in North Carolina and Atlanta. *Bienvenidos* (welcome) to the Deep South and Middle America.

Atlanta, Raleigh/Durham, Oklahoma City and Salt Lake City each experienced enormous increases in their Hispanic communities between 1990 and 2000. Charlotte and Raleigh each saw Hispanic populations soar in the neighborhood of 650 percent. Beating that figure was Kansas City at 714 percent. Bill Clinton's hometown of Little Rock saw a 337 percent boost in Hispanics in that same period of time, while the state of Iowa's Hispanic population grew 150 percent and North Dakota's 66 percent.

Mexicans still represent the bulk of the immigrant population. However, patterns are changing rapidly, in particular among the newest immigrants subsets. Migration is also occurring within the United States. Fleeing the larger urban areas, Mexicans jump from Los Angeles to Salt Lake City. Cubans move from Miami to North Carolina. Thus, the traditionally segmented Mexican Southwest and Caribbean eastern markets are changing character. Historically Cuban Miami grew 16 percent according to the 2000 Census, versus a 64 percent boost in the city's Mexican population, 55 percent among Dominicans and 48 percent for Hondurans. In the meantime, Cuban growth was highest in Arizona (116 percent increase), North Carolina (97 percent increase) and Nevada (58 percent increase). The new Census figures indicated 343,137 Mexicans registered in the New York/Northern New Jersey/Long Island corridor, 42,500 Salvadorans in New York's Nassau and Suffolk counties and 10,718 Guatemalans and 9,083 Colombians in Georgia.

New immigration means new consumers. The Hispanic market, by far, poses the greatest marketing potential for many products and services. Yet, insensitive translations or band-aid public relations attempts can backfire. Just as any solid public relations campaign must rely on well-grounded research and insights; it is paramount to Hispanic public relations.

Inside the Hispanic Real World

Hispanic or Latino. Just one word; yet there is no one word that can describe the complexity of ethnicity for Hispanics in the United States. Following are several people's accounts about their upbringing and Hispanic identification.

Luisa D. does not have a traditional Spanish surname, nor does she fit one of the more traditional classifications.

"My family is from Guatemala, and I was born in Panama. I moved to Falls Church, Virginia when I was three and lived there until age six. There were not many Hispanics living in Falls Church in the 70s, mostly Anglos, African-Americans and Asians. All of my schoolmate friends would ask me if I was black, white or yellow. I was neither. I remember going home and crying with my parents because I couldn't answer the question. My dad said I was 'morenita.' That nickname (meaning dark one) stuck for most of my adolescence. When I moved to Monterey, California, everyone referred to me as Mexican, even though I am not. They called everyone of Latino origin a Mexican. I used to tell my Asian friends that saying I was Mexican was like saying all Asians are from Japan. Monterey is a cultural melting pot, based primarily on the large military base that used to be there. Growing up, I had friends from Guam, Japan, the Philippines, Germany, Brazil, and many others. It was a wonderful experience being exposed to so many different cultures at such a young age."

"I moved to San Bernardino, California after high school. For me, San Bernardino was very different from Monterey because San Bernardino was home to so many Latinos. Still, in San Bernardino, when I would tell my other Hispanic friends that I wasn't Mexican, they accused me of denying my heritage."

Jaci Velasquez, a Houston-born singer/songwriter, author and actress who was featured on more than 60 magazine covers by the time she was 23 years old, rose to the top through her strong Christian faith. Her success was unusual, in part, because she was an award-winning recording artist in English before she "crossed-over" to the Spanish-language market. Although English is Jaci's native tongue, she prefers to sing in Spanish.

"When I was a little girl it was not very popular to be Hispanic. All of my friends had blond hair and blue eyes and spoke only English. My parents decided not to teach me Spanish. The older I got, the more I was interested in my heritage. When I landed a Spanish record deal it was imperative for me to learn Spanish. In spite of how hard they say it is to learn a new language as an adult, I did it. I am very proud of both my ethnic background and my American heritage as well. They both have a very strong part of the woman I am today. In my life, now more than ever, I love being Hispanic. I believe we can make a strong impact on the world."

Latin Grammy winner, Jorge Moreno, an English-dominant Cuban-American is equally at home composing and singing in Spanish or English. His music reflects the cultural mix in which he was born and raised, Miami. His parents both came to the U.S. in pre-Castro days. Jorge grew up surrounded by music. He says he learned a lot from his father, who ran a Latin music label producing records for artists such as Jose Luis Rodriguez (*El Puma*), Oscar de Leon and Frankie Ruiz. Moreno also attributes his learnings and passions to his grandmother who owned a record store where he would hang out after school.

"To go forward, you have to get well-acquainted with your past. I remember going to a few recording sessions with my dad when I was a kid. I'd hang out with the artists when I went with him to a concert, have pictures taken with Celia Cruz after a show, things like that. So I was exposed to show business and Caribbean music at a very young age. As a result, my musical influences are a big mix. They range from the Beatles and Elvis Presley to Perez Prado and DePeche Mode. As a young adult I went to Spain and Morocco where I did some searching for my roots, and at the same time, developed a great appreciation for their diverse music forms."

"My first demos were very alternative, with Arabic music, hip-hop beats, and even a bit of Pink Floyd. From there, my style kept evolving as I mixed my alternative interests with my traditional roots to try to come up with catchy little hooks, but with an edge. On my first CD, I did the time-honored classic Beny More '*Como Fue*,' with a modern alternative arrangement to show how you can cross these worlds without losing your roots. I believe if you are going to cover a song, you have to bring something new to it or just don't do it, and the original by Beny is so beautiful that I didn't want people to come and say 'who does this guy think he is?' Another cut on my first CD, '*Reloj*,' is a bolero inspired by the great, classic Cuban singers like Beny. I'm a big fan of the music of that era. '*Reloj*' was written in today's times as a homage to the sound of yesteryear."

Viana V. was born in South America and moved to Texas in the fifth grade. Although her middle school and high school were diverse, the Hispanic population in her town was predominantly Mexican or Mexican-American.

"People refer to me, or my South American friends, as 'that Mexican girl/guy.' I always tell people I'm from South America or Ecuador. I'm not Mexican. Since Ecuador is not too well known, I'm used to people getting confused about it. But, I've had crazy comments from children, and even their parents. I've had adults ask if there's running water or electricity there. People ask 'do you speak Ecuadorian?' 'That's like Spain, right?' 'So, you're more Spanish than Mexican, then.' 'What part of Mexico is that in?' And, of course they all think we eat Mexican food in South America. I even had someone jokingly ask, 'so are your parents drug traffickers?' I don't see them as being stupid questions, just a reflection of their small-town concepts and lifestyles. We aren't too far from Mexico, but there are lots of people who haven't been out of Texas. Even the Mexican-Americans."

Sonia Q. was born and raised in San Antonio, Texas, where for many years people were discriminated against for speaking Spanish. Consequently, a large portion of San Antonio Hispanics does not speak Spanish.

"I am American; *pero no soy americana. Soy mexicana,* but I am not Mexican. One day while I was sitting in a Mexican-American bi-cultural class, I heard my professor say this and it captured exactly what I have always felt. I feel a sense of pride and patriotism when I say I am an American. Saying 'I am an American' means you stand for something, freedom, to almost do anything you want in this country. But I would never refer to myself as being *americana* and I cringe if a person from Mexico would ever refer to me as being *Americana,* it's stereotypical, it's another word for *gringa.* If I'm called *americana* I am 'the other'—an outsider looking in. If I am *americana,* I'm not really *mexicana,* I shouldn't share my roots and heritage with them. To be *americana* is to be a wannabe, a sell out."

"*Yo soy mexicana.* It's a label I wear with a sense of pride. *Mexicana* equates to my ancestors, sharing their history, having the right to love the music, having the right to sing and wear my *mariachi* outfit, having the right to speak Spanish, having the right to love *mi cultura,* having the right to own the Mexican flag, having the right to care about the poverty that so many *mexicanos* live in and having the right to have compassion for the people who live in a corrupted government. But, I would never want anyone in the U.S. to refer to me has being 'a Mexican'. Somewhere along the way, being a 'Mexican' means people can look down on me, to be beneath everything. Being bicultural and bilingual is a beautiful thing. It means I can live an American way of life but surround myself with Mexican culture. It means I cared that my university didn't have a *mariachi* class but they could teach the History of Rock and Roll. It means I had to set the pace and get a *mariachi* started and have the music department take it seriously."

Maria C. is the daughter of Mexican immigrants. A college freshman at Amherst, she and her siblings all attended Ivy League universities. She describes elements of what make up her Latino identity in the United States.

"Being an individual who falls under the label of Latino brings about many experiences which are mostly meant to subjugate individuals. This term also brings about the denial of a unique and individual identity since Latinos in the United States are seldom looked upon as people who come from different cultures and backgrounds. Instead, they are all lumped into one broad category. Latinos are embraced with open arms into the United States when the work force is in desperate need of workers. They are America's job fillers, but once the need for labor in the United States diminishes, workers are forcefully sent back and the border is shut. Even in today's 'liberal and accepting' American society, blatant forms of discrimination are directed toward Latino immigrants, such as Proposition 187, which sought to rid American society of illegal immigrants. Some Latinos, because of their skin color, will have the choice of either accepting their own culture or to 'enter into' another, which can ultimately make their life easier for them. Other Latinos will not have this choice."

Kimberly J. was born and raised in Laredo, Texas, where 95 percent of the population is Hispanic.

"Having an Anglo father and a Hispanic mother has given me a different perspective. My last name is very much an Anglo name, so people are usually shocked when I can speak Spanish. At the same time, I had a professor once tell me that I don't look like my name because I looked Hispanic. I guess it just depends on who is observing you. In Laredo, I feel more connected with my Hispanic roots. We always joked that my dad was a 'Mexican gringo' because we always celebrated our holidays and birthdays in a very traditional Hispanic style. In Laredo, at least with the crowd I hung out with, we were very 'international' Latinos as opposed to *'tejanos.'* I rarely remember listening to any *tejano* music as a child and young adult; I would occasionally listen to *cumbias* and of course Selena, but not much else. When I moved to San Antonio, I expected the majority of people (especially Hispanics) to speak Spanish, but to my surprise very few did. People would pronounce their surnames like Gonzalez or Salazar with a white accent or twist; this was very new to me. Almost everyone in Laredo spoke Spanish and could pronounce Spanish words or names properly. It was an interesting change and it took some getting used to."

What is in a Name

Presidents of Latin American countries without Spanish surnames
- Nestor Kirchner, elected in 2003 as president of Argentina, second generation Argentine, son of Swiss/German father and Croatian mother
- Vicente Fox Quesada, elected as president of Mexico in the year 2000, Fox was the first non-PRI party candidate in 71 years to

become president of Mexico, son of Basque mother and father of Irish descent

- Carlos Menem, president of Argentina from 1989-1999, son of Syrian Sunni Muslim immigrants
- Reynaldo Bignoni, president of Argentina from 1982-1983
- Leopoldo Galtieri, president of Argentina from 1981-1982
- Dr. Arturo Frondizi, president of Argentina from 1958-1962
- Fernando Belaunde Terry, president of Peru from 1963-1968 and 1980-1985, born to an aristocratic Peruvian family with European ties, educated in France and the United States, worked in Mexico prior to returning to Peru
- Alberto Fujimori, elected president of Peru for two terms, from 1990-2000, was the son of Japanese agricultural workers who arrived in Peru in 1934, currently in exile in Japan
- Patricio Aylwin Azocar, president of Chile from 1990-1994, of Irish and Spanish ancestry
- Abdalá Bucaram, president of Ecuador from 1996-1997, of Lebanese descent
- Jamil Mahuad Witt, president of Ecuador from 1998-2000, son of Lebanese father and German mother, after leaving office taught at the JFK School of Government at Harvard University
- Alfredo Stroessner, military dictator of Paraguay from 1954-1989
- Andres Rodriguez Pedotti, president of Paraguay from 1989-1993
- Juan Carlos Wasmosy Monti, president of Paraguay from 1993-1998
- Luis Angel Gonzalez Macchi, president of Paraguay from 1999-2003
- Julio Sanguinetti Coirolo, president of Uruguay from 1985-1990 and 1995-2000, of Italian descent, worked as a journalist and writer throughout his lifetime and published several books
- Hugo Banzer, president of Bolivia from 1997-2001, of German descent, died in 2002 to complications from terminal cancer
- Dr. Jaime Lusinchi, president of Venezuela from 1984, during the country's economic demise; his Corsican mother was born in Barcelona and raised him without a father

- Ricardo Maduro Joest, elected president of Honduras in 2001 although he was born in Panama to a Panamanian father and Honduran/German mother who was born in Guatemala
- Jose Maria Figueres Olsen, president of Costa Rica from 1994-1998
- Enrique Bolaños Gayer, president of Nicaragua from 2002-2006
- Juan Bosch, president of Dominican Republic in 1962, child of Catalan father and Puerto Rican mother, an accomplished author who lived in exile during the Trujillo regime, died in 2001 in Santo Domingo
- Alfredo Cristiani Burkard, president of El Salvador from 1989-1994
- Oscar Berger, president of Guatemala, 2004-

Suggested viewing:
- Any Gregory Nava production. *"El Norte"* is required viewing
- Most any Edward James Olmos film, especially "Zoot Suit," "Stand and Deliver," "The Ballad of Gregorio Cortez," "My Family" and "Selena"
- Any Emmanuel Lubezki film, in particular, "Like Water for Chocolate" and "A Walk in the Clouds"
- "Tortilla Soup" with Raquel Welch and Hector Elizondo
- "Bread and Roses" with George Lopez and Adrian Brody
- "Real Women Have Curves," with America Ferrera, Lupe Ontiveros and George Lopez

Chapter Summary

- Translations do not suffice.
- On-target strategic public relations demands in-depth understanding of the primary audience.
- If the public relations team is not able to understand the diverse marketplace of today, they need to hire a multicultural marketing specialist or miss a major portion of the marketplace.

- To better address the multicultural arena, one needs to look at how history has shaped today's society and separate stereotypes from reality.
- A Hispanic "look," is what we choose to see, because Hispanics are of all races and ethnicities.
- In the United States, we classify people by their looks and their name and marketers often incorrectly rely on surnames to identify Hispanics.
- To target Hispanics by selecting Spanish speakers shuts out the majority of Latinos who are English dominant or have varying degrees of fluency in both languages.
- It is essential to delve into consumer insights prior to developing a strategic communications campaign.
- Avoid stereotypes at all costs.
- Hispanics represent a multicultural, multiracial and multilingual grouping of peoples with diverse ancestries and histories.
- By the time the 2000 Census numbers came out, marketing pros could not ignore the facts: Hispanics live beyond New York City and Texas; they have large families, are younger, speak English and have money.
- The landscape of America is changing; race is not a black and white issue.
- No longer can you neatly divide Mexicans, Puerto Ricans and Cubans.
- You have to go beyond the barrios.
- An equal percentage of second generation Hispanics are bilingual and English dominant.
- Among third generation Latinos, 78 percent are English dominant, 22 percent bilingual and zero percent Spanish dominant.

About the Author

Deborah Vallejo, Vice President and Managing Director, Bromley/MS&L San Antonio

Deborah Charnes Vallejo is managing director of Bromley/MS&L. Her responsibilities include strategic development of corporate communications plans and implementation of public relations programs geared toward the U.S. Hispanic market. Charnes Vallejo, who has been in the communications arena since 1980, attended the National Autonomous University of Mexico, and earned a bachelor's degree from the University of Illinois-Urbana.

Chapter Four

A Deeper Look into the U.S. Hispanic Market

Derene Allen
Madalyn Friedman

In This Chapter

- An "insider's look" into the Hispanic market
- Definition of Hispanic segments and projected growth to 2009
- Demographic differences between segments including age, income, and education
- Information on Hispanic children relating to growth by age group and cultural impact

Introduction

To understand the emotional drivers behind Hispanic adults' motivating factors linked to purchasing decisions, analyzing beyond strictly level of acculturation or language becomes imperative. Evaluating market segments according to generational distance incorporates both language and culture as well as level of category and brand familiarity. We use generational distance to define the amount of time a Hispanic has resided in the U.S., and this measure has shown to be relatively accurate in predicting both language and cultural influence.

We can identify five distinct generational distance segments, allowing for sizeable segments and identifiable demographic and psychographic characteristics, ranging from a Newcomer who is foreign born with less than one third of their life in the U.S. to an Adapter who is a U.S. born Hispanic, fully integrated into the General Market. Utilizing this segmentation scheme facilitates strategy development (positioning, communications and promotions strategy, public relations and community events, etc.) for marketers wishing to grow their business with Hispanic consumers.

In four out of the five segments, the home country and parents' home country culture is the driving force behind the emotional reasons in purchasing decisions, even though as the resident spends more time in the U.S., noticeable improvements in their English language capability occur. Even the U.S. born Maintainers, while fully fluent in English, have a good command of Spanish, and have chosen to maintain the culture of their parent(s) in their home and with their children. For a marketer, this is critical to understand, and topples the myth that "if they speak English, my English language advertising is reaching them." Yes, they may understand, however they are not being "reached" emotionally, a core element in the purchasing decision-making and brand loyalty generation processes. English language advertising only fully resonates with the Adapter Segment, who account for only 14 percent of Hispanics. Table 1 explains the five segments and their respective characteristics.

Sizing the Segments

Generational Distance	Country of Birth	Percent of Life in U.S.	Language
Newcomers	Foreign Born	Less than 1/3	Spanish Only
Transitionals	Foreign Born	1/3 to 2/3	Spanish Mostly
Transplants	Foreign Born	Greater than 2/3	Equally Bilingual
Maintainers	U.S. Born	100 Percent	Mostly Bilingual
Adapters	U.S. Born	100 Percent	English Only

Table 1 - Five Distinct Adult Hispanic Market Segments

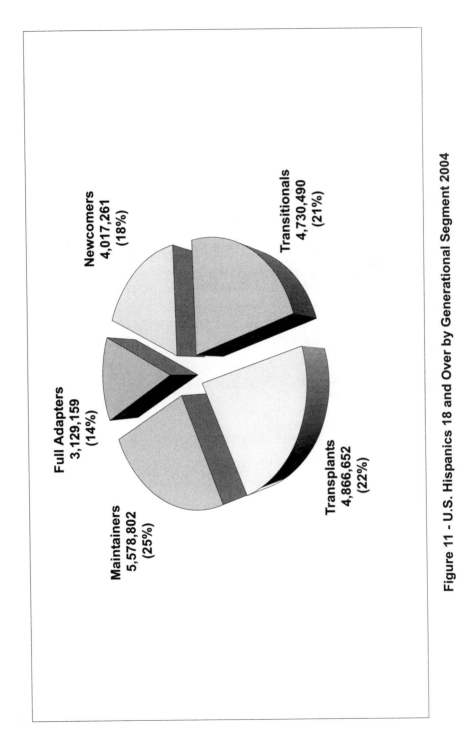

Newcomers
4,017,261
(18%)

Transitionals
4,730,490
(21%)

Full Adapters
3,129,159
(14%)

Transplants
4,866,652
(22%)

Maintainers
5,578,802
(25%)

Figure 11 - U.S. Hispanics 18 and Over by Generational Segment 2004

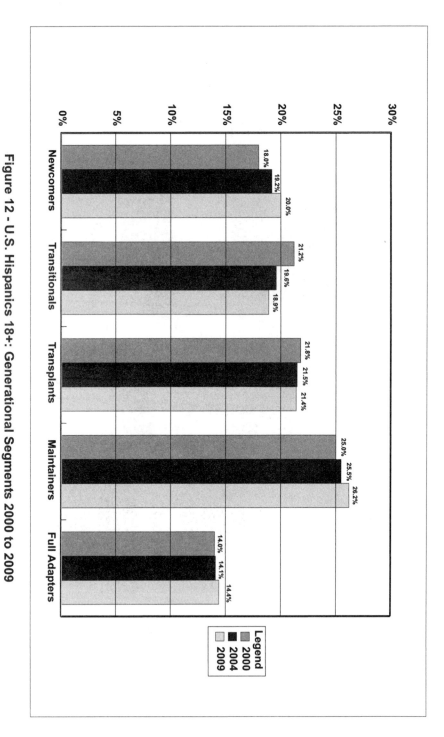

Figure 12 - U.S. Hispanics 18+: Generational Segments 2000 to 2009

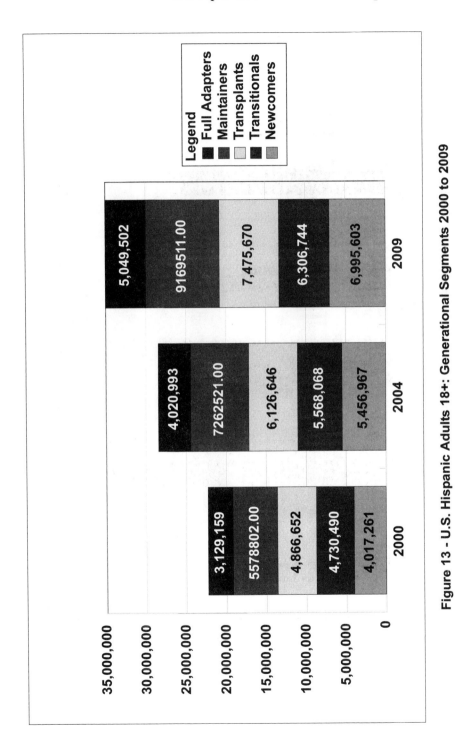

Figure 13 - U.S. Hispanic Adults 18+: Generational Segments 2000 to 2009

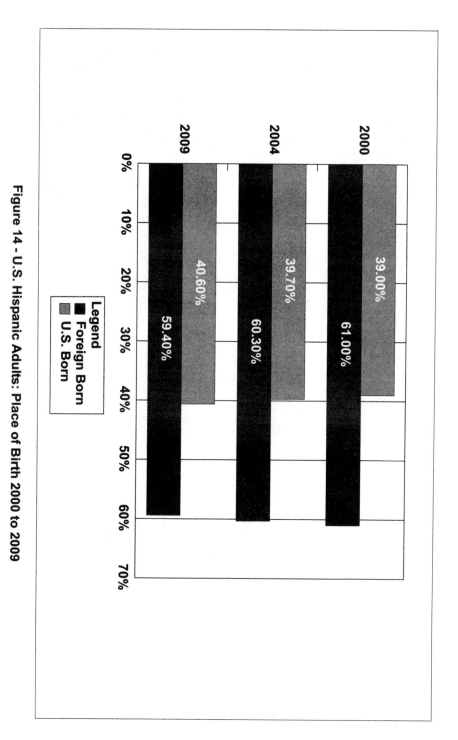

Figure 14 - U.S. Hispanic Adults: Place of Birth 2000 to 2009

Maintainers, born in the U.S., are the largest segment, accounting for 25 percent of the adult population. Transplants and Transitionals follow closely. From a strategy perspective, we can often group Newcomers and Transitionals, and Transplants and Maintainers as they follow similar language usage patterns and are either closer to their home country culture or slightly more acculturated as in the case of Transplants and Maintainers.

The Newcomer and Maintainer segments will see the greatest growth from 2000-2009, rising at a compound annual growth rate of 6.3 percent and 5.7 percent respectively. From a strategy perspective, looking for future growth for your brand, workforce, etc. these are the segments to pay particular attention to, as nearly 7 million additional Hispanic adults will fall into these segments by 2009.

Country of Birth

The majority of Hispanic adults will continue to be foreign born, directly impacting strategy development and the relevance of culture and language. It is important to consider that the overall pie of Hispanics is growing, so the number of English and Spanish speakers is growing. Since 1990, approximately six out of 10 Hispanics have been foreign born, highlighting the importance of including cultural considerations in both product and service development and in the communication of their benefits.

While most U.S. Hispanic children are U.S. born, the majority are born to foreign-born parents, who transfer their cultural impact to their children in the home. Fifty-four percent of Hispanics under age 19 living in the U.S. today were born to at least one foreign born parent.

So while children are being exposed to the English language and general market culture at school and perhaps in the homes of their friends, at home many are speaking Spanish with their parents, "watching" the Spanish language television shows their parents watch in addition to their own shows in English on Nickelodeon or the Disney Channel. They are listening to Spanish language radio shows and music while in the car with their parents, eating foods from their parents' home country and celebrating holidays in an "in-culture" fashion with

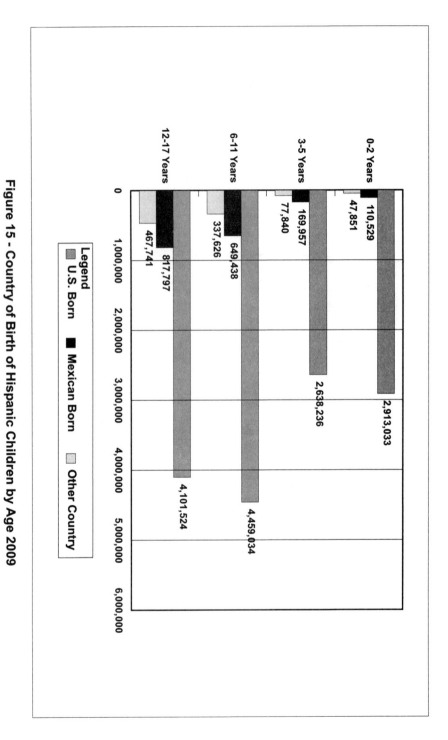

Figure 15 - Country of Birth of Hispanic Children by Age 2009

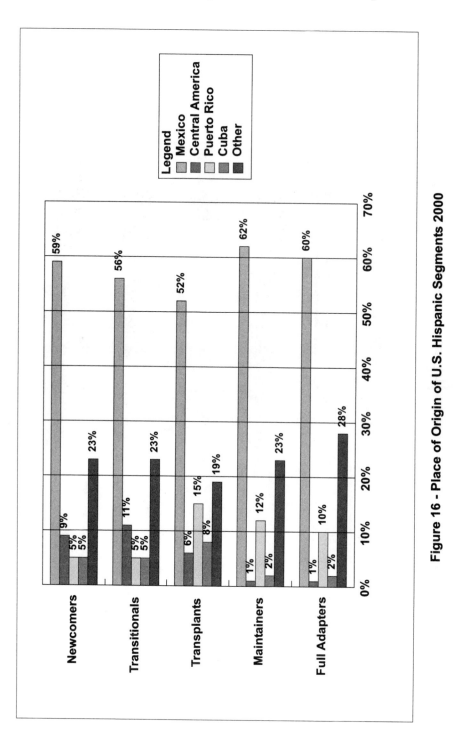

Figure 16 - Place of Origin of U.S. Hispanic Segments 2000

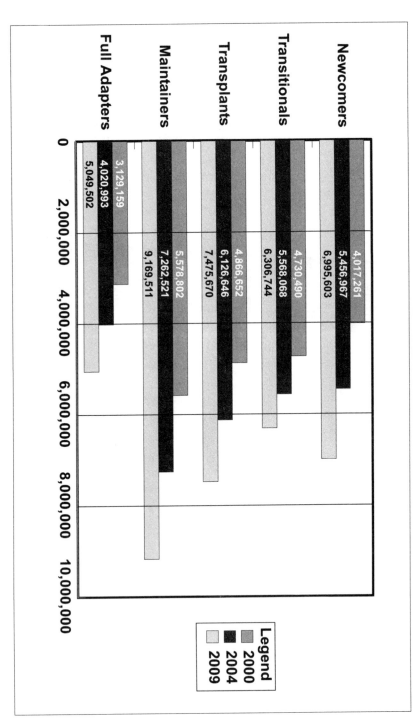

Figure 17 - U.S. Hispanic Adults: Generational Segments 2000 to 2009

piñatas for birthdays, "coming out" parties for the girls when they turn 15 (*quinceañeras*) and so forth. These children truly live bilingual and bicultural lives.

Mexico represents the predominant country of origin across all generational segments, accounting for over 12.8 million of the 22 million Hispanic adults. The influence of Central Americans among more recent immigrants (Newcomers and Transitionals) and that of Cubans and Puerto Ricans among more established immigrants (Transplants) appears in Figure 16. For strategy development purposes, should your product or service be more relevant to those who have been in this country longer, you may wish to target your strategies toward the Transplant and Maintainer segments, which while still heavily Mexican, will have a greater proportion of Puerto Ricans and Cubans than other segments.

Age

Newcomers, Maintainers and Full Adapters skew younger. Newcomers often arrive in their late teens or early twenties, while a large proportion of U.S. born Hispanics, born to an immigrant parent, are the progression of the earlier immigration wave, and their offspring. For products or services targeted to young adults, these three segments are in very different places from a language and culture perspective, requiring that marketers define their lead segment and develop strategies targeted to that core market.

Regional Analysis

Texas and other Southwestern states, traditionally known as states with a significant Hispanic presence, illustrate this history with a higher predominance of U.S. born Maintainers and Full Adapters, with over 50 percent of their Hispanic populations falling into these segments. New "Hispanic states" in the Southeast, Northeast and Midwest each have over 40 percent of their populations falling into the Newcomer and Transitional segments. California's numbers show its role as both a traditional Hispanic state as well as a popular destination for more recent immigrants.

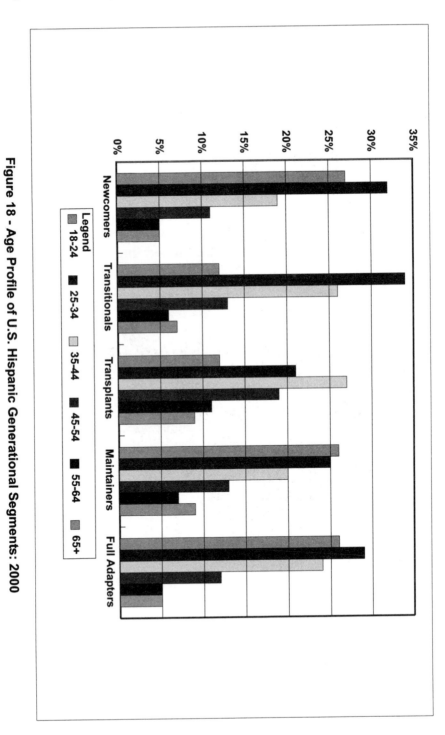

Figure 18 - Age Profile of U.S. Hispanic Generational Segments: 2000

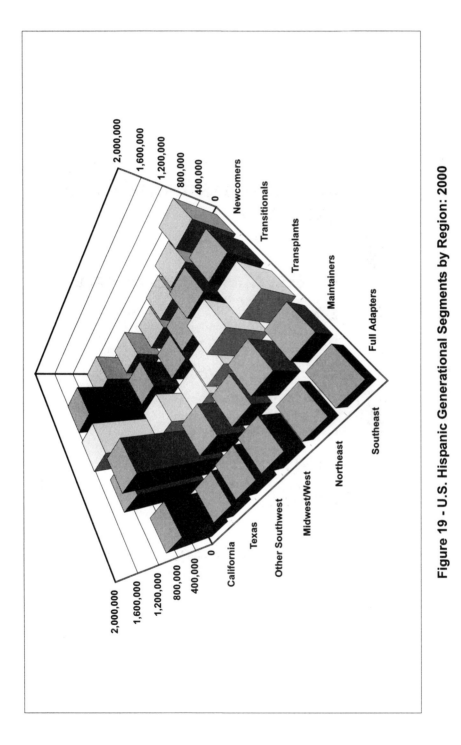

Figure 19 - U.S. Hispanic Generational Segments by Region: 2000

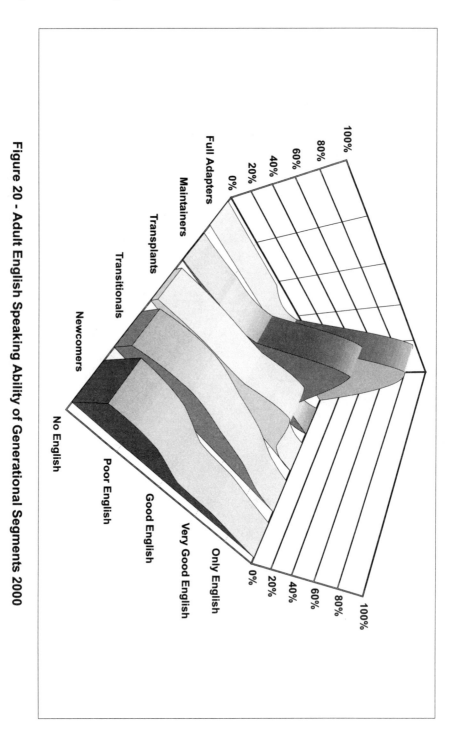

Figure 20 - Adult English Speaking Ability of Generational Segments 2000

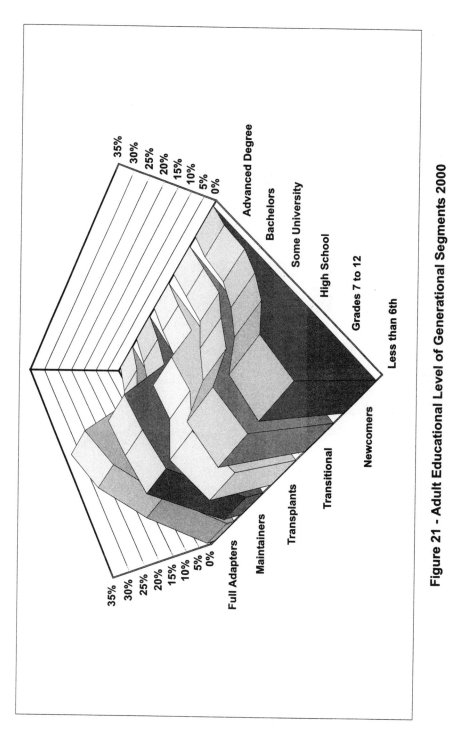

Figure 21 - Adult Educational Level of Generational Segments 2000

Data Table for Figure 18 - Age Profile of Generational Segments

	18-24	25-34	35-44	45-54	55-64	65+
Newcomers	27%	32%	19%	11%	5%	5%
Transitionals	12%	34%	26%	13%	6%	7%
Transplants	12%	21%	27%	19%	11%	9%
Maintainers	26%	25%	20%	13%	7%	9%
Full Adapters	26%	29%	24%	12%	5%	5%

Data Table for Figure 19 - Generational Segments by Region

	Newcomers	Transitionals	Transplants	Maintainers	Full Adapters
California	939,350	1,658,440	1,677,750	1,452,530	1,036,680
Texas	576,125	621,249	684,616	1,815,620	467,557
Other Southwest	331,311	299,033	271,254	697,816	503,401
Midwest/West	507,989	484,315	463,660	498,168	533,531
Northeast	677,020	827,755	957,905	662,527	278,874
Southeast	985,256	839,679	811,467	452,142	309,116

Data Table for Figure 20 - Language by Generational Segment

	Newcomers	Transitionals	Transplants	Maintainers	Full Adapters
No English	34%	17%	7%	1%	0%
Poor English	33%	32%	18%	5%	0%
Good English	14%	26%	25%	15%	0%
Very Good	13%	19%	43%	80%	0%
Only English	6%	6%	7%	0%	100%

Data Table for Figure 21 - Education by Generational Segment

	Newcomers	Transitionals	Transplants	Maintainers	Full Adapters
Less than 6th	31%	31%	23%	7%	3%
Grades 7 to 12	30%	32%	28%	27%	19%
High School	19%	19%	21%	28%	30%
Some University	11%	12%	20%	28%	34%
Bachelors	5%	4%	5%	7%	10%
Advanced Degree	4%	2%	3%	3%	4%

Data Table for Figure 22 - Employment by Generational Segment

	Newcomers	Transitionals	Transplants	Maintainers	Full Adapters
Employed and not Working	1%	2%	2%	1%	2%
Unemployed	6%	5%	5%	6%	5%
Not in Labor Force	40%	40%	38%	34%	26%
Employed and at Work	53%	53%	55%	58%	67%

This regional analysis is useful when looking at marketing program and media efficiencies, enabling marketers to target their efforts to the regions with a higher presence of those particular segments with a higher response propensity to the product or service offering.

Language Ability

Two thirds of Newcomers do not speak English well or at all. Nearly half of all Transitionals fall into these language proficiency categories as well. The predominance of English really only becomes clearly visible among the U.S. born segments of Maintainers and Adapters. Maintainers may speak English very well, but not exclusively. This, along with the maintenance of their parent(s)' home country culture in their home, is what differentiates them from Adapters.

Language is a central element to any marketing strategy; hence, the critical importance of clearly identifying your core target market segments in the Hispanic market. Understanding which language your core segment(s) speak or prefer to speak can eliminate a lot of the discussion related to "do we also need English language media and communications or will Spanish suffice." In addition to language, we must also apply the "culture lens" when developing communication strategy.

Note that the differentiating factor between Maintainers and Adapters is that Maintainers speak at least some Spanish. As a result, if any U.S. born Hispanic reports that he or she speaks only English, he or she is, by definition, an Adapter.

Educational Attainment

Newcomers and Transitionals also have the lowest educational attainment levels with over half not having completed high school. Higher educational attainment is visible in the U.S. born segments. This is a clear driver for product and service strategy and for the development of the communications strategy targeted to these segments requiring a clear transmission of the "why buy" proposition.

In addition to educational attainment, the level of base understanding and knowledge around different product and service groups may vary, requiring you to develop communications from a different frame

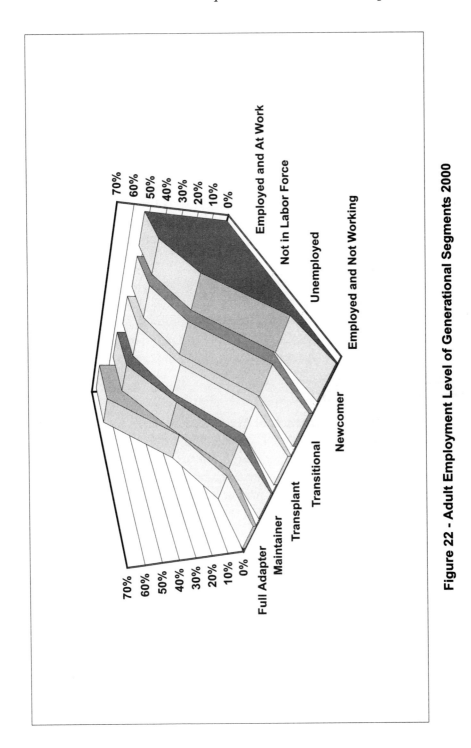

Figure 22 - Adult Employment Level of Generational Segments 2000

of reference; that of your selected target segment, rather than that of the general market. Translation, even a good translation into Spanish, of an English language advertisement may not be effective, given the different perspective and understanding around your product or service category.

Employment

The greatest portion of all segments is employed, followed by those not in the labor force. This is particularly true of the foreign-born segments, which is due to women staying at home and taking care of their families or possibly those in the informal labor market.

Women who are not in the labor force, and are "stay-at-home moms" display different shopping behaviors. These vary from the types of foods they buy (i.e. make meals from scratch or purchase "convenience" foods); to how they medicate their children when they are sick (those that have to work tend to be quicker to medicate so the child can go to daycare or school and mom does not have to miss as much work).

Income

There is a direct correlation between income level and time in the U.S.: the greater the years in the U.S., the greater the propensity to be in the higher income levels. Depending upon the level of basic need for your product, the amount of disposable income can greatly influence purchasing habits. We use the expression basic need here, since higher income segments are not necessarily the most attractive for all products or services.

In our discussion on household size , we see that the same segments that have a higher percentage in the lower income brackets also have a larger household size. These households focus on products that meet basic needs. For certain food and grocery products as well as products like household cleansers, these are highly attractive segments, with lots of mouths to feed and many clothes to wash!

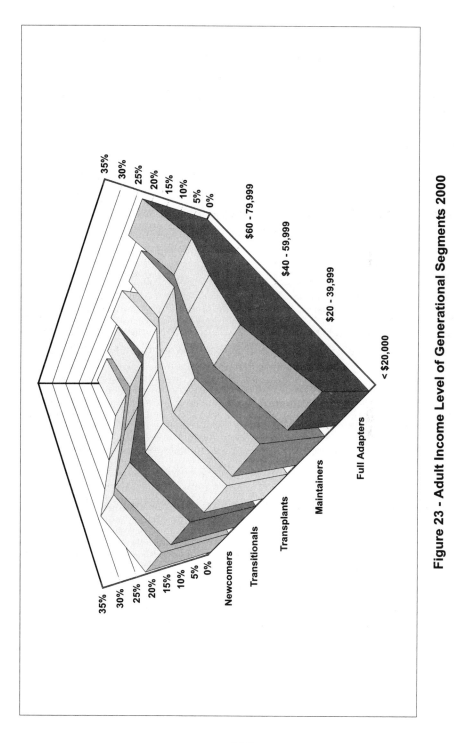

Figure 23 - Adult Income Level of Generational Segments 2000

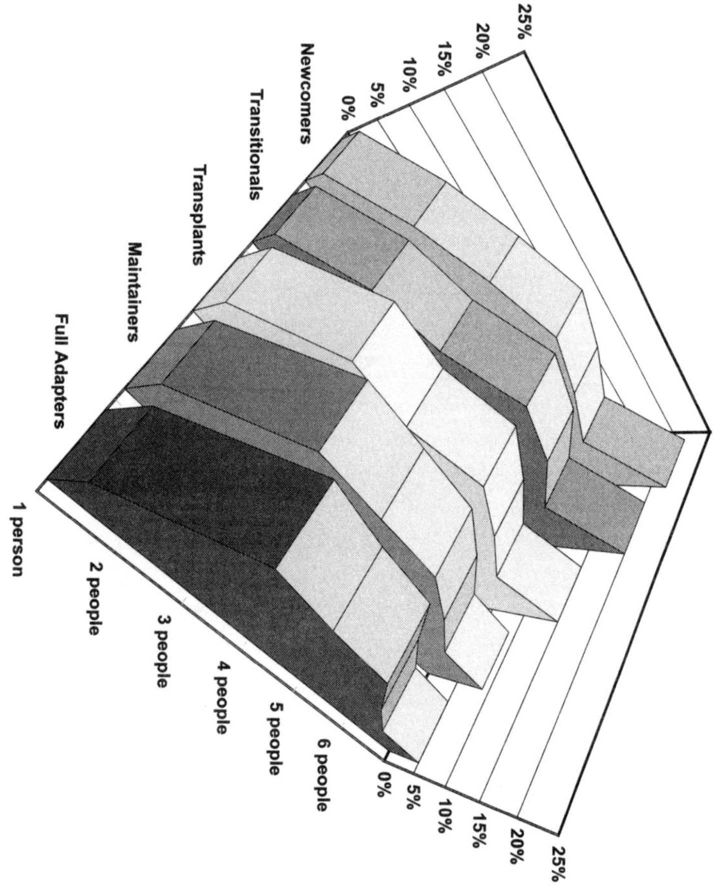

Figure 24- Household Size of Generational Segments 2000

Data Table for Figure 23 - Income by Generational Segment

	Newcomers	Transitionals	Transplants	Maintainers	Full Adapters
< $20,000	23%	22%	20%	21%	16%
$20 - 39,999	30%	31%	28%	27%	24%
$40 - 59,999	21%	21%	21%	22%	21%
$60 - 79,999	12%	12%	13%	14%	16%
> $80,000	13%	14%	18%	17%	23%

Data Table for Figure 24 - Household Size by Generational Segment

	Newcomers	Transitionals	Transplants	Maintainers	Full Adapters
1 person	3%	4%	6%	7%	9%
2 people	10%	11%	16%	20%	24%
3 people	15%	14%	16%	20%	22%
4 people	19%	20%	20%	20%	21%
5 people	17%	18%	16%	15%	13%
6 people	14%	13%	11%	9%	6%
7 people	22%	20%	15%	9%	5%

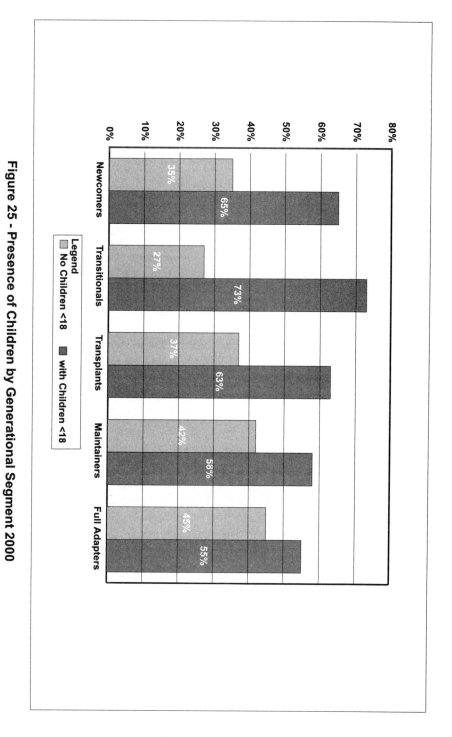

Figure 25 - Presence of Children by Generational Segment 2000

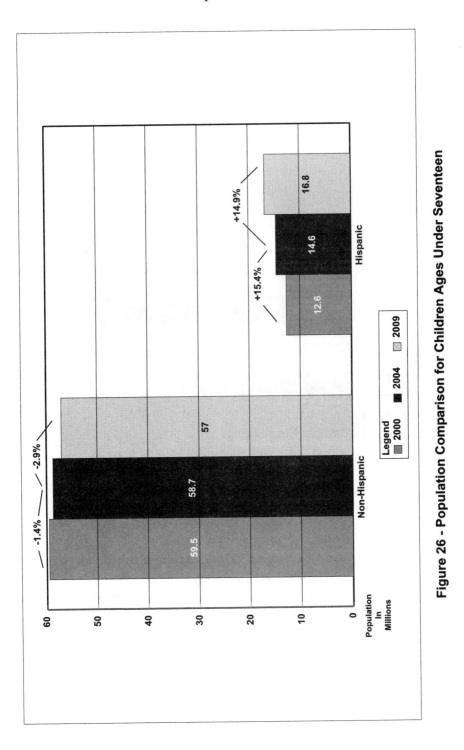

Figure 26 - Population Comparison for Children Ages Under Seventeen

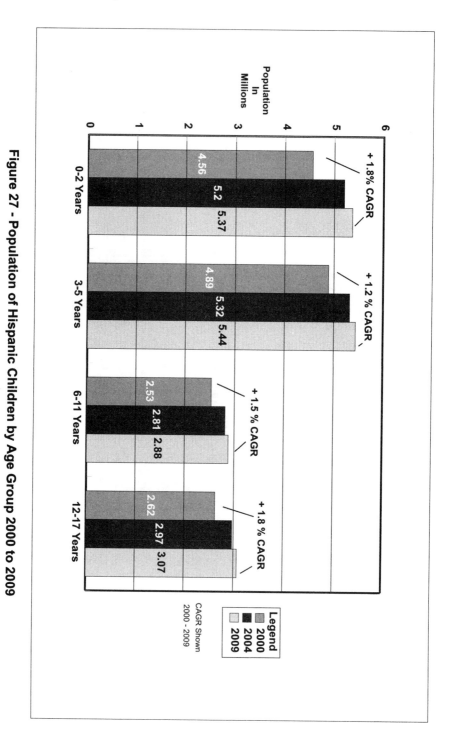

Figure 27 - Population of Hispanic Children by Age Group 2000 to 2009

Population In Millions

	0-2 Years	3-5 Years	6-11 Years	12-17 Years
2000	4.56	4.89	2.53	2.62
2004	5.2	5.32	2.81	2.97
2009	5.37	5.44	2.88	3.07

+ 1.8% CAGR
+ 1.2 % CAGR
+ 1.5 % CAGR
+ 1.8 % CAGR

Legend
2000
2004
2009

CAGR Shown
2000 - 2009

Household Size

Newcomers, Transitionals and Transplants have larger household sizes. This is a critical factor component for many consumer products such as food, beverages, health and beauty, and over-the-counter medications among others. It is also key for retailers interested in attracting these consumers.

Hispanic Children

Transitionals have the greatest presence of children under 18. We may explain this by the fact that many immigrant parents move to the U.S. when their children are very young or they immigrate and then have their U.S. born children.

As a marketer, with a product for children, who needs to reach the decision maker it is critical to understand which segment will have the highest presence of children and develop your strategies around this segment. All of the foreign-born segments have a higher propensity to have children under 18 living at home.

The number of Hispanic children is growing in double digits, while the number of U.S. non-Hispanic children is declining. From 2000 to 2009, U.S. non-Hispanic Children under 17 will decline by nearly three percent while Hispanic children will increase by nearly 15 percent. Looking at it from another perspective, Hispanic children will grow from 17.5 percent of the total under 17 population in 2000 to 22.7 percent by 2009.

For Hispanic youth, less than five years is the largest age category, with nearly two million children per age year, by 2009. All age categories of Hispanic children are experiencing growth.

Implications and Conclusions

From a strategy development perspective, all of the U.S. Hispanic market segments present a potential growth opportunity across the board, for adults and children. Given the core differences between the Hispanic generational segments, the key for the successful marketer is to identify those segments with the greatest opportunity for the target product or service offering. With a more in-depth understanding of the respective segments, we can develop targeted strategies, thereby facilitating successful implementation and business growth generation. The target segment strategy drives all strategy development, which will bring to light language preference, presence of children, regional presence, level of education and employment characteristics of the marketer's selected target segment as well as sophistication of brand repertoire. A fuller understanding of the profile of your selected core target segment will drive efficiencies.

There is no such thing as a single Hispanic Market. There is no single strategy that will appeal equally across all Hispanic segments. Just as there is no single general market strategy which is equally effective across all general market segments.

Acknowledgments

The source of this data is the Census 2000. Nustats demographic consultants mined the Census 2000 data for the 2000 generational segments and demographic characteristics, and projected the generational segments to 2003 and 2008. Santiago Solutions Group projected these segments to 2004 and 2009.

We acknowledge and thank Carlos Santiago, president and chief executive officer of the Santiago Solutions Group, for his never-ending quest to provide further insights into the evolving U.S. Hispanic market. Recognized as one of the leading strategists in this area, Carlos is always questioning and searching for new keys to unlock the secrets for corporate success in growing their participation as well as their contribution to the U.S. Hispanic community.

Chapter Summary

The U.S. Hispanic market offers one of the greatest growth opportunities in the United States today, yet is an enigma to many marketers. Corporations have forayed into the Hispanic market, meeting with differing degrees of success. While not foolproof, the key to unlocking the secrets of the Hispanic market lies in a deeper understanding of the segments.

- Definition of Hispanic segments
- Cultural and language drivers of Hispanic segments
- Demographic differences between segments:
  - Age
  - Income
  - Education
  - Employment
  - Presence of children
  - Regional presence
- Hispanic children:
  - Growth by age group
  - Cultural impacts

About the Authors

Derene Allen, Senior Vice President, Santiago Solutions Group

Derene Allen is a senior vice president with the Santiago Solutions Group, a multicultural business strategy development consulting firm. As such, she has participated in the creation of U.S. Hispanic and African American strategies for such clients as Johnson & Johnson, Nestle, and American Express. Derene is an MBA graduate of Thunderbird and has lived and worked in Latin America and the Caribbean for many years prior to transferring her experience to the U.S. multicultural markets.

Madalyn Friedman, Director, Santiago Solutions Group

Madalyn Friedman brings a comprehensive understanding of the consumer products industry based on twenty-three years of multifunctional experience. She has applied this experience during her eight years in Hispanic marketing strategy and market research. Madalyn earned a Bachelor of Science in Engineering from Princeton University and her Master's in Management from Northwestern University.

Chapter Five

Hispanic Projections

Roger Selbert, Ph.D.

In This Chapter

- U.S. Hispanic market forecasts for size, rate of growth, patterns of dispersion and buying power
- Forecasts summary and analysis

Introduction

Hispanics are now the nation's largest minority group: the number of Hispanics living in the United States was 38.8 million as of July 2002 (not including the 3.8 million people living in Puerto Rico). Hispanics represent 13.45 percent of the U.S. population. Projections for future growth are astounding. The Census Bureau predicts that one in every four Americans will be Hispanic by 2050, growing to one in every three Americans by 2100.

The U.S. Hispanic population increased by 3.5 million, or 9.8 percent, between April 1, 2000 and July 1, 2002, accounting for 50 percent of the nation's population growth of 6.9 million during that period. This high rate of growth (10 times that of the non-Hispanic white population) is driven by immigration (which accounted for 53 percent of the Hispanic population growth between 2000 and 2002); and by natural increase, the difference between births and deaths, which accounted for the remaining 47 percent.

Although this growth rate will moderate over the next 10 years (to merely 35 percent!), the Census Bureau projects a Hispanic population of about 50 million in 2015. Between 1995 and 2025, researchers project the Hispanic origin population will account for 44 percent of the growth in the nation's population (32 million Hispanics out of 72 million persons added to the nation's population).

Researchers expect the Hispanic population to comprise a substantially larger share of the total population in 2025 than in 1995, up from 21 to 32 percent in the West, from 9 to 15 percent in the South and Northeast, and from 3 to 6 percent in the Midwest. This is largely because compared to non-Hispanic households, U.S. Hispanic households are younger (median age 27.6 versus 36.8), larger (averaging 3.4 persons, versus 2.6), and have higher birth rates.

Hispanic Americans are significantly younger as a group than the overall U.S. population. Some 13.34 million (or 34.4 percent of all U.S. Latinos) are under age 18. Another third are in the 25 to 44 age group; 87.8 percent are below age 50. Only 5.1 percent of U.S. Hispanics are over age 65, in contrast to 14.4 percent of non-Hispanics whites.

Changing Sources of Population Growth

Immigration has been key to Latinos' population growth in the past, but the native born will fuel Hispanic population growth in the future. Ten million second-generation U.S.-born children of immigrants make up 29 percent of all Hispanics. Another 11 million comprise the "third generation" (born to two native-born parents) and represent 31 percent of all Latinos. However, by 2025, U.S.-born Latinos will represent 13 percent of the U.S. population; Hispanic immigrants will comprise just 5 percent.

According to the Pew Hispanic Center, Hispanic immigrants are 36 years of age on average and this population will soon pass out of its family formation years. Second generation children of Hispanic immigrants are young, averaging just over 19 years old. Even the third generation is just 26 years of age on average. Third generation Latinos households are smaller than immigrant households are, but they are much larger than non-Hispanic households are. As a result, Hispanic

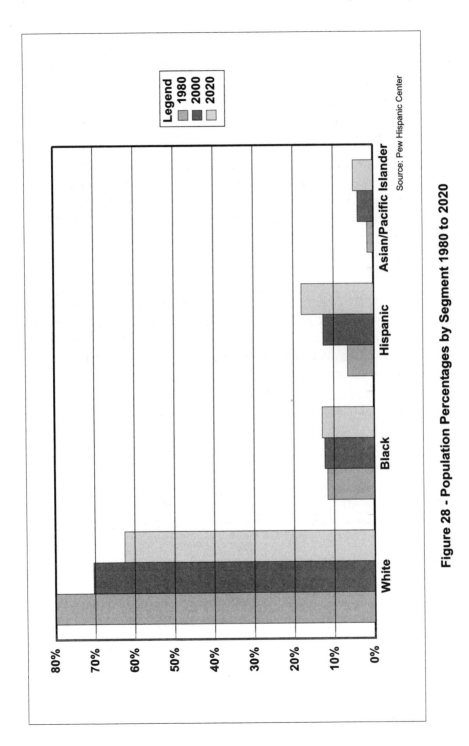

Figure 28 - Population Percentages by Segment 1980 to 2020

Source: Pew Hispanic Center

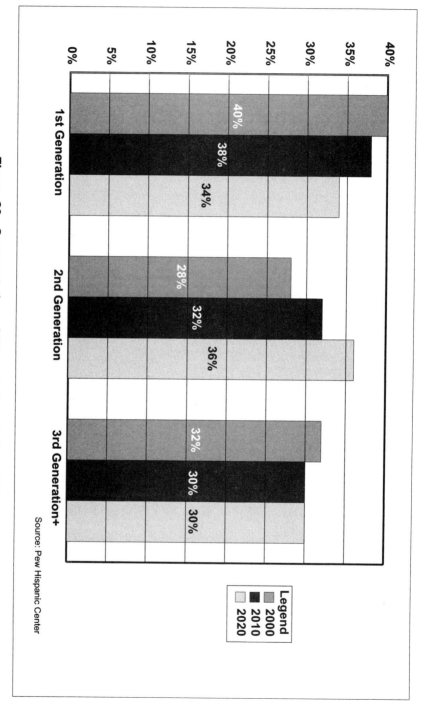

Figure 29 - Segmentation of Hispanic Population 2000 to 2020

Source: Pew Hispanic Center

demography will increasingly be defined by the native-born, even if immigration flows are greater than expected.

Changing Patterns of Population Dispersion

A new study by the Brookings Institution Center on Urban and Metropolitan Policy and the Pew Hispanic Center shows how the rapid growth of America's Hispanic population has played out among the cities and suburbs of the 100 largest metropolitan areas.

The study, "Latino Growth in Metropolitan America: Changing Patterns, New Locations," co-authored by Roberto Suro of the Pew Hispanic Center and Audrey Singer of the Brookings Institution, confirms the wide distribution of Latino population growth during the 1990s, and reveals deep variations in the rate and location of that growth among cities. The report also confirms that the majority of U.S. Latinos now live in the suburbs.

The Hispanic population is growing in most American metropolitan areas. There are four distinct patterns of growth:

- **Established Latino metros** (16 in total) such as New York, Los Angeles, Miami, and Chicago posted the largest absolute increases in Latinos between 1980 and 2000, on top of their already large base populations of Hispanics. These metros represent the Hispanic heartland in America.
- **New Latino destinations** (51 in total) experienced an astonishing and rapid entrance of new Hispanics into their communities in recent years (despite their historically smaller Hispanic population bases). Metros like Atlanta and Orlando charted the fastest growth rates.
- **Fast-growing Latino hubs** (11 in total) began with very large base populations and displayed extraordinary rates of Latino growth between 1980 and 2000. Metros like Houston, Phoenix, and San Diego saw their Latino populations explode by an average of 235 percent over the two-decade period.

- **Small Latino places** (22 in total) posted much lower absolute and relative growth in Hispanics. These included places like Detroit and Philadelphia.

The Latino suburban population grew 71 percent in the 1990s. Fifty-four percent of all U.S. Latinos now reside in the suburbs. The 51 New Latino destinations saw the fastest growth of Latino suburbanites.

Hispanic men outnumber Hispanic women by 17 percent in New Latino destination metros, where the Latino population grew fastest. By contrast, in slower-growing metros with large and well-established Latino communities, a greater number of Hispanics live in family households and gender ratios are more balanced.

Another recent report comes to similar conclusions. According to "Emerging Communities: A Snapshot of a Growing Hispanic America," released by the League of United Latin American Citizens (LULAC), Hispanics dominate U.S. population growth, but the explosive growth of the U.S. Latino population extends beyond traditional metropolitan receiving areas like Los Angeles, Houston, Chicago and Miami. While 58 percent of Latinos live in 10 major metro areas, 42 percent have dispersed to areas not commonly accustomed to receiving clusters of Hispanics, including suburban fringes, small cities and towns, rural areas, and Southern states.

Although presenting challenges to local resources, the study concludes, these newly established communities often bring economic life back to areas sorely in need of revitalization. Some of the report's other findings:

Geographic Dispersion

During the 1990s, the Hispanic population in New Latino destinations such as Orlando, Florida, Little Rock, Arkansas and Washington, D.C. grew 250 percent, even faster than in traditionally Hispanic metropolitan areas such as Houston and San Diego, where it increased 235 percent.

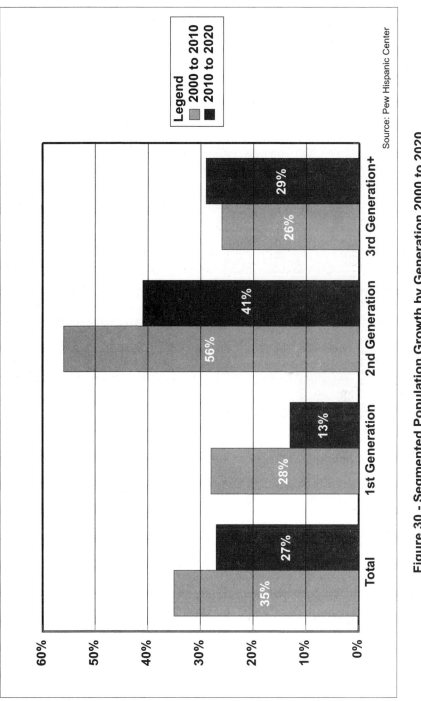

Figure 30 - Segmented Population Growth by Generation 2000 to 2020

An Ethnically Diverse Population

Although two-thirds of the Latino population is of Mexican origin, there are approximately 17 different groups represented in this "national" community.

Similar Traits

While Latinos consist of many national origins, they share similar characteristics. Latinos as a whole are young, have more children, have great family stability, share Roman Catholic roots, and generally have a dominant father figure or male role model. More than half of all Latinos living in the United States are completely bilingual.

An Entrepreneurial Community

In the year 2000, according to the U.S. Census, real household income for Hispanics was more than $42,000; nearly one-third of Latino households had an annual income of $50,000 or more; and Latinos owned 5.8 percent of all small businesses, some 1.2 million firms.

Latinos as Consumers

Latino households spend more on food, utilities and shelter than average, and less on services and health care. Latinos also spend more on clothes, are label conscious and above-average shoppers at discount food and clothing retailers.

Health Insurance and Health Care

Hispanics are the most likely to be uninsured. Over half of Hispanics under 65 do not have coverage, representing one-quarter of all uninsured people in the country. Hispanics are less likely to receive routine health care services compared to non-Hispanic whites.

The Working Poor

Family size, geographic concentration in large metro areas, high costs of living, scarce affordable housing and lack of public transportation contribute to the large number of Hispanic working poor. To escape this predicament many Latinos have relocated to suburbs of the large metro areas or to smaller, less congested cities. While the percentage of Latinos living in poverty is high, extended family and children contributing to the overall income of the household counterbalance it.

Hispanic Buying Power Growth

According to research reports by Standard & Poor's Global Insight and the Selig Center for Economic Growth, Hispanic buying power (total personal disposable income) will grow approximately 9 percent a year over the next several years (and decades), reaching about $1 trillion by 2008 (and $2.5 trillion by 2020).

Over the 18-year period covered in the Selig Center report, "The Multicultural Economy 2003: America's Minority Buying Power," Hispanics' economic clout is projected to rise from $222 billion in 1990, to $504 billion in 2000, to $653 billion in 2003, and to over $1 trillion in 2008. The 2008 value will exceed the 1990 value by 357 percent, a percentage gain that is substantially greater than either the 136 percent increase in non-Hispanic buying power or the 148 percent increase in the buying power of all consumers. In 2008, Hispanics will account for 9.6 percent of all U.S. buying power, up from 5.2 percent in 1990.

Of the many forces supporting this substantial and continued growth, according to the Selig report, the most important is favorable demographics (i.e. a rapidly growing population base), but better employment opportunities also are a factor. A relatively young Hispanic population, with larger proportions of them either entering the workforce for the first time or moving up their career ladders, also augers for additional gains in buying power, which will be even more important in this decade than in the 1990s. The increasing number of Hispanics who are successfully starting and expanding their own businesses is another factor powering the growth.

Because of differences in per capita income, wealth, demographics, and culture, reports the Selig Center, the spending habits of Hispanics are not the same as those of the average U.S. consumer. The most recent Consumer Expenditure Survey indicates that Hispanic consumers spent in total only about 87 percent as much as the average non-Hispanic household spend. At the same time, they spent a higher proportion of their income on goods and services.

Despite their lower average income levels, however, Hispanics spent more on groceries, telephone services, furniture, small appliances and house wares, children's apparel, and footwear. In addition, a higher proportion of Hispanics' total spending was concentrated on restaurants, housing, vehicle purchases, gasoline and motor oil.

The size, growth and spending power of Hispanic consumers is transforming every consumer-oriented industry in America. According to the Global Insight report, sales to the Hispanic population are the fastest-growing sub-market for almost every consumer product or service.

That includes big-ticket items like cars. Car sales to Hispanics over the next decade will increase significantly faster than sales to the general population. On average, car sales to Hispanics will increase 5.4 percent annually versus 1.4 percent for the general population. By 2012, Hispanics will account for 11 percent of all new-car sales, totaling some $32 billion.

The motion picture industry will rely on the Hispanic population for a bigger chunk of its box-office growth over the next decade. Currently, Hispanics account for almost 15 percent of the industry's $9.5 billion in box office receipts. Global Insight predicts that, by 2012, Hispanics will account for 18 percent of some $16 billion in movie-ticket sales.

Over the next five years, Global Insight projects that Hispanic spending on prescription drugs will climb at an annual rate of 15.2 percent, compared with 12.6 percent for spending growth in the category by non-Hispanic households. In part, that will be due to the 10 million newly insured Hispanic employees entering the workforce over the next decade.

Hispanics and the Baby Product Market

According to the U.S. Census Bureau, 40 percent of Latino families have two or more children present, compared with 29 percent of families overall. The Hispanic youth segment (under 5 years of age) is expanding at nearly six times the rate of the U.S. youth market overall. Researchers project that between 2001 and 2010, the number of Latino children under the age of five will increase by 17.3 percent, while the overall number of children in that age range will increase by only 3.3 percent.

As Hispanics continue to make up a growing percentage of this youngest population segment, marketers will direct more baby-related products, marketing and advertising at the Hispanic market. Hispanics already account for about 50 percent of disposable-diaper purchases, and 38 percent of the purchases of children's apparel.

According to Packaged Facts, a New York-based market research firm, by 2005 at least 40 percent of the designs and colors in the children's apparel market will be tailored to appeal to Hispanics and African Americans. And according to New Strategist publications of Ithaca, N.Y., Hispanics outspend the general market by 29 percent on boys' clothing, by 27 percent on girls' clothing, and by 67 percent on apparel for children two years of age and younger.

No wonder mainstream children's apparel companies, and not just urban fashion labels, are starting to tap into these markets. They are coming out with clothes that display brighter colors, have design elements favored by Hispanic mothers, and/or feature characters popular among Latino youngsters (such as Dora the Explorer). Such firms have been featuring more diverse models in their ads for years; now they are increasing their advertising in Spanish-language and Hispanic-directed media as well.

Retailers catering to the baby market are also setting out to exploit the lucrative Hispanic target. Americans spend an astounding amount on baby goods: $29 billion in 2002. New parents spend about $6,000 on baby-related goods and services during their babies' first 12 months.

Babies'R'Us, which operates 183 stores in 40 states and reported revenue of $1.6 billion in 2002, launched a marketing initiative aimed at Hispanics last year. Babies'R'Us:

- Increased its bilingual personnel.

- Made its baby registry available in Spanish.
- Publishes its catalogs in Spanish and English.
- Packages its private-label merchandise with instructions and information in Spanish and English.

Other baby-oriented businesses are plugging into the opportunities the Hispanic market affords and will continue to present for many years to come. Most doll manufacturers, to take another example, now showcase ethnic product lines. American Baby magazine, also seeing the increasing need to market to Hispanics, has launched three Spanish-language magazines in the last four years: "*12 Meses,*" "*Healthy Kids en Español,*" and "*Espera.*" Distributed through Ob-Gyns (obstetricians and gynecologists) and pediatricians, they boast a combined circulation of nearly 2 million.

Hispanics and the Wireless Market

According to an Association of Hispanic Advertising Agencies, AHHA, report, "The Right Spend," Hispanics tend to keep tight bonds with extended family and friends, making them heavy communications users, especially for collect and international calling. Hispanic wireless consumption is already comparable to non-Hispanics, reports the AHAA, which still expects wireless penetration and usage to increase among Hispanics at an incredibly rapid rate.

According to Cheskin Research, a California-based market research firm, nearly half of U.S. Hispanics have mobile phones; this represents a market of roughly 16 million people. According to Insight Research, Hispanics spent nearly $4 billion on wireless communication last year, a figure expected to reach $4.4 billion by the end of 2003.

HispanicBusiness.com reports that the nation's six leading carriers, AT&T Wireless, Cingular Wireless, Nextel, Sprint PCS, T-Mobile and Verizon Wireless, have cast a wide net for Hispanic customers. The firms have established Spanish-language web sites, and planned a barrage of marketing campaigns, product launches and wireless services aimed at affluent and tech-savvy Hispanics.

In its report "The Wireless Future: A Look at Youth Unplugged," Cheskin Research cited several future trends for the industry, especially the development of wireless data transmission that will permit complex games, entertainment, and business graphics to travel on the airwaves. U.S. Hispanic youth, a demographic group projected to grow 62 percent by 2020, compared with 10 percent growth for all U.S. teens, will be a major target market for these services.

Hispanics and the Car Market

Hispanics are the largest minority group in the new-vehicle-buying population. Hispanics, who account for nearly 14 percent of the U.S. population, purchased 8 percent of new cars and trucks sold in the United States last year. And by 2020, when the Hispanic population will have doubled to 70 million people, Hispanics will account for 13 percent of all new-vehicle sales in the country.

That is just one of the conclusions reached by J.D. Powers & Associates in its 2002 U.S. Hispanic Automotive Segment Report, which analyzes the opinions of new and used vehicle buyers who identify themselves as "Hispanic" versus those who identify themselves as another race or culture. According to AHAA, Hispanics account for 25 percent of purchases of minivans and pickup trucks, and 22 percent of entry-level but hip compacts.

Another conclusion of the J.D. Power report is that there is a clear preference among Hispanic buyers for import makes and models. When comparing nameplates based on the percent of owners who are of Hispanic descent or culture, all of the top 10 brands are imports. The high penetration of imports among Hispanic buyers is not only apparent in metropolitan markets, but also across rural and suburban markets. According to the report, Hispanic consumer's predisposition for imported cars is important, especially for domestic car manufacturers, who should closely monitor Hispanic new car buyer's preferences and expectations.

The report also finds that Hispanic buyers rate fuel economy, purchase price and resale value significantly higher in their selection of a vehicle than do non-Hispanics. However, while Hispanic buyers are

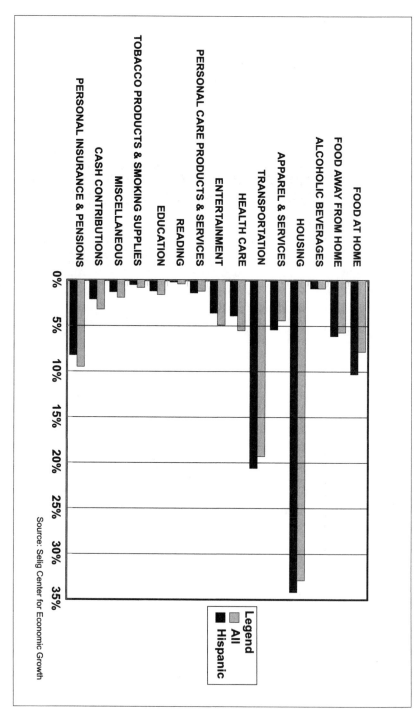

Figure 31 - Item Share of Total Expenditures for Hispanics and Total Consumers 2001

Source: Selig Center for Economic Growth

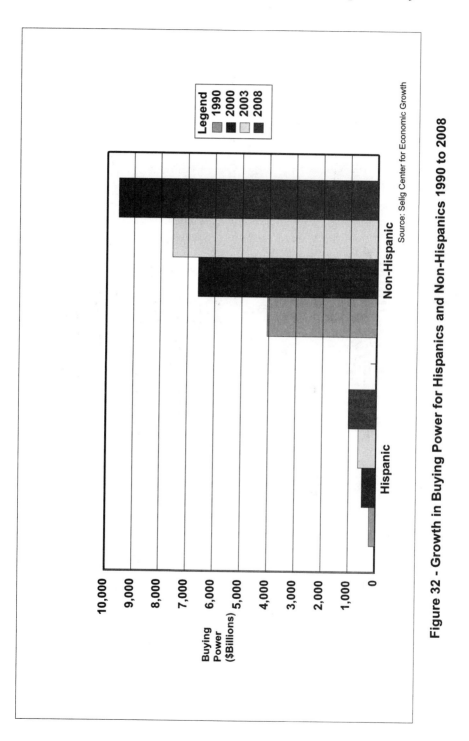

Figure 32 - Growth in Buying Power for Hispanics and Non-Hispanics 1990 to 2008

Source: Selig Center for Economic Growth

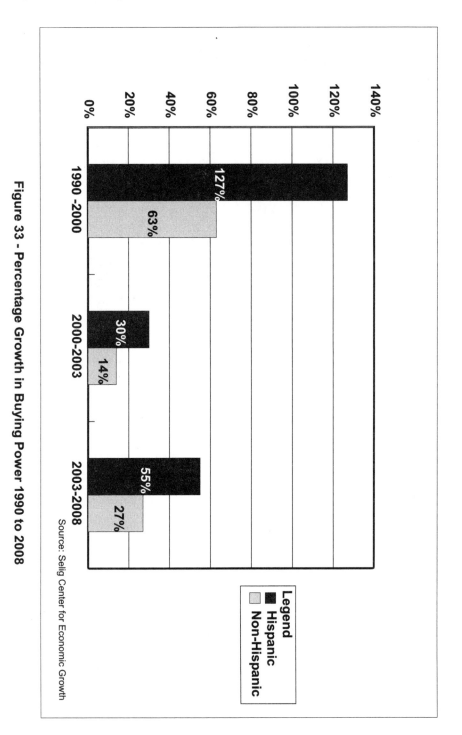

Figure 33 - Percentage Growth in Buying Power 1990 to 2008

Source: Selig Center for Economic Growth

significantly more likely to rate their new vehicle, domestic or import, as "outstanding," they are also much less enthusiastic about their overall experience with the vehicle service process.

According to comScore Networks, an Internet behavioral measurement tool, more than 1.2 million Hispanics, fully 10 percent of the online Hispanic population, visited at least one automotive manufacturer web site during February 2003. Among these visitors, Ford Motor Company attracted 355,000 unique visitors and General Motors drew 353,000 unique visitors.

The comScore analysis revealed even stronger variations in manufacturer rankings among Hispanics who prefer to speak Spanish at home. Among the 2.6 million active Internet users in this segment, Ford led with 89,000 unique visitors, DaimlerChrysler earned the number two ranking with 68,000 visitors and General Motors drew 62,000 visitors.

The comScore data also revealed that in February 2003, 3.7 million U.S. Hispanic Internet users visited third party online automotive resources. With 849,000 unique visitors, AOL Proprietary Automotive content held the number one ranking in this site segment. Autobytel earned the number two rank with 815,000 visitors, and was the growth leader among major third party resources with an 85 percent increase in traffic since October 2002, shortly before the site expanded its Spanish-language *AutoEspañol* research area.

The Internet is a critical element in the buying process for the majority of new car shoppers. The comScore data reveal major differences in automotive site usage between the Hispanic and general markets. These findings further underscore, say comScore researchers, the importance of delivering fresh, compelling content tailored to the fast-growing online Hispanic community.

Hispanics and the Banking Market

Hispanics, the fastest-growing consumer market in America, are underserved by the banking industry. Only 58 percent of Hispanics have checking accounts, versus 93 percent for non-Hispanic whites. About half as many Hispanics have credit cards as the average American. As Hispanic incomes rise, the demand for mortgages, home equity lines, and credit cards is going to explode.

Bank of America intends to take advantage of the Hispanic opportunity. The population of the 21 states where Bank of America does business is growing twice as fast as in the rest of the country, in large part because of Hispanic influence. More than three-quarters of America's Hispanics live in five states, California, Nevada, Arizona, New Mexico and Texas, where Bank of America is either the market leader or a close second (except Nevada, where it is third). In California, Bank of America has the largest market share of any retail bank, including three of every four Hispanics with bank accounts.

"The Hispanic factor is Bank of America's ace in the hole," writes Fortune magazine. America's 39-million-strong population of Hispanics (two-thirds of them of Mexican origin) is young and growing fast. Many are in their prime earning years. In addition, while new arrivals are often unaccustomed to practices like mortgages and checking, their need for them is still acute.

Bank of America already dominates the Hispanic market, and expects to get no less than 80 percent of its future growth in retail banking from Hispanics. To achieve that, it is doing things like stocking its branches with Spanish-speaking tellers and learning to write mortgages secured by the credit of an extended family. It has also introduced SafeSend, which allows a Bank of America account holder to transfer money safely and conveniently. Recipients can access money in the account at ATMs (automated teller machines) in Mexico with a card the bank sends, by secured delivery, to whomever the account holder designates.

SafeSend is proving to be a tremendous success. Not only is volume increasing dramatically, but also, no less than 37 percent of the Hispanics who have signed up for SafeSend open other accounts. This is an intelligent "value migration" strategy, as Hispanics are decidedly more brand loyal than the general market. Indeed, a key insight guiding Hispanic-targeted efforts, says the bank, is that courting this market is all about relationship building.

In addition, according the AHAA, Bank of America has adjusted its advertising allocation to the Hispanic market to match the Hispanic share of its new account growth, estimated at 20-25 percent. Bank of America is also investing in Spanish-language collateral materials and website content

Hispanic Urban Youth Market

The urban youth population is large, growing, and a lucrative marketing target. It is also the most diverse and multicultural population in the United States. Hispanics, for example, comprise 13.5 percent of the American population, but 17 percent of the U.S. teenage population. Over the next 10 years, the number of Hispanic teens will grow by 25 percent (from 3.3 to 4.1 million), and will by then comprise 20 percent of all U.S. teens.

Hispanic youth are clustered in the metropolitan areas of 10 states: California, Texas, New York, New Jersey, Florida, Illinois, Arizona, New Mexico, Colorado and Nevada. Hispanics under the age of 20 number more than 12 million, or 38 percent of the total U.S. Hispanic population. They comprise 58 percent of all youth in Los Angeles today, but will account for 80 percent within a few short years.

What is new, different and unique about the Hispanic urban youth market? What are the trends?

- They are already minority majority.
- They are redefining multiculturalism, away from separate enclaves of ethnicity and race to a mixing, blending and blurring of distinctions.
- They are redefining what is mainstream even as the mainstream influences them.
- "Society" does not alienate or disenfranchise them. They like money, success, getting ahead, acquiring nice stuff and technology (music, video, Internet, television, movies, radio).
- They desire independence, autonomy and control. Most have part-time jobs and have their own money to spend.

- They respect individualism, but identify with their "tribe," young, hip, urban, cool.

Hispanic teens live in two worlds

They embrace the American way of life, but are proud of their heritage (54 percent define themselves as Hispanic only). Multiculturalism is pervasive and largely embraced, but so is pride in one's roots. Peers are a major influence, but so is family. Group identity is important, but so is individuality. Moreover, most Hispanic teens are completely bilingual.

Hispanic teens are big spenders. According to Teenage Research Unlimited, they spend an average of $375 a month, 4 percent more than the average for non-Hispanic teens. In 2000, Hispanic teens accounted for $20 billion in consumer expenditures, or 14 percent of all spending by U.S. teens.

How to reach this large, growing and lucrative market? Here are some key consumer insights, developed from recent qualitative research conducted in several urban markets by LatinWorks, a leading Hispanic market firm:

- Hispanic urban teens live in and embrace a multicultural world.
- Attitude and personality are more important than race and ethnicity.
- Hispanic urban teens believe in authenticity and in being "real."
- Face-to-face interaction is both an urban and a cultural value.
- School is the epicenter of their social lives.
- They are influenced more at the peer level (micro) than by mass media (macro).
- Brands carry a lot of weight, used as a way to express both group identity and individuality.
- Hispanic urban teens want to be spoken to as individuals, not as members of a mass audience.
- Spanglish speaks to their dual worlds, both of which are sources of pride.

Long-range Implications

Two recent books offer some wonderful insights into the future of Hispanic America. "The Other Face of America" (2002), by Jorge Ramos (the Univision news anchor), might be called a defense of the Hispanic immigration to America of the last 20 years from a "quasi-separatist" perspective. Ramos advances the notion that Hispanic immigrants have created a country within a country.

"The New Americans" (2001), by Michael Barone (senior writer for U.S. News & World Report), on the other hand, is a defense of the same wave of Hispanic immigration from an "assimilationist" perspective. Barone agrees with Ramos that the United States is becoming multiethnic, but argues that is fine as long as America retains its distinct national culture. He advances the notion that Hispanics are assimilating in much the same pattern as previous generations of immigrants.

The most interesting part of Ramos' book is also the most humorous: his defense of Spanglish as a legitimate language. Useful words from the Spanglish glossary include *antibaby* (birth control pill), *ancorman* (anchorman), *beseler* (best-seller), *brainstormear* (to brainstorm), *cibernauta* (web navigator), *gufear* (to goof around), *lonchear* (to eat lunch), *mula* (money), *nerdio* (nerd), *queque* (cake), and *sochal* (Social Security number).

The most interesting aspect of Barone's book is his comparison of late twentieth century Hispanic immigrants to early twentieth century Italian immigrants. Both groups came from excessively centralized, politically dysfunctional societies where individual initiative was discouraged, social mobility sharply limited, and ordinary people saw no reason to trust government or look to politics for change. As a result, in America, both groups (at first) rely on family and hard work to sustain themselves, but over time are seen to change habits in becoming part of the American mainstream.

Ramos' greatest fear for the Hispanic American future, especially in the shadow of a long war on terrorism, is latent racism and xenophobia. Barone's greatest fear is the phony multiculturalism of America's elites, which, perversely, only serves to retard assimilation. Who is right, quasi-separatist Ramos, who contends we face an unprecedented situation, or assimilationist Barone, who believes we have been here before?

Both, of course, are correct. How so? Because the future is derived from continuity and change as well as the even more important component of choice. In other words, there will be plenty of separatism and assimilation among Hispanic Americans in the years and decades ahead. That makes the most important factor the autonomous decisions made by millions of individuals. That is the wonder, beauty and efficaciousness of American society and culture: you choose your own future.

Chapter Summary

Population Growth

Hispanics are now the nation's largest minority group: the number of Hispanics living in the United States was 38.8 million as of July 2002 (not including the 3.8 million people living in Puerto Rico). Hispanics represent 13.45 percent of the U.S. population. Projections for future growth are astounding. The Census Bureau predicts that one in every four Americans will be Hispanic by 2050, growing to one in every three Americans by 2100.

Changing Sources of Hispanic Population Growth

Immigration has been key to Latinos' population growth in the past, but the native born will fuel Hispanic population growth in the future. Ten million second-generation U.S.-born children of immigrants make up 29 percent of all Hispanics. Another 11 million comprise the "third generation" (born to two native-born parents) and represent 31 percent of all Latinos. However, by 2025, U.S.-born Latinos will represent 13 percent of the U.S. population; Hispanic immigrants will comprise just 5 percent.

Changing Patterns of Hispanic Population Dispersion

"Latino Growth in Metropolitan America: Changing Patterns, New Locations," co-authored by Roberto Suro of the Pew Hispanic Center and Audrey Singer of the Brookings Institution, confirms the wide distribution of Latino population growth during the 1990s, and reveals deep variations in the rate and location of that growth among cities. The report also confirms that the majority of U.S. Latinos now live in the suburbs.

According to "Emerging Communities: A Snapshot of a Growing Hispanic America," released by the League of United Latin American Citizens (LULAC), Hispanics dominate U.S. population growth, but the explosive growth of the U.S. Latino population extends beyond traditional metropolitan receiving areas like Los Angeles, Houston, Chicago and Miami. While 58 percent of Latinos live in 10 major metro areas, 42 percent have dispersed to areas not commonly accustomed to receiving clusters of Hispanics, including suburban fringes, small cities and towns, rural areas, and Southern states.

Hispanic Buying Power Growth

According to research reports by Standard & Poor's, Global Insight, and the Selig Center for Economic Growth, Hispanic buying power (total personal disposable income) will grow approximately 9 percent a year over the next several years (and decades), reaching about $1 trillion by 2008 (and $2.5 trillion by 2020).

The size, growth and spending power of Hispanic consumers is transforming every consumer-oriented industry in America. According to the Global Insight report, sales to the Hispanic population are the fastest-growing sub-market for almost every consumer product or service.

Hispanic Urban Youth Market

The urban youth population is large, growing, and a lucrative marketing target. It is also the most diverse and multicultural population in the United States. Hispanics, for example, comprise 13.5 percent of the American population, but 17 percent of the U.S. teenage population. Over the next 10 years, the number of Hispanic teens will grow by 25 percent (from 3.3 to 4.1 million), and will by then comprise 20 percent of all U.S. teens.

Long-range implications

Two recent books offer some wonderful insights into the future of Hispanic America. "The Other Face of America" (2002), by Jorge Ramos (the Univision news anchor), might be called a defense of the Hispanic immigration to America of the last 20 years from a "quasi-separatist" perspective. "The New Americans" (2001), by Michael Barone (senior writer for U.S. News & World Report), on the other hand, is a defense of the same wave of Hispanic immigration from an "assimilationist" perspective.

Who is right? Both, of course, are correct. How so? Because the future is derived from continuity and change as well as the even more important component of choice. In other words, there will be plenty of separatism and assimilation among Hispanic Americans in the years and decades ahead. That makes the most important factor the autonomous decisions made by millions of individuals. That is the wonder, beauty and efficaciousness of American society and culture: you choose your own future.

- Hispanics are now the nation's largest minority group.
- Projections for future growth are astounding.
- Native born Hispanics will fuel Hispanic population growth in the future.
- The Latino population extends beyond traditional metropolitan areas to include suburban fringes, small cities and towns, rural areas, and Southern states.
- Hispanic buying power will grow nine percent a year over the next several years and reach about $1 trillion by 2008.
- The Hispanic population is the fastest-growing sub-market for almost every consumer product or service.
- The urban youth population is large, growing, and a lucrative marketing target.
- It is also the most diverse and multicultural population in the United States.
- There will be separatism and assimilation among Hispanic Americans in the coming decades.

About the Author

Roger Selbert, Ph.D., Principal, Growth Strategies Group

Roger Selbert is principal at The Growth Strategies Group, a trend research consulting firm. He is editor and publisher of Growth Strategies, a monthly trend letter formerly known as FutureScan, and senior fellow at the La Jolla Institute, a "new economy" think-tank. His 20-year record of accomplishment in economic, social and demographic foresight is unequaled.

Chapter Six

Qualitative and Quantitative Research Strategies

Miguel Gomez Winebrenner

In This Chapter

- Introduction to qualitative and quantitative research methods
- Critical aspects of choosing your target
- Operational add-ons and resources needed to conduct research with certain types of Latino markets
- Need for cultural relevance
- Parallels and differences between researching the general and Hispanic markets

Introduction

Understanding the logistical and operational challenges when conducting research with Hispanics is important. It is just as important to take into account some cultural nuances. This chapter will familiarize you with some qualitative and quantitative research methods to help you effectively tap into the mindset of the U.S. Latino consumer. To be more specific, it will guide you in the design of research studies that account for several details of the Latino market, which, if ignored, can alter or skew your findings.

141

The chapter is divided into two parts:

- Qualitative Methods
- Quantitative Methods

The qualitative section will discuss the critical aspects of choosing your target, as well as the operational add-ons and resources needed to conduct research with certain types of Latino markets. It will also address the need for cultural relevance in order for the results to be actionable. Similarly, the quantitative section will focus on the parallels and differences between researching the general market and the Hispanic market. We will give particular emphasis to study design and analysis of the results. Overall, this chapter is intended to be a guide for professionals familiar with research who conduct research with the Hispanic consumer rather than an instruction manual on how to conduct market research.

Note: We will use the words "Latino" and "Hispanic" interchangeably throughout this chapter.

Qualitative Research with U.S. Latinos

Qualitative research, as a marketing research technique, has a four-decade heritage in the U.S. Soon after Saul Ben Zeev pioneered the focus group dynamic at the University of Chicago in the early 1960s, it spread quickly, to many places around the world including Latin America where it is still used today along with other qualitative methods.

Overall, the role of qualitative methods is the generation of hypotheses for quantitative validation, and the development of language that will be meaningful to those to whom subsequent questionnaires are administered. These "first principles" are all the more important when conducting research in the U.S. Hispanic market. Marketers, particularly those who are approaching the Hispanic market for the first time, need those hypotheses because the market is outside their own experience. In addition, the language, of course, will not be their own.

Most approaches to conducting qualitative research with U.S. Latinos are based on qualitative research methods employed within general market segments. Therefore, if you are familiar with traditional focus groups, individual interviews, ethnographic research, and the like, you have a good foundation for the formal character of research within the Hispanic market. Ultimately, however, the substance of the research will be different or unfamiliar. Conducting research within the Latino market depends upon special attention to three areas, the target, the operational and the cultural.

Target

As with any type of study, you must first decide whom you want to target. With Latinos, this decision is especially important because there are many different types of Latinos, from the highly acculturated to the unacculturated, young and old, Mexican and Cuban, etc. Not making the distinction clear from the beginning might drive you to have several operational and cultural difficulties.

For example, if your targets are Spanish-dominant Mexicans you may have to have a special type of moderator, an interpreter, and other tools in place. With children, on the other hand, you may not need a Hispanic moderator because many Latino children are fully acculturated. Therefore, you should pinpoint who your target market is before starting qualitative work so that you can determine if you need to hire additional resources, whether your product or service will be culturally relevant, and how (or if) your research needs to be tailored for the Latino market.

Operational

Operational obstacles arise due to cultural differences, but we can often overcome these challenges by hiring or applying more resources. For example, say you are conducting a focus group with Spanish-dominant Hispanics in Miami. Due to language alone, your research supplier will need to hire a real-time interpreter, rent special translation equipment like headsets, and translate the screener and any other materials for respondents. Additionally, you will need to make sure your facility can accommodate the special equipment, and if the facility has not done similar research in the past, you need to plan to get to the facility early to make sure everything is set up properly. When you factor in other obstacles, like thunderstorms if it is July in Miami, planning for

Qualitative Research Phase	Operational Obstacles
Recruiting	• Not all markets have facilities that recruit Hispanics • In many markets, you must contact independent recruiters to get a good group of respondents • Screener must be translated
Moderating	• Moderator must be fully bilingual to communicate with respondents and back-room
Translations	• Need real-time interpreter and translation equipment
Preparing Respondents	• Screener must be translated into both English and Spanish

Table 2 - Operational Obstacles in Qualitative Research with U.S. Latinos

focus groups with a Spanish-speaking segment can seem like a big task. As long as you are well organized and give yourself enough time, planning for groups in the Hispanic market does not have to be difficult.

Cultural

Unfortunately, having adequate resources does not always solve the cultural challenges of conducting research with Latinos. With enough money, you can easily hire the translator, the moderator, and the equipment, but you cannot buy cultural insights and the understanding that comes from working with a bicultural moderator.

For example, say you hired Joe Peterson (a bilingual American moderator) to do your Spanish language Hispanic groups. He would be able to communicate perfectly with respondents and with the back room, thus he apparently solves the challenge of your operational needs. However, because Joe does not understand the Latino culture, it is likely his interpretation of the findings would be biased. The respondents may have expressed themselves in ways Joe did not understand, because while he can speak Spanish, he does not understand the culture of Latinos. Further confounding the situation, the respondents might

Qualitative Research Phase	Cultural Obstacles
Recruiting	• Most Hispanics will only show up if they are recruited by someone they know closely
Moderating	• Moderators must instill confidence and must not be threatening • Unacculturated males and females need to be separated, because in that situation, males tend to dominate the conversation • Groups should be smaller, more intimate
Translations	• Straight translations do not work. Ideas have to be adapted. They need to "transculturate."
Preparing Respondents	• Unacculturated Hispanics need a lot of reassurance that they can be completely honest and that they do not have to please the moderator

Table 3 - Cultural Obstacles in Qualitative Research with U.S. Latinos

have been acting differently in the focus group because they were trying to please Joe because he is American and the respondents (Spanish speakers) are most likely foreign-born and trying to be accepted into American culture. Thus, the fact that Joe is bilingual does not mean he is bicultural. Be cognizant of the fact that Spanish speaking does not equal bicultural.

Qualitative research can be an extremely helpful tool in marketing a product or service, but failure to take into account the logistical and cultural aspects of researching Latinos could render the qualitative research obsolete. For this reason, it is key to partner with researchers who have the operational capabilities to set up groups with Hispanics and can provide bicultural moderators who have ample research experience.

Quantitative Research with U.S. Latinos

In many ways, conducting quantitative research with Latinos is not that much different from general market studies in terms of setting up the study, executing it, and analyzing the results.

Ultimately, as with any project, it is key to have good QCT (quality, cost, and timing) harmony. In almost all cases, when you want to get a project done quickly and cheaply, you may have to sacrifice quality, i.e., higher margins of error or low sample sizes. Conversely, if you want something done quickly and well, you may have to pay a premium, i.e., higher incentives or added resource usage.

In the case of conducting quantitative projects with Latinos, these same rules apply, but we have to give special emphasis to the differences in design, implementation and reporting.

Design

The first major challenge in quantitative research with Latinos is designing the study so that it takes into account all the market-specific and cultural nuances that will have an impact on the execution of the data collection and analysis.

As with the qualitative, it is essential to really understand and be clear on whom you want to target. For example, are you targeting Cubans or Mexicans? Will the product under research be distributed in Florida, home of most Cuban-Americans? Are the targets English-dominant Latinos or Spanish-dominant Latinos? In the end, if the data collected is a reflection of the wrong segment, there is no point in attempting to extrapolate the findings of the research. Assuming you have established the target, it is easy to set expectations for the sample composition. Here are some examples:

Target: Latino adults in the Chicago metropolitan area

Likely Sample Composition, based on secondary data like the census: 50 percent males/females, roughly 70 percent Mexican descent, 15 percent Puerto Rican descent, 15 percent South/Central American, and about 60 percent English-dominant.

Target: Latina television viewers in Miami

Likely Sample Composition, based on secondary data like the census: 100 percent females, roughly 50 percent Cuban descent, 40 percent South/Central American, 10 percent Puerto Rican, and about 25 percent English-dominant.

These are just a couple out of hundreds of possible scenarios. These examples provide an indication of some of the key variables you need to take into account. Of course, other variables are specific to some products and services. For example, if the company commissioning the research is a cable television company, it is likely that the sample would include subscribers and non-subscribers, as well as a mix of light, medium and heavy viewers.

In addition, there are variables that are more difficult, because of their subjectivity, to define. Lately, one of the most important variables for marketers (aside from demographic variables like country of origin or language usage) has been acculturation, because Latinos today are integrating their Hispanic roots with American culture, making them unique shoppers.

The challenge from a design perspective is that there are different levels of acculturation. Obviously, a recent immigrant to the U.S. who had limited exposure to American culture would be less acculturated than a third generation person who has lived here all his or her life. However, it is more difficult to pinpoint the variables that can help us identify the highly acculturated (say a 10 out of 10 on an acculturation scale, where 10 is totally acculturated; and who is a four on the scale). From experience, there are certain variables that are good predictors, like language usage, but they are not 100 percent accurate. Typically, a Spanish-dominant Latino would likely be unacculturated. However, many Latinos who are Spanish-dominant are more likely to act, behave, and shop like someone who is part of the general market. As a result, more sophisticated methods to determine levels of acculturation have been developed that take into account other demographic, sociographic, technographic, and pyschographic variables.

Independent of the variables you choose to define your target, the success of the quantitative research will be highly dependent on whether you are able to make the sample reflect the true nature of your target population. Once you define the target, you can choose among various methodologies. As with the general market, the appropriate approach, such as discrete choice or price sensitivity will depend on the objectives of the study and available data collection alternatives. If it is a concept test and you have many visuals, then a computer-assisted approach will be better than a phone method. If it is a taste test, then mall-intercept might be the best approach.

There are many limitations when dealing with data collection in the Hispanic market. The most obvious one is that on-line studies, which have become a standard form of data collection in the U.S., are not easily conducted with Hispanics because Internet penetration is lower among Latino households, especially among the unacculturated. On-line studies are an option, especially as penetration increases, and it is increasing rapidly. It just means that it might be more difficult to garner accurate data.

Another precaution when designing a quantitative study is to take note of available sample providers and recruiters. It is sometimes difficult to find mall-intercept providers for Hispanics in some smaller markets, and even some larger markets at times. Moreover, once found, there are so few of them that productivity is understandably strangled. You may have to discard mall-intercept (or combine it with another approach) among Latinos if you want to have several thousand interviews in a short period.

If you are conducting a phone study, you will likely have to purchase a list. The results of such as study will vary widely depending on the provider you choose. Many times, these lists are by surname or ethnicity and it is important to remember that these lists are not one-hundred percent accurate. It is always a good idea to ask people if they consider themselves Latino, despite having a list saying they are. For example, the list might say you are talking to Mary Fernández. At first glance, it looks like she might be Hispanic; it is also possible that her maiden name is Wilson and she just married José Fernández two weeks ago.

Ultimately, the design of the study is just as important as the analysis. The difference is that without a good design, the analysis is doomed. A good design will facilitate the process for high-quality analysis and make the implementation of the design smoother.

Implementation

One of the first steps in the implementation of the design will be to get a questionnaire drafted. Aside from helping you make sure you are talking to the right people via the screener portion, the questionnaire will be the decisive tool in correctly communicating your ideas and questions in a way that is appropriate for the Latino market. Assuming you are using the correct scales, unbiased questions and making sure the questionnaire flows correctly, it is also important that the questionnaire be relevant to the Latino culture. Therefore, if the target includes Spanish-speakers, translate the questionnaire. Even more importantly, it has to be "transculturated" a fancy word for taking ideas from American culture and adapting them to Latino culture. For example, everyone in the U.S. knows that "take a seat" means sit down, but if the person translating it does not know this, the idea is lost; the respondent would be told "*Toma un asiento,*" which would probably end up with him or her physically taking the seat home with them instead of sitting in it. Therefore, it is important to have bilingual and bicultural translators rather than just bilingual translators. It is key to have a group of Latinos working with you so that all Latinos understand the transculturation. For example, a "car" can be "*coche*" or "*carro*" depending on whether you are in Colombia or Argentina. "*Vehículo*" spills over nicely into all dialects of Spanish.

Having bicultural staff on a project will also be helpful in implementing the questionnaire during actual interviewing. For anyone who has monitored phone interviews where the respondents are Hispanic, it is apparent that the interviewer has to be fluent in both languages; they could be speaking to someone in English one minute and another person in Spanish the next minute.

It is smart to have bilingual interviewers and interviewers with neutral accents. A neutral accent, just as with English, ensures that the interviewees fully understand the questions. With Spanish, the neutrality of the accent many times depends on the part of Latin America, or Spain the person is from originally. Ultimately, it depends on the individual, which is why it is preferable to have someone who speaks Spanish well approve the interviewers. Another significant language consideration is the impact it has on the questionnaire length, and ultimately the costs. Spanish is a much lengthier language than English is and it rarely has acronyms or shortcuts, like "e-mail," similar to the ones we have in English.

It may be necessary to program the questionnaire into some form of Computer Assisted Telephone Interviewing, CATI, or Computer Assisted Personal Interviewing, CAPI, program. This involves modifying the time line of the project to allow for extra programming time. Overall, good implementation is the result of judicious planning, logistical capabilities and choosing reliable suppliers. Research is an industry that can be confusing because of the amount of suppliers claiming to have expertise in many areas. The choice of a reliable supplier can make the difference between a well-executed job and a lesser one.

Analysis

Once you collect the data and it is time to do the analysis, you need to consider several factors. The first is to allow for analysis by different variables that are key in understanding the U.S. Latino. Depending on the study, these variables will differ. The most common are:

- Country of origin or descent
- Region
- Level of acculturation

Country of origin is important because a Mexican is different from a Cuban. The notion that all Latinos are the same independent from country of origin is false. Data for different products and services has proven that Argentines are not as likely to purchase the same products as Venezuelans are. This is due to many reasons. It has to do with the difference in cultures. For example, the Southern cone of South America has a big Italian and German influence while the Andean region is mostly influenced by the Spanish; climate: Caribbean Latinos eat and like different foods than those Latinos who are from the inlands of South America; and politics: a Colombian has different political worries and agendas than a Mexican.

On a similar note, region will play a big role in part due to country of origin. Most Cubans, for example, are in the Southeast while Puerto Ricans conglomerate in New York City and Chicago; and most Mexicans are in the Western U.S. Consequently, one would think that analysis by country of origin would by default lead to analysis by region. However, it is important to note that not all Mexicans are the same. Mexicans in Chicago tend to be recent immigrants, while Mexicans in Texas and California could have been in the U.S. for several generations. South and Central Americans in the Midwest and West tend to be recent immigrants and have lower incomes than the affluent South and Central Americans in Southern Florida.

Finally, level of acculturation is an integral part of all analysis of the Latino market and key in understanding how you can streamline marketing to capture the most distinct segments in the market.

In conclusion, qualitative and quantitative research is an integral part of marketing to Latinos. By understanding the uses and limitations of the various qualitative and quantitative methods, you will be better equipped to tap into the Latino mindset. As a result, you will develop more relevant products, services, and messages to this growing segment of the American population.

Chapter Summary

- Conducting qualitative and quantitative research among Latinos is somewhat similar to conducting research with the general population.
- The key starting point when conducting both kinds of studies is to think about who the target is in terms of key Latino variables like country of origin, language usage, acculturation, age and geographic region.
- In executing qualitative projects, it is important to select bicultural (not only bilingual) moderators and to select facilities that can recruit and accommodate Spanish-speaking respondents.
- During a quantitative study, the main challenges are selecting a representative methodology, accurate translations, programming

in multiple languages, and asking the right questions so you can place respondents into appropriate Latino segments.

- Among all studies, it is key to "transculturate" documents from English to Spanish, not only translate from one language to another but to transfer and adapt the intended ideas as well.

About the Author

Miguel Gomez Winebrenner, Marketing and Account Manager, C&R/LatinoEyes

Miguel Gomez Winebrenner is marketing and account manager for C&R/LatinoEyes. He has more than seven years of experience researching Latinos in the U.S. and in Latin America. He grew up in Colombia and later attended the University of Iowa, where he received a Bachelor of Science in Economics with honors.

Chapter Seven

Segmentation by Level of Acculturation

Miguel Gomez Winebrenner

In This Chapter

- Integration process for immigrants
- Acculturation versus assimilation
- Acculturation and Latinos
- Acculturation and its Hispanic marketing implications

Introduction

Given the significant population growth of Latinos in the United States, targeting this consumer group presents a market segment with unparalleled profit potential and an enigmatic challenge to marketers in various industries. The key in effectively marketing to Hispanics lies in understanding their various cultural nuances that are best characterized by their individual levels of acculturation.

Twenty years ago, marketers would never have dreamed they would be sitting around the boardroom table discussing the nuances of acculturation versus assimilation. With the tremendous growth of the U.S. Latino population over the last decade, marketers have come to realize how critical the issues of acculturation and assimilation are, and how controversial these definitions can be. Though academics have long

153

analyzed acculturation, there was little discussion about how accultura-tion related to marketing. Once marketers identified the huge buying power of the Latino segment, several important questions began to arise. "Do Latinos assimilate or acculturate?" "Are there different lev-els of acculturation or assimilation?" "What impact does acculturation or assimilation have on marketing?"

First, what are we talking about when we use the terms acculturation and assimilation? On a basic level, if people move to a new country and integrate their original culture with their new culture, they are accultur-ating. Likewise, if people move to a new country and completely aban-don their old culture and immerse themselves in the new culture, they are said to be assimilating.

The latest waves of Latino immigrants to the U.S. have been accul-turating and not assimilating. This trend has not always been the case though. Prior to a few decades ago, Latino immigrants used to assimi-late, because American society was not very open to the Latino culture. Just as with Germans at the turn of the century, the U.S. was stringent about allowing multi-ethnicity among Latinos. As late as the 60s and 70s, Latinos were ashamed of their heritage and tried to shed any trace of their background, including language.

Many factors have influenced the trend of Latino acculturation in-stead of assimilation. Over the years, American society has become more tolerant and open to other cultures. Additionally, as the number of Hispanics has grown, it has become easier for Latinos to maintain their original culture because they are no longer culturally isolated. There-fore, they do not feel ashamed or scared to have pride in their roots. An-other big factor playing into the acculturation trend is that older generations of Latinos are beginning to embrace their heritage. Second and third generation Latinos who had previously assimilated are now beginning to retro-acculturate. They are expressing a renewed interest in learning Spanish, dancing salsa and merengue, and preparing food from their country of ethnic origin. This renaissance creates an interest-ing arena from a marketing perspective because these Latinos are American shoppers with newly acquired emotional connections to their cultural background.

Acculturation and assimilation are processes that occur over a long period. Obviously, a recent immigrant to the U.S. who had limited exposure to American culture would be less acculturated than a third generation immigrant would be. However, pinpointing the variables that can help identify who is acculturated and to what degree is extremely difficult. Certain variables are good predictors of acculturation, but they are not 100 percent accurate. For example, for a long time researchers thought that language spoken at home was the best predictor of acculturation. Therefore, if Latinos spoke mostly English, they were acculturated and if they spoke mainly Spanish, they were unacculturated. However, the Latino population today is becoming increasingly bicultural, due in part to retro-acculturation. This biculturalism results in many people who could easily speak mostly Spanish at home, but who are completely integrated into American culture.

In looking at other demographic, sociographic, technographic, and pyschographic variables, we can more accurately segment Latinos by levels of acculturation. By looking beyond language and delving deeper into areas like self-denomination, length of time living in the U.S., and other variables, it is common to see that there are people who may speak mostly Spanish, but who are fully acculturated. On the flip side, there are people who mostly speak English, but who are unacculturated. The importance of looking at other variables lies in determining who we really need to target as a Latino, independent of their language preference.

Finally, why is all this relevant to marketing? Once you have a solid way of segmenting Latinos by acculturation levels, you will see several significant differences that will affect how you can effectively reach them. For example, unacculturated Latinos are much more likely to be Spanish dominant, meaning that all communications will likely have to be in Spanish. In addition, their values are strongly tied to those in Latin America. They value tradition, family, appearance, personal contact, and a sense of belonging. In addition, their income-expense ratio is higher than that of the acculturated; meaning they tend to spend a bigger percent of their disposable income.

Acculturation or Assimilation

All individuals are imbued with their own cultural distinctiveness. Enculturation is the process for developing culture whereby an individual learns the traditional content of a culture and assimilates its practices and values. Enculturation fundamentally consists of language and ethnic identity. We describe the outcome of this essential process as the individual's original culture. However, what is culture? One scholar defines culture as the system of shared beliefs, values, customs, behaviors, and artifacts that the members of society use to cope with their world and with one another, and transmit from generation to generation through learning[1].

At the heart of the acculturation versus assimilation debate is what happens to an individual's own cultural identity when circumstances

Adaptation		Is it considered to be of value to maintain cultural identity and characteristics?	
		Yes	No
Is it considered to be of value to maintain relationships with other groups?	Yes	Integration (Acculturation)	Assimilation
	No	Separation	Marginalization (Deculturation)

Source: Berry, 1997

Figure 34 - Adaptation Grid

---

1   Bates, Daniel G.

require a sustained exposure to a different culture. For many years, scholars have argued over which social mechanism best represents the process of integration Hispanics use when merging with mainstream American culture. The two methods most commonly invoked are acculturation and assimilation. To understand the breadth of this debate, it is necessary to provide clarity in the fundamental differences of these words.

We describe acculturation as a modification of cultural elements that occur when people of different cultures maintain an interchange; we also know this as integration. This process allows for a compromise between two cultural identities that leads to a melding of both, without entirely losing all components of the original culture. If there is no compromise of cultures within the individual, then we can consider that person unacculturated. In contrast, assimilation is what happens when a person replaces a cultural identity entirely by another. These three concepts define a spectrum for the process of cultural modification or replacement, which Figure 34 illustrates.

Given these definitions, the fundamental question becomes "do Hispanics acculturate or do they assimilate?" The answer is that Latinos mostly acculturate, and they rarely assimilate. To understand how Latinos integrate into American culture, it is best to define the process of acculturation. Explained in simple terms, acculturation has three phases: contact, conflict, and adaptation[2].

At the initial stage of contact, the individual is exposed to new ideas and values that may be alien to their cultural roots. For example, when a Guatemalan first arrives in the U.S., he or she is overwhelmed by the freedom of speech, different work ethics, and idiosyncrasies like "small talk." This individual then confronts the need for personal and inward cultural change, resulting in conflict. He has to choose what to shed and what to incorporate. He may, at times, feel that incorporating U.S. cus-

2   Padilla, 1980

toms or beliefs is betraying his heritage. This conflict can last several years.

The final stage of adaptation is key to the level of acculturation or assimilation the individual achieves. As the person evaluates conflicting cultural values, he or she must compromise on their original set of cultural beliefs. They will ask themselves, "Do I want to learn their anthem? Do I want to watch baseball and go the park? Do I want to celebrate St. Patrick's Day? Do I want to have to speak English this much?"

The level of integration depends strongly on the individual's choice of maintaining various aspects of their original culture, versus sustaining relationships with other cultural groups. This fundamental interchange ultimately defines the level of acculturation reached by the individual.

Another key component of acculturation involves culture shock. They normally experience this phenomenon in several stages, namely fascination, disenchantment, mental isolation, and adjustment or recovery[3]. In the stage of fascination, the person confronts a new culture and environment, the combination of which yields something exciting and intriguing. Disenchantment follows this stage, where differences between cultures become apparent. Afterwards, the person experiences mental isolation, a stage during which he misses his home of origin and seeks out and embraces peers. Finally, the individual reaches the stage of adjustment or recovery, where he reaches a comfort level with the new culture and language.

These experiences can be rather traumatic and seldom follow a predefined path; hence, it is not a linear or homogeneous process. Rather, it varies from individual to individual, as it is a personal journey of adapting to a new culture. This path of integration is dependent on the unique

---

3   Adler, 1975; Juffer, 1983; Schnell, 1996

attributes of the individual, among them, internal and external factors that influence the end result[4].

Internal factors are:

• Ethnicity and nation of origin
• Personality and ability to cope with change
• Age
• Education
• Language proficiency
• Knowledge and understanding of the host culture
• Reasons for migrating

In addition, external or environmental influences also play a large role in the process of acculturation:

• Socio-economic
• Presence of family support networks
• Presence of peers in the community where newcomer lives
• Attitude of host community towards immigrants

These influential factors provide the individual with the necessary internal tools to cope with and adapt to their new surroundings, and contribute greatly to the process of acculturation. Furthermore, researchers have suggested that Hispanics acculturate to varying degrees in two distinct areas, particularly those of value and behavior.[5] Latinos in the United States tend to integrate behaviorally with ease, thus allowing them to move about and interact freely within the surrogate culture. Although, behavioral integration happens readily, value acculturation among Hispanics is less likely to occur.

In summary, the process of acculturation is one where a person, when confronted with a new culture, must choose to meld aspects of his or her original culture with that of the new. Based on the individual's

---

4   Valdes 2002

5   Szapocznik, Scopetta, Kurtines, and Aranalde, 1978

unique internal perspective and experiences, and their external support and environmental influences, this journey of integration becomes personal. It is, therefore, incorrect to assume that all Latinos reach the same level of acculturation in the same manner and at the same time; some may choose to acculturate while others may intentionally avoid this process. This lack of homogeneity within the U.S. Hispanic population makes it difficult to find absolute commonalities within the whole. Understanding these differences is necessary when focusing marketing campaigns effectively towards this group.

Acculturation and Latinos

Among many in academia and the private industry, there has been much debate as to what the differences are between "Hispanics" and "Latinos." By definition, and without getting into too much detail, the word "Hispanic" comes from *Hispano*, which means speaks Spanish derived from the Spanish words *Habla Español*. Many disagree with this term because it excludes non-Spanish-speakers like Brazilians; others disagree because they consider it a cruel reminder of the Spanish colonization of Latin America. The word "Latino" also has its critics. Some say it describes only people from Latin America and excludes those in the U.S. with roots from the region. Others say that it is a condescending term because it refers to people of Latin (European) roots and not the natives from the Americas. All arguments for and against each of the words are valid, and it is an important debate that other ethnic groups have also encountered (Black versus African American).

Although some argue that there are key differences between the meanings and applications of these terms, the lines that differentiate them have blurred with time and with the greater acceptance of Latin American cultures in the United States. It is now common to see these terms used interchangeably, especially with the changes in the cultural landscape currently taking place in the U.S. Unlike many other immigrant groups and given the various factors that influence the acculturation level of the individual, Latinos hold on tightly to their culture and heritage. This process, known as integration, is useful to knowing how the person adapts to their new cultural environment.

This adaptation presents a two-fold challenge to many Hispanics who are trying to retain their original cultural roots, while simultaneously integrating with the American mainstream. On one end, to adapt successfully, Latinos need to integrate as much as possible into the dominant American culture. On the other end, Latinos also strive to preserve their Hispanic identity by celebrating their native cultural roots, as well as conserving their language and heritage. This conflicting dilemma leads to an apparent paradox where the differences in behavioral versus value acculturation provide the necessary solution. Hispanics are realizing that they can integrate behaviorally into the general population, all the while keeping their core cultural values intact. This recognition, combined with a rise in Hispanic pride, is leading U.S. Latinos to become bi-cultural, rather than polarize to extremes on acculturation levels.

Given the increase of bicultural Latinos in the United States, Hispanics now share emotional and cultural underpinnings with the mainstream American and Hispanic cultures. This amalgamation of cultures among Latinos makes it difficult to target these consumers without a full understanding of their acculturation levels. Hence, marketers must understand what factors make the integration of Hispanics into American culture feasible. A deep and true understanding of these variables would allow decision-makers to act preemptively, rather than react to unfavorable marketing campaigns. Many factors make acculturation for Latinos practical. Given the geographic proximity to Latin America, many U.S. Latinos find it easy to maintain strong ties with their culture of origin and their families and friends abroad. Advancements in communication, like email, cell phones, and prepaid calling cards, which allow exchanges of messages and other forms of interaction quickly and inexpensively, greatly enhance this influence. The steady influx of immigration from Latin America serves to replenish the Hispanic cultural base in the United States. These immigrants, in turn, find strong Latino communities to call home. New arrivals to the U.S. find a strong external support network that makes integration into their adopted society an easier transition. Additionally, the interchange between members of these communities slows down aspects of the acculturation process, without necessarily hampering integration into the mainstream culture, thus leading to bicultural individuals.

Another tangible factor making integration feasible is the increased prominence of Hispanics in mainstream media. As they become more visible in various areas, more non-Latinos accept Latino culture. This presents a point of pride to Hispanics. This presence builds a synergy that motivates Hispanics to seek integration, while also contributing their own treasured cultural values to the greater mainstream culture. These factors clearly influence the feasibility of acculturation, and motivate the extent of this integration. It, therefore, becomes important to understand how Latinos segment into various levels of acculturation. These levels range from unacculturated to acculturated, with bi-cultural spanning the region in between.

Unacculturated Hispanics have not or have barely adapted to the U.S. culture. Oftentimes, they are foreign-born recent arrivals. They tend to identify themselves first by their nationality, and secondly as Hispanic or Latino. They are generally most comfortable speaking Spanish at home, at work, and at social settings; and may feel uncomfortable speaking English in all of these situations. In addition, unacculturated Hispanics tend to arrive in the United States as adults, and therefore, base their behaviors and attitudes towards products and services on their experiences in Latin America.

Bicultural Hispanics are in the middle of the cultural landscape. They are fully adapted to American culture, having preserved their Latino roots and heritage. They are often first generation or foreign-born Latinos who arrived in the United States at an early age. They tend to identify themselves by their nationality or that of their parents. They also may identify themselves as a combination of their nationality of origin and American, for example Cuban-American, or Mexican-American. Bicultural Hispanics are generally bilingual, and as a result, are comfortable speaking both languages. In many cases, they have grown up exposed to both cultures, and may have attended school in the United States.

Acculturated Hispanics have completely adapted to the American culture. They, often second generation or later immigrants, are closer to the mainstream culture than either of the previous groups. They generally identify themselves equally by their parent's nationality or as American. They are most comfortable speaking English in all settings, have grown up mostly exposed to the American culture, and have values, perceptions, and ways that are close to the mainstream.

One interesting phenomenon is that of retro-acculturation. This trend has significant impact on second generation and greater Hispanics. This particular segment within the overall Latino market is very interested in rediscovering and celebrating their *Hispanidad* or cultural roots and many strive to share this with their children. They are actively seeking out, learning, and enjoying various aspects of their cultural origin, which may otherwise be lost in the process of integration. This retro-acculturation allows Latinos to meld with the mainstream culture, without ever assimilating into it. This process marks a tidal ebb and flow of Hispanics moving towards integration, then back to retro-acculturation, all the while maintaining a balance between their original and newly adopted culture.

Overall, Latinos undergo a unique process of acculturation that is greatly influenced and made feasible by a number of internal and external factors. These variables combine to yield a middle ground in terms of integration that most clearly manifests itself in producing bi-cultural individuals. These people share strong emotional bonds with Latino and American cultures. As more Hispanics acculturate into mainstream society, they will bring with them their own unique cultural perspectives, thus spurring a greater acculturation within the general social landscape of the United States. Being able to identify these societal trends may allow business leaders to forecast emerging markets; and begin targeting them at crucial moments of development, thus establishing significant brand loyalties among a potentially large and desirable consumer base.

Marketing and Acculturation

The recent acknowledgment of the surging U.S. Hispanic population and subsequently the ever increasing buying power of this group have lead many marketers to ponder the question of how to effectively sell their products or services to the Hispanic consumer. The answer to this question is difficult to attain because there is no single typical Latino consumer in the United States. The market is made up of new immigrants and U.S. born Hispanics, those fluent in Spanish and those who speak only English, consumers who identify strongly with their Latino roots, and those who have fully assimilated the behaviors and values of the United States. Therefore, any successful marketing campaign must first begin with a clear idea of exactly which type of Hispanic consumer to target. In order to do this, you must segment the Hispanic market into groups with relevant and targetable differences.

One way to partition the Latino community into marketable groups is to segment the U.S. Hispanic market based on level of acculturation. In the past, researchers used indicators such as dominant language preference and proficiency, partiality to specific media, and ethnic and social relations, among others, to accomplish this task. The first acculturation scales viewed the process of acculturation as one-way. In other words, in order for a Latino to become more acculturated, he or she would have to relinquish ties to his or her Hispanic culture. Subsequent scales improved upon this idea and made it possible for individuals to acculturate while still maintaining their Hispanic culture. Today, we call such individuals bicultural.

Presently, acculturation scales have become more sophisticated in their ability to segment the Hispanic market. One such scale, the LatinoEyes Approach Scale (LEÁS)[6], results in five distinct categories ranging from Totally Acculturated to Totally Unacculturated. The LEÁS approach takes into account behavior and value acculturation. Dominant language and media preferences are determined, as well as an individual's tendency toward ethnic and social interaction. In other words, the scale determines whether the respondent prefers to speak and receive communication in English or Spanish and whether they prefer social interaction with their cultural peers. Self-identification, length of U.S. residence, and country of origin (U.S. or specific Latin American country) are also taken into consideration. Finally, LEÁS layers on top of these dimensions questions regarding the respondent's attitudes and values, which help to identify their level of acculturation.

---

6   C&R Research, Inc., LatinoEyes Division, Chicago, IL.

The resulting scale has forty-six variables, ten of which are static and thirty-six dynamic. The ten static variables carry the most weight and serve to place the respondent into one of three general buckets: Totally Acculturated, Totally Bicultural, or Totally Unacculturated. The remaining thirty-six dynamic variables fine-tune the respondent's level of acculturation into one of the final five categories: Totally Acculturated, Somewhat Acculturated, Totally Bicultural, Somewhat Unacculturated, and Totally Unacculturated. The LatinoEyes Approach Scale allows researchers to identify accurately a Hispanic individual's level of acculturation. More importantly, the scale allows marketers to segment the entire U.S. Hispanic population, which they can then target more efficiently and track to identify and understand emerging trends within the Latino community.

Attempts to market to Hispanic consumers without considering acculturation are rarely successful. Understanding a Latino's acculturation level will give marketers a much better understanding of that consumer and allow them to tailor their message appropriately. Knowledge of the acculturation spectrum may also allow marketers to capitalize on collapsible markets. Specifically, it may be possible to affect two or more different types of Hispanic consumers with one message. For example, understanding the similarities and differences between the Totally Acculturated and Totally Bicultural Latinos will allow the creation of a marketing campaign that takes advantage of the similarities, while avoiding the differences. Collapsible markets create monetary efficiencies and provide an opportunity to present one united message to a broader target.

Researchers have used LEÁS to successfully identify motivations of Latino groups with varying degrees of acculturation. Hispanics with different levels of acculturation require separate campaigns from the credit card and airline industries. When searching for a credit card, an acculturated Latino's motivation is low interest rates and no annual fee, while an unacculturated Hispanic prefers an easy application process including instructions in Spanish. Likewise, the airline industry will attract acculturated Hispanics with low airfares, whereas unacculturated Hispanics seek an airline with a high safety record, in-flight meals and drinks and Spanish-speaking attendants. Marketers of specific beverages, such as beer, can advantageously collapse the Hispanic market because unacculturated, bicultural, and acculturated Hispanics all have the same motivation for buying and consuming beer, taste.

Chapter Summary

To summarize, the U.S. Latino population is growing rapidly and presents a desirable consumer market to various industries. Unlike general market segments, simply directing a singular campaign towards this group will not necessarily result in a favorable outcome. To target these consumers with the greatest return on investment efficiently, it is vital that marketers understand the many nuances that represent emotional and cultural bonds among Hispanics. Furthermore, excluding collapsible market opportunities, which researchers can identify with acculturation studies, the differing levels of integration among Latinos represent the need for multiple strategies of communication if one is to reach them as potential consumers.

In conclusion, there is no single strategy to reach all Hispanic consumers. However, a deep understanding of Hispanic's motivations, emotional underpinnings, and appreciation for their cultural influences will facilitate a more cost efficient and streamlined approach to tapping into this vital market.

- Significant growth in the U.S. Hispanic population presents an untapped consumer market with considerable buying power.
- Unlike previous immigrant groups, Latinos do not generally assimilate.
- They acculturate thereby integrating their original cultural identity with that of their new environment.
- Effective marketing towards Latinos is complicated by variations in acculturation levels among individuals.
- The acculturation process characteristic to Hispanics is creating an inhomogeneous bicultural segment.
- This segment shares emotional and cultural underpinnings with mainstream American and Hispanic cultures to varying degrees.

- The ability to identify emotional and cultural drivers is fundamental in developing effective marketing strategies for Latinos.
- Segmentation by level of acculturation enables the marketer to identify the specific type of Hispanic consumer they are targeting.
- Additionally, segmentation of the Hispanic market provides the best method of identifying key consumer attributes of a collapsible market.
- Given differing levels of acculturation among Latinos, multiple communication strategies may be required to connect with these consumers.

About the Author

Miguel Gomez Winebrenner, Marketing and Account Manager, C&R/LatinoEyes

Miguel Gomez Winebrenner is marketing and account manager for C&R/LatinoEyes. He has more than seven years of experience researching Latinos in the U.S. and in Latin America. He grew up in Colombia and later attended the University of Iowa, where he received a Bachelor of Science in Economics with Honors.

Chapter Eight

Effective Translations
The Art and Practice of Marketing In-Language

Tony Malaghan

In This Chapter

- Guidelines, recommendations and information to ensure your translated in-language Spanish marketing communications follow "Best Practice"
- How to convey accurate messages that correctly reflect your brand

Introduction

In this chapter, we will discuss in-language written communications with the U.S. Hispanic consumer. We will identify in general terms, some of the current practices in Spanish language business communication in the U.S., the impact poor translations can have on your brand and credibility in the market, and contrast these to what you should expect from "Best Practice" Spanish language translations and marketing. We will highlight salient points to discuss with your Spanish language translator to ensure you receive an accurate translation and key factors to help in the selection of a qualified vendor. Finally, we will discuss the latest trends in the translation industry.

Market Extension and Development

Since the release of the U.S. Census Bureau's 2000 Census results, there has been a lot of hype about the potential of the Hispanic segment of the U.S. market. This reaction is not surprising when you consider that more than one person in eight in the U.S. is of Hispanic origin. To help put this number into perspective, when researchers rank the U.S. Hispanic population alongside the U.S. Census Bureau's estimates of the population of countries in the world, this segment comes in at number 33 out of a total of 228 countries. This means that the U.S. Hispanic market, by population size, is larger than the population of many countries which are considered significant markets in their own right, such as Canada and Australia to name a few. Through natural growth and immigration, forecasters are predicting that by 2050 one in four people in the U.S. will be Hispanic. When you combine these population statistics with estimates of this segment's purchasing power, variously estimated in 2003 to be between $430 & $653 billion, it is clear that U.S. Hispanics represent a significant market opportunity.

Reaching the Spanish-Speaking Community

Many U.S. companies have approached the "U.S. Hispanic" market by treating it as a homogenous group and segmenting by traditional characteristics such as age, sex, family size, educational level, and income. Whilst the Spanish language and a link with Spain serve as a means of considering the "U.S. Hispanic" segment as a single market, diverse ethnic origins amongst the segment, as well as religious, cuisine, music, family beliefs, values, and subtle linguistic variations, make this segment one of the most culturally rich groups in the U.S. today.

The largest group, by far, is of Mexican ethnic origin comprising around 66 percent of the total U.S. Hispanic population. Those from Central and South America total about 15 percent of the population. Puerto Rico represents 9 percent, Cuba 4 percent and the remaining 6 percent are from other countries.

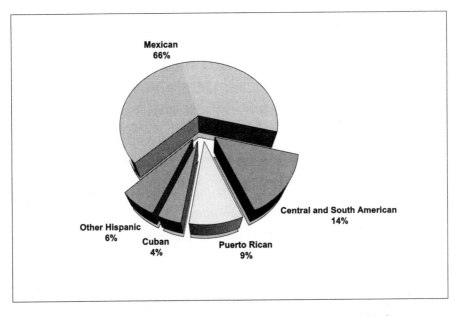

Figure 35 - Hispanics by Country of Origin from the 2000 Census

Effectively reaching and servicing this segment has proven to be a challenge to many companies that have identified the U.S. Hispanic market as a desirable and potentially profitable segment to target. It has been well researched and documented that U.S. Hispanics prefer to be marketed to in their native language. In 2003, Cheskin Research conducted a survey of 6,000 U.S. Hispanics and found that 76 percent prefer to be marketed to in Spanish. While there are many similarities in language between the various sub-groups of the U.S. Hispanic market, there are also distinct differences that marketers must be sensitive to in order to best serve the interests of these consumer segments. A challenging issue for companies is communicating in neutral "Business Spanish" in order to communicate to all the U.S. Hispanic market sub groups.

Reaching the segment with in-language marketing collateral however, is only the beginning. Companies that are truly serious about acquiring and retaining business from this segment of the market need to implement an in-language strategy in all customer communication and across all contact points. If a company is going to create the impression that they are catering to the specific needs of a segment of the market, then they had better live up to the customer's expectations of how to fulfill those needs in the critical areas of customer service and satisfaction.

Impact on Brand

The art of communication is critical for all internal and external business activity; without it, economic activity and commerce would grind to a halt and businesses would fail. Such is the importance of the communication process, that corporations spend millions of dollars every year with public relations companies and advertising agencies to ensure they are communicating messages consistent with their brand, core values, business goals and objectives.

Effective communication takes place when the receiver decodes the message the sender intended; then the receiver provides feedback that allows the sender to judge whether he received the message as it was intended. During this process, distortion of the message can occur from the various physical and psychological elements in our environment. See Figure 36.

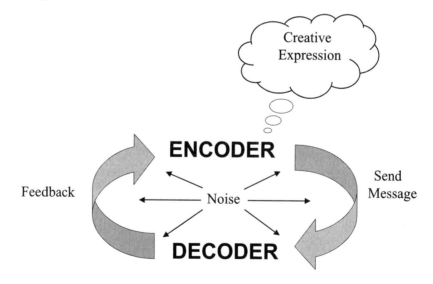

Figure 36 - Effective Communication

Adding the process of translating from one language to another to the communication model increases the complexity of the model. We have an increased risk of distortion of the message with the addition of this new function. In addition, because we want the meaning of the communication piece translated as intended, rather than a literal translation, we introduce the translator's creative interpretation as a new variable. See Figure 37.

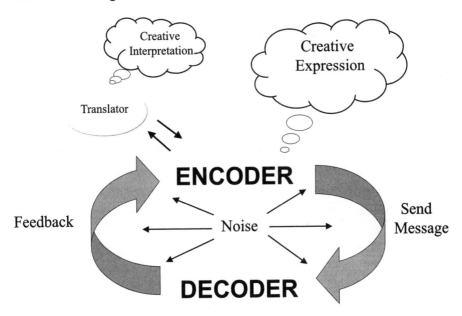

Figure 37 - Effective Communication with Creative Interpretation

A writer's communication style will vary depending on his audience, whether the audience is internal or external to the organization, and according to the specific objectives of the communication piece. In the case of marketing collateral, you are primarily targeting an external audience. The specific objectives can be increased awareness, sales, product information, increased usage and improved customer retention depending on the specifics of the communication piece. The impact of a marketing communication piece however, has wider and longer term consequences than the response to a specific campaign or promotion. A company conveys brand values to its customers in each communication through style, tone, pitch and choice of words. Just as a successful customer communication piece will strengthen the brand value of a company, a communication message negatively impacted by internal or external elements that distort the message can be exceptionally damaging to a company and its brand.

One area of potential distortion you have control over is the quality of your written Spanish language communication. Research has shown that the U.S. Hispanic consumer displays more brand and company loyalty than the general market. Hispanics recognizing high quality customer service and an appreciation of those companies that are marketing in-language and in-culture drive this loyalty.

Nine in ten Hispanics stated in a national study undertaken by Santiago Solutions Group and Hispanic Teleservices Corporation, that a positive customer service experience influences their decision to continue doing business with a given service provider. If the experience is negative, six out of ten will switch to another service provider or product. The study also confirmed that positive word-of-mouth is common practice, with 60 percent of Hispanics sharing their positive customer service experience with an average of seven family members and friends. These research findings reinforce the importance of ensuring your in-language communication messages are accurate and error free. If Spanish language customer service and communication is inferior in quality and contains grammatical errors, spelling mistakes or uses inappropriate words, the effect will be the opposite and the impact on the brand value will be negative.

Given the increased potential for distortion in the communication process when translations are undertaken, and the positive or negative impact Spanish language communication can have on your brand value and perceived image, internally you should mandate the same level of accountability, care and attention to Spanish language communication as is given to your English communication pieces. These mandates should extend to your external translators who should have appropriate internal processes and procedures in place to ensure the result is a high quality professional translation.

The Art of Good Translation

We find individual expression and communication in oral or written form. Oral expression has the benefit of tone, emphasis, body language, pauses, unperceivable perceptions, atmosphere, etc. Language in the spoken form has the added benefit of repetition, explanation, amplification, reticence, or suggestion to aid understanding, something that is not possible in rigid written expression. When the written word is used, there is no way of escaping certain demands that are not attendant in spoken language. Meaning must come from the text, pauses from punctuation, and emphasis or suggestion from the scarce auxiliary signs available.

Translating, or expressing in one language what was written or spoken in another, almost becomes an art when performed with skill. It is not surprising, therefore, that there are times when an effective bilingual speaker does not make an effective translator, and vice versa. Translation is more than concentrating, understanding, and assimilating to create text; it is producing and composing through interpretation. We can see this clearly when we read a single piece translated by different authors, in the same way that a piece of music can sound different depending on the musician who interprets it.

Translation should exactly reproduce the original text, but to an extent, a translation can be a personal version of the text. A translator should be able to rely on a number of skills and carry out various activities, among them:

- Complete understanding of the original language and domain of the object language. This is one of the reasons people who translate into their own language by birth or mother tongue, produce more effective translations.
- Complete understanding of the text. Reading is not the same as understanding. Understanding what you read is essential to structuring the text. For example, a person translating a medical document who has no understanding of the jargon used within the medical industry will produce a translation inferior in quality

than that performed by a person familiar with the terminology used in that industry.

- Adopt a favorable attitude toward the author and the message. Although the translation could be a personal version of the text in terms of style, the writing should express the original idea exactly; here there is no room for personal interpretation of what the author has said. We might dissent from what the author said, but we cannot confuse translation with personal interpretation that pronounces value judgments and obscures understanding of the original message.

- Research the subject to be translated to obtain an adequate level of knowledge in order to be able to understand the text. It is practically impossible to achieve encyclopedic knowledge of any subject, for which reason it is up to the translator to investigate and teach himself about the subject. Glossaries and specialized dictionaries may be necessary according to the subject being translated.

- Faithfully reproduce the message in the object language. The translator achieves fidelity when the translation transmits the message of the original text precisely; that is, if it truly corresponds with the idea the author intended. The translator achieved this if he is aware of the contextual meaning of the words used in the original text, possesses a broad vocabulary, the spelling is accurate, the synonyms are properly used and if the translator knows the grammatical laws of the object language.

Spanish	English
Plato	Dish
Plató	Film Studio Set
Libro	Book
Libró	Avoided, Fought - a battle

Table 4 - Importance of Accents in the Spanish Language

Otherwise, it is easy to distort the message. For example, absences of accents in the Spanish language are considered spelling errors and can change the entire meaning of words.

Bear in mind the tone of the piece, as well as its subject matter and the target audience. It is not the same to translate a scientific paper, a novel, an essay or a verse. The treatment given to the message is subject to the decisions made by the author when selecting and structuring the piece. The translator must bear this in mind when restructuring the code used in the original text. The selection and use of a determined code on the part of the translator should concur with the purpose of the author. The "choice of treatment" could result in the use of a standard that could be cultured, popular, scientific, and literary, etc.

Review the translation. Here translators employ much of their knowledge about the proper use of the object language, such as the correct use of syntax, a varied vocabulary according to normal cultured use, verb-subject agreement, correct punctuation, and so on. It is also advisable to avoid ambiguities created by incorrect syntax, wrongly structured sentences, etc. The best quality translations are those carried out by "four, six, or more hands," that is, those that involve two, three, or more translators and proofreaders. Generally, in these cases each translator speaks a different mother tongue, which guarantees the accuracy and quality of the job.

It is understandable that in order to communicate and connect successfully, it is imperative to translate effectively, correctly and properly aligned to the function pursued, which implies understanding, interpreting, adapting to the target audience, and writing the piece effectively. We should remember that, ultimately, the intention of the writer is to communicate his message to the reader. The job of the translator is to carry that message further.

Best Practice Versus Reality

Despite the negative impact and consequences poorly translated communication pieces have on a company's brand value and image, many U.S. businesses have published Spanish language marketing communication below a standard considered acceptable for formal business communication. These errors occur because of the following five reasons:

Lack of senior management buy-in to Hispanic market extension

Senior management with a lack of understanding of what is required to be successful in this market is a key contributing factor to organizations that are not fully committed to Hispanic marketing initiatives. Without senior management buy-in, Hispanic initiatives are not given the same priority and care that English communication material is given. In this scenario, Hispanic marketing is often under-resourced from a personnel perspective and the department functions in isolation from mainstream marketing.

Internal bilingual resources are not qualified to translate business documents

Companies often use bilingual staff in a capacity that they are not qualified to fulfill. It is common to have Spanish-speaking customer service staff translate customer communication and marketing materials. Companies should not consider a staff member who is not a professional translator proficient enough to translate formal customer communication.

Marketing department staff are unable to proofread translations prior to publishing

Many of the errors that appear in published Spanish language communication material would have been identified if marketing department staff were able to proofread them for errors and omissions prior to publication. Marketing departments without staff proficient in applicable languages to proofread translated material are at the mercy of their translation vendor.

Vendors who use translation software without human intervention

Be wary of translation vendors that offer pricing too good to be true. Chances are they can afford to price lower than their competitors do because they are using computer software to perform the translations without any human input.

Inadequate budget for Hispanic marketing

Hispanic marketing budgets are still proportionately lower than general marketing budgets. According to the Association of Hispanic Advertising Agencies' April 2002 study entitled "Missed Opportunities: Vast Corporate Under-spending in the U.S. Hispanic Market," corporations are only appropriating an average of 3.2 percent of their total national business and marketing dollars to reach the U.S. Hispanic market. The study identified the appropriate spend level for this market should be closer to 8 percent of total national business and marketing dollars.

Inadequate budgets in a competitive environment will result in shortcuts to try to maintain market position or gain competitive advantage. However, these shortcuts will inevitably lead to mistakes that will be costly in the long-term. Spanish language websites, advertisements, marketing collateral and customer letters containing blatant grammar, spelling errors and nonsensical sentences and phrases are all too frequently printed and published, and then circulated in the public domain. The following are some examples of poorly translated Spanish phrases recently found on websites and in marketing collateral:

A bank, promoting services to advise customers to "manage your money and save for the future" unfortunately translated this phrase into "Advance your money and save face to the future." A bank advising customers they could "refinance debt," omitted a letter in a word and was actually advising customers that they could "refinance doubt."

As reported in the *Athens Banner-Herald* on Monday, July 14, 2003, the new Spanish-language Georgia Capitol visitor guide contained so many embarrassing errors, ranging from misspellings and typographical errors to wrong tenses, incorrectly conjugated verbs, missing or incorrect accents and other simple grammatical mistakes, that officials pulled the brochure to rewrite it. Ironically, they had just reprinted the brochure to add two personnel changes when they identified the mistakes. Unfortunately, they had made all the errors more than a year earlier when the brochure was first printed and circulated.

In another example, the author received a statement from a major medical company in the U.S. A number of obvious grammatical errors in the Spanish language statement triggered a call to the marketing manager to bring these errors to the company's attention. The marketing manager, after learning of these errors, said she did not consider them a major problem worth rectifying.

In an example of a practice marketers would consider unthinkable when targeting to the general population, a bank in the U.S. sent a Spanish language letter to Hispanic customers without anyone in the company knowing exactly what the letter said, let alone its style, tone or pitch. The letter, sent manually to Hispanic customers, advised them that the bank did not have the capability to communicate in writing in Spanish and advised the customers to call and speak to a Spanish-speaking customer service representative, if they needed to communicate with the bank and their language of preference was Spanish.

You can be certain that senior management would not tolerate these kinds of errors in their English language customer communication. There are some alleged Spanish language marketing translation blunders that have become folklore and published around the world in marketing textbooks. These are a few examples of how translation blunders can be damaging, costly, embarrassing and get you the kind of publicity your company does not need.

When the Pope visited the U.S., a Miami t-shirt maker printed shirts for the visit. Rather than stating, "I saw the Pope" (el Papa), the T-shirts reportedly said, "I saw the Potato" (la papa).[1] One international corporation had its annual report translated into Spanish. In the sentence "Our vast enterprise achieved record sales," they translated the word *"vast"* as *"basto."* The actual Spanish word is *"vasto,"* but people are often confused because *b* and *v* are pronounced similarly in some coun-

---

1   Winds of Change.Net

tries. Due to this apparent minor error, the sentence read, "Our crude and uncultured enterprise achieved record sales."[2]

When Parker Pen marketed a ballpoint in Mexico, they meant their advertising campaign to say, "It won't leak in your pocket and embarrass you." The company mistakenly used the word "*embarazar*" which they thought meant, "embarrass." Much to their embarrassment the ad read, "It won't leak in your pocket and make you pregnant."[3] Translators mangled chicken-man Frank Perdue's slogan, "it takes a tough man to make a chicken tender," terribly in another Spanish translation. A photo of Perdue with one of his birds appeared on billboards all over Mexico with a caption that explained, "It takes a hard man to make a chicken aroused."[4] When a well known airline wanted to advertise its new leather first class seats in the Mexican market, it translated its "Fly in leather" campaign literally. Unfortunately, "vuela en cuero" means "Fly naked" in Spanish.[5]

The above examples highlight the reliance U.S. companies have on their translation vendors to do the job right. The extent of the vulnerability is highlighted by the fact that many U.S. businesses do not have the internal resources to proofread Spanish language customer communications prior to printing and publication. These are not isolated examples; they demonstrate that U.S. companies have some way to go to attain "Best Practice" Spanish language communication and customer service.

2   International Business, Betty Jane Punnett, David A. Ricks

3   International Business, Betty Jane Punnett, David A. Ricks

4   Winds of Change.Net

5   Winds of Change.Net

Ensuring Culturally Appropriate and Accurate Translations

Many communication pieces targeting the U.S. Hispanic are direct translations of their English counterparts. Any in-language written message needs to be consistent with your English communication in pitch, tone and style; culturally appropriate and error free. We developed the checklist below to assist you in ensuring your Spanish language communication meets the expectations of the target audience and is written with an appropriate level of professionalism for business communication.

1. Use Neutral Business Spanish

Just as business communication in English has its own discipline, rules and conventions that set it apart from informal communication, the same applies to Spanish. They require that we use formal language, appropriate terminology and follow specific grammar rules for professional communication in Spanish. Whilst an individual may claim to be bilingual, does he or she have the necessary skills to communicate in formal business communication, or is their vocabulary restricted to informal communication with family and friends? A growing trend in the U.S. is to test the language capabilities of bilingual job candidates and staff to assess their competency and suitability for a position requiring specific language skills.

U.S. Hispanics come from more than twenty countries and, depending on their origin, use the Spanish language differently. This raises an issue: the U.S. Hispanic market is not comprised of one homogenous group and there are subtle differences in language use and cultural differences that set one group apart from another. Just as there are differences between a person from England and a person from the U.S. even though they speak the same language; there are differences in the words and phrases used, how certain words are spelled and distinctive cultural differences in their personal and professional lives. Table 5 shows examples of these differences.

The settlement patterns of the different ethnic origins of U.S. Hispanics have created distinct regional differences of Spanish speakers in

English	American	Example
Cheque	Check	Can I pay for my meal by cheque?
Colour	Color	Your credit card can be either Gold or Platinum in colour
Petrol	Gas	I filled the car with premium petrol
Bill	Check	Waiter, can I have the bill for the meal now, please?
Biscuit	Cookie	I have just eaten the last chocolate chip biscuit

Table 5 - Differences in English and American English Words

the U.S. Many Spanish speakers who live in the East are of Puerto Rican, Dominican Republic or Cuban-American origins. In the West, the heritage of Spanish speakers is mostly Mexican and Central American. Then, there are people from South America, who live all over the U.S., who speak yet a different variation of Spanish. A simple example of a commonly used Spanish word is *"cancelar."* A non-speaking Spanish person might understand this word to mean, "to cancel." In Mexico, for example, this word does mean, "to cancel." However, in Puerto Rico, Venezuela and other countries, the word *"cancelar"* is used primarily to mean "to pay." There are more than nine verbs in Spanish that signify

English	Mexico	Puerto Rico & Caribbean	Central & South America
Balance	Saldo	Balance	Importe
Statement	Factura	Estado de Cuenta	Resumen, Extracto
To Pay	Abonar	Cancelar	Bonificar

Table 6- Spanish Language Credit and Collections Glossary

"to pay." We highlighted regional differences in Spanish in the Spanish Language Credit and Collection Glossary. Notice the contrast in the banking and financial services language in Mexico, Puerto Rico and Caribbean, and Central and South America.

A challenging issue for companies when communicating with U.S. Hispanics in writing or verbally is using "Neutral Spanish" in order to communicate to all the subgroups that comprise the U.S. Hispanic market. Table 7 shows a "Neutral Spanish" example for each of three words in the Spanish Language Credit and Collections Glossary.

English	Neutral Business Spanish
Balance	Saldo
Statement	Estado de Cuenta
To Pay	Pagar

Table 7 - Neutral Business Spanish Credit and Collections Glossary

Communicating in "Neutral Spanish" in business communications will help prevent alienating one or more of the subgroups that comprise the U.S. Hispanic market, minimize misunderstandings and prevent confusion and frustration amongst customers on important customer communication.

2. Ensure Communication is Formal rather than Informal

When communicating to U.S. Hispanics, it is important to be cognizant of the degree of formality necessary in a given communication piece. In Spanish there are two distinct ways to say "you," formal ("*Usted*") and informal ("*tú*"). Each usage requires a different conjugation of verbs. Misuse of "*tú*" and "*Usted*" and the appropriate accompanying verb is a common mistake we see in business Spanish communication in the U.S.

3. Use In-Culture Communication

To capture the heart and mind of the Hispanic consumer, the written message needs to be in-language and the communication piece needs to be in-culture. Culture can be defined as the set of basic values, beliefs, perceptions, preferences and behaviors that shape how we think and behave as human beings. Therefore, marketing in-culture means demonstrating an intimate understanding of the country of birth, perceptions, preferences, and the impact that all of these have on images, symbols, colors, and purchasing behavior.

4. Use Appropriate Style, Tone, Pitch and Attention to Detail

In each communication with your customers or prospects, you are representing your organization's brand and core values. Speak to customers in a consistent brand voice regardless of the language used. Consistent writing styles, tone, pitch and choice of words creates a recognizable approach, which results in increased brand recognition and enhanced awareness. The tone of your written message reflects your position, how you see yourself and how you want others to perceive you. A useful tool to help ensure consistency is to develop a Spanish language style guide and glossary of terms defining the words and phrases you want to use, and the specific ways you want to use them.

5. Translate the Meaning

The purpose of translation is to represent accurately the meaning or intent of a communication piece from one language to another. Literal translations are word-by-word translations using grammatical and lexical forms of the source text language. Literal translations are not always accurate and, in some cases, can be misleading. To preserve the context of what you are saying, the best approach is to translate the meaning of the word or phrase using natural grammatical and lexical items of the receptor language.

6. Make Sure Editing is Part of the Process

In the absence of suitably qualified internal resources to proofread translated material prior to printing, have a second translation vendor edit the work of the original translator. Although this is an additional cost, the long run benefits of detecting errors and omissions before costly print runs, will justify the additional cost.

7. Minimize Technology or Software Translators

Determine if your vendor uses computer software in any part of the translation process. Software can be used to perform the translation, as is the case with "Fully-Automated Translations," or to assist a human translator, as is the case with "Computer-Aided Translations." Obvious benefits of machine translations over human translators are speed and price. However, we must share a word of caution; machine translation software should not be used in isolation for business and professional translations. Fully automated translation software provides a useful tool to someone who has a basic understanding of the language; however, it is prone to errors and incorrect use of semantics, morphology, syntaxes and lexicology. Software provides one meaning, (and not necessarily the correct one). For example, we can translate the verb "to be" into two different verbs in Spanish, "*ser*" or "*estar*," and a live translator reading the paragraph can identify which one is correct. If your vendor uses machine translations, ensure there is a human being who performs the final edit.

8. Hire Native Speakers

The best translations are those performed by native speakers translating into their native language. Translators who are native Spanish speakers are intimately familiar with the language and understand cultural nuances, colloquialisms and idioms. To ensure the purest translation, select a vendor that uses a combination of native Spanish and native English speakers on each translation project. An expensive step, but one that will help ensure accuracy, is to request that your translation vendor perform "backtranslation." This involves translating the communication piece into Spanish and then having a second translator translate the Spanish version back into English. You then compare the original document to the "backtranslated" version and make necessary changes until it mirrors the meaning of the original version.

9. Implement an Audit Process

Use a vendor that has an internal audit procedure to check the translation against the original document. This differs from "backtranslation" in that the document is not translated back into the original language; a comparison is made between the translated version and the original to ensure accuracy, and that the translated document retains its original tone and meaning. This is a critical step. It may be the only proofreading undertaken prior to printing or going live on the Internet since many companies do not have Spanish speakers in-house.

Vendor Selection

There are many options to consider when looking for translation services. With advances in technology and the relatively low cost to enter the industry, there is no shortage of vendors. When selecting a vendor to undertake your translation work there are a few key criteria to consider in the selection process that will help ensure you are getting a professional quality translation:

- Choose a vendor who is familiar with your industry and the specific terminology, jargon and technical terms used. A firm specializing in translating for the financial services industry will have a better understanding of the terms and phrases used in the banking industry than a firm that primarily translates for companies in the pharmaceutical industry. For example, specialized terms such as loan to value, unsecured credit card, grace period, balance transfer and wire transfer are specialized terms in financial services communication that must be translated accurately.
- Use a vendor with an internal audit procedure to check the translation against the original document. This step is essential and even more so if you lack the internal resources to proofread translated material in-house. Request a minimum of "four hands," two independent translators involved in the translation and editing process, carry out your translation. This will ensure accuracy and that the translated document retains its original tone and meaning.

- Do not underestimate the benefit of local knowledge. Translators who are intimately familiar and/or native Spanish speakers understand cultural nuances, colloquialisms and idioms.
- To ensure the purest translation, use a vendor that has a combination of native Spanish and native English speakers on each translation project.
- Do not entrust machines, without human intervention, to edit or to undertake professional translations. Progress in technological translation capability has been impressive over recent years, but still has a way to go to reach the intellect, understanding and reasoning capability of human translators.
- Choose a reputable professional translator who can provide you with credible references. Check with the references to ensure they are happy with the quality of the work and turnaround times.

Supporting Your Spanish Language Marketing

Companies are entering the U.S. Hispanic market with various degrees of marketing efforts. At one end of the continuum there are companies developing specific strategies and products or services to meet the needs of the Hispanic market. At the other end, there are companies that translate their English materials and websites into Spanish verbatim with little or no back-office support to service this segment.

With the growth in the use of the Internet as a marketing tool, we have seen an increase in the number of websites translated into Spanish. Companies serious about capturing this segment of the market need to do more than translate their English website into Spanish. Hispanic marketing initiatives do not start and end when you translate websites, brochures, and letters into Spanish verbatim. A company's Hispanic marketing and communication strategy must be fully integrated across all communication mediums, (marketing collateral, websites, brochures, advertisements, letters, voice response units, call center scripts, etc.), in-language and in-culture, across all communication mediums and supported in the back office.

If a customer receives a solicitation in Spanish, that customer has the reasonable expectation that they can call and accept the offer and be able to talk to a Spanish-speaking customer service representative. Supporting your Hispanic marketing with bilingual customer service representatives, bilingual Interactive Voice Response, IVR, capabilities, Spanish language letters, and statements demonstrates that your company is respectful and sensitive to your Hispanic customer's needs, values, beliefs and culture and truly values their business.

Translation Services Trends

According to Allied Business Intelligence, the market for translations has grown from over $11 billion in 1999 to close to $20 billion in 2004. There are a number of contributing factors in the growth in translations. A primary one is technology advancement, its lowering cost structure, and its impact on the globalization of markets. The rapid pace of change in the field of technology in recent years, in particular communication infrastructure technology, combined with the increase in Internet usage and e-commerce has had a significant impact on how we do business and the erosion of traditional geographic borders.

Increased competition and the use of the Internet to market products to new audiences around the globe has been a major catalyst for the increase in translation services. Technology has facilitated growth in demand while email and downloadable files have provided the means for service providers to service clients from anywhere in the world in a cost effective and timely fashion. The relatively low cost structure required to set up and operate as a translator has prompted an increase in smaller service providers competing directly with the traditional larger firms. These smaller firms tend to be proficient in one or two languages and/or have industry specific expertise.

A rising trend is the use of computer-assisted software by translation firms to translate business documents and websites. Software will never replace a person performing translations. The use of a word or phrase can change the meaning of a sentence completely. "Home," for example, can be a noun, adverb, or verb. Software provides one meaning, (and not necessarily the correct one), but only a trained professional can differentiate the appropriate meaning depending on the context; and only the translator reading the paragraph can tell which one should be used.

Another emerging translation tool is the use of on-line translation services. Scores of these are available free of charge on websites and enable the user to translate text from one language to another. Often these tools perform literal translations, which in many cases are non-sensical and should not be used in a professional capacity. Technology has fueled growth in the market. At the same time, the purest and most accurate translation results from a professional translator who speaks the mother tongue, has the benefit of local knowledge and understands cultural nuances, colloquialisms and idioms. This is still the best option for professional translations.

Chapter Summary

There is no denying that the U.S. Hispanic market represents a significant opportunity to those marketers wishing to target this segment of the U.S. economy proactively. Statistically this segment will become even more powerful in the future, with the U.S. Census Bureau predicting that it will comprise 25 percent of the total population by the year 2050.

Before embarking on a program to target the U.S. Hispanic consumer proactively, formalize your market extension strategy. This entails developing a formal business case and marketing plan presented to senior management to get their buy-in. Senior management needs to agree to the vision, understand the necessity to research the target market, and adequately resource and budget the initiative.

A key success factor when designing your U.S. Hispanic market extension strategy is to recognize and understand the differences between the U.S. Hispanic market and the general market, as well as the similarities and differences between the various ethnic origins that comprise the U.S. Hispanic consumer. One of the differences between Hispanics that marketers often overlook is the subtle difference in language use. All customer communications should be in "Neutral Business Spanish" in order to cater to every Hispanic consumer, regardless of their ethnic origin.

Due to the high percentage of Hispanics who prefer to be marketed to in-language, translating websites and marketing collateral into Spanish is an essential component of any proactive Hispanic marketing strategy. Marketers should ensure the elements of the communication mix are not translated in isolation; and any decision to market in-language and in-culture should be part of an integrated approach touching all customer contact points. It is reasonable for a Hispanic consumer, who receives a solicitation in Spanish, to expect service in Spanish.

Ensuring your in-language Spanish communication is accurate and error free should be a fundamental requirement before signing off for print or publication. However, current practice in the U.S. demonstrates that marketers do not give the same care and attention to Spanish language communication that they give to English marketing communication. This is due in part to ill-equipped internal resources performing tasks outside their capabilities or sphere of expertise or a lack of care and/or process by the translation vendor. We should not underestimate the negative consequences of translation errors or misinterpretations with this very loyal segment of the market, particularly on brand value and perceived image.

The potential for distortion occurs in all communication through noise in the environment. By adding translations into the communication mix, the risk of errors or misunderstanding increases. Your choice of translation vendor and their suitability to translate for your industry will play a critical role in the overall quality of the finished product. Utilizing checklists to identify and select the optimum vendor and asking pertinent questions about audit procedures will identify you as an informed client and ensure you minimize additional risks as much as possible. Sample questions may include: how many 'hands' will be involved, whether they utilize native speakers, perform back-translation, and use software in any part of the process.

- The U.S. Hispanic market is a heterogeneous group of consumers for which the Spanish language is a unifying factor.
- U.S. Hispanics prefer to be marketed to in Spanish.

- Due to the diverse ethnic origins of the sub groups that comprise the U.S. Hispanic market, marketing material must be written in "Neutral Business Spanish."
- Adding translations into a communication model increases the complexity of the model and the risk of distortion.
- Customer communication messages containing errors can be exceedingly damaging to a company and its brand.
- Mandate the same high levels of accountability, care and attention to detail in Spanish language communication as is given to English communication.
- Inferior Spanish language marketing communications are occurring because of a lack of senior management buy-in, using unqualified internal resources, inadequate or nonexistent proofreading, use of translation software and inadequate budgets.
- Speak to your audience in a consistent brand voice regardless of the language used.
- Preserve the context of what you are saying by translating the meaning of the word or phrase, not by using a literal translation.
- A skilled translation is one that is undertaken by a professional translator who:
  - Completely understands the original language and domain of the object language
  - Understands the text
  - Has a favorable attitude toward the author and message
  - Has a working knowledge of the subject matter
  - Is aware of the target audience and required tone for the message
  - Proofreads his or her work and checks the translated material to the original document
  - Is carried out by four, six, or more hands. In other words, it involves two or more translators and proofreaders
- Utilize translators that translate into their native language; they are intimately familiar with the language and cultural nuances.
- Mandate your translation vendor have an audit process to check the translated document against the original.

- Many U.S. companies, who do not have the internal resources to translate or proofread Spanish language materials, rely heavily on translation vendors. When selecting a vendor:
  - Choose one familiar with your industry
  - Mandate an audit process to check the translated document against the original
  - Do not underestimate the benefit of local knowledge
  - Use a combination of native Spanish and native English speakers
  - Do not entrust translation software without human intervention
  - Choose a reputable translator with credible references
- Support all in-language marketing to the U.S. Hispanic consumer with integrated in-language customer service across all customer contact points.

About the Author

Tony Malaghan, Chief Executive Officer, Arial International

Tony Malaghan, chief executive officer of Arial International, has a Bachelor of Business Studies with a major in Marketing from Massey University. He brings more than 23 years of professional experience in the marketing and financial services industries to Arial International's management team. Since joining Arial International, Tony's focus has been on Hispanic marketing projects in the U.S.A.

Chapter Nine

Marketing to U.S. Hispanics Online
Research and Perspectives

Richard Israel
Cynthia Nelson

In This Chapter

- Brief history about marketing and advertising to U.S. Hispanics
- A glimpse of the significant contributions of those that made U.S. Hispanic online marketing what it is today
- Clear and concise tips on how to best leverage this growing market

Introduction

This chapter is intended for everyone interested in the U.S. Hispanic market, not just marketing or statistical experts. Developed as an easy read, it is based upon the historical experiences of the founders of this industry, current quantitative and qualitative research as well as interviews from up-and-coming online industry icons.

While our chapter title, "Marketing to U.S. Hispanics Online" is about the Internet population, we first take you though a brief history of marketing and advertising to the U.S. Hispanic segment, and provide a glimpse of the significant contributions of those that made ethnic marketing what it is today.

Our goal is that you move quickly, find interesting anecdotes, quotes and some clear and concise tips about how to best leverage this growing market. Ideally, this chapter will stimulate your interest enough to continue research on your own, and share the simple experience with others who may also be curious.

In the Beginning

To understand how the U.S. Hispanic market has become "an overnight success," we must first appreciate and give credit to a handful of people who have become icons of this industry. These people made it happen above all odds, and with just a little bit of luck, they helped transform the advertising world.

In the beginning, there were only a handful of people interested in the U.S. Hispanic market. The idea of "ethnic marketing" was just a glimmer in the eye of people like Daisy Exposito, former chief executive officer, C.E.O., of the Bravo Group, the largest U.S. Hispanic advertising agency. Speaking about her career, Exposito said,

> "Fresh out of college, I started working on marginal television programs on public television, the kind you'd need to be an insomniac to catch on the air. I was associate producer on 'Realidades,' a pioneering show in English designed and aimed at New York's Latino population. Then I went to Conill Advertising, an agency that was pioneering the Hispanic market. That marked my true start in advertising for U.S. Hispanics, with a brief departure and a stop at NBC's New York station. Then came Bravo and a passionate romance with Hispanic communications that has lasted more than 22 years. Along the way, I've even polished my Spanish, because my beginnings were completely Anglo in as far

as the language of the business at hand. I guess I'm one of the few rare instances of 'reverse crossover.'"[1]

Advertising to U.S. Hispanics was not fashionable or profitable; and it definitely was not popular with most advertising agencies. The world, at least the Madison Avenue advertising world, was not prepared for the imminent changes.

Many also consider Leticia Callava, a 25-year veteran of Telemundo, and Arturo Villar, publisher of *Hispanic Market Weekly* early pioneers of Hispanic marketing. While Callava considers her start in Hispanic marketing accidental, Villar attributes his start in Hispanic marketing to the recession in 1981-1982 in Latin America. As his previous career stalled, he had recognized a need for Hispanic newspapers in the United States.

"It started accidentally, really. It was a time in South Florida when the [Hispanic] television industry was very immature," Callava said. "I didn't have any experience in broadcast, or reporting for that matter. What I did have was the ability to speak, read and write in both English and Spanish and I was Cuban. I came to Florida during the Castro regime in the 50s. I understood the Cuban culture and issues first hand and started reporting and writing for a very small station in Miami in the 70s. We had no budget for anything and we did our 'network production' in a room the size of a small garage. We did trades for everything, wardrobe, gasoline, you name it. We sometimes didn't even have enough money for the electric bill. We tried to imitate the mainstream network anchors but provide information for the Cuban community. I also did weather, wrote and taped segments and

---

1   From phone & written interview January 28, 2003

co-anchored. You did everything, you learned and you made mistakes"[2]

"I was publishing a magazine in Latin America in 1985 and when the economy crashed, I was out of work," said Arturo Villar. "I realized that there was not a publication aimed at the Hispanic community. There was little if any distribution available and we knew through research that Hispanics did indeed read. I worked to develop an insert in several national newspapers in Chicago, San Antonio, and Houston and developed a 500,000 circulation. I had the freedom to do what I wanted since the main newspaper publishers didn't understand the inserts."[3]

These trailblazers faced a myriad of challenges. Along the way they, and countless others, pioneered the U.S. Hispanic marketing and communications industry. Their independent actions and small steps have accumulated into giant leaps for the entire industry. There were stereotypical and monetary challenges as well, the silent challenges, according to Daisy Exposito.

"With the invisible challenge of breaking down stereotypes and succeeding in what very much remains a male-controlled industry, I've had to work harder than 10,000 Egyptians building a pyramid," stated Exposito."We have also learned from people like Eduardo Caballero who recalls the challenges of educating general market experts about the importance of marketing to Hispanics, only to be met with doubt about Hispanics' usage of the most basic, everyday products," said Ingrid Smart, C.E.O. of Mendoza Dillon and past

2   From personal interview January 27, 2003

3   From personal interview January 28, 2003

president of the Association of Hispanic Advertising Agencies, AHAA.

What the critics of the time did not understand was that this small group of pioneers had a vision. A vision filled with real life experiences of immigration, acculturation and confrontations borne out of bias and prejudice. These pioneers were real people with real experiences who knew in their hearts that they somehow had a higher calling: they needed to change the way marketers and advertisers thought about and communicated to U.S. Hispanics.

When asked who had particular influence on them and their careers, these pioneers mentioned Joaquín Blaya of Radio Unica; Raúl Toraño, retired from Univision; Eduardo Caballero, media pioneer; and Alicia Conill repeatedly as true industry icons. To them we owe a debt of gratitude.

U.S. Census in 2000

With the publishing of the 2000 U.S. Census, advertisers and marketers finally "discovered" the Hispanic market. "First, it took decades to move. Lately, it has evolved at the speed of sound, maybe the sound of money. The motivation to market to U.S. Hispanics has transitioned from informed intuition to factualness to financial desirability," according to Daisy Exposito. "Only a decade ago we were preachers. Today we are practitioners."

The turning point for everyone was indeed the U.S. Census 2000. No other document has received such broad, general market distribution or review. No other piece of research is as highly debated for its accuracy, yet simultaneously regarded as the bible of measurement of the U.S. Hispanic community. The results of the Census in 2000 left no doubt. For the first time, America faced a new population reality, the 35.3 Hispanics now among its ranks. The 2000 census gave legitimacy to the Hispanic market in the eyes of corporate America.

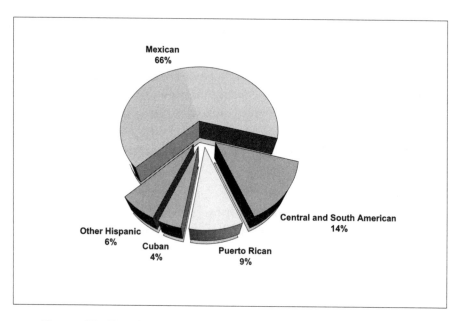

Figure 38 - Breakdown of National Origin of Hispanics in 2002

Continued Growth, Census 2001 and 2002

The Census in 2001 reconfirmed that the growth of the U.S. Hispanic population had not slowed. With a population increase of more than four percent over 2000 levels, the decade-long growth pattern continued as the U.S. Hispanic populace expanded 14 times faster than non-Hispanic whites. In 2002, there were 37.4 million Latinos in the civilian non-institutional population of the United States, representing 13.3 percent of the total U.S. population. Among the Hispanic population, the breakdown of national origin is shown in Figure 38.

In 2001 natural growth contributed about 60 percent of the total Hispanic growth (already 21 percent of all U.S. babies are born to Hispanic moms). The continuous wave of immigrants, mostly adult Mexican and Latin Americans, accounted for 40 percent (up to 60 percent in some markets) of the total 1.7 million annual population increase.

The U.S. Census predicted that by the year 2010 Hispanics will account for 13.5 percent of all Americans, and 22.5 percent in 2050 (or one in five people). Of the total U.S. population, Hispanics were more likely than non-Hispanic whites to reside in the West and South regions of the country and less likely to live in the Northeast and Midwest.

Nearly half of all Hispanics lived in central cities within a metropolitan area (45.6 percent) compared with slightly more than one-fifth of non-Hispanic whites (21.1 percent) who lived in similar areas. More than one-third of U.S. Hispanics resided in just three markets: Los Angeles, New York and Miami.

Hispanics' disposable income is expanding at a rate 60-70 percent faster than sheer population growth, with yearly disposable income gains of 7.3 percent[4]. In 2003, Hispanic U.S. and Puerto Rico buying power was forecast to reach $685 billion[5], surpassing that of African Americans for the first time ever.

Impact of Television and Internet on Hispanics

Using television as a benchmark in the media industry, we can start to visualize how content, developed for television and ported onto the Internet, has affected the growing U.S. Hispanic audience[6]. The sources for this information include Strategy Research Corp., Thomas Rivera Policy Institute, *Hispanic Business* and Nielsen Media Research.

In most of the markets there are only two local Spanish-language television stations, while viewers have a choice between several non-Spanish-language stations. The advent of the Internet has presented consumers, of all races and ethnicities, with an unprecedented choice of outlets from which to receive information. Unlike television, the Internet also enables consumers to seek information of interest to them, from any available source, at the time of their choosing. Given these new realities, U.S. Hispanics are forming the following habits.

4   Selig Institute 2002

5   The Santiago Solutions Group analysis based on 2001 Census trends and Selig 2002

6   September 2004 comScore Media Metrix

In September 2003, with 9.7 million unique visitors, AOL Time Warner sites reached 76 percent of all U.S. Hispanic Internet users. During the same period, there were 9.6 and 9.4 million Hispanic unique visitors on the Yahoo! and MSN-Microsoft sites respectively. The popularity of these sites, which are primarily available in English, points to Hispanics comfort level with English language sites. Of the top Spanish-language websites Terra, Yahoo and Yupi lead the pack.

At the national level, Univision is the fifth largest television network in the United States after CBS, NBC, FOX and ABC. Television is the medium of choice for U.S. Latinos. On the Internet, however, Univision.com ranks fourth. The Nielsen Hispanic Television Index (NHTI) indicates Hispanic households tend to be larger and their television usage greater than the general market. Due to larger household size, viewing levels among Hispanic households tend to be most comparable to total U.S. households with three or more members.

The same holds true on the Internet. More Hispanic household members equal more users on the Internet. Hispanics watch more television; 3.6 hours on weekdays compared to 3.2 hours for all Americans. On the Internet, we are starting to see a shift parallel with what the general market reported. U.S. Hispanics are starting to watch less television and use the Internet more for entertainment. While television still dominates, the Internet is having an impact and driving share shift in the market.

The Tomás Rivera Policy Institute Study, in a telephone survey conducted among 1,013 Hispanics in five states, found that half of all respondents reported watching equal amounts of English and Spanish-language television programming. Hispanics who regularly watch television in both languages reported significantly more viewing time than those who watched in one language. This is another interesting parallel to the Internet. U.S. Hispanic online users tend to conduct research, transactions and communications in both languages depending upon the content or subject matter.

This newly acquired validation with the U.S. Census and other important studies manifests itself in a spectacle that is pure capitalism: the U.S. agency conglomerates fighting for a piece of the market, developing Hispanic marketing capabilities; and forming, buying and investing in the Hispanic marketing and advertising industry.

Although marketers are now aware of the size and buying power of the U.S. Hispanic population, the level of advertising and marketing dollars spent by Fortune 500 companies to reach this important market is still only 40-50 percent of what they should invest to reach a market of this size. As a result of this under-investment the Association of Hispanic Advertising agencies (AHAA)[7] which maintains the strongest and longest running organization dedicated to the Hispanic media market, along with the Santiago Solutions Group, conducted studies entitled "The Right Spend" and the "Right Spend II." They developed these studies to help highlight and provide solid research for large corporate marketing departments about the vast level of underspending in the U.S. Hispanic segment.

The Santiago Solutions Group designed a series of studies for AHAA in 2002 to define a straightforward systematic approach to calculate recommended allocation levels for targeting Spanish-dominant and bilingual Hispanics across major industries. While this study concentrated on offline media spending (television, print, radio, outdoor, etc.), we can draw parallels to the online advertising world. The study grouped three years of corporate resource allocation trends into a scorecard by category, identifying "Developing" and "Underdeveloped" industries.

Developing industries have traditionally better recognized the value and allocated more dollars against the Hispanic segment, and underdeveloped industries have historically allocated dangerously low levels resulting in underdeveloped categories not yet delivering their full potential growth from the Hispanic segment to their stockholders.

"Developing" Industries include the following:

- Food and beverage products
- Food services

---

7   Information from http://www.ahaa.org

- Children's products
- Personal care
- General merchandise
- Telecommunications

Underdeveloped Industries (for which higher allocation levels offer substantial growth opportunities) include:

- Insurance
- Automotive
- Specialty retail
- Securities and financial services
- Travel and entertainment
- Computers and software
- U.S. government
- Pharmaceuticals

The study concludes that advertisers as a whole are missing significant opportunities associated with this important segment and are underspending (by up to 200 percent) in several key categories. Visit www.ahaa.org for the entire study. At the end of this chapter, there are case studies on several of these key segments, including insights on how smart marketing managers are starting to purchase media and benefit from the Internet.

How advertising agencies have evolved to penetrate this market

In the past ten years, U.S. Hispanic agencies across the board have taken on investments, monetary as well as through mergers and acquisition, from large media conglomerates and other general market agencies. This indicates an improved level of understanding by large non-Hispanic companies of the importance of the U.S. Hispanic market.

Today, only a few top 10 agencies have not invested in strengthening their Hispanic marketing capabilities. These investments have helped agencies gain access to additional resources and research that would have otherwise been difficult, if not impossible, to attain. In many cases, they have also opened doors to general market clients and opportunities. Numerous general market agencies are encouraged to bring in

Rank	2003 Revenue ($M)	Parent Company	Agency Name
1	32.9	Publicis 49 percent stake	Bromley Communications
2	31.8	WPP	The Bravo Group
3	23.0	Omnicom	Dieste Harmel & Partners
4	16.4	Independent	Zubi Advertising Services
5	14.2	Independent	La Agencia de Orci &Asociados
6	12.4	Publicis	Lapiz Integrated Hispanic Marketing
7	12.1	Independent	Lopez Negrete Communications
8	11.2	Omnicom	DellRivero Messianu DDB
9	11.0	WPP Group	Mendoza-Dillon & Associates
10	10.7	IPG	Casanova Pendrill Publicidad, Inc.

Source: Hispanic Fact Pack, 2004, *Advertising Age*

Table 8 - Top Ten Hispanic Advertising Agencies in 2003

their Hispanic market specialists to gain access to current and prospective clients seeking to target the critical U.S. Hispanic segment.

"No longer are the agencies so small, so undercapitalized and 'forgotten.' Hispanic agencies have grown and become as professional as any general market agency," states Arturo Villar.

Even the agencies with outside ownership of over 50 percent remain fiercely independent. They remain for the most part to do what they do best, help clients navigate the Hispanic segment. Table 8 highlights the investment that general market agencies and media conglomerates have dedicated to this growing segment.

Significance to Marketers

Marketers cannot afford to overlook the fast-growing and ever changing U.S. Hispanic segment when developing marketing and advertising plans. Even in a slow economy, it is evident that brands are recognizing the importance of allocating Hispanic marketing and advertising dollars. America is, among other great things, about numbers.

Preparation Avoids Panic

Armed with the wisdom of industry veterans, important census statistics, and an understanding of how agencies have taken notice of the Hispanic market a review of marketing to U.S. Hispanics online is in order. Before developing a marketing plan, it is essential for companies to understand how their target segment interacts with and utilizes the medium they intend to use to advertise their products and services.

Understanding online consumer behavior, including that of U.S. Hispanics, is vital for the Internet to flourish as a viable marketing channel. Given the Internet's vast size and scope, measurement of consumers' behavior online is not an easy task. Measurement of Hispanics' online behavior must address additional considerations, including:

- Sample diversity and size: Accurate measurement of online usage among U.S. Hispanics requires a large and diverse sample in order to ensure representation of the varied sub-segments, including Hispanics of Mexican, Puerto Rican, South and Central American, Cuban and Caribbean descent.
- Language preferences: When measuring the U.S. Hispanic population, it is important to note that there are five distinct language preference segments: Spanish only, Spanish dominant, bilingual, English dominant and English only. A large segment of the U.S. population is comprised of individuals who identify themselves as Hispanic, yet speak little Spanish.

- Measurement across all multiple Internet users per household: To ensure accuracy, an Internet audience measurement system tracking behavior of U.S. Hispanics must quantify usage for specific household members; and highlight key behavioral differences in types of sites visited, amount of time spent online and details of purchases made online.
- Broad industry support: The majority of large portals serving the U.S. Hispanic audience must support a viable online audience measurement system. The research must be considered the industry standard.

The comScore Media Metrix Hispanic Services team made data for this chapter available. This included data from its panel of more than 50,000 U.S. Hispanic Internet users. At the time of this writing, comScore is the only reliable source measuring U.S. Hispanic Internet usage, offering more than a year's worth of reliable usage data on the Hispanic segment. The comScore sample represents the only database able to measure the online behavior of U.S. Hispanics.

ComScore Media Metrix Hispanic measurement services are based on a continuous measurement of the Webwide buying and surfing behavior or a representative panel of 50,000 U.S. Hispanic Internet users, spanning all key markets and language preferences. In adherence to U.S. Census Bureau convention, comScore classifies each panelist based upon his or her self-defined ethnicity. In addition to comScore Media Metrix data, selected sections from the AOL/RoperASW Hispanic CyberStudy are also included in this chapter. The AOL/ RoperASW Hispanic Cyberstudy was conducted via telephone among a random sample of 301 Hispanic home Internet online subscribers. The interviews were conducted from October 1, 2002 to October 28, 2002. The margin of error is plus or minus 6 percent for the total sample. The margin of sampling error for subgroups may be greater.

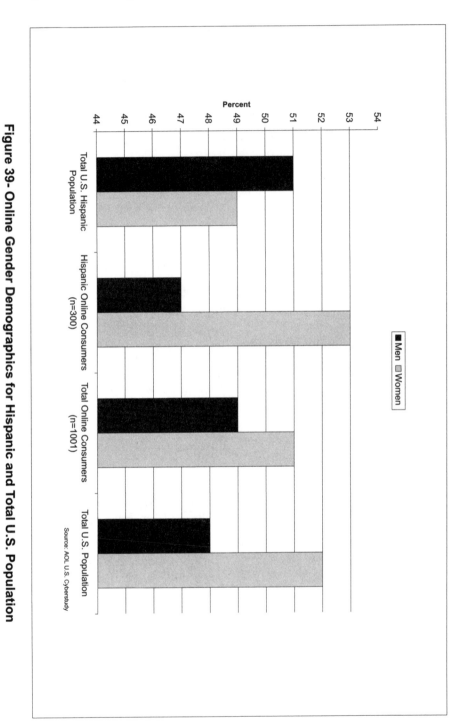

Figure 39- Online Gender Demographics for Hispanic and Total U.S. Population

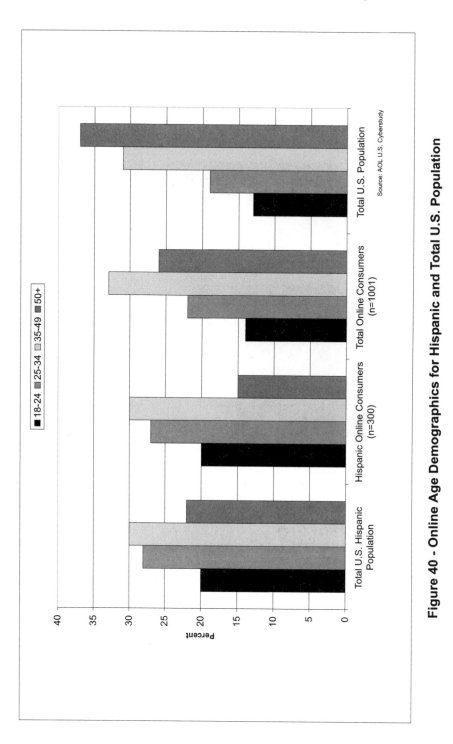

Figure 40 - Online Age Demographics for Hispanic and Total U.S. Population

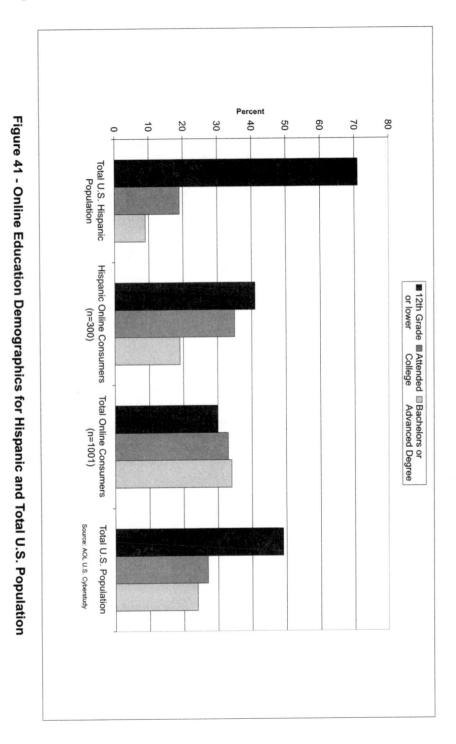

Figure 41 - Online Education Demographics for Hispanic and Total U.S. Population

Profiling Hispanic Online Consumers

U.S. Hispanics are Younger than U.S. Population

Any demographic analysis of U.S. Hispanic online consumers needs to be viewed in the context of the larger demographic picture in the United States today. U.S. Hispanics are generally younger than the general U.S. population overall (20 percent versus 13 percent are between 18 and 24).

Hispanic Online Consumers: Upscale Mass Market

The U.S. online consumer population appears to be an upscale mass market when compared to the general U.S. population. It is not surprising then that U.S. Hispanic Internet users are more educated than the general U.S. Hispanic population.

One of the key trends revealed by the U.S. Cyberstudy research is the progressive broadening of the online consumer population to include more consumers that are diverse. This trend is clearly exemplified by Hispanic online consumers, relatively new arrivals in cyberspace. Hispanics are twice as likely as the average to have come online in the past two years; half of Hispanic online consumers joined the market in the past two years alone (48 percent versus 21 percent of total U.S. online consumers).

Despite the relative newness of their arrival in cyberspace, Hispanic online consumers are generally as confident in their online skills and abilities as the online consumer population as a whole. One in five describes themselves as novices (22 percent of Hispanics versus 20 percent of the total); while one in seven describe themselves as experts (14 percent versus 16 percent).

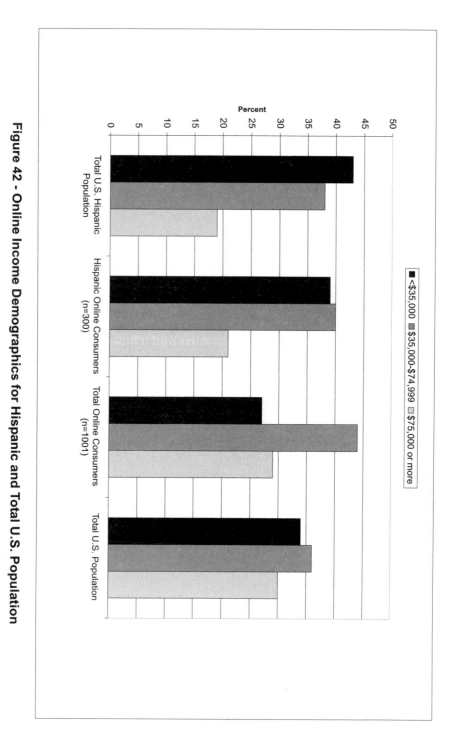

Figure 42 - Online Income Demographics for Hispanic and Total U.S. Population

What do Hispanics do online?

According to comScore Media Metrix[8], a year-over-year analysis of usage intensity among the 13.8 million U.S. Hispanic Internet users found that the amount of time spent online and the number of Web pages viewed by the average U.S. Hispanic Internet user has increased dramatically. Specifically, Hispanic Internet users spent an average of 26.5 hours online in September 2003, up 24 percent versus 21.4 hours in October 2002. Growth in content consumption was even more dramatic, with the average U.S. Hispanic user visiting 2,791 pages in September, an increase of 30 percent versus the previous year.

These trends indicate the Internet is playing an increasingly important role in Hispanics' lives. Many are developing online preferences and loyalties that will last well into the future. As with any major dislocation in consumer behavior, the nimble marketer will benefit. Smart marketers seeking to engage Hispanics are already identifying the destinations and content with which these consumers are most engaged.

In 2001, 33 percent of U.S. Hispanics had Internet access at home[9]. While home Internet access was less pervasive in the Hispanic community when compared to the U.S. population as a whole (where 55 percent of households reported having Internet access), U.S. Hispanics are increasingly connected to the online medium at home. In fact, nearly half of Hispanic online consumers (48 percent) joined the online medium in the past two years alone. Signifying the buzz about the Internet is traveling fast among this segment; 65 percent say they have suggested to a family member or friend that they use the Internet. Online Hispanics reportedly spend an average of 9.5 hours a week online at home, logging on frequently (a reported average of 4.2 days a week).

8   AOL/RoperASW Cyberstudy published in November 2002

9   Source: CPS Computer and Internet Use Supplement 2001

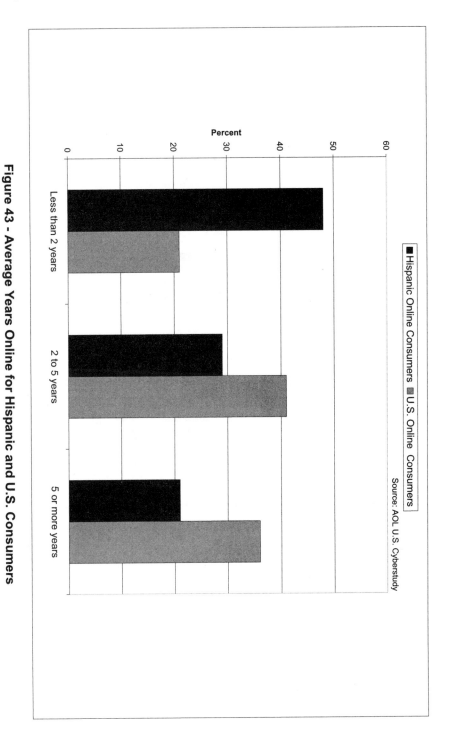

Figure 43 - Average Years Online for Hispanic and U.S. Consumers

Activities	Hispanic Adult Online	U.S. Adult Online
	percent	percent
Doing research of any kind	78	88
Communication with friends and family	76	90
Sending and receiving pictures	69	63
Getting information about products to buy	68	77
Online instant messages	66	48
Getting driving directions and/or maps	63	67
Checking the weather report	56	66
Listening to music like you do on the radio	50	40
Getting local entertainment information	49	51
Downloading music files	44	33
Looking up addresses and/or telephone numbers	43	45
Communication with business associates	40	50
Watching video clips	36	29
Downloading books	16	10
Going online using a portable device like a cell phone	15	9

Table 9 - Online Activities Engaged in by Hispanics

Music and Entertainment: Important Hispanic Touchstones

According to the Cyberstudy, when comparing online usage habits of U.S. Hispanics to other online consumers, several trends emerge. For example, Hispanic Internet users emerge as more avid consumers of entertainment-related online features and activities, perhaps in part because they are younger overall. Music, in particular, proves to be a more important touchstone for online Hispanics. Half of all Hispanic Internet users report that they regularly or occasionally "listen to music like you do on the radio" while only 40 percent of total online consumers do the same. Forty-four percent (compared to 33 percent for U.S. general population) say they "download music files." Just over one-third (36 percent) of Hispanic Internet users report they regularly or occasionally "watch video clips," compared to 29 percent of the total online consumer population.

Communication Key Online Activity

The Cyberstudy also states that communication and research are the top activities Hispanic online consumers engage in. Although online Hispanics are less likely than online consumers as a whole to say they communicate with friends and family online (76 percent versus 90 percent), they are more likely to say they use online messaging (66 percent versus 48 percent). Similarly, at least two-thirds regularly or occasionally send and receive pictures online (69 percent) and use online instant messaging (66 percent).

Where do they go?

According to comScore Media Metrix, the Hispanic population surfs and visits sites in parallel with their general market counterparts. Sites in the travel category top the list of sites that Hispanics visit. Websites within the computer hardware, apparel, event tickets and consumer electronics categories are also popular destinations for this audience.

Figure 44 illustrates the percentage of Hispanics versus the general market in each of the top five categories. What can we learn from this? For one thing, the U.S. Hispanic segment is as large as and sometimes larger online, than its general market counterpart.

Language Preference

The AOL Cyberstudy states that Hispanic consumers' top uses for the online mediums parallel the general market and include doing research (78 percent regularly or occasionally engage in the activity online), communication with friends and family (76 percent), sending and receiving pictures (69 percent), and getting information about products to buy (68 percent).

At least two-thirds of Hispanic online consumers prefer conducting online activities like communicating and newsgathering in English.

216

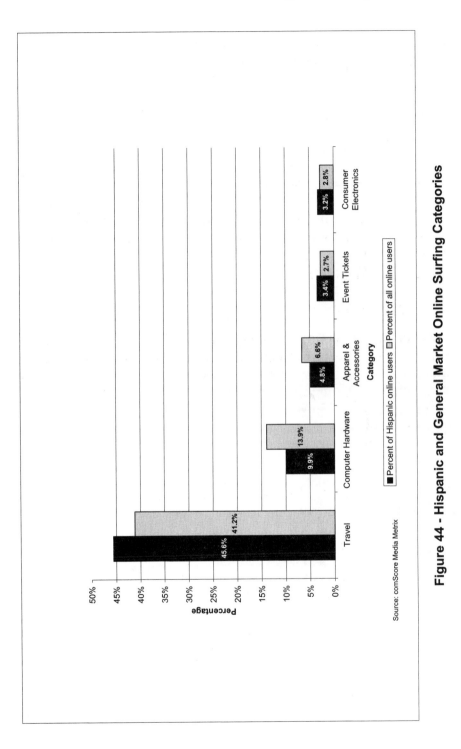

Figure 44 - Hispanic and General Market Online Surfing Categories

Source: comScore Media Metrix

■ Percent of Hispanic online users □ Percent of all online users

217

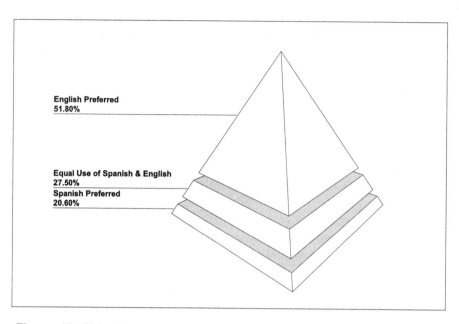

Figure 45 - U.S. Hispanic Internet Population by Language Preference
September 2003

Marketers consider the English (83 percent) and Spanish (53 percent) content important. However as the population broadens and more Spanish-speaking Hispanics get online, the Spanish language may become increasing necessary and important. These statistics hold true with the comScore panel as well. Recruitment for the comScore panel was conducted in Spanish and English. This approach helps ensure accurate representation of the five key language segments that comprise the U.S. Hispanic population.

The data indicates that 52 percent or the 13.8 million U.S. Hispanics who use the Internet prefer to speak English, but 49 percent either prefer Spanish or use Spanish and English equally. While English content can and does reach large numbers of Hispanics, to reach U.S. online Hispanics effectively, marketers must also provide relevant Spanish language content.

	Unique Visitors	Rank Among U.S. Hispanic Users	Rank Among Total U.S. Internet Users
Total U.S. Hispanic	12,566	N/A	N/A
AOL Time Warner Network	9,744	1	2
Yahoo! Sites	9,641	2	3
MSN-Microsoft	9,365	3	1
Terra Lycos	5,428	4	6
Ebay	5,347	5	4
Google Sites	4,663	6	5
Gator Network	4,155	7	9
About/Primedia	3,883	8	7
Verisign Sites	3,087	9	11
Amazon Sites	3,004	10	8
Source: comScore Media Metrix			

Table 10 - Top Properties U.S. Hispanic Internet Users Visit 2003

Surfing Patterns, Segments and Priorities

Data from comScore indicates that with 9.7 million unique visitors, AOL Time Warner reached 76 percent of all U.S. Hispanic Internet users in September, while Yahoo! and MSN-Microsoft had 9.6 and 9.4 million unique visitors. Terra Lycos also has a significantly higher reach among Hispanics than in the general market, with 43 percent of the U.S. Hispanic online population visiting Terra Lycos in September compared to 34 percent of the total U.S. Internet population.

Top Spanish-Language Networks

With 1.5 million unique visitors, Terra Networks is the number one Spanish-language network among U.S. Hispanics. Moreover, the average amount of time spent by visitors on Terra Networks sites has grown by 50 percent in the past 12 months. At a close second, Yahoo! Spanish

219

Site Name	Unique Visitors
Terra Networks Spanish Language Sites	1,451,000
Yahoo! Spanish Language Sites	1,446,000
YupiMSN	1,274,000
Univision	1,245,000
Wanadoo Spanish Language Sites	784,000
AOL Latino	407,000
Source: comScore Media Metrix	

Table 11 - Top Spanish-Language Sites U.S. Hispanics Visit September 2003

language sites garnered 1.4 million U.S. Hispanic visitors, representing growth of 14 percent in the 12-month period.

These data points clearly highlight the importance of quality and culturally relevant Spanish-language content in attracting visitors from the sizable segment of Hispanics who prefer to surf in Spanish.

E-Commerce Activity	Hispanic Adult Online Percent	U.S. Adult Online Percent
Getting information about products to buy	68	77
Making purchases	44	60
Booking travel reservations or tickets	40	50
Banking	30	36
Filing or paying your income tax online	20	20
Taking part in an online auction	18	24
Tracking your stock portfolio	18	28
Getting coupons online	15	17
Trading stocks	11	10

Table 12- Percent of Hispanics Who Engage in E-Commerce Activities Online

E-Commerce Activities

E-Commerce and Online Hispanics

Overall, Hispanic online consumers are less likely than the total online consumer population to shop online; 44 percent say they regularly or occasionally make online purchases compared to 60 percent of the general market. They are also less likely to book travel reservations or tickets online (40 percent versus 50 percent).

While these commerce activities are less frequent, getting information about products to buy is the top e-commerce activity for Hispanic (68 percent) and total (77 percent) online consumers alike. Hispanic online consumers engage in other e-commerce activities such as banking (30 percent versus 36 percent) and trading stocks (11 percent versus 10 percent) with similar frequency compared to all other online consumers.

Strong Tenure Effect for E-Commerce Activities Only

	Total Hispanic Online Shoppers Percent	Total Online Shoppers Percent
Concert, event or movie tickets	42	38
CDs or DVDs	40	37
Consumer electronics	40	30
Computer hardware or software	38	44
Books	34	49
Flowers	28	25
Groceries delivered to the home	13	5
Stamps	7	3
Pet food delivery	5	3
Count of Survey Particpants	(183)	(734)

Table 13 - Percentage That Purchase Items Online

If Hispanic online consumers appear to be behind the e-commerce curve, think again. Hispanic online shoppers reported spending an average of $439 in the past three months[10]. Suggesting e-commerce enthusiasm, Hispanic online shoppers are also as likely as others to recommend specific shopping websites to family and friends (53 percent versus 55 percent of total).

Trends revealed in the U.S. Cyberstudy research over the past five years suggest that the longer online consumers are online, the more likely they are to shop online. Since the Hispanic consumer population is still relatively new to the online medium, e-commerce is likely to increase as experience grows. Interestingly, e-commerce activities are the only activities asked about in the Hispanic Cyberstudy that increase in tandem with online tenure.

For example, 74 percent of Hispanics who have been online at home for five years or more make purchases, compared to 49 percent of those online two to fewer than five years and only 30 percent of those online less than two years. Sixty-six percent (66 percent) of the most seasoned users say they regularly or occasionally book travel reservations or tickets online, compared to 43 percent of those online two to fewer than five years, and 28 percent of those online under two years. The most seasoned users are twice as likely as newcomers to bank online (47 percent versus 21 percent). These concerns also top the list among non-shoppers in the total online consumer population.

Where Do They Come From?

Hispanic Online Consumers at Work

Similar to online usage at home, Hispanic online consumers, when compared to all U.S. online consumers, are less experienced at logging online at work, but they are moving online at a higher rate. While Hispanic online consumers are similar to all U.S. online consumers in terms of the number of days they log online at work, they spend a

---

10   Interviews conducted October 1 through October 28, 2002.

greater number of hours logged on at work. A typical Hispanic online consumer who has an Internet connection at work logs on 3.8 days and 13.8 hours each week. In comparison, all U.S. online consumers who have an Internet connection at work log on 4.0 days and 9.6 hours each week at work.

Doing Personal Chores at Work

With so little time in the day and so much to do, many online consumers are using their online connection at work to catch up on some of their personal responsibilities, and Hispanic online consumers are no exception. Similar to all U.S. online consumers with an online connection at work, the majority of Hispanic online consumers with a work Internet connection (56 percent) say they check the news when they are at work. In addition, around four in ten shop for personal items at work (40 percent), plan a vacation (38 percent), and do online banking (38 percent) while on the job. Smaller proportions arrange social events online (29 percent) and track their stock portfolios or trade stock while at work (22 percent).

New Market Segments: U.S. Hispanic Women and Mothers 18-34

As with their general market counterparts, Hispanic women 18-34 tend to be the decision makers concerning what is right for their family. They do the majority of the shopping, comparison research, and play a key if not dominant role as decision makers regarding the purchases for the family.

From a pure economic view, the numbers are staggering[11]; AHAA states Latinas represent 62 percent of the buying power of U.S. Hispanics, which researchers estimate will reach $900 billion by 2007. What is unique about this market is that Hispanic families are larger. Between the ages of 18-34, the average mother is trying to get pregnant, pregnant or raising children under the age of six.

---

11   AHAA Right Spent II 2003

"Having a baby is a life changing moment in any culture, and especially so among Spanish speaking families. The numbers tell the story: on average, Hispanic families have three children, and in major urban markets like Los Angeles and Miami, more than 50 percent of births are Hispanic," said Gillian Sandler, chairman and C.E.O. of TodoBebé™.

Issues surrounding a mother or mother to be[12] and the ability to communicate and research information, have made the Internet a top "go to place," only second to immediate family for information about pregnancy and child rearing. In addition, research and purchasing of products and services not normally associated with pregnancy and babies are directly impacted because of this life change including:

- Automotive: need a larger car as family grows
- New home purchase
- Home updates, additions or remodeling
- Insurance: increase health, life and auto insurance
- Finance, banking and credit cards: having a baby is the time when you spend more and simultaneously start thinking about saving
- Cell phones and long distance: communication with family and friends

"Keep in mind these startling statistics when marketing to the U.S. Hispanic Latina," states TodoBebé's Sandler.[13] At any one time, over 4 million U.S. Hispanics are planning, expecting or raising babies. They tend to spend more on their babies than non-Hispanics, upwards of $8,000 in the first year on baby showers, christenings, significant birthdays, and holidays; as well as general consumer goods, toys and apparel.

---

12   Miami Baby Fair Survey, TodoBebé™ 2004

13   Research from TodoBebé™

Bilingual Hispanics prefer Spanish for pregnancy and baby information. There is a comfort level in using their native or "mother tongue" to communicate about their pregnancy or newborn. Speaking Spanish is also important when communicating with relatives in the U.S. and abroad. Following are some interesting statistics:

- A significant percent of the newborns in major cities are born to Hispanic mothers: more than 50 percent in Miami, Los Angeles, and Phoenix; 34 percent in New York City and Chicago.
- At the same time, Hispanics have the highest number of children per family of any ethnic group: 3.1 versus 1.9 for the total U.S.
- 85 percent of Hispanic women give birth by age 40
- 49 percent of Hispanic new and expectant mothers recently moved to a new home or are planning to move in the next 12 months
- 40 percent of new and expectant moms purchased a new vehicle in the past year or plan to during the baby's first year
- 61 percent of Hispanic new and expectant moms say their beauty and skin care regimen has changed since becoming pregnant
- More than 30 percent of Hispanic new and expectant moms are online, spending 6 hrs/week on average
- Products in U.S. retail stores and pharmacies are always in English, even at those situated in mainly Spanish speaking areas[14]
- Up to 21 percent of baby-related advertising spending in the U.S. should be in Spanish!

Conclusions

The ability to connect with a Hispanic mother during this important time of life, in a language that is familiar and comforting, is key to developing a branding bond that will continue as the family grows. The market is large, growing and controls a large percentage of the buying power of the U.S. Hispanic. The time of life is unique and short, but

---

14   AHAA Right Spend Study, see http://www.ahaa.org

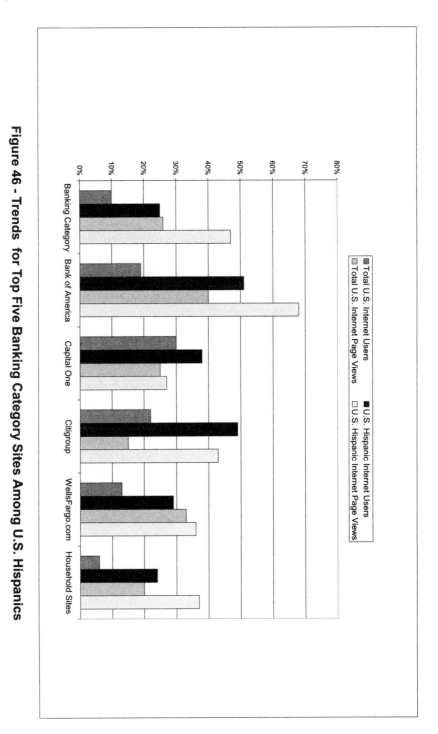

Figure 46 - Trends for Top Five Banking Category Sites Among U.S. Hispanics

when communicated to properly, marketers can develop a lifelong brand association with the woman and her family segment.

Case Studies

- Online Banking
- Baby and Pregnancy

Case Study 1

Online Banking Grows by 25 Percent among Hispanics[15]

The country's major consumer banking and lending institutions were among the earliest investors in Spanish language content and online marketing to the Hispanic population. An analysis of visitation to major online banking sites among U.S. Hispanic Internet users reveals this investment has paid dividends.

Banks enjoyed a 25 percent increase in U.S. Hispanic visitors in the past year compared to a 10 percent increase among general market Internet users. In fact, among the five largest banking category properties, four sites experienced more than double the increase seen in the general market. Each of these companies features Spanish-language content.

The number of U.S. Hispanic visitors to bank sites increased, and so too have user's engagement levels. Overall, comScore found a 47 percent increase in page views by Hispanic visitors at banking category sites compared to a still-impressive 26 percent increase in the general market. Bank of America drew 51 percent more Hispanic visitors versus the previous year, and recorded a remarkable 68 percent increase in page views.

---

15   comScore Media Metrix 2003

Case Study 2

Babies and Pregnancy Equals Kraft Comida[16]

Kraft Objectives
- Support the launch of www.ComidaKraft.com Kraft's Spanish-language website for U.S. Hispanics
- Create awareness of the new website and drive traffic to it
- Reinforce Kraft branding among growing Hispanic audiences

Strategies
- Concentrate on Kraft's core competencies (food products and recipes that include them) for branding and consumer loyalty
- Leverage the holiday season (Christmas and New Year) to generate buzz about the new website and provide special holiday recipes.
- Capitalize on Hispanics' family values and traditions to establish a relationship with the visitor

Tactics
- Sponsorship of www.TodoBebé.com Recipe Corner
- Divided in categories for ease of search
- Updated on a weekly basis
- Selection of recipes that appeal to Hispanics
- Promotion of section through a prominent button in home page, weekly email newsletter to U.S. Hispanic registered users and co-branded banners

Sponsorship of Special Edition Newsletters

Sent "Special Dishes for the Holidays" electronic newsletters to U.S. Hispanic registered users

---

16   TodoBebé™ Case Study 2003

Kraft-banners

Aimed at channeling traffic to ComidaKraft.com

Results

During the six-week campaign www.Todobebe.com delivered:

- More than 300,000 page views that helped increase brand awareness
- More than 250,000 banner impressions with a click-thru rate to the Kraft Comida site three times as high as the industry average
- More than 7,500 electronic newsletters to targeted U.S. Hispanic registered users, reinforcing the Kraft brand with products and recipes for the Hispanic consumer

Ready to dive in?

Daisy Exposito put it best when she was asked what you needed before marketing to this segment: "First, understand the culture. It is rich as it is complex and varied. It's about Mexican-Americans in its largest percentage. And it's about a whole continent that starts in Spain and Portugal and goes as far down as the Southern Cone. It's endured pain that's morphed into wisdom and joy. They were here before anyone else. Second, their fullness is many times connected to another place. It's in that faraway place that we can find their otherness. There's nothing wrong with that. It's a plus, an added dimension. And thirdly, I've learned that this country is a perfect prismatic mirror to capture and reflect the splendor of these many different lights. It's a fantastic show of diversity linked by the same Hispanic pathos. Only in America!"

Chapter Summary

- The Hispanic population is growing and will reach 22.5 percent of the population by 2050.

- Many of the top Hispanic advertising agencies have merged with or are partly owned by large general market agencies.
- Hispanics are not "one size fits all."
- Relative acculturation, language and heritage play an important role in branding and marketing.
- Preparation avoids panic.
- Make sure your research has a large enough sample size.
- Hispanics are younger online than the general market, online and offline.
- Television is the medium for offline entertainment for Hispanics.
- Univision is the fifth largest television company after CBS, NBC, FOX, and ABC.
- Hispanics exceed online usage in entertainment, travel and communication over general market.
- Advertisers continue to under spend in most categories for Hispanics.
- Hispanics use English and Spanish language sites.
- Bilingual mothers-to-be and new parents prefer Spanish language sites for pregnancy and parenting information.

About the Authors

Richard Israel, Vice President, Hispanic Marketing Solutions, comScore Media Metrix, a division of comScore Networks

Richard Israel, as vice president of Hispanic Marketing Solutions for comScore Networks was instrumental in the development and launch of the first ever Hispanic Internet audience measurement tool reporting details of website usage in the U.S.

Cynthia Nelson, Chief Operations Officer TodoBebé™, Inc.

Cynthia Nelson is responsible for operations and business development of the Spanish language media company, TodoBebé™, Inc. This leading integrated media company (television, radio, online, events) is dedicated to providing information around babies and pregnancy for Spanish speakers worldwide.

Chapter Ten

Hispanic Public Relations and Its Emergence as an Industry

Dora O. Tovar, M.P.Aff

In This Chapter

- The rationale for creating a Hispanic public relations industry
- What is at stake for Hispanic public relations professionals?
- How the Hispanic advertising industry serves as a precursor for Hispanic public relations and presents unique insights and opportunities for practitioners
- Lessons Hispanic public relations professionals can learn from that sister industry
- How the growth in the Hispanic media market has created demand for Hispanic-focused public relations expertise
- What has led to the rapid development of a Hispanic public relations monitoring infrastructure to aid practitioners
- Effects of the "marketing of *Latinidad*"
- Case studies for cultural relevance in Hispanic public relations initiatives
- Distinguishing characteristics between public relations, advertising and event marketing to Hispanics
- Why Hispanic public relations professionals choose this industry

- Common mistakes and misrepresentations that affect Hispanic public relations professionals

In 2000, Hispanic[1] marketers promoted the census results as a ringing-in of a new era. This new era underscored the shifting demographics and need to prepare for a change in audiences, messages and U.S. cultural context. Those early believers are reaping their rewards in double digit growth and profits. The wake-up call was a rallying cry by Hispanic advertisers to gain the attention of corporate business and policy leaders to employ a more effective business strategy, embrace change or find themselves cut off from a rapidly growing segment of their prospective customer base. Even with this compelling call to action, the message has been slow to sink in.

There is no doubt that the Hispanic 'boom' has lead to a growth in demand for services to support corporate advertising efforts. It is also the reason for the increase in the number of Hispanic-focused public relations firms and offerings[2]. The result is the opportunity to distinguish these services from the Hispanic advertising market and advocate for a separate but parallel Hispanic public relations industry from its earliest and nascent beginnings. Until 2001, no formal research or history of the Hispanic advertising industry existed. In "Latinos Inc: A Making and Marketing of a People," Arlene Davila, Ph.D., provides a close examination of the emergence of Hispanic advertising and its impact on Latina culture and language in the U.S.[3]

This chapter examines the development of the Hispanic advertising industry as a significant precursor for the influences on the emergence

---

1   The word "Latina" appears throughout the chapter instead of constant gender specifications such as Latino/a. Latina refers to the shared cultural experience and language unifying various Hispanic subgroups in the U.S. from Mexico, Central and Latin America. Although it may appear that Latino and Hispanic are used interchangeably, Hispanic refers to state or federal data and business sources.

2   The Association of Hispanic Advertising Agencies directory was the primary source of data on public relations services given that there is no professional association serving Hispanic public relations professionals compiling such data at the time of publication. The Public Relations Society of America has a directory and conducts an annual survey yet its data is not as comprehensive as that available from Hispanic-focused associations.

3   Davila, Arlene. "Latinos, Inc.: The Marketing and Making of a People." Berkeley, CA: University of California Press. 2001.

City	Total Population	Hispanic Population	Percent Hispanic
New York, NY	8,008,278	2,160,554	27.0
Los Angeles, CA	3,694,820	1,719,073	46.5
Chicago, IL	2,896,016	753,644	26.0
Houston, TX	1,953,631	730,865	37.4
Philadelphia, PA	1,517,550	128,928	8.5
Phoenix, AZ	1,321,045	449,972	34.1
San Diego, CA	1,223,400	310,752	25.4
Dallas, TX	1,188,580	422,587	35.6
San Antonio, TX	1,144,646	671,394	58.7
Detroit, MI	951,270	47,167	5.0
El Paso, TX	563,662	431,875	76.6
San Jose, CA	894,943	269,989	30.2

Table 14 - Hispanic Population in Metropolitan Areas

of the Hispanic public relations arena, including significant events in the Hispanic advertising industry. For Hispanic advertisers the development of Spanish-language television networks created an opportunity and demand for advertising coupled with Hispanic growth that would give them their own unique marketing platform and infrastructure[4]. Continuous growth of this same platform provides a similar opportunity for a distinction in communications services primarily consumed by corporate America and the government. In the case of Hispanic communications services and public relations professionals,

---

4   The word infrastructure refers to the critical services that collectively allow the advancement or development of a particular objective or, in this discussion, U.S. industry.

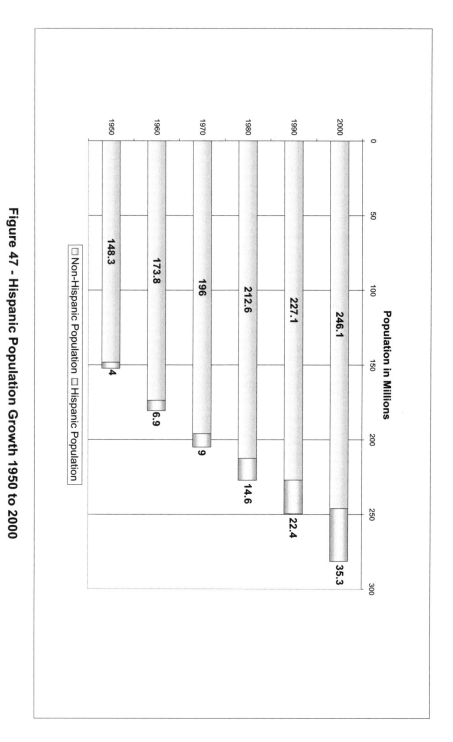

Figure 47 - Hispanic Population Growth 1950 to 2000

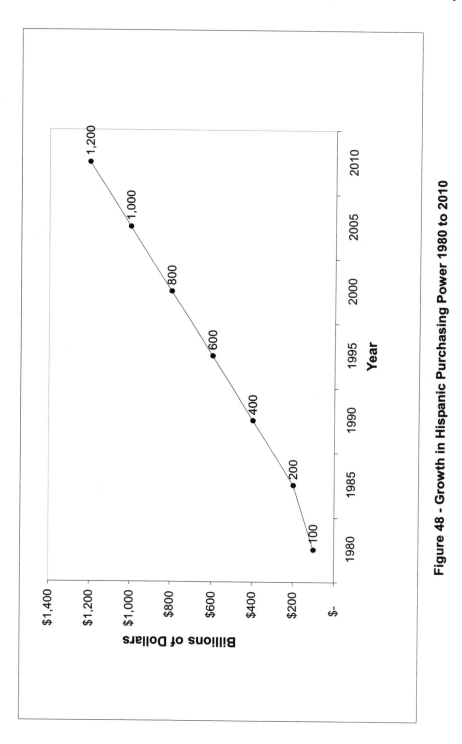

Figure 48 - Growth in Hispanic Purchasing Power 1980 to 2010

has posted consistent profits annually since Jerrold A. Perenchio first purchased the network in 1992, capturing about 85 percent of the market.[10] Univision moved quickly to consolidate its existing radio assets by purchasing HBC radio at a $2.8 billion all-stock deal.[11] The merger added 65 radio stations to its already 62 television stations, also broadcasting to TeleFutura its sister network with unrivaled Hispanic reach. By the end of 2003, Univision posted over $100 million in net profits for the previous nine months.[12]

Spanish-language television advertising expenditures reached $1.9 billion in 2003; they are estimated to reach almost $3 billion by 2005.[13] Even so, the Hispanic advertising industry reports consistent corporate under-spending in the market since industry representatives began to monitor Hispanic ad spending in 2002. Advertisers on average are spending about 3 percent reaching Hispanics compared with the 13 percent Hispanic population growth and relative to the almost 89 percent increase in Hispanic purchasing power.[14]

Hispanic Advertising Industry as Precursor

The early believers have been those sectors closest to the changing customer base, consumer goods. Procter & Gamble, Unilever, Coors and McDonald's were some of the earliest brands that advertised to a Spanish-language dominant audience in the U.S. The first precursors of the industry were marketers early resistance and complexities associated with simply "translating to Spanish." Just as marketers were devel-

10   Tovar, Dora O. Census "1990 Redistricting in Texas: Hispanic Political Gains." Lyndon B. Johnson School of Public Affairs. August 1991.

11   Suro, Roberto, "Latino Growth in Metropolitan America Changing Patterns, New Locations." Pew Hispanic Center and Audrey Singer, Brookings Institution Center on Urban and Metropolitan Policy.

12   Ibid. "Latinos, Inc.: The Marketing and Making of a People."

13   U.S. Hispanic Media Markets 1999-2005. April 2004, HispanTelligence Report.

14   Selig Center for Economic Growth. Hispanic purchasing power has grown by 88.7 percent since 2002. Whereas, the Census Bureau reports that the Hispanic population has been growing by 42.2 percent beginning in 2000.

Hispanic-Focused Agency	Inception	Ownership	2002 Billings ($M)	2003 Billings ($M)	% Change
Publicis-Bromley Communications	1986	Publicis Groupe	$184.00	$276.00	50
The Bravo Group	1980	WPP	$280.00	N/A	N/A
Dieste Harmel & Partners	1995	Omnicom	$140.00	$180.00	29
Lapiz Integrated Hispanic Mktg	1987	Publicis Groupe	$175.00	$180.00	3
Casanova Pendrill	1984	Interpublic Group of Companies/51% Hispanic-Owned	$120.00	$140.00	17
Zubi Advertising	1979	100% Hispanic-Owned	$130.00	$147.00	13
Wing Latino Group	2000	GCI/WPP	$96.79	N/A	N/A
The Vidal Partnership		100% Hispanic-Owned	$85.00	$102.00	20
Mendoza Dillon & Asociados		WPP	$89.00	N/A	
The Cartel Group	1994	100% Hispanic-Owned	$81.17	$95.29	17
La Agencia De Orci	1985	100% Hispanic-Owned	$100.00	$92.00	-8
Del Rivero Messianu		Omnicom/51% Hispanic-Owned	$75.00	N/A	N/A
Accentmarketing	1994	Interpublic Group of Companies/51% Hispanic-Owned	$63.40	$99.00	56
Lopez Negrete Communications	1985	Independent/51% Hispanic-Owned	$53.50	$70.00	30
Arvizu	1991	100% Hispanic-Owned	$57.50	$65.20	13
Ornelas	1988	100% Hispanic-Owned	$47.50	$59.40	25
Siboney U.S.A.	1983	Interpublic Group/51% Hispanic-Owned	$40.00	$50.00	25
Castells & Asociados Advertising (Formerly AD Americas)	1985	30% Hispanic-Owned	$38.70	$49.50	29
Latinworks	1998	100% Hispanic-Owned	$42.00	$48.00	14
Euro RSCG Latino	1997	RSCG Worldwide	$40.00	$45.00	13

Table 15 - Top 25 Hispanic Focused Agencies

Hispanic-Focused Agency	Inception	Ownership	2002 Billings ($M)	2003 Billings ($M)	% Change
The San Jose Group	1981	100% Hispanic-Owned	$35.20	$43.00	22
IAC Group Inc.	1978	100% Hispanic-Owned	$34.00	N/A	N/A
Marti, Flores, Prieto & Wachtel Hispanic	1972	100% Hispanic-Owned	$28.00	$25.00	-11
Reynardus & Moya	1999	100% Hispanic-Owned	$24.00	$28.00	16
Anita Santiago Advertising	1987	100% Hispanic-Owned	$24.00	$24.00	0
Creative On Demand	1998	100% Hispanic-Owned	$19.00	$22.00	15

Source: AdAge 2004, *Hispanic Business*

Table 16 - Top 25 Hispanic Focused Agencies (continued)

oping a compendium of positive marketing cases, there were also those who had been "burned" in the Hispanic market. The introduction of "Nova" by Chevrolet is one example. Early marketers forgot to consider how to translate the brand effectively into Spanish prior to the campaign launch revealing that Nova in Spanish means, "Does not go or run."

That was the first wake up call for marketers to see that their entry into the Hispanic market needed to be strategic. The most adept at promoting the value of the Hispanic market and changing U.S. demographics has been Spanish media. For advertisers, they produced videos to illustrate the change in vivid images of Hispanic leaders, young families and the strong family ties that would connect them to a new segment of U.S. consumers, and eventually position their brands across borders, oceans and continents to their Hispanic cousins.

Top corporations set out after the pot of gold. Most enlisted the assistance of their own internal Hispanic "experts" to conduct the search for external Hispanic market advice. Most corporations focused on the size of the pot. They also worried that left unattended competitor's hands would reach it instead. Few knew or evaluated the expertise on a spe-

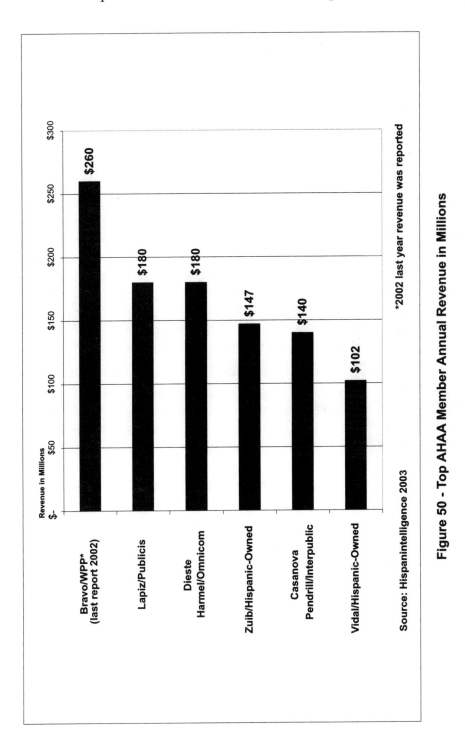

Figure 50 - Top AHAA Member Annual Revenue in Millions

cific strategy required to embrace it. This "open field" also created some unfair advantages resulting in geographic or segment prefer-ences, which largely reflect today's concentration of Hispanic market-ing agencies in New York, Miami and Los Angeles.

It was also responsible for placing the greatest market influence in the hands of the most visible Hispanic segments behind Spanish media companies, and those behind the cameras displaying the media mes-sages that dictate the commodification of our own *Latinidad* and the myths about the U.S. Latino experience. *Latinidad* is the making and marketing of images for Latinos alongside the promotion of consumer products. This gives way to a complex web of economic and social in-terests sometimes referred to as a collective language and cultural expe-rience or community. Dr. Davila explains that Hispanic marketing promotes "the public reconstitution of these images for the purpose of creating belonging and cultural citizenship in public life." A handful of Hispanic advertising agencies, mostly in New York and Cuba, created the earliest popular images of Hispanics.[15] Twenty years later, Hispanic advertising revenues have reached $3 billion.

Timing was enormously important for the early believers. Most of the top 10 Hispanic independently owned ad agencies dating to 1990 have been purchased by one of the three global advertising conglomer-ates. In addition, although the advertising consolidation in the Hispanic category follows the same trend in the general market, the impact on the Hispanic community and its independent and entrepreneurial assets are much more severe because of the size and percentage of the market.

The first Hispanic agencies in the U.S. were born in Cuba because of transnational companies needs to create a "one stop" marketing pres-ence for corporate clients.[16] Today there are over 61 Hispanic-focused advertising agencies with 23 percent of these owned by transnational conglomerates targeting Hispanic consumers. The same advertising conglomerate, Interpublic Group of Companies (IPG), owns seven of the Association of Hispanic Advertising Agencies (AHAA) member

---

15   Davila, Arlene. "Latinos, Inc."

16   Ibid.

agencies. The WPP, headquartered in England, owns three Hispanic agencies and Omnicom owns two, see Table 15 and Table 16. Omnicom, IPG and WPP round out the world's "Big Three" advertising conglomerates. We will discuss the issues of conglomerate ownership and corporate under-spending further when we address the value these agencies bring to the Hispanic community. Nonetheless, the events in the advertising industry are important when considering the implication of these for the growing Hispanic public relations field.

Hispanic agencies have experienced phenomenal growth compared to the general advertising market. Researchers reported that more than 90 percent of the top 25 Hispanic agencies increased their billings in 2003.[17] Some agencies saw their billings increase by tens of millions almost mirroring the explosive rate of the overall Hispanic population growth. The individual agency increases confirm that for those agencies "well positioned" in the Hispanic marketing arena, the opportunity to increase their revenue is a given.

When AHAA was formed, it made specific reference to allocating membership upon agencies 49 percent owned by Hispanics. This detail, omitted in the public relations service market, should be considered a valuable and distinguishing factor in the approach toward contract awards. The larger negative implication is a new industry focused on culture, again dominated by non-Latinos, in which we work to create the relevance but have no significant control over its objectives or future.

Marketing of *"Latinidad"*

The issue of profitability is not a question for Hispanic marketers. There is however, a question of the role advertising and public relations professionals have in the direction that *Latinidad* is heading. Our shear numbers have assigned a particular economic value to the Hispanic market in direct proportion to the value the general market places on Latino images in the U.S. Until recently, the mainstream media had sole

---

17   *Hispanic Business Magazine.* "Top 25 Hispanic Ad Agencies," December 2003

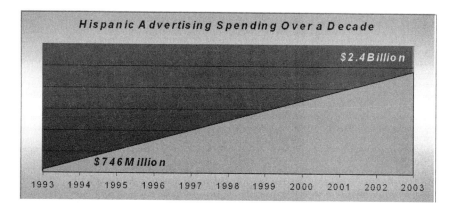

Figure 51 - Growth of Hispanic Advertising Spend Over a Decade

control of the Latino images put forth on general market television through sitcoms, movies and network newscasts. Society has typecast Latinos as workers, maids, a voting block to be mobilized in election years and sometimes as gang-members or political exiles. Lately, we have seen the images of Ricky Martin, Jennifer Lopez, Daisy Fuentes, Salma Hayek, Enrique Iglesias and countless others in mainstream and Spanish language media.

Dr. Davila principally asserts that the images of Latinas created by the Hispanic advertising industry for Spanish and mainstream media have led to a "commodification" of U.S. "*Latinidad.*" In turn, Hispanics in the industry have replicated many of the same images that perpetuate the class and race struggles of their native countries. These images divide us and prevent Latinos from enjoying the collective gains from our increased influence. Other Latina scholars use the term "New Latinos" to refer to the blending of Latino cultures by virtue of our collective U.S. experience.[18]

18   Ilan Stavans, "The Hispanic Condition: The Power of a People." Stavans defines, "The New Latino": a collective image whose reflection is built as the sum of its parts in unrestrained and dynamic metamorphosis, a spirit of acculturation and perpetual translation, linguistic and spiritual, a dense popular identity, with its diameter everywhere and its center nowhere. We shall never be the owners of a pure, crystalline collective individuality because we are the product of a five-hundred-year-old fiesta of miscegenation... round trip from one linguistic territory and cultural dimension to another, a perpetual bargaining."

Our greatest influence on U.S. culture is our ability to negotiate new positioning through a "merging" of cultures.[19] However, like other groups, Latinas also expect that our increased visibility will translate into greater political influence and greater inclusion in the rights of citizenship.[20] Recent studies confirm that although language unites Hispanics, the differences between various subgroups are significant enough to affect the outcomes of local and state elections.[21]

As Latinas, the process of constant negotiation and translation of our experiences, perspectives, roles and contributions in the U.S. is reflected in the emergence of new venues and markets for our professional services. We will illustrate this further in our discussion of the growing influence of Latinas on U.S. policy and electoral influence. Each election year, Hispanic political influence becomes even more significant.

According to Davila, the Hispanic marketing industry has tried to ignore the differences of class and race, yet perpetuate these in the images put forth to corporate clients, hence the implication of her book title, "A Marketing of a People."[22] At the same time, the growth and consolidation of the industry by global interests has become one dominated by corporate intellectuals of Latin American background. The results for Latinas are reflected in a concerted attempt to "merge" the uniquely U.S.-centered Latina experiences with those of Latin Americans. The resulting complexities of creating "appendages" of class and race, the images of white-looking Latinas in the media continues to be a long-standing problem. Recently this topic received national attention

---

19   Habell-Pallán, Michelle and Mary Romero. "Latino/a Popular Culture." New York University Press. Copyright 2002

20   McAllister, Mathew. "The commercialization of American Culture: New advertising, Control and Democracy." London Sage. 1996.

21   Habell-Pallán, Michelle and Mary Romero

22   Davila, Arlene. Latinos, Inc.

in the May 2004 issue of *Latina Magazine*,[23] criticizing Univision for the negative images projected by their programming.

Hispanic Market and Community Values

Carlos Santiago and Isabel Valdez, Ph.D., among other Hispanic market gurus, acknowledge the critical value Hispanic community "influencers" play in the development of successful Hispanic marketing efforts. According to Valdez' two-volume Hispanic marketing primers, there is an intrinsic value that Latino community leaders and non-profit organizations have in providing and facilitating a "sense of belonging and cultural heritage for Latinos."[24] The use of Spanish by vendors, churches, and neighbors strengthens relationships and provides information validating our presence in the U.S. These informal and formal community structures serve as the infrastructure for the acculturation process and the constantly revolving transition between cultures that define Latino aspirations, preferences and purchasing decisions thereby distinguishing us from general market consumers.

However flawed or scrutinized, we contend and embrace the Latina tendency to create a uniquely relevant U.S. experience whether through our respective geographic and ethnic enclaves or our unique cadre and menu, and preference for Latina professional services. In this way, our examination of the evolution of Hispanic public relations infrastructure is closely mirrored in the same need to create a "parallel and intersecting" Latino infrastructure to that of the general market.

Carlos Santiago, principal architect of the AHAA research, has developed a model together with Dr. Valdes that highlights the integrated communications effort relevant to Hispanic consumers. This model places community influencers as central to effective marketing effort to Hispanic consumers. Figure 52 further illustrates the evolution and in-

---

23   May 2004 issue *Latina Magazine*.

24   Valdés, Isabel M. and Marta H. Seoane. "Hispanic Market Handbook: The definitive source for reaching this lucrative segment of American Consumer." Gale Research Inc. 1995.
        Valdés, Isabel M. "Part 2 - Marketing to American Latinos: A Guide to the In-Culture Approach." Paramount Market Publishing, Inc. 2002.

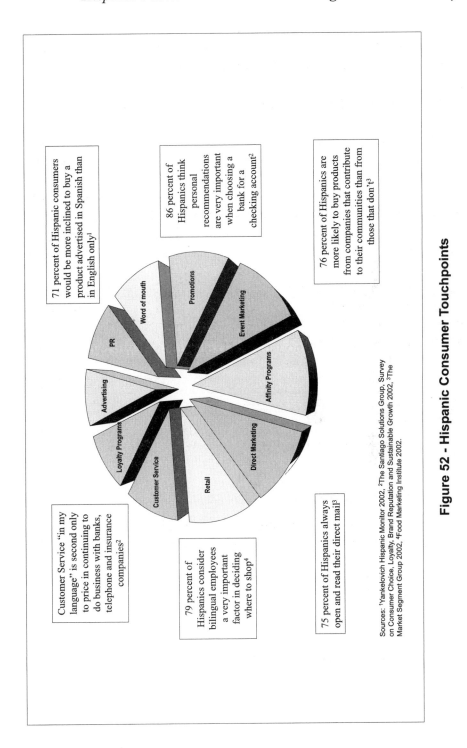

71 percent of Hispanic consumers would be more inclined to buy a product advertised in Spanish than in English only[1]

86 percent of Hispanics think personal recommendations are very important when choosing a bank for a checking account[2]

76 percent of Hispanics are more likely to buy products from companies that contribute to their communities than from those that don't[3]

Customer Service "in my language" is second only to price in continuing to do business with banks, telephone and insurance companies[2]

79 percent of Hispanics consider bilingual employees a very important factor in deciding where to shop[4]

75 percent of Hispanics always open and read their direct mail[3]

Word of mouth

Promotions

Event Marketing

Affinity Programs

Direct Marketing

Retail

Customer Service

Loyalty Programs

Advertising

PR

Sources: [1]Yankelovich Hispanic Monitor 2002, [2]The Santiago Solutions Group, Survey on Consumer Choice, Loyalty, Brand Reputation and Sustainable Growth 2002, [3]The Market Segment Group 2002, [4]Food Marketing Institute 2002.

Figure 52 - Hispanic Consumer Touchpoints

tegration of all elements of communications with the Hispanic consumer as 'touch points' emphasizing and integrating marketing messages.

Hispanic Public Relations Market

Integrated Communications Versus Specialized Public Relations Services

The emergence of Hispanic public relations had its nascent development in the area of corporate social responsibility in the early 1970s and 1980s primarily in response to Hispanic community leadership criticisms about corporate efforts or the lack thereof. For some companies it was enough to learn from the troubles of their competitors to motivate the development of their own corporate Hispanic outreach efforts. It was mostly these proactive initiatives that the Hispanic advertising agencies had a hand in encouraging and expanding.

Some of the earliest brand campaigns involved extending a company's brand to a new medium or forum outside of the product environment or aisle. For example, Coors developed an immigration awareness campaign shortly after the 1986 Immigration Reform and Control Act. It was an outgrowth of their close relationships with Raul Yzaguirre (then president of National Council of La Raza), and an effort to rebuild their Hispanic brand value after a financially devastating product boycott by Mexican-Americans that lasted into the late 1970s.[25]

The Coors citizenship campaign was unique because of the tremendous positive value it had in turning around the Coors image with Mexican-Americans and immigrants encouraged by the policy change to seek U.S. naturalization. The first part of the campaign consisted of an extensive Spanish immigration and naturalization handbook with detailed explanations of the naturalization process including sample questions for the citizenship test. This campaign has continued in various forms over the past decade including a Spanish video widely distributed by Hispanic advocacy organizations. As a result, the campaign

---

25   Interviews with Raul Yzaguirre, National Council of La Raza, President. 1998-2003

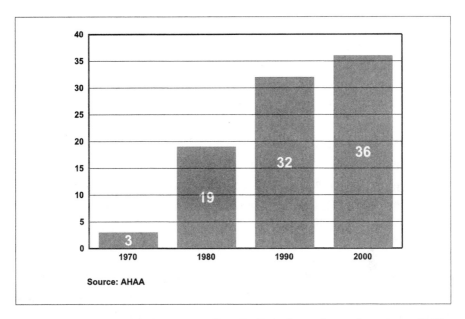

Figure 53 - Growth of Hispanic Public Relations Agencies since 1970

had visibility among potential new voters and key Hispanic influencers who had previously questioned Coors commitment to Hispanic employees and community leaders. The relationship between Coors and Latino leaders has "rebounded" reflecting positive positioning in the Hispanic market and current campaign efforts include MANÁ, among other top Latino musical groups, raising funds for the Hispanic Association of Colleges and Universities.[26]

Many other consumer brands woke up, took notice of Coors' efforts and developed a brand presence that existed in parallel to their product campaigns. However, these early efforts did not necessarily reflect an integrated approach until much later. In fact, the convergence of the corporate social responsibility initiatives with Hispanic product marketing merged with corporate participation at national Hispanic conferences and community events. Corporate brand marketers began to call upon their Hispanic advertising agencies to develop event campaigns

---

26   Interview with Olga García, Corporate Relations Manager, Coors Brewing Company.

for their products and appropriate communications messaging for their executives that included speech writing and presentations highlighting their commitment to the consumer market. It was the latter communications services few agencies were able to maintain client interest in on a long-term basis. Perez, Valencia and Echeveste, founded in 1988, touts social responsibility as one of its tenets distinguishing itself as a top Hispanic public relations firm.

Hence the reason corporate product promotions and event participation have been a focal point of integrated communications at Hispanic advertising agencies, and the absence of such services provided by Hispanic and general market public relations firms. This has been a factor in describing Hispanic public relations services as lacking in "sophistication" because a significant number of Hispanic advertising and public relations efforts focus first on product promotions. The criticism has developed primarily because there has not been much evolution in other areas of public relations services such as public affairs, crisis communications and reputation management just to name a few. Those of us that practice in this area find this perception has more to do with the constant education process required of Hispanic practitioners in developing client and market understanding for first-time entrants, and with practice infrastructure issues that will be addressed later in the discussion.

Hispanic agencies unique positioning of products, brands and the intersection of these with Hispanic consumers have been central tenets of integrated Hispanic marketing communications. This reflects the evolution and use of "integrated Hispanic communications and marketing" by several Hispanic agencies to define their services and practice.

Hispanic Public Relation's First Appearances

The oldest and earliest appearances of public relations efforts in the Hispanic market were primarily product promotions with community-wide presence. Many public relations professionals have acknowledged that their early attempts were "shots in the dark" and campaigns closely resembling activities already executed in the general market.[27]

In the early years, several Hispanic advertising agencies found themselves responding to their client's demand for public relations or product promotions efforts. Those involved in some of the early efforts readily acknowledge they did not know if the Hispanic specific campaigns they developed primarily in response to their clients would be effective.[28]

"When we started we had just a hope and a prayer," Margarita Hernandez says of her firm's first entry as a Hispanic agency in 1983[29]. The hope was that Chicago-based companies would see the value of the market and understand the importance of having "relevance" for Hispanic consumers. Their public relations efforts began as event marketing and media relations related to client events that later expanded into a full-service agency. "Our selling point was our relationship with Spanish media and print outlets here in Chicago. It was difficult for clients to get access to Hispanic consumers and community 'influentials' without reaching out to the media," says Hernandez.

"However, since those early days, few Hispanic public relations professionals have really understood the unique role that they played in connecting corporate America to the grassroots community," explains Zeke Montes, publisher and former president of the National Association of Hispanic Publications (NAHP). The National Association of Hispanic Publications has been wrestling with this issue as it makes its own pitch to corporate America about the value of Hispanic print. "Hispanic print has been at the forefront of laying the infrastructure for many Hispanic marketing professionals, yet there seems to be an absence of community-minded and oriented professionals that bring value to their clients and the community. And, believe me I understand

---

27   *Hispanic Market Weekly*, "Special Public Relations Report," February 2002

28   Ibid.

29   Interview with Margarita Hernandez of Hernandez and Garcia Inc.

PR Service Offerings	Hispanic Integrated	Hispanic PR	GM PR Firms
Hispanic PR services focus	Varied depending on original owner ethnicity	Since inception	Began Hispanic focus in 2002
Full Hispanic PR services	Product campaign and event focused	Campaign and outreach focused	Only 1 respondent provides all services
Philanthropy communications	Least provided services	Least provided services	Events and campaign driven focus
Hispanic-Specific Crisis Communications	Only 1 agency has provided services	1 Firm affirmed service delivery	Have not delivered service in Spanish
PR Clients	**Hispanic Integrated**	**Hispanic PR**	**GM PR Firms**
Product or Brand Marketing Client	Majority of PR clients are marketing office	Some corporate communications clients	Campaigns from government clients and corporate clients familiar w/PR offerings
Hispanic Distinction	**Hispanic Integrated**	**Hispanic PR**	**GM PR Firms**
Hispanic Service Distinction to Clients	Some try to integrate multicultural from Hispanic services	Only one agency categorized itself as providing strictly Hispanic Services	Only one respondent was Hispanic focused
Promotions & PR Bundled Services	**Hispanic Integrated**	**Hispanic PR**	**GM PR Firms**
Do you include promotions in your PR offerings?	Most agencies offer promotions as part of their public relations service offerings but depending on the client's need	A handful of firms continue to offer promotions from previous agency experiences	Non-existent bundling in the general market respondents
Hispanics in the Profession	**Hispanic Integrated**	**Hispanic PR**	**GM PR Firms**
Do you find it difficult to find and retain employees	Several hire from Cuba and Latin America for PR services	Firms see a lack of fully bicultural & bilingual professionals	Most draw up Latin American sister agencies

Source: Tovar Manriquez Survey 2004

Table 17 - Hispanic PR Agencies by Service Designation

254

Media Outlet	2002 Billings (in $ Millions)	Percent of Total
Internet	28.16	1.35
Print	172.92	8.28
Radio	409.71	19.62
TV	1,187.82	56.88
Other	289.57	13.87
Total	2,088.18	100.00

Source: *Hispanic Business* magazine

Table 18 - Latino Advertising Spend by Outlet

that television is sexy, but print delivers much more in a sustained fashion for corporate brands." [30]

Montes and Hernandez statements reinforce the value of the touch points model of integrated consumers put forth by Santiago. Hispanic public relations professionals serve a unique role of interdependence and support for the Spanish media vehicles closest to the community. However, the rapid evolution of these vehicles underscores the critical need to maintain an open dialogue between the media, public relations professionals and the communities they each service. Even tipping the scale of outlet preferences slightly can have a dramatic impact on the community and its perception of these brands. The nuances are not slight but many times imply the Hispanic community is "slighted" by corporate America and the agencies representing their interests. This of course, can have negative implications for the community and the corporate brand.

[30] Interview with Zeke Montes, Jr. President of Teleguía de Chicago and immediate past president of the National Association of Hispanic Publications.

By Service	2002 Billings (in $ Millions)	Percent of Total
Strategic Planning	394.93	18.91
Media Buying	477.93	22.89
Creative/Production	650.30	31.14
Research	54.63	2.62
Web Site	47.17	2.26
Public Relations	106.71	5.11
Promotions/Events	201.42	9.65
Translation Services	67.77	3.25
Budgeting/Finance	23.83	1.14
Other	63.49	3.04
Total	2088.18	100.00

Source: *Hispanic Business* magazine

Table 19 - Latino Advertising Spending by Service 2002

General Market Firms Enter Hispanic Arena

General market public relations and public affairs conglomerates such as Fleishman-Hillard, Burson-Marsteller, Ketchum, Porter Novelli and Edelman set their sights on the multicultural markets beginning in the 1980s. Some acknowledge that they had limited success at first. Now, these firms have been able to command influence and access to critical relationships in corporate communications departments. Many times their existing clients were the same ones they now serve with multicultural campaigns.

The playing field is not level given that their general market relationships allow them to dominate major corporate and government assignments as well. We will say more about current competition for these assignments in examining the under-representation of Hispanics in the public relations industry in general. Nonetheless, general market firms will face greater competition as clients and the market grow more sophisticated in discerning appropriate and relevant approaches. In the meantime, Hispanic-focused public relations firms need to get their "arms around" their unique insights and value to various client sectors.

Although the client sectors between public relations and advertising vary little, the nature of the campaigns, the objective and the training is vastly different. We discuss this difference in services and approach in the context of the unique U.S. Latino experience and a culture distinct from those offered in native Latin American marketing segments. Dr. Davila makes the clear distinction that those services, although similar and unifying in language, are almost extraneous to establish relevance for U.S. Latinos.[31]

Recently, Burson has 'Latino-branded' their Hispanic-focused services to underscore their insights as uniquely relevant and community-focused. Previously, they and other conglomerate-owned shops had been somewhat deferential to their Hispanic "sister" shops as "owning" the U.S. Hispanic market platform while they focused on the Latin American markets. That changed in 2001, because of the declining economic circumstances abroad and the consolidation of agencies, which made internal competition among shops acceptable and even encouraged. It was then that some of the conglomerate-owned Hispanic shops began to concede the Hispanic public relations platform to their "PR specialty" shops rather than fight for that piece of the market.

Some Hispanic agencies had already begun to lose their top public relations directors and staffs to the general market shops who were preparing their entry into the "multicultural" public relations services market. In some cases, the conglomerate-owned Hispanic shops had difficulty vying for the Hispanic public relations specialty internally while others simply let it go to the general market shops. Even though the Hispanic agencies did not formally concede the specialty, they would have lost the traditional "hands-off" protection from the owners.

---

31   Davila, Arlene. "Latinos, Inc."

In 2001, Burson won the public relations assignment for the Latin Grammy's, which signaled a new era of competition for Hispanic assignments. Previously, Bravo, Bromley and others won key Hispanic accounts with their public relations approach. Now, as competitors, some of the Hispanic agencies have lost accounts or new public relations business to the general market shops. It was this factor, conceding Hispanic expertise, to the general market firms, which gave general market firms unprecedented access and unparalleled competition from Hispanic agencies.

However, this inequitable advantage by general market agencies is entirely dependent on the retention of the Hispanic staff, not their insights or expertise. It remains to be seen whether Burson can maintain their edge now that their top Hispanic practice leader has left their shop.

Infrastructure Supporting Hispanic Specific Public Relations Industry

Hispanic public relations professionals have access to sufficient communications infrastructure to demonstrate the value and accessibility for consumption of Hispanic relevant messages constituting a unique industry infrastructure in function and parallel to the general market. Of course, their use has largely reflected the development and demand for these by Hispanic practitioners.

New public relations measurement and tracking mechanisms to support the growing media infrastructure appeared only recently. Practitioners have expressed a constant frustration that these services have not grown as rapidly, as the outlets sometimes serving as a barrier, and even at times undermining the efforts of Hispanic public relations practitioners.

"It makes evaluating my efforts more difficult when I can't count on quick access to print articles or even more so, video footage of Hispanic-centered campaigns," said Edna Ruano, Southwest Airlines multicultural specialist. "The general market monitoring services fall short and sometimes make little attempt to deliver these materials to existing clients for both market segments," Ruano added.

Cable Company	Markets and Reach	Spanish Channel Distribution
Comcast Cable Communications, Inc.	24.4 million subscribers with markets in 35 states & D.C. #1 in the industry	Offers three basic Spanish channels, however an optional package is offered that includes more Spanish channels.
Time Warner Cable	12.9 million subscribers operating in 27 states	Offers Galavision and Telemundo as basic packages but additional Spanish channels can be bought.
Cox Communications	6.6 million subscribers in 21 states	Two Spanish channels with optional packages available.
Charter Communications, Inc.	6.5 million subscribers in 40 different states	Again offers limited Spanish channels on it's basic service but additional packages can be ordered.
Cablevision Systems Corporation	3 million subscribers in the New York City area	More Spanish channels than industry competitors as part of it's basic service.

Source: Cable Company Websites 2004

Table 20 - Cable Companies that Feature Spanish Language Channels

At the behest and leadership of public relations practitioners serving the Hispanic public relations segment the market is making the greatest contributions towards closing the gap between the public relations services. Manny Ruiz, president of Hispanic PR Wire has grown his business, enjoying double-digit expansion, and developed new business alliances and services that have grown the Hispanic public relations services arena by leaps and bounds. "As a public relations practitioner, my vision has been to fill the void in the measurement tools and services to support the unique demands and needs of the Hispanic public relations industry. Hispanic PR Wire has been fortuitous in attracting partners that allow us to grow and expand our product services" Ruiz underscored.[32] Ruiz recently announced the launch of Con-

32   Interviews with Manny Ruiz, president, Hispanic Public Relations Wire.

Company	2003 Advertising Expenditures	Percent change in 2003
1. Procter & Gamble	$11,188,958	(+32%)
2. General Motors	$7,093,081	(+166%)
3. Ford Motor Company	$6,441,104	(+34%)
4. L'Oreal U.S.A., Inc	$3,600,185	(+4%)
5. DaimlerChrysler	$3,563,831	(+209%)
6. Toyota Motor Sales, U.S.A.	$3,453,585	(+23%)
7. Colgate-Palmolive	$2,099,908	(+40%)
8. Pfizer, Inc.	$1,871,844	(+138%)
9. KF Holdings	$1,871,657	(+50%)
10. Johnson & Johnson	$1,571,659	(+122%)

Source: HispanicMagazineMonitor, a service of Media Economics Group

Table 21 - Top Ten Advertisers in Hispanic Magazines in 2003

texto Latino, a bilingual editorial features service to reach U.S. Hispanic audiences.

In 2003, the growth of the Hispanic media: broadcast, cable and satellite, radio and Internet provided new and virtually untapped opportunities to position client messages. The overall increase in these properties is difficult to track placing greater value on various Hispanic and multicultural buying resources such as the Latino Print Network and American Multicultural Marketing services.

Opportunity and Social Responsibility

The main premise for accepting the emergence of Hispanic public relations should be affording the "space" which understands our own subordination, especially as reflected in the ownership of the media that serve us our own self-image. As professionals, we need to ask ourselves whether they are the images that speak positively of our struggles and contributions. Are the messages ones that will engender positive action by our family members? Do we offer a message that reflects our values and inspires us to fulfill our dreams? Quite clearly, because Latino communications are building infrastructure for the message of many communities it may require us to look beyond our own self interest. It is necessary to refocus on the long-term since we know short-term solutions are not what we deliver to clients. So why should our communities deserve less? In 2004, 6.7 million Hispanics were expected to vote, according to the 'Tomas Rivera Policy Institute. Hispanics represent an influential group for marketers and politicians.

Although these populations have historically lacked access to public venues of self-representation, it is in the market and through marketing discourse that they are increasingly debating their social identities and public standing. These issues are consequently reduced and correlated with their "advertising worthiness and marketability." They are cautioning us against the facile celebration of Latinos' commercial popularity as an infallible sign of their "coming of age" and political standing.[33]

To a certain extent, the commodification of *Latinidad* may be as constitutive of political struggles and political disenfranchisement. The more "native" groups have carried the Latino political agenda for others that upon arrival have the opportunity to diminish or relinquish ownership in the name of accommodating to participate. This trend is also reflected in the transnational conglomerates dominating public relations and public affairs. These agencies' ability to interject themselves as "experts" in the public affairs arena garnering critical contracts diminishes the Latino's community to "negotiate" our own image and rules of engagement on critical policy issues such as health and obesity, for example. The strategy created by these campaigns dictates the rules of engagement of community advocates and elected leaders to discuss the strategy, embrace or even reject the approach. A case in point is the recent assignments from the Centers for Disease Control (CDC), the Department of Health and Human Services and others that are almost mirror images of general market initiatives and language

---

33   Ibid.

relevance, yet miss the demographic relevance and instead use reach as a sole measurement.

Measurement in the general market public relations industry is heavily reliant on media impressions as indicators of success. The infrastructure for the Hispanic market is in "development." according to The Bravo Group's managing partner Meg Bernot-Rodriquez, "There is little in terms of measurement. We don't have the same matrix as in the non-Hispanic market. Once we can achieve this, it will give our market greater sophistication and it will let us be perceived as more reliable."[34] Hispanic public relations professionals continue to be held to the same measurements standards commonplace for the general market primarily because the differences in infrastructure are not widely discussed or acknowledged among clients. Instead, this creates an uneven playing field for public relations professionals in the Hispanic market. Practitioners need to play a role in developing unique Hispanic measurements that account for cultural, brand, campaign message, and language relevance and "good will" values. These factors are critical to Hispanic consumers in addition to impressions alone. Ruiz from Hispanic PR Wire notes that the demands for such Hispanic public relations measurements and monitoring services increase faster than the market can develop them.

Although culturally specific, many regarded marketing as a viable means to correct stereotypical and commercial portrayals. The issue of community credibility must also be a factor. The government has awarded most Latina health education contracts to non-Latino firms. These campaigns further perpetuate the original offense because, regardless of intent, the campaigns lack true community and grass-roots relevance. For example, the Centers for Disease Control and Prevention's (CDC) campaign entitled "verb" and its Spanish translation "go out and play" or "sale y juega" took the form of a billboard campaign in the top Hispanic markets. Unfortunately, the message was lost for the target audience because billboard placement requires even greater Hispanic community insights to ensure relevance is delivered to the target.

---

34   "Special Report: Shopping Around, a Look at Media Planning and Buying." *Hispanic Market Weekly*, Volume 7-Issue 36. September 8, 2003.

Instead, they positioned the billboards in communities where gang activity has increased raising the ire of the Hispanic community and where the message of *"sale y juega"* even appears insensitive to Latino families concerned about their children's safety and their inability to play in their own yards.[35] The campaign demonstrated that good intentions do not deliver results even though they placed the ads in high Hispanic traffic areas. This CDC campaign served to undermine the overall campaign message and exposed the absence of relevance for Latinos in East Los Angeles (Los Angeles).[36]

The implications are severe and we should examine them closely with a frank discussion about the benefits of furthering success for others while Latina images continue to negatively impact generations of Latinos. Together marketers and agencies have embarked in an "educational" campaign about the value of the Hispanic marketer. In 2004, greater awareness and focus should equally be placed on education since the media has the potential of moving the American political needle. Political influence is measured by votes and as a community, we need to vote to be full participants; and we need to have economic equity, our greatest strength and ultimate drivers.

Although the programming and images of Latinas are degrading, they are mired in the guise of entertainment. Yet, why do we ascribe unacceptable standards for the general market, but not hold our own to the same standards? Is it a surprise that there are no women on Univision's board of directors? Would we find this acceptable if Univision lacked such high Hispanic "affinity?" Most Latinas are completely unaware that Univision is not Latina-owned.

This premise is the most significant argument for both distinguishing the services currently provided from transnational agencies and Hispanic agencies because the former have no "vested ownership" in developing positive images of Latinos in the U.S.; whereas, the latter

35   Vega, Miguel Angel. *"Piden protección en Boyle Heights: Se recrudesce la violencia y aumentan las victimas de las pandillas en la zona." La Opinión*. March 18, 2004.

36   "New CDC Program Addresses Major Concerns Cited in Recent Report on Inactivity Among Los Angeles County Children". December 18, 2002.

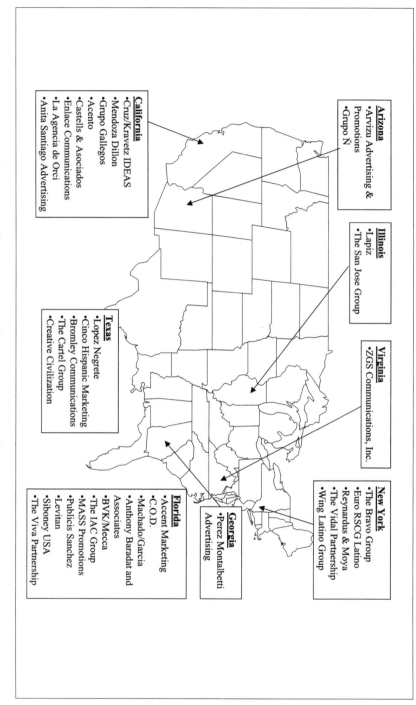

Figure 54- Hispanic Advertising Agencies with PR Capability

Arizona
- Arvizu Advertising & Promotions
- Grupo Ñ

California
- Cruz/Kravetz IDEAS
- Mendoza Dillon
- Grupo Gallegos
- Acento
- Castells & Asociados
- Enlace Communications
- La Agencia de Orci
- Anita Santiago Advertising

Illinois
- Lapiz
- The San Jose Group

Texas
- Lopez Negrete
- Cinco Hispanic Marketing
- Bromley Communications
- The Cartel Group
- Creative Civilization

Virginia
- ZGS Communications, Inc.

New York
- The Bravo Group
- Euro RSCG Latino
- Reynardus & Moya
- The Vidal Partnership
- Wing Latino Group

Florida
- Accent Marketing
- C.O.D.
- Machado/Garcia
- Anthony Baradat and Associates
- BVK/Mecca
- The IAC Group
- MASS Promotions
- Publicis Sanchez
- Levitan
- Siboney USA
- The Viva Partnership

Georgia
- Perez Montalbetti Advertising

are focused on the commodification of those images for the purpose of selling a product. As a result, the public relations sector, although a segment within the Hispanic marketing industry, is a unique segment with a shared cultural identity and values of the consumer group.

The factor differentiating Hispanic advertising agencies and transnational agencies for the purposes of establishing membership in AHAA, is that agencies must have 75 percent of their total billings in the U.S. Hispanic market. AHAA maintains that the wholly owned conglomerate member agencies should have a strong voice where they do business and their presence somehow "validates" the value of the Hispanic segment. Dr. Davila makes a historical notation that the issue of ownership was debated in the organization's early history. However, today this issue was recast in favor of conglomerate participation.[37] The Association of Hispanic Advertising Agencies (AHAA) uses staff composition to further "Hispanize" such agencies by requiring at least 65 percent of agency staff be Hispanic. The last criterion requires member agencies to offer media, creative and account services for consideration as a full-service agency.

As Horacio Gavilán, executive director of AHAA explained, "We have found a way to leverage our role and make the business argument for hiring Hispanic marketing expertise and not necessarily excluding major players by focusing in on the ownership composition or entitlement argument. I think some Hispanic organizations are not served by this strategy." However, the ownership argument is one that has been quite lively among agencies when competing for government contracts. In addition, AHAA's contention, further contradicts reports that Hispanic-owned businesses remain severely underutilized and under parity in corporate America[38]. According to Hector Barreto, U.S. small business administrator, "by law 23 percent of more than $200 billion in government contracts must go to small business owners. The President wants the fastest-growing segment of small businesses and Hispanic-owned small businesses, to take a share of those contracts." Organiza-

37   Davila, Arlene. "Latinos, Inc."

38   SBA Administrator, Hector Barreto comments in the HACR *Corporate Observer*

tions such as the United States Hispanic Chamber of Commerce (U.S.H.C.C.) and the Hispanic Association on Corporate Responsibility (HACR) continue to raise procurement as a critical economic stumbling block for Hispanic-owned business in America. As such, the issue of Hispanic-ownership and procurement will remain front and center and cannot be dismissed in order to advance the argument of the conglomerate owned Hispanic agencies.

It is difficult to assess who bears the responsibility for educating corporate America. It seems the spending in-balance, requires an inclusive and long-term public relations strategy. It is difficult and somewhat self-serving to have the Hispanic advertising agencies advance the argument for greater Hispanic corporate investment without also examining the direct and indirect benefits at-stake for the larger Hispanic community. Traditionally, Hispanic community leaders would be the ones to advance the Hispanic causes. In the case of Hispanic marketers, corporate under-spending might be a larger rallying cry for Hispanics if there was a clear benefit or implications for the Hispanic community. It would also be necessary to examine the role of such agencies for the Hispanic community. It would require quantifying the value of the contributions these agencies make to the community in philanthropic donations.

Our collective Latina clout is dependent on our ability to capture the economic and political influence in the role we have in defining the Latino cultural machine.[39] In addition, although contradictions riddle our images, our greatest opportunity as public relations professionals is to redefine these images for the benefit of our own community's integrity while also benefitting our client's positioning. In this way, we have the best opportunity to create our "own" unique Latino presence in the public relations industry. It is up to us as public relations professionals to take issue with inappropriate and denigrating Latino images in the media. The appeal to professionals is not exceptional in that this is the primary purpose of professional associations, to maintain the integrity of the profession. As Hispanic public relations practitioners, we have a

---

39   Habell-Pallán, Michelle and Mary Romero. "Latino/a Popular Culture." New York University Press. Copyright 2002

tremendous opportunity to lay the professional infrastructure that will encourage growth, demand and integrity of our profession and Hispanic expertise.

By developing Hispanic public relations "Best Practices" case studies we have an opportunity to advance these images and provide leadership within our profession. "Best Practices" is not to be confused with sponsorships or awards. Too many times in the developing industry, Hispanic public relations practitioners are too focused on accumulating industry awards rather than laying a foundation that increases understanding and standards of practice. Now, perhaps this tendency persists precisely because those standards or case studies do not exist. However, too many times campaigns receive awards in the multicultural category that are not necessarily based on any standard of "cultural relevance" as a measurement of audience reach. Part of this reflects the industry's fixation on impressions as a measurement tool. Given the previous discussion of Hispanic media, we need to bring greater validity to the widely acknowledged "cozy" buying relationships that determine campaign media impressions in the Hispanic market and not necessarily campaign message relevancy.

We should not leave such circumstances to "free market forces of competition" as some in the Hispanic advertising industry might argue. Instead, rapid growth requires a tempered strategic vision for the Hispanic public relations industry. The vision should be accompanied by a specific set of industry case studies and best practices outlined by practitioners vested in the industry's distinction. When appropriate, awards should be bestowed for integrity and industry contributions that reflect the unfettered contributions and participation of Hispanic professionals at all levels of the industry. We are not there yet. We should look critically and carefully at the awards given without the merits of standard reflecting the vision for the industry. Most agency and practitioner awards currently given to multicultural and Hispanic campaigns are awarded without regard to relevance of message or community impact. The awards are a mirror image of those given by the general market and by practitioners alone with only audience reach or creativity as measurements.

Cultural Relevance Case Study and Challenges

The following paragraph illustrates the common practice that leaves Latina community relevance by the wayside. It was part of a press release announcing a $12 million corporate grant for Hispanic after school education. Organizers also purportedly intended to highlight corporate commitment to their Hispanic consumers.

A portion of the funds will be used to translate the homework assistance program, "Program X's" into Spanish, a direct effort to address the dropout rate among Latino youth. According to the U.S. Department of Education, 37 percent of Hispanics do not finish high school, compared to the national average of 15 percent. Company X is addressing this important issue by funding bilingual after school learning activities for early childhood development.

"English Program X" in Spanish helps Latino youth succeed academically, and it fosters a lifetime love of learning," said the company spokesperson. "That is why the Spanish translation of 'Program X' is a priority for our partnership with non-profit partner."

Spanish press release excerpt: *"El programa Nombre en Ingles en español ayuda a que los jóvenes latinos triunfen académicamente, fomentando sus deseos de superarse mediante el aprendizaje durante toda la vida", comentó representante de la empresa. "Esta es la razón por la cual la traducción al español del programa Nombre en Ingles es una prioridad en nuestra alianza con asociación no-lucrativa.*

One of the most glaring shortcomings of this seemingly benign effort is the lack of thought given to positioning the program for Hispanics appropriately prior to making the grant announcement. That the program and grant announcement proceeded the development of a relevant Spanish language and Hispanic branding effort for the program demonstrates a lack of thought by sponsors and partners at best. At worst, it represents disrespect for the Hispanic children and parents this program is supposed to serve. The lack of appropriate positioning reflects poorly on the corporation. It reflects negatively on the non-profit organization, demonstrating that it is "out-of-touch" with its Hispanic constituency.

268

Too many times, corporations do not give much thought to the selection of appropriate non-profit partners for Hispanic public relations or community initiatives. Sometimes this is a result of budgetary limitations; other times these errors are a result of poor advice from Hispanic advertising agencies or general market public relations agencies. In this particular case, the effort was well funded eliminating budgetary constraints as the problem. The company's Hispanic agency of record (AOR) does not offer public relations services; they offer interesting thoughts regarding Hispanic public relations services (discussed later). The next potential culprit is the general market public relations agency for the company and/or the non-profit. More times than not, such nuances are missed and pervasive when the corporation and the non-profit share the same general market public relations firm driven by the thought that the general market value (impressions) of the program would simply "cross-over" to Hispanics. However, in discussion with the company's public relations Hispanic team member, they shared that the idea for the "Hispanic program" came from the company's non-profit grantee on the basis that the program had been especially successful for them with the general market.

Clearly, this initiative demonstrates the lack of strategic thought given to Hispanic community relations programs not to mention the negative implications for their corporate partners in following their advice however well intentioned. It is also curious that Company X had not thought to have their Hispanic AOR take a cursory look at the effort prior to such a launch. This further highlights the fact that such corporate efforts fall below the "Hispanic" radar of internal or external review either because they are borne out of Company X's "general market" relationships (because the "expansion" idea originated with the general market non-profit) in philanthropy or corporate communications rather than the more "enlightened" ethnic marketing departments familiar with such nuances. There are many other critical issues that have been omitted in this discussion for brevity that merit review such as: the relevance of the program for Hispanic parents; translating programs that may not work for Hispanics; and the actual amount or percentage of the $12 million dedicated to reaching Hispanics. All of these issues could be raised by members of the Hispanic media and be further points of contention for Company X.

Marketing and Hispanic Celebrity Spokespersons

In this particular example, they used a Latino celebrity to further improve media coverage. Sometimes, large corporate clients refer to the use of celebrities in a Hispanic public relations campaign to raise the ante for companies. The results often do not reflect the benefits of the exorbitant expense. Clients with sufficient experience in the Hispanic market have begun to recognize these efforts are "unique tactics" of the general market firms with Hispanic practice. One corporate executive commented that they used the celebrity investment as a way to justify the disproportionately high fees to de-emphasize or overcompensate for the fact that the firm was visibly removed from the Hispanic media and community by using the celebrity as collateral instead. Although this practice is not unique or uncharacteristic for the general market, these techniques are always exceedingly effective in the Hispanic community when the objective is to engender "good will" in the community for that corporate brand. The faux pas indicates the stark difference between the insights of a Latino-focused campaign and the costly client "nuances" of a general market entrant into the Hispanic public relations market without invaluable Latino expertise.

Corporate clients have become somewhat skeptical about using Hispanic celebrities as brand and product spokespersons for public relations efforts. Hispanic marketers not adept at the public relations nuances of proper talent preparation for the client event have produced less than favorable results from celebrity interactions with the media. It is critical to ensure that the talent understands the client's brand profile and positioning developed by the Hispanic AOR.

In several instances, poor talent performances or interactions demonstrated the celebrity's lack of preparation by misstating the endorsing client's brand at a media launch event where Hispanic media were present. This reflects poorly on the agency, and equally so for the brand and client that they are seeking to promote.

Although they could have easily averted the poor performance or preparation by ensuring the talent received event briefings, communications and media training; most agency account staff or public relations staff has no such training or expertise in these areas. As a result, the risks and mistakes in this area seem to abound with celebrity talent simply because most agency experience has been limited to controlled on-camera interactions or agency staff has never "tested" talent for real unscripted public appearances.

The same is true for talent appearances with Hispanic media and radio in particular. It is an agency's responsibility to provide product brand and media training for talent regardless of their career experience or trajectory. The radio interviews or appearances are vastly different when promoting their records versus promoting a brand or a cause tied to a brand. Few Hispanic agencies are equipped with the experienced staff to prepare celebrity talent for their public relations functions adequately.

The public relations responsibilities and preparation of celebrity talent need to be stipulated in their representation contracts. Agencies must seek out the appropriate expertise internally or externally to maintain and build upon client confidence in this area. This is a contributing factor for Hispanic agencies losing significant public relations assignments to general market public relations agencies with Hispanic-focused services. It is also, why Hispanic public relations professionals have begun to distinguish their expertise from the advertising industry. The training, objectives and purpose of the two industries can be complimentary though the training and skills required for the two industries are significantly dissimilar.

English Dominance and Spanish Cultural Relevance

Though language relevance is the most understated skill, it is also the most critical determinant of success for public relations professionals. These professionals need to first dominate the English language and understand that we must be able to articulate communications strategies convincingly to clients before these strategies can be embraced as effective brand positioning. One contributing factor has been that many transnational companies redirected their Latin American marketing efforts to the U.S. in response to the economic downturn abroad, and simply tried to rename these efforts "Hispanic." Although much has already been said about the implications of these efforts for Hispanic campaigns, many professionals are not prepared to have positive interactions with corporate communications officers. As Carlos Santiago states, "it is unfortunate yet it still occurs far too often that Hispanic marketers venture into the Hispanic public relations arena unprepared to offer appropriate and relevant corporate counsel only further setting back the profession and the entire Hispanic marketing objective." As a result, Hispanic public relations professionals must be English dominant for corporate and client purposes. At the same time, they must equally connect for Spanish community relevance; giving greater depth to the notion of fully bicultural and bilingual professionals.

The Industry: Growing Hispanic Professionals

The previous discussion was not meant as a simple indictment or admonishment of existing Hispanic public relations initiatives but reflecting the urgency to rely on expert counsel from Hispanic public relations professionals. Even though many companies are proceeding without this counsel as in the case of Company X, more and more companies are looking to hire Hispanic communications professionals in their corporate communications departments signaling a growing acknowledgment of the value of Hispanic talent.

Like other industries and academic disciplines, Hispanics are severely under represented in the communications and public relations field. In 2003, the Public Relations Society of America undertook a survey of the public relations membership and found that only 3 percent of respondents were Hispanic.[40] The lack of diversity no doubt serves as a barrier to Latina professionals. The void of Latina professionals in the industry reflects the profession's inability to embrace a more relevant vision and does a disservice to the industry and clients. Agencies can-

---

40   Shortman, Melanie. "PRSA Survey Spotlights The Industry's Lack of Diversity." *PRWeek*. September 1, 2003.

not possibly reflect a true vision for clients when more than 14 percent of American society is made invisible.

This is both an opportunity and a challenge for educational institutions and Latina practitioners. Our professional networks are more extensive and valuable than many professional recruiting firms. However, we also bear responsibility for mentoring and developing the cadre of professionals that we will rely on for counsel and insight. Currently, few institutions offer Hispanic communications and public relations theory or practice course work. For the past several years, the University of Florida has led the way in the area of Hispanic communications offerings. This is one reason the region boasts so many Hispanic practitioners.

Until recently, the country's West and Southwest region had virtually no relevant communications course offerings in the area of Hispanic communications or public relations. This is ironic when considering that this region accounts for the largest segments of Hispanic population, Mexican-Americans. In 2003, the University of Texas at El Paso (UTEP) established the Ruben Salazar Spanish Language Media Program on the heels of establishing the Sam Donaldson Center for Communications Studies in 2001.

Patricia Witherspoon, Ph.D., chairman of the Department of Communications and center director, recently addressed the NAHP likening the role of Hispanic publishers and editors as "agents of change, public voices on public matters."[41] Similarly, public relations professionals operating in the corporate and public arenas such as public affairs are challenged to serve as agents of change. Much of the Center's efforts are focused on building binational and bicultural communications education.

"Our Hispanic communications students are optimistic and enthusiastic about the contributions they are preparing to make to both journalism and public relations fields. Most have been raised in predominantly

---

41   Witherspoon, Patricia D. PhD. "Newspapers: Sites of Change in the 21st Century." Comments delivered on March 18, 2004 to the National Association of Hispanic Publications in Los Angeles, California.

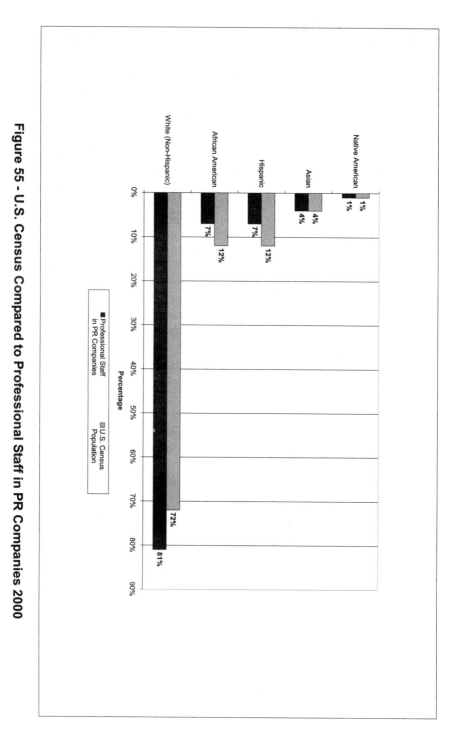

Figure 55 - U.S. Census Compared to Professional Staff in PR Companies 2000

Hispanic communities along the border affording them tremendous insights from their own daily 'inter-cultural' experiences straddling two worlds and cultures," exclaimed Frank Perez, Ph.D., professor of communications at UTEP. He also noted that many students have participated in Hispanic market internship or employment opportunities that reflected the degree to which their insights and skills are undervalued by the Hispanic media or agencies. Dr. Perez further elaborated, "It is unfortunate that several students have returned from these experiences somewhat disheartened by their experiences in the lack of depth and community relevance of their employers in 'top' Hispanic market service industries."[42]

Although the efforts of Drs. Witherspoon and Perez are encouraging in that they are developing critical curriculum for the Hispanic public relations industry, it is disappointing that we are not paving the way for them to have more positive experiences that truly value their contributions by offering financially rewarding and intellectually stimulating experiences. This was also a recurring theme expressed by interns at New York agencies participating in minority programs such as the American Advertising Agency Federation and the American Association of Advertising Agencies. Most noted the differences between themselves and other Latino participants in that few shared their commitment to serving as "agents of change" themselves in the industry; they saw themselves as solely reaping the benefits of their personal marketability.

It seems obvious that there are tremendous synergies to be captured by public relations industry leaders and the Public Relations Society of America in preparing for the change that our inevitable presence and contributions beckon. Yet, this also requires our own service as mentors and models of change in an industry that to date is far from reflecting our own images.

---

42   Interview with Dr. Frank Perez, Professor of Communications at the University of Texas
      at El Paso. May 2004.

An Industry versus Niche Services Market

The dilemma of "native" Hispanic versus external (conglomerate or general) infrastructure is continually posed by the ever-growing influence, dominance and general disregard for the unique value of Hispanic public relations professionals. A partner in one of the top Hispanic-focused advertising agencies responded the following when asked why they do not provide Hispanic public relations services: "we don't provide Hispanic public relations services and if we really want that expertise, we will rely on Ketchum for Hispanic public relations expertise. They know everyone in the client circles; this saves us from building these services ourselves even though our clients have requested these services."[43] Ironically, the agency, once Hispanic-owned, was the first to cry "foul" when they lost large government assignments to conglomerate-owned Hispanic-focused agencies. Putting the offense of this comment aside, the relevant point here is that the road for the Hispanic public relations industry is familiar to that traveled by Hispanic marketers and advertisers early on. As practitioners, we should be ensuring that the infrastructure established indeed reflects the image of the industry we want to call our own.

Given the burgeoning Hispanic demographics and that marketing services grew to over $1 Billion, these investments underscore that the Hispanic market might have been considered a niche in 1980. One cannot dismiss the eye-popping earnings posted by Univision together with NBC's $2 billion purchase of Telemundo. Even non-believers cannot dismiss these as a fluke or reflecting a niche; instead, they fit the characterization of a growing behemoth. In addition, although the Hispanic electorate has yet to become the "waking giant" in 2004, the language-driven cultural infrastructure in the U.S. is sufficient to support entire industries not simple niches. The only limitation for Hispanic public relations professionals is a hesitancy to build the unique infrastructure that reflects our cultural values and integrity.

---

43   Conversation between agency partner and client. Quote provided on condition of source anonymity. April 2004.

Challenges for the Industry and Campaign Opportunities

As a community, *Latinidad* has its challenges ahead. Communications professionals, like journalists, have high standards and are passionate about their contributions for the future. There is much room for introspective and constructive debate. However, we need to engage our colleagues, especially the non-believers in the industry and the community that we purport to understand and reflect.

In an attempt to open this dialogue with the community, the Dallas-Forth Worth Network of Hispanic Communicators sponsored a community dialogue entitled, "The Role of the Hispanic Media and the Community" in February 2004. The event was an effort to engage participants in assessing the value of various local properties and their role in promoting the interests of the Latina community. One of the issues raised was whether there is a different role and expectation of Hispanic television properties. More specifically, are these companies first and foremost entertainment companies? On the other hand, should we hold them to the same standard of professional integrity since they are the sole connector and promoter of Hispanic culture in the U.S.? Many of these issues remain unresolved and serve as a healthy and productive debate.

It seems that left unaddressed, community advocates will raise these until companies respond to the pressure and negative publicity or before the Federal Communications Commission (F.C.C.). One recent example is the discussion of Latina images portrayed by Spanish programming on Univision and Telemundo published in *Latina Magazine*. The article provides valid and repeated examples and criticism of the sexually explicit images of Latinas on Univision network programming. Public admonishment of such programming will require foreign programmers to adjust to a "new," possibly more enlightened audience influenced by the U.S. experience and that will demand a new standard for companies seeking to reach U.S. Latina audiences. Perhaps the hybrid experience and increased advocacy and influence in the U.S. will move Hispanic-serving companies to increase the level of programming to resonate with the culture and the language. Jeff Valdez needs to be commended for his tenacity in developing unique U.S. Hispanic programming such as Nickelodeon's Garcia Brothers and Network Sí TV. Corporate America and the Latina community are well served by his efforts demonstrating that cross-purposes can and must be achieved in this arena.

These issues are worth highlighting because our industry will be best served by increasing our awareness to lead eventually to their dismantling. Future generations of Latinos cannot afford to reconstruct the same system of hierarchies that we have surpassed and blindly reimpose them on future generations of Latinos. Race and class are the most sensitive challenges to our unity. We are best served insisting we accurately reflect the hue of our true colors as a tapestry we verbalize to corporate America. We are responsible for realigning these images; otherwise, we become party to our historical and cultural distortions and invisibility.

This premise of "cultural citizenship" reflects the extent to which the marketing of Hispanics becomes the platform by which we negotiate with U.S. institutions and the infrastructure we build to sustain our community's future. Rosaldo and Flores discuss the extent to which Latino visibility is directly related to political influence as an opportunity for Latinos (and other groups) to claim "space" and the potential to claim rights.[44] The Association of Hispanic Advertising Agencies, AAHA, continues to assess the business value corporate America holds of Latino cultural capital. The Hispanic Association on Corporate Responsibility, HACR, asserts the responsibility and the success of Hispanic inclusion lie in the hands of "senior corporate management." Whom will we look to for leadership in developing standards and practices that reflect inclusion and diversity in our own industry? Will we take leadership positions in the Public Relations Society of America and be agents of change for the public relations industry?

---

44   Rosaldo, Renato, and William V. Flores. "Latino Cultural Citizenship: Claiming Identity, Space, and Rights." Ed. Rina Benmayor and William Flores. Boston, MA: Beacon Press. 1997

The current relationship between Hispanic ad agencies and Hispanic public relations professionals is primarily of ambivalence. There is a growing interest being assessed formally by AHAA but this interest mostly focuses on the growing number of public relations assignments in the private and public sectors. The relationship that has been proposed is one of an "associate" member status for Hispanic public relations agencies in the association. This subtle delineation has begun to raise eyebrows among professionals and question the value of this designation given our unique and significant long-term contributions. Not to mention, the need to recognize our unique perspectives as both central and invaluable to their member agencies. Many corporations assume that the two are one and synonymous yet agency budgets, training and experience indicate otherwise.

The Association of Hispanic Advertising Agencies has taken only a cursory examination of the serious inclusion issues their corporate clients receive by Hispanic community leaders and could be seen levied upon their conglomerate owned members. Until now, the dotted line between the Hispanic agencies and practitioners has been recent and limited to holding corporations accountable. These tables will soon turn to require the same levels of accountability being imposed on their corporate owners in the future for adequate inclusion of Hispanics at all levels of their business and that their community contributions be measured as well.

We should look to the National Association of Hispanic Journalists and embrace strategies that deliver results in the media industry. We believe and embrace our own marketing statistics and hype; at the same time, there are multitudes of issues that require addressing. If left unaddressed, these will continue to affect our collective ability to make long-term gains in the U.S. Among them:

- The number of Latino workers will grow by 36.3 percent by the end of this decade. Latino immigrants are the most likely to die because of work place injuries.
- The National Agriculture Workers Survey found that half of all farm workers earned less than $7,500 per year and that half of all farm workers had below poverty-level incomes.

- Latinos have the highest rate of being uninsured in the United States at 34 percent, compared with 22 percent for African-Americans, 20 percent for Asian/Pacific Islanders, and 12 percent for whites.
- About six in 10 (64 percent) of Latinos ages 18 through 24 have completed high school. By comparison, more than eight in 10 African-Americans (83 percent) and nine in 10 whites (92 percent) of the same age group completed high school.
- In addition, only 11 percent of Latinos ages 25 years and older received bachelor's degrees or higher in 2000, compared with 27.7 percent for whites.
- Latinos are more likely to be incarcerated for drug offenses, although they are no more likely than members of other racial and ethnic groups to use illegal drugs, and less likely to use alcohol, the report noted. Latinos accounted for 43 percent of the total drug offenders in 2000, more than three times their proportion in the general population.
- Latinos have the third highest incidence of heart disease, the highest for chronic obstructive pulmonary disease and second highest incidence of diabetes.
- Latinas continue to outpace other groups in teen pregnancies.

The opportunities and challenges for public relations practitioners are many. Change has occurred quickly and opportunities have multiplied, although the context of many of these opportunities is based on some antiquated practices. The growth of Hispanic media has created a competitive environment for advertising and a demand for Hispanic-focused content. Corporate America, although lagging in its Hispanic marketing investment is stepping-up quickly, even though its messages sometimes lack resonance and long-term benefits for Hispanic consumers in the way of positive or empowering media images.

We can learn much from the "buy-out" of Hispanic advertising agencies. Owners of groundbreaking agencies that previously touted greater consumer relevancy because of their minority-ownership were silenced by their new majority-owners. Agency principals remain silent when facing unflattering images of Hispanics or have lost their zeal to examine the impact of such changes on the Hispanic-owned communications infrastructure.

The general market public relations firms just recently set their sights on the Hispanic public relations practice mostly by approaching the market as part of a larger multicultural practice. Hispanic advertising agencies have largely looked the other way at their entry in the arena since many share the same owners; and conglomerates maintain a policy of open competition within 'sister' Hispanic agencies. Although some consider it too strong a statement, Hispanic public relations practitioners are under assault by the general market public relations firms. Their importation of Latin American talent to gain Hispanic access produces a cadre of professionals devoid of commitment to Latino community needs and struggles with the potential of turning back our full participation in the American dream. The uneven playing field Hispanic practitioners and firms face almost requires an affirmative action style intervention to germinate the industry and ensure public relations industry diversity is attainable. The situation requires an agenda of industry social responsibility.

The myriad issues faced by Hispanic consumers require an increase in advocacy campaigns to enlist and encourage better long-term public policy in the U.S. A great number of governmental Hispanic outreach efforts have been placed in the hands of general market agencies without question or requirement of any Hispanic inclusion. The impact of some of these failed campaigns is outlined in previous pages. These under-the-radar practices endanger the diversity of the entire industry. The gains made by the early Hispanic marketing pioneers and advanced by AHAA advocating Hispanic leadership and representation have given way to dominance by the new conglomerate owners devoid of substantive commitment to the Hispanic community.

Hispanic consumers place a high value on a company's commitment to Hispanic causes. All practitioners will need to be cognizant and mindful of the Hispanic community's needs if they are to position their client's products and services in a relevant manner. Hispanic consumer loyalty, regardless of its strength and longevity, must be gained from the onset and maintained long-term. This requires a heartfelt commitment to our unique community and communications infrastructure; and more than a simple "cause-related" general market approach. Our community will distinguish between the two approaches and measure the efforts by true investment not simple positioning.

Welcome new practitioners. Our journey is long and full of challenge and promise.

Chapter Summary

- The Hispanic community and Hispanic practitioners benefit from efforts to formalize our contributions to the industry.
- Hispanic advertising is different from Hispanic public relations in very specific and formal ways.
- It is critical that Hispanic public relations professionals also increase the value of their contributions to the public relations industry.
- With a collective effort, the Hispanic public relations industry can move from a "niche" to a formal practice area.
- Consolidation trends witnessed in Hispanic advertising could seriously affect Hispanic public relations practitioners and the industry.
- Growth in the industry provides Hispanic practitioners unique opportunities.
- It is important to gain a better understanding of ownership relative to Hispanic advertising and learn about different practice areas.

About the Author

Dora O. Tovar, M.P.Aff., President, Tovar Public Relations

Dora Tovar has more than 17 years of experience providing strategic counsel to nonprofit, governmental and corporate clients in the areas of Hispanic marketing, crisis and litigation communications and public affairs. Along with her extensive communications expertise, she provides clients with public policy insight and advocacy efforts that promote relevant cultural competency practices. Dora received a master's degree in Public Affairs from the LBJ School of Public Affairs at the University of Texas at Austin and an undergraduate degree in Political Science.

Chapter Eleven

Latino Media: A Cultural Connection

Federico Subervi, Ph.D.
Heidi Eusebio

In This Chapter

- Kinds of Latino media in the United States
- Why reaching out to Latino communities through Latino media is essential
- How to communicate effectively through Latino media

Introduction

Latino media in the United States are vast, growing, complex, and continuously evolving to reflect the progression and demands of the nation's developing Hispanic populations and markets. For a veteran Hispanic marketing or communications specialist, this comes as no surprise. It is part of our everyday reality as we disseminate or gather news and information for our clients. Even for experienced practitioners, the complex dynamics of Latino media may require additional guidance.

The purpose of this chapter is to provide an overview of the Latino media landscape. We start with a brief introduction of the best terms and categories to use when referring to the variety of Latino media and describe some of the audiences and functions of these media. We then feature the major media in Spanish and in English, each with pertinent groupings of broadcast, print and "other" types available to Latino populations across the country. The chapter also provides Latino media resources, and ends with a series of suggestions to succeed when dealing with Latino media and populations. The map emerging from these pages should serve as a media guide and a guide to leverage the power that Latino media provide to connect with the ever-growing Hispanic community.

Terms and Categories

For this chapter, we use Latino media to cover all electronic, print, and other types of media directed primarily to Latino populations in the United States.[1] The focal point of the term is the main audience of the media, as would be the case when saying, for example, "youth media." This term would not imply that only young people access that media or that the owners of such media are only young people. This is the case with Latino media; the main, though not necessarily the only, audiences are Latinos, and the owners of such media are Latinos as well as non-Latinos.

An alternative term, and possibly a more accurate one, is Latino-oriented media. This term is used mostly in academic settings.[2] Regardless of which of these terms is preferred, communicators should keep the following three points in mind about the media directed primarily to Latinos in the United States.

---

1   For this chapter, media in Puerto Rico are excluded. First, because they are much more numerous than can be addressed in these pages. Second, while the island is a territory of the U.S., the cultural and political frameworks of the media and the audiences are different in the U.S. On the island, the media and the audiences are not "minorities." Therefore, the Puerto Ricans there, all of whom are Spanish-speakers, are the majority and the mainstream. Also, the Spanish-language media on the island are the general market media. Nevertheless, some of our work as public relations professionals will require us to know about the media in Puerto Rico and in many other Latin American countries.

2   The first author prefers the term Latino-oriented media because it helps avoid any incorrect impression that Latinos are the owners of such media. In professional circles, however, the most common term is certainly Latino media.

First, Latinos own many Latino media outlets. However, increasingly, many are owned by non-Hispanics. Do not assume Latinos are the ones who own the "Latino media." Second, Latino media include Spanish-language media as well as English-language media and even bilingual media directed to Latinos. Therefore, do not use the term "Spanish-language media" as an umbrella label for all media directed at Latinos. Third, Latino media encompass media programs fully produced outside of the United States; or only partially produced in the U.S., as long as the content is aimed primarily at U.S. Latino audiences. For example, we can still consider a television program, newspaper, magazine or website fully or partially produced outside the United States but with U.S. Latinos as a target audience part of Latino media.

General-market media is a common umbrella term used, especially in the advertising industry, to refer to media produced for the predominantly English-speaking populations in the United States as a whole. The term implies the content of such media is produced for broad and diverse market groups, not narrowly defined niche groups, be these based on race, ethnicity or other factors. We commonly use the term mainstream media also to encompass print, broadcast and other outlets geared for the same broad markets. It is correct to use this term. However, in some communities, what is considered "mainstream" may also be minority-focused. This happens in locations where Latinos are the majority (at least numerically, although not necessarily in terms of political or economic power).

For example, in Laredo, Texas, the Spanish-language and other elements of the Latino culture would be the "mainstream." Even so, the local Spanish-language media would not automatically be general market because they are not geared to the broader (also English-speaking) population of the area. Thus, the term general-market media is preferred as the contrast to the focus of this chapter, the Latino-oriented media.

Language and Audience

When referring to particular subgroups of Latino media, additional terms apply. Spanish-language media is the most appropriate term for media produced in Spanish. Depending on the type of medium, terms that are more specific might be more appropriate. For instance, there are Spanish-language newspapers, magazines, radio, and television.

When dealing with Spanish-language media, it is important to keep the audience in mind. Spanish-language media are produced for two main markets. The first is U.S. Latino-oriented, that is, media produced primarily for the U.S. Hispanic market. The second is non-U.S. Latino-oriented, meaning media produced primarily for broader Spanish-speaking markets in the Americas and Spain. Some of the media of the second type may be distributed in the United States but the main market is not U.S. Spanish-speakers.

Regarding non-U.S. Latino media in Spanish, three additional distinctions are relevant:

- One group is originally produced for Spanish-speaking audiences across one or more Latin American countries including, though not exclusively, for U.S. Latino populations.
- A second group is the media produced and intended for residents of Spain or a specific Latin American country.
- The third entails the Spanish-language versions of English-language media; the audiences of these are similar to the first of this subset.

All of these Spanish-language media, mostly in print but also via broadcast, cable, satellite, and the Internet, are increasingly available in the U.S. thanks in part to the ease of international transportation and telecommunications. In major U.S. metropolitan cities with large concentrations of immigrants from one or more Spanish-speaking countries and in border communities across the southwestern U.S., there is an abundance of Spanish-language media. Many of these media are produced in Mexico primarily for Mexican nationals, including the recent migrants who are still more focused on the news and entertainment ongoing in Mexico. The same is the case with media in Colombia, Peru, Puerto Rico, Venezuela and other Latin American countries and available in the U.S. Those media are not produced for the long-settled Hispanics in the U.S. Even so, U.S. Hispanic audiences of those media are profitable secondary markets because they tune into or read the

Spanish-language media and the advertising messages those media carry. Given their different target audiences and places of production, it should be evident that all Spanish-language media are not the same, nor should we consider all of the outlets to be oriented to U.S. Latinos. We highlight selected examples of each of these in a separate section. The key issue is that specificity is indispensable even in the terms referring to the various types and categories of Spanish-language Latino media.

In addition to the vast array of Latino media in Spanish, there is an increasing number of English-language Latino media. This term applies to the print, broadcast, video and Internet-based media for which the primary audience is U.S. Latinos.

There are not as many subcategories of these if the assessment excludes the general-market, English-language media and any other media produced outside the United States. One distinction, however, is English-language media produced abroad, but available in the United States. Puerto Rico's daily newspaper, *The San Juan Star,* is one such example. A regional example is the Latin American, English-language edition of *Time* magazine. Neither of these or similar types should be considered Latino media even though they may be part of the media diet of some English-speaking U.S. Latinos.

A final language-based subcategory of Latino media encompasses material produced in Spanish and English, i.e. the bilingual Latino media. In print or Internet-based media, the text in Spanish is followed side-by-side or in a separate section by text in English. *Latina* magazine is an example of such a media outlet.

In broadcast and cable media, the term bilingual may be applicable because a separate soundtrack, such as second audio programming, is made available. Some media are bilingual because they produce two separate editions of the same program, for example newscasts, and then broadcast them at different times. Bilingual can also describe media that mix the two languages side-by-side in one sentence, paragraph, or page.

Ownership and Functions

In addition to terms and categories related to language and audience, we should consider the characteristics of ownership, function and content when referring to, labeling or categorizing particular subgroups of Latino media. Ethnic heritage of capital investors, license holders (for broadcast media), and/or other primary decision-makers is important as it may influence the patterns of content of the material produced, and the level of involvement of those decision-makers with the local community. Regardless of the language in which they are produced, many Latino media are Hispanic-owned or Hispanic-operated. Still some media are not owned or operated primarily by Latinos (i.e., the top decision-makers of the organization are not Latino), though the content is directed to this population or particular niches within it.

Other ownership characteristics with bearing on the labels and categories depend on whether the media are for-profit commercial operations privately owned by an individual, a family, a small or large company or one that is part of a conglomerate based in the U.S. or some other country. There are also non-profit publicly owned, cooperative outlets, or community-based for-profit or non-profit Latino media. A few are free while others require purchase or subscription. Latino-oriented as they may all be, the main function(s) and thus breadth or specificity of the content of these media differ accordingly. This means that depending on the particularities of these factors, Latino media will offer content of which the main function is, for example, entertainment, information, education, political, advocacy, cultural, religious, or any combination of these or other categories.

In summary, specificity is indispensable with respect to the terms and categories for the various types of Latino media. These media are not homogenous or monolithic in the language in which they are produced, or with respect to their primary target audiences. Moreover, ownership, function and content factors also have bearing on the terms and categories used to best describe the multiple Latino media in the U.S. In the next section, we apply these terms and categorizations as we continue mapping the current landscape of the major Latino media in the U.S.

Latino Media Landscape

Newspapers, magazines, radio and television specifically geared to Latinos in the United States have been around for decades. Print media date back to the 1800s and Spanish-language radio programs began in the mid 1920s, almost immediately after the inauguration of commercial broadcasting in this country. Television programs in Spanish also started shortly after general market programs hit the air.[3]

During the last decade, there has been exponential growth in the number and types of Latino media, including a recent spurt in Internet sites. Spanish-language, English-language and bilingual Latino media can be found across the United States. Without a doubt, Latino media are solid testimony to, and the outcome of, growing Latino populations, their purchasing power, the value they give to and the strength with which they hold on to their culture, the positive sense of identity among Latinos and the entrepreneurship of Hispanics and non-Hispanics.

A challenge facing communication professionals is the lack of a single media guide that includes all Latino media. Hopefully, this general map can help public relations and marketing specialists take the first step in understanding the diversity of Latino media to help them better serve their clients.

Sources of Connection, Culture and Information

According to the U.S. Census Bureau's American Community Survey, 70 percent of Latinos speak Spanish at home. The majority of Latinos say they are more comfortable being spoken to in Spanish than English. Therefore, it only makes sense that more than 70 percent of Latinos say they watch television or listen to the radio in Spanish.

---

3   For an overview history of Latino-oriented media in the United States, see Subervi-Vélez, Federico A., with Charles Ramirez Berg, Patricia Constantakis-Valdés, Chon Noriega, Diana I. Rios, and Kenton T. Wilkinson. "Mass communication and Hispanics" (pp. 304-357). In Handbook of Hispanic cultures in the United States: Sociology, Edited by Félix Padilla. Houston, TX: Arte Público Press, 1994.

Spanish-language media outlets provide a sense of familiarity and cultural connection, and are a vital source of information. Oftentimes, Spanish-language media are the sole sources of news from a Latino's home country. Everything from corporate websites to health-related brochures is written primarily in English. When there are Spanish versions, they often are translated literally. This is inaccurate and insensitive. For these reasons, many Latinos rely on Spanish-language media, which makes working with these media outlets imperative. Following is an overview of specific types of Spanish-language media and examples of how some companies have communicated their messages through various outlets:

Radio

For communication professionals looking to reach Spanish speakers, Spanish-language radio is a powerful tool. There are approximately 567 stations[4] offering all types of music, from Mexican to Tejano, from rock *en español* to ballads, and from salsa and merengue to romantic. The stations also offer news and talk shows, and some even cover national and international sports.

In Latino households, where music is an essential part of culture, the radio often is switched on starting early in the morning. Even people who do not speak Spanish can rely on this medium for musical entertainment. This makes Spanish-language radio an important source to affirm many elements of *Latinidad,* the personal or collective sense of being part of or identified with the Latino heritage, and helps disseminate the culture and other information across generations. As illustrated in the following example, Spanish-language radio also provides oppor-

---

4   The number excludes Spanish-language stations in Puerto Rico, where there are approximately 59 stations. The data were provided by the librarian at the National Association of Broadcasters, who inquired with various sources, primarily the Broadcast & Cable Yearbook. We state approximately because of two reasons: First, given the many sales and format changes in these media, the number changes almost daily. Also, when we inquired with Inside Radio, a radio consulting business in New Hampshire, the number of stations was listed as 633, including Puerto Rico. In sum, the numbers are dynamic and even greater if we take into account that there are many more stations, particularly public stations in university settings that carry part-time programming in Spanish.

tunities to communicate messages in greater depth than other media outlets.

Case Study Illustrates the Power of Radio

A pharmaceutical company enlisted Edelman Diversity Solutions to help raise awareness about the health risks of obesity and the treatment option of the medication it manufactured. Part of the campaign included informing listeners about free health screening with Latino doctors in 15 top Hispanic markets. At those screenings, the pharmaceutical company disseminated Spanish-language information that addressed the specific needs of the Latino community. Those who could not attend the screening were invited to call a toll-free number to get information in Spanish about obesity and the company's product.

Radio was one of the most effective vehicles Edelman used to provide this health information and encourage the Latino community to go to the screening. Local Latino doctors went on-air in the different markets to talk directly to the community, and were provided ample time to do so because obesity is an important issue in Latino communities. In Los Angeles, for instance, though a Latino doctor was on an hour-long health talk show, the long list of callers exceeded the air time. The radio station continued to patch callers through well after the show was over so listeners could get the information they needed. The campaign was a huge success, with 10,000 information packets disseminated and more than 1,500 calls placed to the pharmaceutical's toll-free information number. This shows how one radio interview can amplify a message and broaden a media campaign from the airways to the community.

The following Spanish-language radio operations are among the most important in the United States:

- Univision Radio is the largest Spanish-language radio broadcaster in the United States.[5] The company, owned by Univision Communications, Inc., with corporate offices in Los Angeles, owns and/or operates 68 radio stations in 17 of the top 25 U.S. Hispanic markets (four of those stations are in Puerto Rico).
- The major company devoted solely to radio broadcasting is Spanish Broadcasting Systems, Inc. Based in Miami,[6] Spanish Broadcasting owns or operates 19 stations in the top 10 U.S. Hispanic markets (eleven of those stations are located in Puerto Rico). The company also operates LaMusica.com, a bilingual website providing content related to Latin music, entertainment, news and culture.
- One of the very few large radio networks owned by a Latino is Border Media Partners, based in Houston, Texas. With Tony Castro at the helm, this radio company holds 20 stations in the Rio Grande Valley area where it has at least nine stations. By the end of 2004, when Border Media receives Federal Communications Commission, FCC, approval for its purchase of part of the Amigo Broadcasting network (see below) and the Austin-based García stations, this radio network could consist of up to 35 stations in the Southwest region.[7]
- Clear Channel Communications, Inc., with corporate offices in San Antonio, Texas also has a significant presence in Spanish-language radio with eleven stations and potentially

---

5   See http://www.univision.net/corp/en/urg.jsp

6   See http://www.spanishbroadcasting.com/

7   Border Media Partners did not have a company web site at the time of this writing. This link offers a summary of the company's recent acquisition of Amigo Broadcasting stations, and its capital investment partners for that venture: http://www.hispanicprwire.com/news_in.php?id=2882&cha=14

another 20-25 on the way.[8] Five are in California, and the others are in Arizona, Massachusetts, Oklahoma, South Carolina, and Texas.

- Two examples of smaller regional networks are Amigo Broadcasting and Radio Lazer Network. Amigo Broadcasting with corporate offices in Irvine, Texas, has 12 Spanish-language radio stations, all in that state. Pending FCC approval Amigo's stations in Austin, Dallas, Waco and Laredo will be part of Border Media Partner's network. Meanwhile, Amigo Broadcasting may venture with other Spanish-language radio stations. Radio Lazer Network, owned by Alfredo Placencia and based in Oxnard, California, has seven stations in that state.[9]

In the arena of Latino public radio, the oldest and largest is Radio *Bilingüe*, based in Fresno, California.[10] It broadcasts *"Noticiero Latino,"* a weekday series of news and news bulletins, across the network's 40 stations in the United States, two in Puerto Rico and five in Mexico. The network also airs *"Línea Abierta,"* a two-hour weekday program of news, news-related interviews, debates and other information on current events.

Radio *Campesina*, with eight stations in three Western states, also is an important public radio network in the United States.[11] From its offices in Bakersfield, California, it produces a variety of programs though its main mission is educational, and it specifically targets recent immigrants from rural Mexico and Central America.

Another important avenue for dissemination of news and information via Spanish-language radio to Latinos is CNN en *Español* Radio,

---

8   See http://www.clearchannel.com/- On September 17, 2004, this company announced that it would convert 20 to 25 of its stations to Hispanic format within a year or a year and a half. Dow Jones News service item published in the *Austin American Statesman* page C3.

9   See http://www.radiolazer.com/00-S-LBC-!.htm

10 See http://www.radiobilingue.org/

11 See http://www.campesina.com/

based in Atlanta.[12] Though not a network of owned and operated stations, it produces and offers top-of-the-hour news programs to approximately 50 Spanish-language stations in the United States that subscribe to this service. It is produced exclusively for U.S. Latino audiences.

From its offices in Washington, D.C., Hispanic Radio Network (HRN) can help disseminate information to Latinos via radio.[13] The Hispanic Radio Network does not own or operate any stations. It does public relations campaigns for its federal, non-profit and corporate clients interested in reaching Latinos across the United States. It produces nine programs that are broadcast on more than 100 popular Spanish-language radio stations in this country.

Across the nation, many regional private operations and community stations offer full-time or part-time programs in Spanish. The rapid changes in this industry require that public relations and marketing specialists aiming to reach Latinos keep up-to-date documentation on the new developments in this arena.

Television

Spanish-language television has such a high following that Nielsen rating assessments show some of these stations frequently surpass their general market counterparts. For example, the number one news program in Los Angeles is on a Spanish-language station. There are more than 120 Spanish-language television stations in the United States. The two major networks are Univision and Telemundo, which respectively can reach up to 97 percent and 91 percent of the total U.S. Spanish speaking Latino households. There are other networks and independent television operations.

The Univision Television Group, which is also part of Univision Communications, Inc., is the largest Spanish-language television com-

---

12   See http://www.cnn.com/espanol/radio/index.html

13   See http://www.hrn.org/

pany.[14] The television group owns and operates 17 full power and seven low-power stations. It also works with 56 broadcast television affiliates and 1,789 cable affiliates that together provide the core distribution of the Univision Network all across the U.S.[15] TeleFutura Television Group is another branch of Univision Communications, Inc. This network owns and operates 18 full power, and 13 low-power stations; and works with 30 broadcast television affiliates and 98 cable affiliates to provide the core distribution of TeleFutura's programs nationwide.

The other major Spanish-language television enterprise is the Telemundo Communications Group.[16] In the United States, it owns and operates 14 full-power stations and nine low-power stations. It also has 32 broadcast affiliates and 450 cable and wireless systems, which together disseminate the network's programming[17] The Telemundo Communications Group also owns Telemundo Cable, composed of Mun2 in the United States, and Telemundo Internacional, covering Latin America.

A third major network emerging on the Latino television scene is Azteca America, which reaches approximately 69 percent of the Hispanic market, but mostly in the Southwest.[18] This network, owned by TV Azteca S.A. de C.V. based in Mexico City, has 33 stations transmitting or relaying its programming.

14   Univision Communications, Inc., is itself is owned primarily by A. Jerrald Perenchio, Mexico's Grupo Televisa, S.A., and Venezuela's Venevisión International Corporation. See corporate section of the company's extensive web site: http://www.univision.net/corp/en/index.jsp

15   In Puerto Rico, the Univision Television Group has one non-Univision full-power station and a program management agreement for two full-power stations.

16   Telemundo is an operating subsidiary of NBC, which is wholly owned by General Electric. See http://www.telemundo.com/telemundo/2449824/detail.html

17   In Puerto Rico, Telemundo has one full-power station. The name Telemundo stems from the station in Puerto Rico, which the network purchased early in its corporate development.

18   See http://www.aztecaamerica.com/. Because most of its programming stems directly from Mexico, this is an example of a Spanish-language TV network oriented to Latinos in terms of reaching that market in this country, but whose content is not necessarily U.S. Latino-oriented, except for some segments of news production.

In addition to the major networks, Spanish-language cable and independent television stations are proliferating. The leading cable network nationally is Galavisión, launched in 1979 to provide additional viewing options to the growing Latino population. According to owner Univision, Galavisión is the only Hispanic cable network to offer more than 50 hours of live programming per week.[19] Other local cable stations operate in large metropolitan areas with high concentrations of Latinos. Examples include CNN's NY-1 Noticias and Time Warner's channel 35 in New York City. This latter cable outlet is wildly popular for its programming from the Dominican Republic.

Today, various top general market networks are venturing into the Spanish-language markets. NBC's ownership of Telemundo is one of these ventures. Further U.S. media corporations have also made capital investments in Univisión and additional Spanish-language media companies as they venture into the Latino and Latin American markets creating Spanish-language networks and original programming. Examples of these are Time Warner's HBO Latino, The Walt Disney Company's ESPN *Deportes* and The History Channel *en español*, Fox's *"Deportes en español*," and Nickelodeon's (Viacom) "Dora The Explorer" (bilingual).

All of these networks, their partner broadcast and cable operations, as well as the independent stations feature a wide range of programs produced in the United States and in Latin America, including news, sports, variety and reality shows, sitcoms, movies, and *telenovelas* (soap operas). The audience reach for cable outlets is vast, as these are viewed in the United States and in other Spanish-speaking countries where the cable company operates.

Telenovelas are among the most popular programs on Spanish-language television. They are similar to U.S. soap operas, however *telenovelas* run only for approximately two to three months and at times can include direct references to contemporary social and political developments in the region. This is one reason why they have a wide following across social classes, age, and gender in Latino communities in

---

19   See http://www.univision.net/corp/en/galavision.jsp

the U.S., and even more so in Latin America. For marketers in particular, *telenovelas* are important sources for spokespersons, as the stars of these shows are extremely popular with Latino audiences and have significant media clout.

Daily Newspapers

Spanish-language newspapers were the original Latino media in this country. Starting with *El Misisipí* (the first Spanish-language paper launched in 1808 in New Orleans), and continuing through modern times, Latino-oriented newspapers and magazines have been serving Hispanic communities across the land. After many years of stagnation and uncertain futures, the Spanish-language newspaper and magazine industries directed to U.S. Latinos and Spanish speakers in the hemisphere are growing.

Every day, approximately 1.7 million Spanish-language newspapers are printed across the country. Their advertising revenue is growing with circulation in sharp contrast to the declining circulation of some of their English-language counterparts. Marketers spent approximately $854 million advertising in Spanish-language newspapers in 2003, up from $785 million in 2002 and $596 million in 2000.[20]

Daily Newspapers by Region[21]

The Spanish-language newspaper industry is among the most vibrant. Since 1995, the number of daily newspapers in this language and serving primarily Latinos has more than tripled. Weekly publications also have soared in numbers, circulation and the locations where they are available.

---

20   Information obtained from the National Association of Hispanic Publication's sales coordinator.

21   In this section we indicate approximate circulation numbers for the newspapers listed. These circulation figures often vary by day of the week. Likewise for the average number of pages indicated. For many daily newspapers, the Wednesday and the Friday editions have more pages as they carry more inserts and advertisements.

In the Northeast, the oldest is *El Diario-La Prensa*, which since 1913 has been serving the greater metropolitan New York City and the Latino communities in New Jersey, Connecticut and Pennsylvania.[22] This tabloid of approximately 56 pages is published daily, Monday through Sunday. Its circulation, audited by the Audit Bureau of Circulation (ABC), is 50,000. ImperMedia, LLC, currently owns *El Diario-La Prensa*.[23]

Another Spanish-language daily newspaper serving the same region is *Hoy*, launched in 1998 by the Tribune Publishing Company.[24] This tabloid newspaper runs an average of 60 pages per day for its Monday through Friday editions. In addition, it publishes a weekend edition that is heavy on marketing. Its circulation, also audited by the Audit Bureau of Circulation (ABC), is approximately 50,000.

In the Southeast, there are four Spanish-language dailies, three of them in Florida. The oldest is *Diario Las Américas*, founded, owned and published in the Miami area since 1953 by the Aguirre family.[25] This daily broadsheet paper averages 24 pages weekdays and 40 on weekends, and has a Standard Rate & Data Services (SRDS) certified[26] circulation of approximately 61,000 and 65,000 respectively.

The largest Spanish-language daily in the Miami area is *El Nuevo Herald*, a publication of the Knight Ridder Corporation since 1976.[27] Published Monday through Sunday, it is a broadsheet of approximately 48 pages with a circulation of more than 88,000 audited by ABC.

22 See Subervi-Vélez, et al., for a brief history of the paper. Since that writing, the paper has changed ownership two times. For more current information about *El Diario-La Prensa*, see the corporate website at http://www.impremedia.com/

23 See http://www.impremedia.com/

24 See http://www.holahoy.com/

25 See http://www.diariolasamericas.com/

26 Circulation figures based on Standard Rate & Data Services certification, which stem from annual sworn affidavits from the newspaper.

27 See http://www.miami.com/mld/elnuevo/contact_us/#english. This newspaper was published from 1976-1987 under the name of *El Miami Herald* and circulated at the time as an insert to *The Miami Herald*.

The newest daily in the Southeast is *El Nuevo Día-Orlando*.[28] The Ferré Family, which also own Puerto Rico's largest daily, *El Nuevo Día*, launched this tabloid in 2003. Published Monday through Friday with of an average of 48 pages by Enterprises of Puerto Rico, the Orlando edition, has a rapidly growing (but still not audited) circulation of about 25,000.

A fourth daily in this region is *La Visión*, which began operations in 2000 in Lawrenceville, Georgia.[29] CHL Communications Inc. publishes this independently owned 24-page tabloid Monday through Friday. Half of its news and information content is in Spanish, the other half in English. Its circulation is approximately 12,000.

In the North Central region, the only Spanish-language daily at the time of this writing is the Tribune Publishing Company's Chicago edition of *Hoy*. Launched in 2003, this tabloid circulates Monday through Friday.[30] On Thursdays, it provides its readers a *The Wall Street Journal* Spanish-language insert; on weekends, it distributes *Fin de Semana*, a "total market coverage product," which is light on news, but available for advertising and pitching stories, free.

On the West Coast, the oldest and largest continuously published Spanish-language daily newspaper is *La Opinión*.[31] Founded in 1926 and still operated by the Lozano family, this seven day a week broadsheet averages 60 pages and has a circulation of more than 128,000 audited by ABC. In January 2004, Lozano Enterprises and CPK Media, the owners of *El Diario-La Prensa* at the time, joined corporate efforts to create ImpreMedia as a national newspaper company. In October of the same year, ImpreMedia purchased Chicago's weekly *La Raza*.[32]

---

28   See http://www.endiorlando.com/

29   See http://www.lavisiononline.com/

30   Because the newspaper was still in a startup phase, the circulation figures were not available at this writing.

31   See http://www.laopinion.com/

32   It would not be surprising if *La Raza* converted into a daily in the near future.

The most recent addition to the dailies in this region is the Los Angeles edition of *Hoy*, which is also owned by the Tribune Company. That west coast edition tabloid averaging 48 pages was launched in March 2004 and is published only Monday through Friday.[33]

The Southwest, more specifically Texas, is the most vibrant region for daily newspapers in Spanish. There are currently at least ten full-fledged publications and more are on the way. Since 1995, Latinos in Houston have had the daily *El Día*, owned by the Budini family enterprises.[34] This is a 56-page tabloid published Monday to Saturday, with an ABC audited circulation averaging 40,000.

In the Fort Worth metropolitan area, *La Estrella*, which started as a weekly, increased its production to five days a week, Tuesday to Saturday, in early September 2003.[35] Owned by the Knight Ridder Company, this is a broadsheet 36-page publication with a Certified Audit of Circulations (CAC) audited circulation of 25,000.

The second Spanish-language daily in the Dallas-Fort Worth area is *Al Día*, launched in late September 2003 by the Bello Corporation.[36] This Monday-to-Saturday publication is a broadsheet averaging 40 pages with a yet to be officially audited circulation of approximately 40,000.[37]

One of the newest daily publication in Texas is *Rumbo*. a tabloid launched in 2004 with editions in San Antonio (distribution 25,000), Houston (distribution 35,000), and the Valley in South Texas (distribution 25,000).

33   Circulation figures for this emerging daily were not available at the time of this writing.

34   This newspaper's website is currently not operating. The paper was a broadsheet from its start but changed format in 2004.

35   See http://www.dfw.com/mld/laestrella/

36   See http://www.aldiatx.com/ The parent company also owns many other general market broadcast and print media, among them the *Dallas Morning News*."

37   Because of the recent launch of this paper, the circulation figures have yet to be fully audited.

In addition to these major metropolitan dailies, there are various Spanish-language border dailies. The oldest, published since 1926, is *El Tiempo*. This paper consists of four pages Monday through Friday and six pages on Sunday available as an insert to the *Laredo Morning Times*.[38] The ABC circulation figures for the *Laredo Morning Times* are more than 21,000 daily and 23,000 Sundays.

Another border newspaper is the broadsheet *El Nuevo Heraldo* published daily in Brownsville since 1934.[39] It is an independently circulating paper that runs an average of 24 pages Monday through Sunday, and has an ABC audited circulation of approximately 7,000 weekdays with slightly higher numbers on Wednesday and Sunday. The newest Spanish-language daily in the border region is *La Frontera*, published since July 2004 by *The Monitor* in McAllen, Texas.[40] This 18-page

Quite an Impression

Pass-along readership and the number of people within households who listen to or watch Spanish-language or other Latino media is much higher than in the general market. Hispanics households have more members than non-Hispanics ones (four people per household versus 2.9 for non-Latinos). When measuring results from a Latino media campaign, public relations professionals habitually use a higher multiplier to determine the impressions a news story generated. General-market, newspaper circulations are multiplied by 2.5 or 2.7 (depending on organization) to calculate impressions. With Latino media, multiply by 3.5.

---

38   See http://www.lmtonline.com/tiempo/tiempo.htm On Fridays, this paper also publishes a supplemental entertainment magazine *Qué Pasa*, a little over half of which is in English and the rest in Spanish.

39   See http://www.elnuevoheraldo.com/ Prior to October 2000, the paper's name was *El Heraldo de Brownsville*.

40   See http://www.themonitor.com/

broadsheet is produced Monday through Saturday, with an average circulation of 15,000.

Publication	Revenue in Millions of U.S. Dollars
1. El Nuevo Herald (Miami, daily)	93.48
2. La Opinión (Los Angeles, daily)	13.53
3. El Diario/La Prensa (New York, daily)	9.42
4. Hoy New York (daily)	7.18
5. Hoy Chicago (daily)	6.61
6. La Raza (Chicago, weekly)	3.24
7. TV y Más (Phoenix, weekly)	2.60
8. Lawndale News (Chicago, weekly)	2.40
9. Nuevo Mundo (San Jose, CA, weekly)	2.30
10. El Sentinel (Orlando, Fl, weekly)	1.71
11. Washington Hispanic (weekly)	1.47
12. Diario Las Américas (Miami, daily)	1.45
13. La Voz (Phoenix, AZ, weekly)	1.40
14. Al Día (Dallas, daily)	1.26
15. La Nación U.S.A. (Arlington, VA)	1.26
16. Prensa Hispana (Phoenix, weekly)	1.20
17. Excelsior (Orange County, CA, weekly)	1.08
18. El Latino (San Diego, weekly)	1.03
19. La Voz (Houston, weekly)	1.01
20. Mundo LA (Los Angeles, weekly)	1.00

Table 22 - Top Twenty Spanish-Language Newspapers According to Advertising Revenues

Top Twenty Spanish-language Newspapers

Table 22 shows the top 20 Spanish-language newspapers, according to ad revenues in U.S. dollars during January-April 2004:[41]

Weeklies

In addition to these daily newspapers, hundreds of weekly newspapers are published for Latinos across the country. Some weeklies have been published for many decades; others are new ventures. A few are community-based or grass-root advocacy newspapers produced by individuals and families for whom community information and activism takes precedence over financial gains. Individuals and companies, some affiliated with general market media, for which commercial profits are the main goal of the business, publish other weeklies. Many of those weekly publications have a strong following at community levels, and cover a wide range of topics and issues from local events to news from their readers' home countries.

Because the list is too long to include even succinctly in these pages, the reader should consult the resources mentioned later in this chapter. Those sources regularly publish updated lists of most of these weekly publications. For the full list of all the publications in a particular community, consult more than one source. Even then, additional inquiries may be necessary to learn about any newly launched paper not included in those directories.

Supplements and Inserts

Another way to reach Latinos via printed media in Spanish is the regularly published supplements and inserts that cover a variety of topics or specific themes. In recent years, there has been a proliferation of these publications, which are distributed in and by top daily and weekly

---

41   Source: TNS Media Intelligence/CMR, a company that provides advertising expenditure information, trends and insights. See http://www.tnsmi-cmr.com/

Title	Freq.	Circulation	Content	Language
Fútbol Mundial (Sensación Marketing)	Monthly	1,000,000	Soccer news	Spanish, some English
MLB en español (MLB Properties)	3 times per year	1,100,000	Baseball news	Spanish, some English
Nueva Salud (Laureti Media, Papel Media)	Quarterly	1,500,000	Health information	Spanish
NYP Tempo (New York Post)	Monthly	678,012	Youth-oriented news, entertainment	English some Spanish
Sobre Ruedas (Magazines Publications)	Monthly	650,000	Automotive news	Spanish
Wall Street Journal en español (Dow Jones)	Weekly	350,000	Business & finance	Spanish
Vista (Hispanic Publishing Corporation)	Monthly	1,000,000	Culture, leaders	Bilingual

Table 23 - Spanish-Language Newspapers and Supplements

newspapers. Some of the supplements and inserts are placed in general market newspapers; others are placed in newspapers destined only to the Latino neighborhoods. *Vista* magazine, a bilingual publication based in Miami, was the first supplement of this kind.[42] Launched 20 years ago, it is currently the most widely recognized publication of this type in the country.

Table 23 shows a few of the main Spanish-language newspaper supplements and inserts, the publishing company (indicated in parenthesis), frequency, circulation, main content, and language. For

---

42   See http://www.vistamagazine.com/ In addition to being an insert in selected newspapers, *Vista* is also distributed via subscriptions.

information about the circulation and distribution of these, which is subject to change, see the respective publication's website.[43]

Magazines and Other Periodicals

Spanish-language magazines circulating in the United States are too numerous to list in these pages. They run the whole spectrum of topics from the serious to light, from highbrow to lowbrow, from religious to outright sexual and outlandish. Many of those magazines are published in the United States with Latinos as the main audience, such as *People en Español* (Spanish-language) and *Latina* (bilingual), the largest Hispanic magazines in the country.

Others are distributed throughout Latin America and the United States, with different versions tailored to each market. For many of these magazines, the U.S. Latinos are a complementary or secondary market. Examples include *Selecciones del Reader's Digest* (which has a special U.S. Spanish-language edition), *Vanidades, Mecánica Popular, Cosmopolitan en español, Marie Claire en español, Harper's Bazaar en español, National Geographic en español, Men's Health en Español,* and *Playboy en español.* Still others are Conde Nast's *Vogue en español, Glamour en español, Men's Fitness en español,* and *Architectural Digest en español.*

Many media corporations, who recognize the importance and power of the Spanish language, have extended their brand equity by keeping their general-market media names. For a complete list of these magazines, their owners, advertising rates, main audiences and circulation, consult the resources mentioned later in this chapter.

---

43   Publication websites: *Nueva Salud* http://www.nuevasalud.com/ NYP Tempo http://www.nypost.com/tempo/ Wall Street Journal in Español http://www.online.wsj.com/public/page/0,,2_0137,00.html?mod=2_0137 *Vista* http://www.vistamagazine.com/

The Internet

The Internet clearly is another important avenue of communication with Latino audiences. Hispanics are rapidly embracing the Internet and have become the fastest-growing online community today. Several companies have invested in quantitative and qualitative research that validates this claim. According to winter 2004 Media Metrix research, more than 14 million Latinos have access to the Internet, and that number is on the rise. Latinos are more avid Internet users than the general U.S. market, spending 9 percent longer online and viewing 15 percent more Web pages.[44]

The 2004 Annual American Online/Roper ASW U.S. Hispanic Cyberstudy found that Hispanics recognize the value the Internet brings them and are quickly making its tools and features part of their daily lives. Based on the study, Hispanics use the Internet far more frequently than the general online population to listen to music (54 percent versus 30 percent), purchase a car (6 percent versus 2 percent) and communicate via instant messaging (64 percent versus 48).[45]

As with other media vehicles, Hispanic online tools have been increasing with the growth and influence of the population. Following is a list of the top Spanish-language portals that include search engines, as well as general news, entertainment, sports, and lifestyle:

AOL Latino:	aollatino.com
MSN Latino:	latino.msn.com
StarMedia:	us.starmedia.com
Terra:	terra.com
Univision:	univision.com
Yahoo En *Español*:	espanol.yahoo.com

---

44   ComScore Media Metrix, the audience measurement division of comScore Networks, a global information provider and consultancy to which leading companies turn for consumer behavior insight. .http://www.comscore.com

45   AOL Latino is a leading Internet service provider for U.S. Hispanics. RoperASW, a leading global marketing research and consulting firm.

These portals target the universe of Spanish-speaking consumers, though most include U.S. versions with tailored information. In addition to the portals, there are numerous websites featuring a variety of topics (e.g., health, automotive, finance, etc) and targeting different Latino segments (e.g., youth, professionals, and women). Many newspapers, television and radio media outlets have websites with information on programming. Depending on the story, these portals and websites are useful tools for marketers to further communicate a story and reinforce messages consumers hear and read about offline.

Latino media: Commerce, Style and Youth

In addition to the innumerable Spanish-language Latino media, there also are many English-language media specifically directed toward U.S. Latino audiences.

What is a Blog?

A new trend in marketing, blogs or "web logs" are websites compiled by marketing professionals to offer information about and insight into new trends. These can be great sources for communication professionals. Blogs can highlight a trend to which to link a story, making it more newsworthy, culturally relevant and therefore more likely to be placed. Many Hispanic marketers are using blogs to stay up with trends, read the perspective of others in the industry, and stay connected. A good blog is Juan Tornoe's Hispanic Trending,[46] a daily information source of issues within the Hispanic community from his perspective and the perspectives of others in the industry. Some marketers connect with bloggers and help shape perception to communicate a message to its audience. A blog is a good source to reach the professional Hispanic or to hear the opinion of some thought leaders.

---

46   See http://juantornoe.blogs.com/hispanictrending/

Targeting Acculturated Audiences and Professionals

Acculturated Hispanic adults are a growing and stable demographic. For many years, several outlets have targeted this influential professional Latino group in business and politics. The topics of the media directed to them vary, but always reflect issues important to them such as current affairs, business and politics.

Television and Cable

"Hispanics Today," since 1999 produced monthly and now weekly by the U.S. Hispanic Chambers of Commerce, is a nationally syndicated half-hour English-language television show that highlights issues related to business, entertainment, politics, culture, lifestyle and sports.[47]

Publications

There are no English-language daily newspapers specifically directed to U.S. Latinos in any city or region. However, there are a few English-language periodicals and various magazines. Much like any professional or networking group, Latinos follow English-language publications to stay connected and informed of opportunities and new developments in business and politics.

The *Hispanic Link Weekly Report* is a national news weekly that covers Hispanic issues and trends.[48] Although not a newspaper or magazine per se, it is one of the nation's most influential English-language sources of news and information about Latinos and Latino issues. Published in Washington, D.C., since 1983 by Charlie Erickson and his family, this eight-page newsletter is packed with succinct sum-

---

47   See http://www.ushcc.com/hisp_today_tv.htm

48   See http://www.hispaniclink.org/ Hispanic Link is also a news service that syndicates opinion, analysis and feature columns to newspapers and magazines throughout the Americas through the Los Angeles Times Syndicate.

maries of the major issues and events related to Latinos and Latino policy.

The major English-language business magazines include *Hispanic* owned by Hispanic Publishing Corporation and published since 1988,[49] *Hispanic Business* published in Santa Barbara, California, by Hispanic Business, Inc. since 1979,[50] and the more recent *Latino Leader* and *Hispanic Trade.*

Most public relations and marketing trade publications in print or on-line are in English or bilingual. These are useful sources for communication professionals trying to stay informed about Latino audiences.

Examples include:

- *Hispanic Market Weekly*
- *Hispanic PR Monitor* (the trade newsletter of the HPRW)
- *Hispanicad.com*[51]
- *Hispanic Target*[52]
- *Marketing y Medios*[53]
- *InterAccion*, a newsletter published three times a year since 1996 by the nonprofit Hispanic Marketing and Communication Association provides Hispanic marketing information. Complimentary subscriptions are available through the association website at www.hmca.org.

---

49   See http://www.hispaniconline.com/magazine/

50   See http://www.hispanicbusiness.com

51   See http://www.hispanicad.com

52   See http://www.reporterinformativo.com.ar/target/

53   See http://www.marketingymedios.com

Among the English-language publications geared to the young adult and professional female, we can list *Latina Style*[54] published in Washington, D.C., since 1994, and *Latina*.[55]

Targeting Bilingual, Bicultural Youth

The Hispanic youth market is the fastest-growing youth demographic in the nation. The exponential growth of this market is well recognized in media outlets from television to magazines. In the past few years, several outlets have been launched, all vying for the attention of the young, bicultural, bilingual and professional Latino.

Though topics vary by media outlet, most programming reflects issues important to this demographic, including music, entertainment, lifestyle, and current affairs, mostly communicated in English, Spanish, or sometimes "Spanglish."

Television and Cable

Already mentioned in a previous section were Telemundo's Mun2, and Univisión's TeleFutura. Two new emerging networks are SíTV and Voy Network. SíTV, launched in February 2004, is geared specifically to English-speaking Latinos, and to crossover audiences.[56] This network with "Latino vibe and multicultural appeal" is currently available via DISH satellite and on select cable systems. The Voy Network is a lifestyle cable channel "targeting the acculturated, English-speaking Latin audience and those discovering Latin culture."[57] Additional tele-

---

54   See http://www.latinastyle.com

55   See http://www.latina.com

56   See http://www.sitiv.com

57   See http://www.voy.tv The company that is developing Voy TV also has ventures in Latino music, books, pictures, and a non-profit foundation. See the "What is Voy" section of the website.

vision efforts include Urban Latino TV,[58] and American Latino TV,[59] nationally syndicated programs that celebrate American and Latino culture in the United States. An education-oriented outlet is the Hispanic Information & Telecommunications Network, Inc[60]. It was established as a non-profit organization to provide a network of non-commercial telecommunications facilities to help advance the educational, social, cultural and economic aspirations of Hispanics in the U.S. and Puerto Rico.

Publications

The magazines directed to this group are constantly emerging and growing. Examples include *Urban Latino,*[61] and *Urban Sofrito* (a monthly supplement of *Diario-La Prensa*),[62] *I Caramba U* oriented to Latino college students,[63] and the music themed *Batanga,*[64] *¡Boom!-nación alterlatina,*[65] and *La Banda Elástica.*[66]

---

58   See http://www.urbanlatino.com/ultv/ultv_home.html

59   See http://www.americanlatino.tv/

60   See http://www.hitn.org

61   See http://www.urbanlatino.com

62   See http://www.eldiariony.com/suplementos/sofrito/index.aspx

63   See http://www.icarambau.com/magazine/

64   See http://www.batanga.com/sp/magazine/

65   See http://www.boomonline.com

66   See http://www.labandaelastica.com/magazine/home/home.cfm

Internet

There are many new Internet sites directed to English-speaking and/or bilingual Latino youth, including:

- Latinitasmagazine.org, a bilingual webzine and organization launched in 2002 to empower Latino adolescents and teenagers though media and technology[67]
- Bilingual sites dedicated to inform about and promote Latino music and artists[68] lamusica.com and musicalatina.com
- Migente.com and iCaramba.com, subscription-based chat rooms for Latino youth[69]

There are many Latino-oriented media of various types, from print to broadcast to Internet sites, in Spanish, English or in both languages side by side. Learning more about the particular characteristics of these media, including their locations, content, audiences, and other operational matters will be profitable for public relations and marketing professionals, as well as students aspiring to work for these media or to work for companies that will have to do business with these media.

Resources

Because there are thousands of Latino media outlets, we cannot list all of them in these pages. Following is an abridged list of resources, in alphabetical order:

Association of Hispanic Advertising Agencies (AHAA): The mission of AHAA is to grow, strengthen and protect the Hispanic marketing and advertising industry by providing leadership in raising awareness of the value of the Hispanic market opportunities and en-

---

67 See http://www.latinitasmagazine.org/ This magazine and non-profit community based organization in Austin, Texas, has its genesis in a class project under the mentorship of the first author of this chapter when he was a professor at the University of Texas at Austin.

68 See respectively http://www.lamusica.com and http://www.musicalatina.com

69 See respectively http://www.migente.com and http://www.icaramba.com

hancing the professionalism of the industry. AHAA has extensive lists of Hispanic media outlets and current ad revenues.[70]

Bacon's: Develops comprehensive books of media contacts in the United States. The company also has the capability of monitoring U.S. media and evaluating results through quantitative and qualitative methodologies. While Bacon's has made strides to cover the burgeoning Hispanic media, it is a general market service that only includes top-tier Hispanic media.[71]

Burrelle's: A monitoring service that includes print, broadcast, news wires and the Internet. Like Bacon's, Burrrelle's is a comprehensive general market media monitoring service that only incorporates top-tier Hispanic media.[72]

HispanicAd.com: Launched in 1999, HispanicAd.com provides news and information, including photos and data from the U.S., Latin America and the Caribbean. It is owned and operated by Hispanic Media Sales, Inc.[73]

Hispanic Market Weekly (HMW): Provides news, research, and information about Hispanic media and marketing. The online version of this magazine has a directory of all national and regional accounts and brands active in the U.S. Hispanic market with a direct reference to the advertising agency that handles each account and the assignment for each agency.[74]

Hispanic Marketing & Communication Association (HMCA): Established in 1996, the Hispanic Marketing & Communication Association is a national volunteer driven nonprofit professional association

---

70   See http://www.ahaa.org/

71   See http://www.bacons.com/

72   See http://www.burrellesluce.com/

73   See http://www.hispanicad.com/

74   See http://www.hispanicmarket.net/

dedicated to Hispanic marketing excellence. The Association provides networking opportunities for practitioners in marketing, advertising, media, public relations, and other communication fields who have an interest in the Hispanic market. Through its website, roundtables, seminars, and conferences HMCA provides forums to discuss interesting, timely issues, and encourage professional development.

Hispanic PR Wire (HPRW): A news distribution service reaching U.S. Hispanic media, organizations and opinion leaders nationwide. This company features a menu of Hispanic media circuits that includes the options of national, state and U.S.-based pan regional Latin America distributions.[75]

Hispanic Public Relations Association (HPRA): Founded in 1984, HPRA strives to be a resource for communication professionals and for those seeking insights into the Hispanic market. This regional organization has more than 150 members representing public relations, marketing and advertising professionals from agencies, government, non-profit and corporate companies.[76]

Independent Spanish Broadcasters Association (ISBA): A collaborative group of independent Spanish-language broadcasters and networks whose mission is to pursue ownership opportunities and capital sources amidst industry consolidation, and help expand media employment and management opportunities for Latinos. The 13 founding companies own roughly 20 television and 40 radio stations as well as Spanish-language radio networks.

L-Watch: A web-based Spanish-language clipping service created by Reporte Informativo (reporteinformativo.com) and PR Newswire (prnewswire.com). L-Watch processes and classifies Spanish-language print and on-line news articles published in the U.S., Latin America and the Spanish-speaking Caribbean.[77]

---

75   See http://www.hispanicprwire.com/

76   See http://www.hprala.org

77   See http://www.l-watchreport.com/

LatinClips: A web-based media monitoring service capturing news daily from 350 U.S. Hispanic, 900 Latin American, 70 Caribbean sources, 65 U.S. Black media as well as more than 5,000 U.S. general market online sources. LatinClips[78] tracks online, dailies, weeklies, semi-weeklies, monthlies, wire services and portals.

Latino Print Network (LPN): Founded in 1996, is the oldest and largest Hispanic owned Hispanic print rep firm in the U.S.A. The company has a database of Hispanic publications in the U.S.A., with over 1,550 publications, including, editorial sections, circulation, audit status, format, frequency, day of publication and key staff members.[79]

Latinos and Media Project (LAMP): Serves as a guiding light for information and resources about a variety of issues related to Latinos and the media. It contains an annotated and searchable bibliography of over 300 items related to Latinos and the news media. It is most valuable for academics and students developing research in this field and on this topic.[80]

National Association of Hispanic Journalists (NAHJ): Established in April 1984, NAHJ is dedicated to the recognition and professional advancement of Hispanics in the news industry. The organization has approximately 2,300 members, including working journalists, journalism students, other media-related professionals and journalism educators.[81]

National Association of Hispanic Publications (NAHP): A non-profit organization with a membership of over 200 publications throughout the United States. These publications combined have a circulation of over 12 million, produce over 15 billion pages of information annually and reach over 50 percent of the Hispanic households on a

---

78   See http://www.latinclips.com/

79   See http://www.latinoprintnetwork.com/

80   See http://www.latinosandmedia.org/ Additional annotated and searchable bibliographies about Latinos and entertainment media and Latinos and advertising will be added in subsequent years.

81   See http://www.nahj.org/

weekly basis. The Association recently published a media kit and resource book.[82]

New Generation Latino Consortium (NGLC): Launched in January 2003, this organization with an informational website has as its primary goal raising the marketing profile of a burgeoning, yet underserved segment of the U.S. Hispanic population: predominantly U.S. born second, third and fourth generation Latinos who consume mostly English-language media and represent more than $300 billion in purchasing power.[83]

National Hispanic Media Coalition (NHMC): A nonprofit coalition of Hispanic organizations that have joined together to address a variety of media related issues that affect the U.S Hispanic community across the nation.[84]

Standard Rate and Data Service (SRDS): In operation for over 85 years, this company's database of media rates and information is the largest and most comprehensive in the world containing more than 100,000 U.S. and international media properties, including Spanish-language media in the U.S. and abroad. The SRDS Media Solutions also provides media planning and list rental information for advertising and direct marketing.[85]

Video Monitoring Service (VMS): This company records and monitors thousands of hours of television and radio broadcast news in over 100 top U.S. and international markets. Video Monitoring Service operates 16 full-service offices and two monitoring centers in major cities throughout the U.S. Company staff monitor select Spanish-

82   See https://www.nahp.org/

83   For more information, visit http://nglc.com/

84   See http://www.nhmc.org/

85   See http://www.srds.com

language national television programs and some local programs in top Latino markets.[86]

None of these sources provides a fully comprehensive list of the Latino periodicals or magazines. Some directories include entries only for the companies that purchase space in their pages. Not all newspapers or magazines publish space in every directory. For example, the NAHP's directory does not include, among other well-known print media, Miami's *Diario Las Américas.*

Communicating Your Story to Latino Media

Once communication professionals have an understanding of Latino markets and media, the next step is to reach out to the Latino audience through Latino media. Below is a short guide to help practitioners in these efforts.

Seven Steps to Success with Latino Media

1. Do your research

Although research is paramount to any communications campaign, it is even more essential to multicultural marketing. It is imperative to know your target audience to make a story relevant to them. This is not always easy as Latinos are highly diverse. Depending on what you are trying to communicate, you may need to reach one or more Hispanic market segments, such as Dominican or Mexican or youth. Doing your homework before you pick up the phone will ensure that you can answer reporters' questions about the importance of your story to Latino communities.

2. Tailor your messages

Once you have completed your research, integrate your findings into key messages. Follow the example of the pharmaceutical company's obesity awareness campaign mentioned earlier in the chapter. Rather

---

86   See http://www.vmsinfo.com/

than creating general messages about obesity in America, the company presented facts about the number of Latinos struggling with obesity or obesity-related complications such as diabetes or cardiovascular ailments.

3. Use the right spokesperson

A credible spokesperson is always the best communicator. Spanish-speaking Latino doctors are the most trusted to talk about health issues, for example. Latinos are the best spokespersons for Latino audiences, but as Latinos are not homogenous, it is important to find the right spokesperson for your target audience. For example, a young Latino is ideal to address issues facing Latino youth. Also, Puerto Rican communities will relate best to a Puerto Rican spokesperson. If it is not possible to get a Latino spokesperson, it is doubly important to make sure that your spokesperson's messages are tailored and culturally sensitive to your target audience.

4. Build relationships with Latino reporters

As family and relationships are important to Latinos, it makes sense that they are equally vital to Latino media. When a Latino journalist knows a communication professional and trusts his or her judgment, that reporter usually is more receptive to his or her ideas. It is important to build and maintain relationships with Latino journalists.

5. Reach multiple media genres

Even with limited budgets, communication professionals should reach out to multiple Latino media outlets. This is because Latinos get information from multiple sources, and are more likely than the general market to discuss what they hear or read with family and friends. For example, a teenager who reads information about a new product on the Internet is likely to talk about that product with his or her parents. Reaching out across media genres, even if you target just a few of each type, will help ensure a wide audience receives your messages.

6. Pitch stories in Spanish whenever possible and appropriate

Since the vast majority of Latinos are more comfortable speaking Spanish, it makes sense to serve their needs and communicate information in their preferred language. In some cases, it is necessary, such as for Spanish-language television B-roll (background video) or video news releases. Other times, pitching stories in Spanish is not necessary, though doing so demonstrates a cultural sensitivity and helps build a connection with Latino journalists. For English-language media, it is more appropriate to pitch stories in English.

7. Consider enlisting the help of Latino marketing specialists

There are a growing number of public relations, advertising and marketing firms specializing in Latino audiences. Many large agencies also have divisions that focus solely on multicultural marketing. These organizations already have long-term relationships with journalists, are abreast of the latest developments with Latino media and have the Spanish-language skills to communicate your stories. These professionals can help you reach target markets and avoid making mistakes.

Case Study

Acuvue Contact Lenses

When Johnson & Johnson marketers wanted to promote their Acuvue brand contact lenses directly to Latino consumers, Edelman Diversity Solutions knew the task required more than placing Spanish-language advertisements. Before Acuvue could gain brand recognition, it had to become relevant to Latino audiences. This was accomplished in several steps: First, by creating targeted information; then, selecting the right spokespersons. Finally, these spokespersons delivered information through multiple media outlets and community events.

Targeted information

When Acuvue decided to promote its contact lenses, it discovered that there was not much Spanish-language information about general eye health. In order for consumers to make an informed decision about whether contact lenses may help them, they need to have some basic knowledge about eye care. Edelman's first job was to fill this information void by creating an awareness campaign. The company did this by building on and tailoring existing information to address health and cultural issues specific to the Latino community. Brochures, information kits and a website included information about eye problems common among Latinos, and a toll-free number was established with Spanish-speaking representatives. The previous lack of information also helped position eye health issues as a long overlooked subject in the Latino community. This made the story newsworthy, and seeded the marketplace to receive more information.

Relevant Spokespersons

Acuvue enlisted the help of and media trained Latino eye care professionals in major Hispanic markets. These doctors speak Spanish and are accustomed to talking to Latinos about eye care issues, creating a foundation for trust, which opened the door to effective communication.

Multiple media outlets

Edelman enlisted "spokes-doctors" went on local market media tours to talk about eye health in six top Hispanic markets, including Los Angeles, New York and Houston. Media tours generated extensive coverage, including a live spot on Telemundo's national morning show, *"De Mañanita,"* as well as features on CNN *en español*. Radio coverage included BBC Radio Latinoamerica and Hispanic Broadcasting Corporation. Print media also were targeted, and stories that quoted spokes-doctors were featured in leading Spanish-language dailies and long-lead magazines, such as *Men's Health en Español* and *Marie Claire en Español*. Internet coverage was high, with yupi.com and Terra.com using Acuvue B-roll as streaming video. Finally, the campaign itself was watched closely in the communications industry, and stories were written about it in *Hispanic Market Weekly* and "Marketing to the Emerging Majority." The newsworthiness of Acuvue's story was heightened by creating action steps for consumers, such as attending eye health seminars at well-known Hispanic festivals and calling toll-free numbers for consumers to get more information.

Community involvement

The company's sponsorship of and presence at major Latino festivals such as Calle Ocho in Miami and Fiesta Broadway in Los Angeles generated a lot of the media buzz in Acuvue's campaign. Acuvue leveraged large turnout at these events to disseminate important health information, and have a little fun. In addition to health seminars, Acuvue promoted its new line of color contact lenses with a Web simulator that allowed consumers to see photos of themselves with various eye colors. These images were kept online so people could go to Acuvue's website after the festivals and show their pictures to family and friends. This helped drive traffic to Acuvue's website after the event. This cross-promotional program generated more than 82 million impressions, and won the 2003 *PR Week* Multicultural Campaign of the Year.

Chapter Summary

- The Latino population is the fastest-growing minority and ethnic group in the United States.
- They represent an audience that cannot be ignored.
- One of the main ways to reach Latinos in the United States is through Latino media, an important source of information for this community. When doing so, keep in mind that:
  - A "one size fits all" approach does not work.

- As the Latino population becomes increasingly diverse, audiences are changing and the growth and evolution of Latino media outlets reflect these changes.
- There are many Spanish-language media in the U.S.
- Many, but not all, of those media have U.S. Latinos as their main audience.
- All information should speak to Latinos directly, highlighting news relevant to Latino communities and families.
- Direct translation of English, general-market information is not as effective and can lead to major gaffes with the intended message.
- Finding culturally appropriate spokespersons is paramount, as is providing information in Spanish whenever possible.
- Communication professionals must stay informed about issues affecting Latino communities and the changing media environment.
- Doing so will help ensure that marketing messages are conveyed in a relevant, culturally sensitive manner.

About the Authors

Federico Subervi, Ph.D., Professor, School of Journalism and Mass Communication Texas State University, San Marcos Director, The Latinos and Media Project

Federico Subervi directs the Latinos and Media Project, an emerging non-profit organization dedicated to the gathering and dissemination of research and resources pertaining to Latinos and the media. For over twenty years, he has been teaching, conducting research, and publishing on issues pertaining to the mass media and ethnic groups, especially Latinos in the United States. He is currently finishing a book on mass media and Latino politics and teaching at Texas State University, San Marcos.

Heidi Eusebio, Vice President, Edelman

Hidekel (Heidi) Eusebio is vice president at Edelman, the world's largest independent public relations firm. She has more than 10 years of experience in marketing communications. Heidi manages Edelman's national Hispanic marketing practice, and specializes in Hispanic media relations, consumer and event marketing, healthcare communications, and advocacy relations. Heidi's current responsibilities include developing marketing strategies and managing the implementation of programs targeted at the U.S. Hispanic market on behalf of a variety of clients. Heidi holds a Bachelor of Arts in Sociology and minors in Political Science and Spanish Literature from New York University.

Chapter Twelve

Electronic Publicity and Broadcast Public Relations

David Henry

In This Chapter

- Tools to reach television, radio and Internet news programming
- Most effective ways to implement and employ these tools
- How to best employ these tools to reach Latinos in the United States via Spanish-language broadcast media

Introduction

Electronic publicity or broadcast public relations utilize certain tools that allow an organization to get its story effectively on television, radio and Internet news programming. This chapter will address the various tools used to reach these media and the most effective ways to implement and use those tools. It will focus on the U.S. Hispanic market and how to best use these tools to reach Latinos via Spanish-language broadcast media.

Many different surveys have shown that the majority of people in the United States get their news from television. Broadcast media can be the most effective way to reach the most people with your organization's news. Reaching out to broadcast outlets is significantly different than reaching out to print outlets. One needs to utilize and implement the right tools to engage these media effectively. Done properly, the results can be fantastic.

Electronic publicity or broadcast public relations is the art of pitching and placing stories on television and radio news outlets. More specifically, it involves assessing the news environment at these various outlets, developing and creating the appropriate messages and content, and utilizing the most appropriate tools to deliver those messages and content to the media.

The purpose of broadcast public relations is to give the broadcast journalist your story information in their medium. As one gives a press release (words) to a print journalist, one needs to give video to a television journalist and audio to a radio journalist. One could give print, video and/or audio to an Internet news site, depending on its format and capabilities. All of the tools and information in this chapter are targeted to getting your (or your client's) message onto broadcast news outlets.

Broadcast Versus Print Publicity and Media Relations

While the underlying principles of pitching broadcast media are similar to print media, there are immense differences that make pitching broadcast media quite dissimilar to print. First, and most obvious, is that each medium relies on a different format to reach its readers, viewers or listeners. When reaching out to print media, one needs to send press releases and other material in print form. Written words are the medium.

When pitching television, a press release may prove ineffective. Television uses video to tell its stories. To engage television reporters and producers effectively, one needs to provide compelling video that tells a story and engages the viewer. Similarly, one needs to provide compelling audio to radio stations. It is also important to determine the best means of delivering that video and audio to the stations. A variety of factors can influence the choice of the delivery vehicle.

Like a press release, one must have some kind of "news" in order to make broadcast public relations effective. There has to be some element of the story that is new. Once we decide to distribute our news to television news outlets, there are a few more things to consider.

First, one has to consider the typical television news audience. This audience is, in general terms, made up of consumers. Therefore, only stories that have some relation to the consumer and general public will be effective. For example, stories about products, services, businesses, or legislation that directly affect or touch the general consumer would be appropriate for one of the many broadcast public relations (PR) tools. A product or service sold by one business to another business (business-to-business or B-to-B) is generally not a story that would play well on television news, as it does not directly affect the consumer audience.

Elements of a Good Broadcast Story

Key Elements for a Good Broadcast Story Are:

- *A consumer angle*
- *A news hook or tie-in to news*
- *Human interest (health, kids, money, etc.)*
- *Highly qualified expert sound bites*
- *Cannot be promotional … It's not an advertisement*

It is highly recommended that one spend time studying the various broadcast media to understand the types of stories each covers, how they cover them, what elements they use to communicate those stories and the style in which they communicate the stories. There will be differences between national, cable and local news. There will also be differences between cities or television markets.

One must take into account the kind of news that typically airs on those television outlets. Usually, stations are interested in news about health, money, family and children. When taking the U.S. Hispanic market and Spanish-language television news into consideration, one needs to delve a bit further. The general market English-language media cover news that affects all people in the United States. Spanish-language media has one focus, the U.S. Hispanic population. In the case of the local market station, its focus is the local Latino population.

Spanish-language Broadcast Media

Spanish-language stations continue to mature and grow. There are currently more than 120 television stations with Spanish-language news programming in the U.S., compared to the 700-800 English-language stations in the U.S. with news programming. Many Spanish-language stations are among the top stations in their respective markets. For example, the number one television newscast in the Los Angeles market is from a Spanish-language station.

Moreover, several Telemundo and Univision stations (the two main Spanish-language networks) had the top newscasts in their markets during 2005 rating periods. According to the Nielsen Station Index, Univision stations in New York, Los Angeles, Miami and Phoenix out-paced their English-language and Spanish-language competitors during the November 2003 sweeps, achieving greater year-over-year household ratings growth across the entire broadcast day than any other station in those markets.

In addition, according to studies by Horowitz Associates, a New York-based research company, Hispanic urban households watch more television than Asian and white households do. At the same time, Spanish-language television is growing and getting more attention. It has become popular with many Fortune 500 companies. Advertisers like Pepsi, Ford Motor Company, the Walt Disney Company, Nabisco and many other consumer products companies have fully embraced this powerful market.

Univision and Telemundo

Univision and Telemundo are the two major Spanish-language broadcast television networks in the U.S. The vast majority of local Spanish-language stations in the U.S. are affiliated with one of these networks. Univision and Telemundo respectively reach 97 percent and 91 percent of the total U.S. Hispanic market. Both networks provide an extensive line-up of programming produced in the United States and throughout Latin America. Programming includes news and information, sports, movies, children's shows and cartoons, comedies, talk and variety shows and *novelas* or soap operas. Univision also owns the TeleFutura network, a 24-hour broadcast network with programming distinct from Univision and Telemundo. Telemundo is a subsidiary of NBC and General Electric. Telemundo also owns the Mun2 network, a bilingual network aimed at Latino youth with original programming and video mix shows. Mun2 programming is decidedly different from any other Spanish-language network.

A third network is making headway in the U.S. In the past two years, Azteca America has grown to cover 78 percent of the U.S. Hispanic market and is growing quickly. TV Azteca, the largest broadcaster in Mexico, owns Azteca America.

How are Spanish-language Broadcast Media Different?

1. Los Angeles	10. Brownsville - McAllen, TX
2. New York	11. San Diego
3. Miami, Ft Lauderdale	12. Fresno - Visalia, CA
4. Chicago	13. Sacramento - Stockton-Modesto
5. Houston	14. El Paso, TX
6. San Francisco, Oakland, San Jose	15. Albuquerque - Santa Fe
7. Dallas - Ft. Worth	16. Denver
8. San Antonio	17. Philadelphia
9. Phoenix	18. Washington, DC

Table 24 - Top Twenty Hispanic Markets

There are many similarities in how Spanish-language and general market, English-language media work. The same tools are used to reach Spanish-language and general market media. The dissimilarities make all the difference in ultimate results. It is imperative that one understand how Spanish-language media differ from other media in order to be successful.

One of the most obvious differences is that U.S. Spanish-language media have a specific audience, Hispanics in the United States. They cover stories that have an impact on U.S. Hispanics. General market media must keep the entire U.S. population in mind when covering news. Spanish-language stations are primarily focused on the Hispanic population. Though this may seem like an obvious observation, it has implications on the kinds of news the stations will cover. With that said, Spanish-language stations are looking for news stories and issues that directly affect Hispanics in their respective markets.

It is also important to understand cultural differences and nuances when pursuing Spanish-language broadcast news. For instance, the footage one shoots to send to these stations needs to show images consistent with the audience. In order to save money, many organizations try to use the same footage they shot for a general market story, recycled for a Spanish-language story. Unfortunately, this usually does not work. The problem that often arises is that the people in the existing footage are not representative of the Hispanic audience. In most cases, there are no Latinos in the footage at all! The settings may differ from those found in Hispanic communities. If the footage shows images not common to the average Latino, it will be harder for them to identify and relate to the story. Stations may decide against airing the story simply because the footage is not culturally sensitive or appropriate.

Another difference between mainstream media and Spanish-language media is the size of the staffs in the newsroom. The budgets at most local-market English-language network affiliates are substantially higher than at the local Spanish-language stations. In most cases, this is because these are better-established stations that garner higher ratings and, more revenue, though this may not be the case in all markets. Obviously, this allows these stations more effective staffing. Spanish-language stations, with smaller budgets, have to get the same amount of work and reporting done, usually with less staff. This means that producers and reporters are usually multi-tasking and do not have much time to take pitch calls. This can present a challenge when trying to get your story on the news.

Challenges in Reaching Spanish Language Media

There are some inherent challenges in reaching out to Spanish-language media. They are not unlike mainstream media, though they may be a bit more obvious. First, most stations will not have the same size staff as their mainstream media counterparts. This means that news staff have more responsibilities and perhaps more than one function. That translates into less time to deal with everything, including you! While you can usually feel the weight of a deadline anytime you talk to a reporter, you will usually hear it more at a station with a small staff. It is important to have all of your ducks in a row before you approach the station. It will also be helpful if you have prepared everything to make that reporter's job as easy a possible.

Second, it may take longer to get your story on the air. With most mainstream television news outlets, you have a finite time to pitch the story and get on the air before the story is considered old news. With Spanish-language media, it may take many phone calls just to get through to your contact and several more to be able to get a decision on whether they will use the story.

Before You Approach Spanish Language Media

It is important to know what these stations are looking for before you pitch a story. First, Spanish-language media are looking for materials in Spanish. While there are instances in which they use English-language video footage and dub a Spanish-language voice over the footage, this is not their preference. Spanish-language radio stations insist on material in Spanish. Second, understand the station (or network), the program, and its audience. Do they use outside material? If so, how?

Translating from English to Spanish has its challenges. A direct English to Spanish translation will often result in a document that does not convey the same messages and meaning as the original document. In the cases that it conveys the messaging and meaning, it may not be in a tone appropriate for the audience. When working with an English document adapt it to Spanish. This means you are adapting the mes-

SURVEY OF SPANISH-LANGUAGE TELEVISION STATIONS

Do Spanish-Language stations VNRs/B-roll Packages? . . . . . . Yes   100%

Do VNRs and soundbites need to be in Spanish? . . . . Yes   88%
        No   12%

Would Spanish-Language stations use soundbites in English? . . No   59%
        Yes   41%

Should a story be voiced in Spanish or English? . . . . Spanish   95%
        English   5%

If the story is received in English, but without a Spanish
translation, what is the likelihood it would be used? . . . . Not Likely   72%
        Likely   28%

Do Spanish-Language stations participate in SMTs? . . . . Yes   68%
        No   32%

What kind of news stories are most Spanish-language
audiences interested in watching?
        Health · · · · · · · · · · · · · · · · 96%
        Consumer · · · · · · · · · · · · · · 86%
        Kids · · · · · · · · · · · · · · · · · 75%
        Entertainment · · · · · · · · · · · · 61%
        Finance · · · · · · · · · · · · · · · 57%
        Business · · · · · · · · · · · · · · · 32%
        Immigration · · · · · · · · · · · · · 28%
        Hi-tech · · · · · · · · · · · · · · · · 26%
        Latin America · · · · · · · · · · · · 18%
        Education · · · · · · · · · · · · · · 16%

What language should be used for slates? . . . . Spanish   68%
        Both   28%
        English   4%

What are the common mistakes seen in VNRs/packages sent to you?
        VNR is all in English / not in Spanish
        Proper Spanish is not used (no accent marks on CG/scripts)
        Lacks cultural sensitivity
        No NAT (natural) sound
        Too long
        Poor production
        Too commercial

How do Spanish-Language stations prefer to be notified? . . . . . Fax   75%
        E-mail   64%
        Telephone   14%

How do Spanish-Language stations prefer to receive the story? . . Beta   93%
        Satellite   32%
        DVC Pro   28%

What other support materials are useful? . . . . Press releases   89%
        Press kits   60%
        Scripts   11%

Source: TeleNoticias, 2004

Figure 56 - Survey of Spanish Language Television Stations

sages in English to Spanish so the result communicates the original meaning.

Broadcast Public Relations and Electronic Publicity Tools

There are several common tools or vehicles used to communicate a message to television and radio media. They are:

- Video News Release (VNR)
- B-Roll Package (B-Roll)
- Satellite Media Tour (SMT)
- Audio News Release (ANR)
- Radio Media Tour (RMT)
- Public Service Announcement (PSA)

Video News Release

The Video News Release, or VNR, is one of the most common tools used to get an organization's news to a television news station. Simply put, a VNR is the video version of a press release. It has many of the same characteristics as a press release; and its sole job is to inform the television news producer or reporter about a news story including the information necessary for him or her to develop a complete story.

A VNR package will include the edited VNR (a scripted and voiced 90-120 second story) accompanied by additional B-roll footage (we describe B-roll in the next segment). The VNR package is roughly the video equivalent of a press kit. The actual VNR is similar in content to the lead press release. The additional B-roll footage is like the backgrounders, fact sheets and other materials found in a press kit.

Though VNRs have been in existence for more than 30 years, they became most prominent in the early 1980s. Since that time, many companies have been created that specialize in producing and distributing VNRs and other broadcast public relations tools. Some of those companies produce several hundred VNRs each year. Today, television newsrooms across the country receive many VNRs each day, via satellite, tape and electronic distribution. The competition to get a story on the television news has become tough. It is more important than ever to ensure one has a story relevant to the television news audience. With such a story, one produces a VNR that the television news outlets can use easily.

Marketers typically use a VNR for a story that needs some explanation or in the instance that they need to deliver a specific message to the news station and audience. Health and medical stories are a good example. Most stories involve concepts or messages that need explanation. For example, it is important to explain why a new product works better than other similar products already on the market. Another example would be to explain why people should keep their cholesterol low. In both cases, the key messages require a fair amount of explanation to communicate the idea, which makes a VNR the perfect tool. It allows one to script a story that communicates and explains an important issue. It also allows one to communicate specific messages to the audience.

A good VNR will start with a well-written script. Though this may sound obvious, there are probably more badly written scripts than good ones. As one would write a press release in the style of a print news story, one needs to write a VNR script in the style and manner of a television news story. If you are not familiar with this style, spend some time watching network, cable and local news programs. You will see a pattern and style emerge. Your best bet when working on a VNR is to work with someone who has written and produced many in the past. In general, a VNR should not exceed 90-seconds in length. Usually, the rule is the shorter, the better. The purpose of the VNR is to communicate your concept to the news producer and reporter so he or she understands the story and can decide if it makes sense for the station's newscast. The better you communicate that story, the better your chance of getting it on the air. If the news producer or reporter has to spend an inordinate amount of time to figure out the story, chances are you will lose his or her interest quickly and he or she will move onto the next story idea. A well-written script will make the entire VNR process efficient and serve as the basis for the video shoot and edits.

Depending on the client, the script may be written in Spanish; or, more likely, in English first then translated to Spanish. Keep in mind it takes longer to say something in Spanish than in English. If the goal is a 90-second to two-minute scripted package in Spanish, the English script will need to be significantly shorter than it would be normally. As many corporate personnel that have to approve the script do not speak Spanish, it is usually developed in English first. After they approve the script, it is translated to Spanish and carefully reviewed to ensure an accurate translation and meaning.

In a recent project, TeleNoticias produced and distributed a VNR for an existing drug pending Federal Drug Administration (FDA) approval. TeleNoticias was asked to take an existing script in English, translate it and adjust the script to ensure the messaging was consistent, and to adjust for length. Much of the script needed to be cut to ensure the Spanish-language package would be short enough. This can be challenging when dealing with complicated issues and/or issues where specific language and messaging must remain in the VNR. As is the case with most VNRs dealing with a pharmaceutical product, there is specific regulatory language and guidelines that we must follow. It is important to keep these in mind while translating and adapting for a Hispanic audience. The final Spanish-version of the script contained all necessary messages, and was still at an acceptable length.

Once the script is written (and approved!), the next step is to shoot the video. It is greatly helpful to schedule (if possible) all elements in a one-day shoot. This requires that all spokespersons and locations be scheduled and approved prior to the shoot day. This includes getting any necessary permission or permits to shoot at specific locations. Most companies, stores, hospitals, etc. require advance approval before one can show up with a video crew and shoot. Once everything is scheduled, proceed and capture all of the video for the entire VNR. This usually means you will significantly over-shoot at each location. It is always better to have too much footage or too many takes of the same sound bite, then to find (at a later time) that you do not have what you need.

Upon completion of the shoot(s), the edit or post production phase can begin. This is when the actual voiced VNR package is first edited,

337

along with the B-roll and any other information (including animation and graphics) necessary for the entire VNR. In most cases, we can produce this first edit or "first cut" in one day. Production of the final version, or "master" waits for any required approval process to complete.

Once the VNR is completed and approved, it is distributed to the target stations. Before the VNR is distributed, a station advisory or notification must be written to let the stations know what the story is about, what they will see on the video and when they will receive it. Since the advisory is the first thing a producer or reporter will see about the story, it needs to attract their attention quickly and succinctly and convince them why to air the story. The advisory should be no longer than one page. In many cases, the advisory will make or break your chances with the producer. It is an especially important document.

After the advisory is written (and approved, if necessary), the distribution process can move forward. This process begins by distributing the advisory via blast fax or email, followed immediately by aggressive telephone pitching. One can distribute the actual VNR in days or up to a week, depending on the story and lead time. VNR distribution will involve a combination of satellite feeds and hard copy (tape) distribution.

When targeting Spanish-language media, it is prudent to budget for a fair amount of hard copies (tapes) of the VNR. Staffs at many Spanish-language stations are small and busy (they still have to produce the programs). It may take a while to pitch someone and send him or her the information. Many stations may have missed the satellite feeds. It is important to be able to plan for the possibility of extra hard copy distribution.

After you distribute the VNR, it is imperative that you effectively track VNR usage. The most reliable electronic encoding available is the SIGMA system. It is the best method available for the mainstream market; it covers most every English-language television news station. Though it is not as effective in monitoring Spanish-language stations, it is still the best electronic tracking available. It is also worthwhile to secure a good monitoring service. Be sure to check the service's coverage of and ability to track Spanish-language stations before you sign an agreement.

The final results of a VNR should be detailed in a monitoring report with the total number of airings, the total audience figure, and a station-by-station detail of each airing, including the date, time, station call letters, program name (if available and applicable), market, market rank, network and audience figure for that airing. The results of the VNR in the drug example were excellent, even though the Spanish-language version was distributed more than a week after the FDA approval and the distribution of all the English-language components. The VNR garnered 56 airings with an audience of more than 4.6 million viewers, including airings on Univision and CNN en *Español*. That represents more than 12 percent of the total U.S. Hispanic population.

Video news releases rarely air as produced, just as press releases are not printed verbatim. Stations will typically create their own package or story using elements from the package you sent them. There is never a guarantee that you, your product or message will appear on the air. This emphasizes the need to prepare and provide stations with a usable, well-written and produced piece that meets their needs and yours.

Remember, the VNR is not a commercial. Frequent product mentions and overly commercial video will surely result in your video news release not airing. News producers and reporters understand you are sending them a VNR and that there is a message that you are trying to communicate about your organization, product or service. If you are not careful in how you produce the VNR, you will be sure to have few airings. If you are careful and distribute a well-written and produced VNR, it should deliver the results you are looking for.

The cost range for an average VNR, including story and script development, script translating from English to Spanish, a one-day shoot, edit and post production, distribution and monitoring and tracking, should be between $20,000 and 30,000. The cost will decrease or increase if the project parameters change. For example, if there is more than one shoot day or extensive animation, the cost will be higher. If on the other hand, the project only requires a half-day shoot and distribution to a limited number of stations and markets, the cost could be lower.

B-roll Package

B-roll is a term used to describe footage provided in an un-packaged format. B-roll refers to sound bites (the video term equivalent to a "quote" in print) and other video footage and video elements provided to stations for their use in coordinating a story. A B-roll package is a series of sound bites and extra footage edited together to send to news stations. It is not a scripted, voiced-over package like a VNR. Rather, it gives stations the video footage or elements needed for the news producer or reporter to create his or her own news package. You can also use B-roll to describe the additional sound bites and footage not used in the VNR package.

The term B-roll, originated in film, has evolved to mean extra footage. Typically, a B-roll package will include story information, several sound bites from experts or consumers, and additional footage to support the story.

Use a B-roll package when the video elements tell the story without further explanation. In other words, anyone can look at the footage in the B-roll package and fully understand the story and any messages that need to be communicated. For instance, let us say that McDonald's is opening a new restaurant across the street from the White House in Washington, D.C. The story is that a McDonald's restaurant is opening near the White House. Nothing requires explanation here. The B-roll package would include a McDonald's executive's generic sound-bite about the opening; a sound-bite from a consumer saying how happy he or she is to see this restaurant opening; footage of the new restaurant including its proximity to the White House. From that footage, any television news station will have the resources it needs to make their own story. The video tells the story.

There are two schools of thought with regard to using a B-roll package versus using a VNR package. One school thinks VNRs are a waste of time, because stations never use a voiced VNR. Rather, stations take the parts of the VNR and accompanying B-roll and edit an original package. The other school of thought thinks that the VNR is an important tool in explaining a more complicated story. They agree that stations rarely use the voiced VNR and that the station will edit its own package. They believe that by explaining the story through the VNR, more producers and reporters will understand the story and messages and use the story. If you find yourself planning a B-roll package requiring a great deal of explanation, consider a VNR.

The B-roll production process is similar to that of a VNR, without a scripted, voiced piece. It is usually helpful to prepare for the shoot by drafting questions and suggested sound bites in advance to ensure the shoot is productive and captures all necessary sound bites. It is useful to prepare a short list for a B-roll shoot to ensure you capture all basic video. Once the shoot is complete, the edit and post production phase begins.

When producing B-roll for the Hispanic market, the footage must be relevant to the culture and the demographic. Re-purposing existing footage produced for the general market may not work or may not be as successful as footage shot for the Hispanic market. In general, that means not using footage of Anglos or the typical "white" family for distribution to the Spanish-language media. It will not resonate well with the viewers. It also means making sure messages are appropriate and make sense. Further, the footage should represent the typical lifestyle and life of the U.S Hispanic. Hispanics want to be marketed to and communicated to as Hispanics. It is essential to keep that in mind.

The distribution process for a B-roll package is the same as for a VNR. It starts with a well-written advisory, proceeds to satellite or hard copy distribution and concludes with the monitoring and tracking process. The average cost for producing and distributing a B-roll Package is between $15,000 and $25,000, depending on project parameters.

Satellite Media Tour

A Satellite Media Tour or SMT is a series of live interviews conducted from one location with television stations around the country. The first SMT was conducted in the early 1980s as a logical extension to the traditional media tour. The cost of the traditional media tour (where one takes a spokesperson from market to market, setting up interviews with media in each market) continued to rise. Further, it required a great deal of staff time to travel and accompany the spokesperson to each market. The SMT was a great solution, allowing a spokesperson to "travel" to each station via satellite.

An SMT is an excellent tool if you have a strong spokesperson or a celebrity spokesperson closely tied to the story. It can also be a great vehicle to show off a specific location or to use when a location enhances the story. For instance, if a record company's artist has a new album coming out in conjunction with the Grammy's or the Latin Grammy's, an SMT from the city or location of the award show can be a great tie-in to launch the new album. If there is a sports personality (player, coach, etc.) as a spokesperson, it might make sense to conduct an SMT from the location of a predominant upcoming sporting event (game or match) to enhance the story.

Though a typical SMT is usually two to three hours in length, SMT's can be as short or as long as one likes. As with other broadcast public relations vehicles, the story usually dictates the direction of the project and, the length of the SMT, which can originate from a television studio or from most any remote location. It is possible to feature one or two spokespersons; more than two tends to create problems. First, it makes for an awkward shot (three people on screen); second, as these segments tend to be only a few minutes, it is difficult for the television anchor or reporter to engage all three people. There are exceptions to this rule, for example a music group with several members.

An SMT targeting Spanish-language media may not be as long (number of interviews) as a general market SMT. There are a lot fewer stations than with the general market news media and, there are fewer staff members at these stations. That creates more of a challenge when pursuing an SMT in this market. It is important that the story and spokesperson resonate well with the news producers and reporters, and ultimately the Hispanic audience. It is also essential to leave ample time to pitch and book the interviews.

Once you have decided to move forward with an SMT, the first step is to determine where to hold the SMT, the date and the time. Most SMT's originate from a studio, which is more cost effective. It is more expensive to conduct a tour from a remote location.

Unlike a VNR or B-roll Package, the pitching process happens before the production. An advisory is developed similar to one used for a VNR. It has much of the same information and needs to grab the attention of the news producers quickly and succinctly. The pitching process usually begins three to four weeks prior to the actual SMT, though they certainly can be booked in less time.

The rule of thumb is that you can conduct roughly six interviews an hour. Therefore, you are looking to secure at least 12 interviews for a two-hour SMT and 18 interviews for a three-hour SMT. Sometimes it is possible to squeeze a few more interviews into the allotted time.

Once the advisory is written and approved and the date, time and length of the SMT is firm, you can begin pitching and booking interviews into specific time slots on the schedule, until the grid or schedule is filled. Depending on the nature of the project, try to book interviews with top market stations or focus on a list of specific target markets or geographical areas.

During this process, all production arrangements are made for the date of the SMT. This includes securing the studio (or remote location or satellite production truck), satellite time and other necessary production equipment and staff needed to produce the SMT. This is the time to media train or prepare the spokesperson(s) for the SMT.

On the day of the SMT, everything has already been arranged. The interviews are booked and the production team and studio are in place. It then becomes a matter of execution. In a best-case scenario, everything occurs according to the plan; all interviews are completed and the spokesperson(s) delivers his or her messages.

There are, of course, small roadblocks that can arise during the SMT. First, one may encounter breaking news (either nationally or locally) that can affect a booked interview. A local fire may cause a station to cancel their previously booked interview for your SMT. Another potential problem is technical glitches. Sometimes a station has a difficult time locking in the satellite or the audio feed. This can cause a delay in the SMT or the loss of an interview. It is possible the spokesperson is not doing an effective job of staying on message or delivering the proper or complete message.

These are all potential problems that one can prepare for, but cannot always solve. You can rarely do anything about breaking news. It is the nature of the business. On the other hand, Spanish and/or bilingual media training can help a spokesperson stay on message. If the spokesperson has never been in a media interview or is uncomfortable with the media, media training becomes imperative for the success of the project. Further, it is possible to coach the spokesperson in between interviews to help him or her stay on message.

Once you complete the SMT, you can begin the tracking and monitoring process. It is important to use an electronic system like SIGMA to track the usage. You can use other broadcast clipping services to supplement the electronic monitoring. At the end, a final report is generated similar to those of the VNR or B-roll Package.

A two-hour Satellite Media Tour produced out of a studio will cost between $14,000 and 15,000 depending on the parameters of the project. A three-hour SMT from a studio will cost between $18,000 and 19,000, depending on project parameters. A remote SMT will cost at least $7,000 to 10,000 more than the above costs, as a remote SMT requires transporting all the production equipment to that location.

Audio News Release

The Audio News Release (also called a Radio News Release) or ANR is the radio version of a VNR. It follows a similar format to a VNR: it is a scripted and voiced piece. Most ANRs are exactly 60 seconds long since most radio stations prefer this length; it is easier to work with. For smaller stations, it is easy to drop the ANR into their programming, if necessary.

Audio News Releases are often underutilized and can be a highly effective means to deliver your message(s). This is especially true for the Hispanic community. U.S. Hispanics tend to listen to more radio than the mainstream as a whole. Further, it can be easier to get a message placed on radio than on television. Said another way, some stories that may not garner a great deal of television news coverage, will often get coverage on radio.

Audio news releases and video news releases are similar. The scripting process will be almost identical. If you produce an ANR and VNR simultaneously, the scripting process becomes easier. Often one will wait until the VNR script is final and approved to cut the script down to the 60-second ANR requirement. Remember, it takes longer to say something in Spanish than in English. This will have a dramatic effect on the ANR script because of the exact 60-second requirement.

TeleNoticias distributed an ANR along with the VNR for the above-mentioned FDA approval. It was necessary to cut the English ANR script down significantly to meet the 60-second requirement; we had to edit out approximately 30-35 percent of the script to meet production requirements. This can become tricky when you need to communicate specific messages. Usually, it is necessary to determine the most important message or messages and eliminate the others.

The production process is easier than with a VNR; it is only necessary to capture the sound bite, or in radio terminology, the actuality. You can accomplish this in many ways. One might simply record the sound bite onto tape, digitally onto a CD or an MP3 file. You might record the actuality via ISDN (integrated services digital network) or telephone lines. The result is the needed actuality or sound bite. Once you record this, you record the voice-over and edit the entire piece into a 60-second ANR.

There are several ways of distributing an ANR. One way is to make copies of the ANR on CDs or cassettes and send them to stations via mail, messenger or overnight delivery. It is possible to create an MP3 file and email it to stations; or invite stations to download the MP3 directly from an Internet site. Many will include a combination of the above for distribution. The challenge in ANR distribution at this time is that there are no means to track radio programming electronically, as there are with television. Careful consideration is necessary because Radio remains a difficult medium for ANR distribution and usage tracking.

A popular means of distribution is reaching out to certain radio networks for ANR distribution. Many of the networks can offer guaranteed placement of your ANR. With a guaranteed placement, it is possible to know exactly when and where the ANR has been placed, making it possible to provide a report detailing this activity, with dates, times, stations names, and audience numbers. This means of distribution has become the standard in the industry. The average cost for the production and distribution of an ANR is between $7,000 and $12,000.

Radio Media Tour

The Radio Media Tour or RMT is the radio version of a satellite media tour, a series of individual radio interviews scheduled over a set period with a spokesperson. Like the SMT, it is a great tool to utilize when one has a celebrity or expert spokesperson for the story. For the most part, the same criteria apply to the radio media tour as for the satellite media tour. Since Hispanics listen to more radio than the Anglo or non-Hispanic population, an RMT can be an effective tool to reach this audience. It can also be an effective tool to reach specific markets or regions in the country.

An RMT is usually booked in one or two-hour intervals and can be spread over several days. Typically, an RMT has capacity for three to six interviews in an hour. After you decide how many interviews are appropriate for the story, budget and spokesperson you can schedule the RMT accordingly. For instance, you might decide to conduct an 18 to 20-interview RMT for a given project. The spokesperson may be available for two or three days during which you can schedule daily interviews in hour to hour and a half segments.

With RMTs you have the opportunity to book interviews with individual radio stations and affiliates. You also can book interviews with syndicated programs and networks and network radio shows and feeds. Since there are far more radio stations in the U.S. than television stations, it is usually easier to book a solid RMT successfully. An RMT with five to six interviews costs between $5,000 and 6,000. One that schedules 18-20 interviews costs between $9,000 and 10,000.

Public Service Announcement

A public service announcement or PSA delivers a message geared to serve the public interest. A PSA may also try to persuade the viewer to take some sort of action or to take a certain view on an issue, cause or organization. Public service announcements may be informational in nature or support government causes or community service activities. In any case, a PSA will have a message for the general benefit of the viewing public. PSAs are appropriate for television and radio.

In most cases, stations will air the PSA free of charge at a time determined by the station. There are certain guidelines you must meet before the piece can be a PSA. The most important one is that a non-profit organization with a 501C tax status must sponsor the public service announcement. If contracting union actors or actresses, it is also necessary for the Screen Actors Guild (SAG) to deem the piece a PSA officially.

Many times a celebrity will serve as a spokesperson to deliver the message or promote the cause. Michael J. Fox, for example, has been an effective spokesperson for Parkinson's disease. A PSA may also focus on a campaign to stop smoking or for drug abuse awareness. Most people have seen the Ad Council PSA campaigns on drug abuse, disease prevention, drunk driving, and infant and child nutrition, among others.

A good PSA will have a simple and memorable message. It will also make use of strong visuals and sounds to help communicate its message. It is important to work with a professional who has experience writing and producing PSAs. In some cases, PSAs can be complicated to execute and become quite expensive. The important point is to understand what you want from the PSA before you begin. This will dictate the project's production, complexity and budget.

TeleNoticias produced a radio PSA for the Planned Parenthood Federation of America to alert the public about their march on Washington in April. In this case, it was to be a 60-second PSA and there was a lot of information to be communicated. The goal was to get people to attend the march. One major challenge was how to communicate some of Planned Parenthood's messages so a Spanish-language listener would understand them. In this context, most English-speaking people would understand the term "choice." However, this does not translate directly in Spanish. Using a direct translation for "choice" would not infer the same meaning. It was therefore necessary to adapt the message to resonate with the listener. It required many more words to communicate "choice." This illustrates the challenges involved in translating and adapting messages into Spanish.

Like most broadcast public relations tools, PSAs are sent more frequently to mainstream, English-language stations than to Spanish-language stations. This creates an obvious opportunity for PSAs relevant to the Hispanic community.

Public service announcements are primarily distributed via hard-copy (either tape to television stations, or via MP3, CD or cassette to radio stations). PSA distribution usually relies on free air time provided by stations. Though in 1985 the FCC removed the requirement for stations to air PSAs, they continue to air them to support their communities and show their commitment to their audience. Stations usually utilize PSAs to fill unsold advertising time gaps.

Where the PSA message is time sensitive, it may be necessary to purchase air time to ensure it gets the play necessary to be effective. In many cases, stations will also provide free time to complement the time purchased. This is particularly true with radio stations.

A comprehensive report will detail the PSA usage, including day, time, station, station affiliate/network, and audience figures. These reports may also include demographic information about the stations that aired the PSA. Television PSA production begins from a low side of $10,000-15,000 to a high of $100,000 or more. Radio PSA production starts around $5,000 and can reach $10,000 to 20,000, if it is a high-end production.

Tips for Success

Here are a few tips to help you pitch and approach Spanish-language broadcast media.

Know the Media

This should go without saying. Know the station, network and program you are pitching. Find out: What kind of stories they cover, how they cover them, and how you can help.

Know the Audience

Know the end audience; in other words who is watching and listening. Be prepared to provide information in Spanish and English, and make sure that you are using proper Spanish. Many stations complain about poorly written or poorly translated materials. Make sure any translations to Spanish truly reflect the meaning in English. Many literal translations will have a completely different meaning. Often English phrases or euphemisms do not translate directly to Spanish. This can cause your English campaign themes or slogan to have a different meaning in Spanish.

Understand that it takes longer to say things in Spanish than it does in English. If you have a VNR or ANR script written in English that you are planning to distribute to general market media and want to distribute a Spanish version to Spanish-language media simultaneously, you will need to substantially edit down the length of the scripts. Experts estimate it takes about 30 percent longer to say things in Spanish. Media specialists and media pitchers should be bi-lingual.

Chapter Summary

There exist great opportunities to reach Spanish-language broadcast media with your news. While many companies and organizations routinely utilize broadcast public relations tactics to get their news onto general market, English-language media, few routinely target Spanish-language media. This represents an excellent opportunity. For those organizations willing to spend the time to target Spanish-language broadcast stations, the results will be well worth the effort.

- Know and understand the media you are pitching.
- Understand the opportunities and roadblocks that exist with Spanish-language broadcast media.

- Each broadcast public relations tool has a specific use; it is important to know when to use which tool.
- Many do not understand how these broadcast tools work; it is helpful to explain the process and benefits before undertaking a project.
- It is important to understand that the landscape of Spanish-language media changes on almost a daily basis; it is necessary to keep on top of these changes.

You may find examples of broadcast public relations tools at:
http://www.telenoticiasusa.com/hispanicmarketing&publicrelations.htm

About the Author

David Henry, President and Founder, TeleNoticias

David Henry is president and founder of TeleNoticias, a broadcast public relations company that targets the U.S. Hispanic market. He has nearly 15 years of experience providing broadcast strategy and counsel to a diverse client base. He brings a complete understanding of and experience in all facets of electronic media. David holds a Bachelor of Science in Journalism from the University of Maryland.

Chapter Thirteen

Maximizing Public Relations Results with Entertainment

Claudia Santa Cruz

In This Chapter

- Selecting event and audience specific talent
- General versus entertainment media issues
- Managing entertainment events

Introduction

According to the latest census figures, Hispanics are now positioned as the largest minority in the U.S.; more importantly, their purchasing power continues to rise, increasing the interest of companies across the board. While retailers utilize proven methods, such as entertainment marketing campaigns, to gain brand awareness and consumer loyalty, it comes as no surprise that they are now doing it with a Latin twist. The catch phrase "crossover appeal" has become the latest approach for companies that want to reach this prosperous market.

"Hispanic entertainment specifically, is one of the best communication vehicles to establish an emotional connection with Latinos," says Max Gallegos, director of marketing at McDonald's Corporation. He indicated that Latino culture, music and entertainment go together and are an intrinsic element of today's Latino lifestyle. In addition, that the brand loyalty and affinity are born of an emotional tie developed while the Latino consumer is still defining his or her likes and choices.

Whether it is Mexican singer and actress Thalía endorsing her new clothing line in Kmart, Rock Latino groups Molotov and Maldita Vecindad on tour with McDonald's or Hollywood actress Salma Hayek drinking Coke, corporations are banking on Hispanic celebrities and events to reach this coveted segment of the population. For this reason, the public relations effort takes on a critical role in supporting and securing the success of this new marketing strategy.

Selecting the Right Talent for an Event and Audience

Prior to selecting a celebrity or "talent," as they are called in the industry, one must clearly define the target core group within the marketing strategy. The talent's ability to connect and relate to this particular group is critical to assure reception of the message. Credibility and reputation are the most important factors when choosing a celebrity to endorse a product.

When the Centers for Disease Control were searching for a spokesperson for their Aids Act Now campaign, "they wanted Marc Anthony, but we recommended Jerry Rivera," says Mayna Nevarez, an independent publicist with more than eight years of experience in the entertainment arena. She indicated that although Jerry was not as popular as Marc, he had a great reputation; had been married for 13 years; and was a wonderful father. Nevarez has worked in the career development of Pablo Montero, Los Tri-o and Gisselle, among others, as well as the Spanish-language CD launch of Cristina Aguilera. A negative reputation can be detrimental to the campaign, and this does not rely solely on personal image.

Other factors to consider are what the artist represents, whether it is music containing offensive lyrics, or a television show filled with controversy. The main lesson is not to leave any stone unturned. If a celebrity is selected to endorse a product or company, steps need to be taken to assure that he or she will provide positive representation, and will not be detrimental to the product's or company's reputation. Where it involves endorsing a cause rather than a product, obtaining an artist who can associate himself, or herself, with the cause increases credibility immensely. A good example, because of her personal fight against breast cancer, is singer Soraya. She is the perfect spokesperson for the cause because she brings her own personal experiences and emotions to the table, and can deliver a passionate and compelling message.

Another factor to consider is language capability. If the spokesperson will be handling Spanish-language ads or interviews, it is important that he or she be fluent in the language. A strong accent and grammatical mistakes will cause a message to get lost. Just because a celebrity is Hispanic, does not mean they are fluent in the language.

Also, consider an artist's relationship with the media. How open is he or she to promoting a product or cause? It is incredibly difficult to work with a celebrity who is never available, or who simply does not want to dedicate the effort. If they do not like to promote their own CD or film, imagine them promoting your company's product. There are many celebrities who are a pleasure to work with, and who will assist you in getting the message across.

Sometimes, working with talent is not as difficult as working with their managers or publicists. In the Hispanic community most talent have managers, although few have their own publicists. This creates some challenges, since they do not always have press materials such as a bio and photos available. Many have not had media training to conduct good interviews. The managers usually pick up these responsibilities, but not always.

Having everything in writing is essential to maintain a positive working relationship with talent, as well as their managers and publicists. Details are extremely important in entertainment public relations, much more so than in any other area. Public relations professionals need to make sure to take care of the client and the celebrity. This leaves no room for mistakes.

One disgruntled celebrity can cause an entire event or campaign to fall apart. Always plan ahead as much as possible. If an artist is scheduled for an interview or a taping, logistics must be executed flawlessly.

The best way to do this, just as in events, is to visualize, and always have a contingency plan. Visualize the talent's participation from the moment they are in your care (be it at the arrival area in the airport, or from their home) until their return. Issues to organize include: communication with the talent so they know what to expect (with copies to the manager and publicist); transportation to and from the venue; security on location; greeters to make sure the talent has a familiar face to go to with questions or problems; a green room or place where they can wait prior to their appearance; meals, if there is no time for breaks; and consideration regarding hours of work.

An overtired and hungry artist will be grumpy and difficult, rightly so. The worst assumption companies can make in working with artists is that they can be treated just like any other employee. Artists, who have garnered recognition through their talent, expect a certain amount of respect. This is true in the general market and in the Hispanic market. The happier a talent is with the care that went to secure their comfort, the more likely he or she will return the favor through positive attitude and participation.

During a two-week six-city Toyota tour with actors Manolo Cardona and Paola Rey, there was not much time for rest and relaxation. The team endeavored to make the talent's travel, transportation, meals, and stay in each city comfortable. Although the working hours were sometimes grueling, the talent in turn, did what they could to maintain the best attitude we could hope for, making our jobs easier and allowing us to deliver great results.

When all of these factors fall into place, celebrities and entertainment as a whole are successful tools within a marketing strategy. An example was McDonald's launch of their *"Lo McXimo de la Música"* initiative, a multi-media, non-traditional inclusive approach to reaching young Hispanic adults. First, they identified the strategy and core targets. LoMcXimo celebrated the essence of a unique Latino insight: our deeply rooted pride in our Latino heritage.

LoMcXimo del Espiritu Latino served as the strategy to reach the 18-24 year old target market. To accomplish it, they selected the two most inherent passions of this young demographic: education and music. With extensive research, knowledge of their core customer target, a solid strategy endorsed by the corporation, and with tremendous support of their franchisees, LoMcXimo became McDonald's most recent success in its 30-year pioneering tradition and legacy in Hispanic marketing.

The music approach led them to the Spanish Rock genre with the support of an extensive internal agency network and Clear Channel's Vivelo! team as thought partners. They identified Molotov, El Gran Silencio, Maldita Vecindad, Rabanes, Nortec, and Yerba Buena as the line-up for what was to become a national sold-out U.S. tour. Education was embedded into the campaign by creating awareness for the largest Latino scholarship program for high school students in the nation, the Ronald McDonald House Charities' HACER Latino Scholarship Program. More so, the corporation and its respective franchises fully funded and contributed to the program's costs so that all ticket sales from the national tour would benefit Latino scholarships.

Richard Castro, a McDonald's owner operator who has contributed close to $15 million to date and over one million dollars annually to Latinos pursuing higher education founded the HACER program in 1985. The strategy included a multi-media approach with in-store merchandising, television, digital, radio, print and outdoor grassroots advertising in both English and Spanish-language outlets. The program accomplished key partnerships, and 10 key objectives by:

- Positioning McDonald's as a relevant and contemporary brand to the elusive 18-24 Latino demographic.
- Distinguishing McDonald's as a brand that grows and evolves with the different phases of its customers' lives. In this case, by becoming the first in the quick service restaurant industry to launch such an inclusive and extensive national campaign anchored to an untapped and "irrelevant" genre, Spanish Rock.
- Raising awareness of the importance of higher education among Latinos (especially since this group has the highest drop out rate in the nation).
- Airing a national special in Spanish and English-language television through Telemundo, mun2, and select NBC affiliates nationwide.

- Raising over $200,000 for Latino scholarships.
- Providing true customer access to genuine passion for music through affordable ticket prices, despite a solid class act lineup ($20 admission tickets for a non-stop 4-5 hour performance), a national tour billed as the most aggressive and platinum AAA lineup of its kind, with reviews that included *The New York Times* and *Billboard* magazine.
- National sweepstakes winners enjoyed an all expense-paid trip to attend the concert in the city of their choice.
- Increasing on-line traffic to McDonald's bilingual Web site at http://www.lomcximo.com building momentum for sweeps entry, ticket and merchandising purchases, and post recap of concert tour gallery.
- Showcasing a solid business case and success story of how Hispanic brand marketing is integral to driving business by increasing brand awareness among the 18-34 Latino target.
- Increasing traffic to restaurants with the ultimate goal of building sales and winning customer visits.

Difference Between Entertainment and News Media

According to Alberto Sardiñas, producer and on-air personality for the Spanish Broadcasting System, entertainment news is information that is not truly necessary though the audience does not want to give it up. This contrasts with general news, which focuses strictly on current events. Whereas general news media reacts to issues taking place in the world every day, entertainment media is busy searching for angles and stories to cover.

For public relations, this is a plus since entertainment media is waiting for a pitch. However, their thirst for information also means that you have to be prepared for crisis public relations at a moment's notice, as they are turning stones to seek reports of possible interest to their public. With very little effort, news surrounding celebrities and entertainment events can take on a gossip angle or a bigger-than-life magnitude that can often get out of hand.

Maintaining a positive relationship with entertainment media, therefore, is critical in order to assure fair and balanced coverage. This relationship is built over time and not over night. One of the biggest mistakes public relations people make with Hispanic media is to treat them like general market media. Hispanic media representatives like Hispanics mix business with pleasure. It is common to know the reporter from work and be aware of their family, the area they live in, their likes and dislikes. Calling only during times when you make a pitch will not get you far with a Hispanic reporter; he or she will feel you are only using them for your convenience. You also need to become a resource for them. Make yourself available when they seek information, press materials and background; provide a spokesperson when they need an interview; and respect their deadlines and specific needs.

The most difficult part of dealing with entertainment media is keeping focused on the message. The draw to their stories is many times controversial and gossipy. Staying away from this is not always easy, and this is where media training takes on a critical role. After singer and actress Lucero's presentation at a theater, her bodyguard pulled out a gun on the media representatives waiting for her to appear. The next day, Lucero called a press conference, and demonstrating complete annoyance at the constant media harassment, stated that she supported her bodyguard's actions. This made her unpopular with media and fans alike. Although it is true that the spotlight is not always a fun place to be, this was not the best way to handle this situation.

An experienced publicist would have immediately relayed the message that the young actress was waiting for the results of the investigation prior to making any statements to the media. Once this investigation was finalized, a different approach would have worked to her advantage; having all the facts would have allowed for a more educated decision. The advice the actress received was not that of an experienced publicist. Today, Lucero is working hard to regain her previous reputation as the sweet little girl who grew up in front of the screen.

Because people and events can cause immediate news, working with entertainment public relations means you are constantly on deadline. Successful public relations practitioners will learn to respect media deadlines and understand them. Be aware that some reporters will take advantage of public relations professionals by waiting for the last minute to request items they could have requested with anticipation. There should be mutual respect for a positive working relationship.

Putting oneself in the shoes of the reporter helps in gaining further understanding of their needs. If it is a small medium with few resources, they will be counting more on the public relations person for information and support materials. If it is a television show, visuals will be necessary to make the story more interesting and appealing to viewers. "People who do good PR are people who think like the journalist and who are responsible and help out with the story," says Renzo Devia, executive producer of urban Latino television and supervising producer at Maximas Productions.

On the other hand, a big "peeve" for reporters is when public relations professionals pitch them on a topic unrelated with the areas he or she covers. In other words, the public relations professional did not do his or her homework. Positive publicity does not mean a constant plug of your product or talent. Media will not respect you if the interview you provide them sounds like a rehearsed commercial, or if your spokesperson's only concern is to mention the product as many times as possible. According to Sardiñas, producers are constantly in search for content and the best way to position a story is to link your client's message with the program's style.

Events

When handling public relations for an entertainment event, details are critical. Keep in mind that you are seeking to make your client, and the participating talent, who are many times much more demanding, happy.

When considering the venue for an event, take into account how easily people will find the venue, parking, entrance for the public, secure entrance for the talent and VIPs, and the façade (especially if media will cover a red carpet area). Take into account ambient sound that could affect television crews covering the event, space for a green room where talent can wait comfortably, a press area, the location of bathrooms, and indoor and outdoor lighting.

If you want to be sure your talent will arrive promptly to the event, provide transportation. In the end, it will not add that much to your cost. It will provide you peace of mind to know the media representatives will not be waiting for hours prior to talent arrival. In addition, security is extremely important, as fans are not always predictable. The talent's needs should be a top priority: whether it is arranging for passes for their companions, food and beverage while they wait for the show to begin, or talent flow to get them from the red carpet into the venue to start the show on time.

As far as media logistics, consider the type of media that will cover the event. If the media ranges from print to broadcast, keep in mind their needs to make their story more interesting, such as visuals like photos or video. This means that if they are allowed inside the main event, they can obtain their own photos or video. If they are in a press-room instead, they will be counting on you to provide them with backstage photo opportunities, as well as video feeds. In the end, it is up to you to decide the type of coverage they will have, and what will be used for print and broadcast. This is a huge responsibility, since it can mean positive or negative coverage. In addition, having many media at hand means that if a crisis erupts they will be seeking first-hand information. It is important to have a crisis plan in advance, so you can control the message.

Case Study: Billboard Latin Music Awards

In 2003, Telemundo broadcast the Billboard Latin Music Awards for the fifth consecutive year. The public relations role was significant in developing the event's image, garnering awareness, and positioning the Awards as the biggest night in Latin entertainment. The key responsibilities in public relations included the following:

Credentialing

Almost 1,000 journalists applied for credentials to cover the awards. Keeping in mind the limitations of space the venue had, we were able to credential 139 media outlets (323 journalists) to cover the event. Telemundo coordinated the credentialing process through its press website.

Journalists filled out a credential form on-line that provided information to help us decide which media to approve. Some of the factors considered included circulation, local, national or international coverage, and relationship with the network.

The website was a means to garner credential requests and a vehicle for communication. Through it reporters obtained additional information about *Billboard*, Telemundo, finalists and the awards. They were also able to download pictures and additional information about each artist. After the rehearsals, we also made an audio news release with various bytes from artists available for download. In order to promote the website, we sent various media alerts to the press including a CD we mailed, which provided a direct link to the site.

Once approved, credentials were made available for pick up at the hotel where *Billboard* held the annual music conference, three days prior to the Awards. This made it easier for reporters, since most were covering the conference, and could take advantage of their presence there to pick up their credential package. This was important because many reporters from other states and countries flew in to cover the Awards.

The registration area also served as another opportunity to brand Telemundo. A monitor with a looped tape of Telemundo's music specials was shown constantly to promote other productions attractive to people from the music industry. The credentials were color coded to differentiate the areas reporters would be covering. Media covering the photo room (photographers) had a different color credential than media (reporters and television crews) covering the pressroom or the exclusive one-on-one room.

Pre-Publicity

Once the website was up and running, a time line was set and the following press materials were disseminated prior to the show:

- CD mailed to media outlets with link to a Web page for credentials registration

- Release emphasizing Telemundo as the producer and broadcaster of the event and the exclusive agreement with *Billboard* (including date and venue)
- Media alert inviting media to register for credentials, providing them with website information, and emphasizing the deadline
- Release announcing finalists
- Viewer's Choice Award release encouraging voting at telemundo.com
- Releases announcing hosts, performers and presenters
- Final call for media to register
- Local media alert to broadcast outlets inviting them to cover rehearsals

Rehearsals

Top broadcast media were invited to cover rehearsals (local television stations, Extra, Access Hollywood, Telemundo shows, and the event's radio partner, Hispanic Broadcast Corporation, HBC). Reporters had access to one-on-one interviews with talent, and they were able to cover preparations, such as the laying of the red carpet.

Red Carpet

On the day of the event, we divided the red carpet area into four sections for media: live broadcast, broadcast with red carpet access, print and on-line, and wire and radio. This allowed public relations representatives to facilitate certain needs, such as accessible satellite truck parking for media that would go live from the red carpet (including Telemundo's local station that broadcast its entire newscast from the red carpet); in the case of television crews, an entire red carpet view. We also provided lighting and risers to facilitate coverage.

In addition, communication channels were developed to make the names of arriving talent available on a timely basis for the announcer, the media and the rest of the public relations team. A fact sheet of the event, as well as a list of talent (with descriptions of each), were provided. We assigned a Telemundo photographer to the red carpet and made his pictures available on the press website. Although celebrities were allowed to walk with their own personal publicists, Telemundo public relations representatives were available at each media section to facilitate interviews and information.

One-on-One Room

The one-on-one room allowed Telemundo and NBC shows, as well as the HBC Awards radio partner, to obtain exclusive interviews backstage, once the talent had received their awards. Each one-on-one station was given lighting and a power drop, a monitor with headset to keep abreast of the show, and a poster of the show they could use as a backdrop. A Telemundo representative secured a make-up artist for touch-ups prior to these interviews. Staff were assigned to escort them from the backstage area into the one-on-one room, the photo room and press room.

Press and Photo Rooms

We made a pressroom available to the media. Monitors in this room allowed them to watch the show. Once the artists received their awards, the reporters were able to ask them a few questions and take additional pictures of the artists holding their awards. In addition, we brought a live feed of the show into the room so that television crews could record specific moments of the show for their news coverage. A separate feed allowed television and radio crews to record audio from the press conference taking place at the pressroom.

We made the photo room available to print photographers only. Artists entering the stage in this room would not answer any questions; they would just pose in front of the repeat wall. The repeat wall is a backdrop containing logos of the main producers or sponsors, in this case Telemundo and *Billboard*. A Telemundo photographer was placed inside the Arena, and another at the photo room to make these pictures available for downloading the next morning.

One key factor in both rooms was the access to telephones and teleports we provided media who needed to send in their stories and/or pictures that same night. This was important, particularly for the dailies and wire services, such as Reuters and AP (Associated Press). The release announcing the winners was distributed at the pressroom making the information accessible to reporters while they wrote their stories on the spot.

Post Publicity

Once the event was over, we distributed the winners' release through the wire and posted it on-line along with photographs for downloading. In addition, an audio news release produced during rehearsals utilizing bytes from different artists was distributed to promote the broadcast of the show, which took place three days after the event.

Results

Top local, national and international media outlets from Hispanic and general markets attended. Coverage included four of the top five networks (ABC, CBS, NBC and FOX), as well as major wires including Reuters, AP, Getty, Wire Image, Notimex, and EFE. There were 46 television cameras, 56 newspapers and magazines, 15 radio stations, eight on-line publications, and 13 wires. The public relations campaign resulted in maximum pre-publicity for the event and on-air show, which helped fill up the venue and increase ratings. It also positioned the event as one of the most important Latin music events in the world.

Chapter Summary

Utilizing entertainment to gain brand awareness and consumer loyalty within the Hispanic market has a proven success record. Top things to remember are the careful selection of events or talent in order to assure your message the best reception. This marketing strategy can be supported by a comprehensive public relations campaign, playing a significant role in achieving the ultimate goal of the company.

- Prior to selecting a celebrity define the target core group within the marketing strategy.
- Credibility and reputation are the most important factors when choosing a celebrity to endorse a product.

- To select a celebrity, consider what the artist represents, their language ability, and their relationship with the media.
- Having everything in writing is essential to a positive working relationship.
- Make sure you look after the client and celebrity.
- Understand general news and entertainment media needs.
- Maintaining a positive relationship with entertainment media is critical to ensure fair and balanced coverage.
- The most difficult part of dealing with entertainment media is keeping focused on the message.
- To be successful you must respect and understand media deadlines.
- When handling public relations for an event, details are critical.
- When considering a venue for an event, take into account location, parking, and public and talent entrances.
- Take into account ambient sound, space for a green room and press area, restroom location, and lighting.
- Provide talent transportation to ensure their timely arrival.
- Prioritize talent needs.
- When coordinating media coverage, take different type of media needs into account.

About the Author

Claudia Santa Cruz, President, Santa Cruz Communications Inc.

Claudia Santa Cruz, who has 13 years of experience in the communications field, is a seasoned public relations professional dedicated to the development of strategic campaigns and programs that synergize and support client marketing and public relations goals. Her clients include mun2 television, Conill Advertising, Telemundo, Billboard Latin Music Awards, Mapa Communications (Ford, American Association of Retired People, Verizon), and R.L. Public Relations (Sears, Johnnie Walker, Cover Girl). Claudia received her Bachelor of Arts in Journalism from California State University, Northridge.

Chapter Fourteen

Hispanic Public Relations Return on Investment
Miracles on a Dime:
An Outline of Hispanic Communications Measurement Tactics

Christine Clavijo-Kish
Dalia Paratore Salazar

In This Chapter

Tactics you can include within a Hispanic marketing communications plan to yield measurable results

Introduction

Measuring the true impact of any communications campaign is a challenging task. Translating the achievements of a Hispanic-community targeted outreach effort is literally harder to report. If you plan to summarize exactly what audiences within the many layers of Latinos and Hispanics your efforts actually reached, the first phase of your campaign must include an outline of the appropriate messages and select the corresponding media that will potentially carry those messages most effectively.

There are many expensive resources to measure the reach and impact of communications initiatives. Unfortunately, few options are yet available to calculate the penetration of multicultural audience messages appropriately. The outline within illustrates what we lovingly refer to as *Milagros con Poquito* or "Miracles on a dime," tactics you can strategically sprinkle within a Hispanic marketing communications plan to yield measurable results. These are the kind of results possible within a limited budget, which can demonstrate the investment viability for this market.

Of course, we understand the goal of any new or ongoing multicultural marketing initiative is to sustain or even increase the organization's investment in the effort and more importantly, in the community. We present these tactics with that goal in clear sight.

Research From the Beginning

Conduct grassroots phone research or work with a firm to determine customer needs and ongoing issues facing your audience. Make sure to keep results fresh and relevant through "research updates." This will help your program and budget. You should benchmark these initial findings and then conduct comparisons with follow-up field research to determine if any further awareness of your message or campaign has been achieved. Also, be sure to keep an eye on top competitors who may implement response programs to diminish your efforts.

Tactic in Action: A national cancer awareness organization sought to inform Hispanic women age 65 and over regarding the importance of cervical cancer screening and continued PAP exams after child bearing years. This effort was specifically targeted to help reduce the increased incidence of the cancer among this age segment. The initial program phase included phone research among the core target to determine their media and communications preferences. The result: the campaign benchmarked concluded that all communications efforts must also reach the younger segment of 18 to 45 year old Hispanic women, the daughters and granddaughters, who would inform "Abuela" of her need to return to the gynecologist's office. Research also illustrated the taboos associated with older Hispanic women and their attitudes toward continued gynecological care. The data positively impacted the campaign message development and served to more accurately access subsequent media coverage.

Media Relations Strategy, Back to Basics

Make sure that you are clear on what Hispanic segment you are targeting and why. Keep your message or communications with those audiences relevant whether it is Latina moms, *abuelas* (grandmothers) or *jovencitas* (young girls) and use their preferred media. Do not get caught up on impressions only. For example, *"Despierta America"* has great viewer ship but this may not be your target audience nor serve to target your secondary audience either. Perhaps a lifestyle magazine would better communicate with your target directly.

Tactic in Action: A national cereal manufacturer was launching a new line-up of vitamin-fortified cereals and including Hispanics among its targeted campaign audiences. The company wanted to reach Latina moms and their children directly. Their public relations outreach media line-up included shows skewed to younger audiences and radio outreach complimented by local on-site sampling of the product via a special effort with PTA (parent teacher association) groups in schools with significant Hispanic student concentrations.

Include a "Call-in" Show

Making a "call-in" show such as radio or cable television part of your media outreach provides you with simple, measurable results, as audience impact is immediately available. This can help you tweak your campaign. Also, be sure to include promotional offers such as a "give away" for every caller. This will require delivery (of some sort) to each winner, thus building a link to and knowledge of your targeted campaign consumer.

Request that the Hispanic communications program lead the pure advertising initiative (at least until results can be measured.) Isolate your public relations or cause-related marketing efforts and then measure any sales hikes, giveaway requests, visits to a website, calls to a dedicated line, etc. These efforts can now be more closely attributed to the communications tactics because you do not have to compete with your own advertising group.

Tactic in Action: As part of a cervical cancer awareness program, a highly recognized and respected Hispanic oncologist fielded questions during an on-air radio interview early in the communications campaign. The tone, type of caller, length and depth of the questions were subsequently analyzed. The follow-up press releases and campaign messages were altered to communicate with the targeted audiences more effectively. Television interviews were also better managed and delivered as a result of earlier analysis.

Include Call-to-action Tactics and Offers in Your Program

Establish dedicated call-in numbers with bilingual capability. The same applies to websites, free informational packets and any other offers.

Tactic in Action: As part of a national effort to launch a new line-up of vitamin-fortified cereals, the communications campaign included a new fully dedicated "toll free" call-in number. This number was presented on all campaign materials and featured during all media interviews. The call-in center was staffed with bilingual nutritionists and operators providing key data from a recent study that indicated a link between a healthy breakfast and higher academic results among children. Additionally, all callers received a complimentary informational kit sent to their homes. A bilingual website also was developed specifically for the initiative.

Media Coverage Retrieval and Analysis

Not all organizations have the budget for high-level analysis. Clipping, for relatively little, can show demographics and quantitative data regarding a campaign's reach. For example, if a story was published or aired in a certain market segment it must have had greater resonance there. News stories also reflect qualitative data. What is being said, and how and when? Monitoring and clipping related articles can illustrate the overall effectiveness of the campaign's strategic tactics.

Events

The decision as to whether an event should be small, medium or large and during what time of year it should take place is highly subjective and should directly correspond with the initiative's communications goals. It is wise to partner with a retailer, organization or educational institution to drive an event since attendance creates word of mouth or *referencias* among Hispanics.

Develop relationships or push Hispanic participation in nontraditional groups within the culture, for example:

- Parent Teachers Association (PTA's)
- Girl or Boy Scouts
- Medical Support Groups

Establishing a rapport with such organizations affords the ability to measure membership increases and potentially align those results with your initiative. Many of these organizations are hungry for new opportunities to align themselves with quality Hispanic programs; it could be a perfect match.

Tactic in Action: The large street festivals held annually within traditional Hispanic markets may not be appropriate for all communications initiatives although they reach mass numbers of consumers. A national manufacturer of baby care products was debating whether participation in such an event was a key component for an upcoming initiative.

The strategic decision was made based largely on past research and results among their Latina "mom" target audience, that smaller, more personalized events were preferred. The brand team negotiated with local retail stores on a national basis and created "baby fairs" that included their products and bilingual data about early child care, nutrition and other key messages and brands that elevated their initiative. Results later benchmarked as an integral component of the "fairs," included questionnaires regarding awareness among the audience about the brand and other important data.

Use Hispanic "Experts" to Drive Messages

Using Hispanic experts makes quotes easier to deliver and creates more targeted story opportunities. Experts can be a number of people from doctors to nutritionists or fitness experts and financial planners. Ensure campaign messages are simple and clear to deliver while being "helpful" to key life aspects, issues or values among your Hispanic target audience. Always remember to carefully train all spokespersons on your particular messages no matter how well versed or spoken they may be in general.

Tactic in Action: A recent breast-cancer awareness program driven/adopted by a manufacturer of baby related products featured a highly recognized Latina singer who had supported her mother through the illness diagnosis and treatment. While not a traditional "expert," her personal knowledge and vast education on the matter helped her clearly communicate messages of early detection and treatment and build keen awareness regarding the issue. A Hispanic female oncologist who focused on the clinical aspects endorsed and delivered the program's message points during media interviews. The campaign's success was attributed to this strong spokesperson combination, supplemented by an informative bilingual website.

Build a Database

All of the illustrated call-to-action tactics above require registration, calling or mailing, etc. These are all easy ways to build a database of your target audience for subsequent marketing and sales purposes. The Hispanic marketing communications efforts can now drive your organization to better "communicate" with its audiences in general.

Final note: These methods have been tried and tested by savvy public relations practitioners familiar with the nuances of both the Hispanic market and the challenges of a small budget. ¡Adelante!

Chapter Summary

- Conduct grassroots phone research to determine customer needs and ongoing issues facing your audience
- Keep an eye on top competitors who may implement response programs to diminish your efforts
- Be clear on what Hispanic segment you are targeting and why
- Keep your message or communications with those audiences relevant
- Make a "call-in" show part of your media outreach
- Include call-to-action tactics and offers in your program
- Monitoring and clipping can illustrate the effectiveness of the campaign's strategic tactics
- Partner with a retailer, organization or educational institution to drive an event
- Use Hispanic "experts" to drive messages

About the Authors

Christine Clavijo-Kish, Partner, LatinClips Inc.

Christine Clavijo-Kish directs all sales and marketing strategies, and jointly overseas the overall operations and client services for the company. She has spent more than ten years as a public relations and marketing practitioner and is an expert in developing multicultural, multilingual strategies and promotions for the U.S. Hispanic and Latin American markets. Clavijo-Kish is a graduate of the University of Miami with a bachelor's degree in Communication and English Literature.

Dalia Paratore Salazar, Partner, LatinClips Inc.

Dalia Paratore Salazar directly oversees all of the development, technology and research aspects of LatinClips Inc. She is directly responsible for all monitoring and developing of resources in addition to the LatinClips client management systems. Paratore Salazar, who holds a Master of Science in Information Studies and a Bachelor of Science in Psychology from Florida State University, also collaborates in the creation and promotion of new products and services.

Chapter Fifteen

Cultural Understanding Key to Effective Hispanic Media Training

Elena del Valle, M.B.A., J.D.

In This Chapter

- Key aspects of effective media training
- Hispanic market interview cornerstones
- Major media models
- Media interview benefits
- Crisis management considerations

Introduction

In this chapter, you will find an outline of the key elements of a Latino oriented media training program. Assume for purposes of this discussion:

- The terms Hispanic and Latino are interchangeable
- Hispanic is an ethnicity not a race
- Latino media training refers to training oriented to reach Latino audiences effectively
- Latinos are categorized based on self perception and may be multiracial

- Hispanic media training can be in English, Spanish or both languages
- Hispanic media refers to U.S. based media and media targeting U.S. Latino audiences in either English, Spanish or both
- Mainstream media refers to U.S. based general media targeting the overall American population

As of the 2000 Census, Latinos are America's largest minority, representing (even by conservative estimates), 13-15 percent of the overall market. Although many Hispanics are Spanish dominant, a significant percentage of the Latino population is highly acculturated and English dominant or bilingual. Approximately 28 million of 33 million Hispanics speak Spanish. This makes for a complex Hispanic media mix.

There are hundreds of U.S. based newspapers, magazines, television and radio programs and online websites targeting Hispanic consumers in the U.S. and beyond. In addition, because Latino consumers spend a high percentage of their disposable income on food, transportation, clothing and housing, an increasing number of communicators and marketers are beginning to focus their efforts on them.

There are plenty of examples of Hispanic market campaigns. The question we are here to ask is, "how can media training help you create a successful Hispanic market campaign?" Many have heard of one or more unsuccessful outreach efforts targeting Latinos. Examples include the prominent airline which invited travelers to fly "naked," the slogan for pork as "the other white meat" and a beer company whose advertising campaign made a veiled reference to Hispanic women.

In an effort to promote their new business class leather seats, an airline invited passengers to fly *"en cuero."* It was not until they had launched the campaign that airline executives realized *"en cuero"* means naked in colloquial Spanish. Oops! The Tecate beer tagline "Finally, a cold Latina" sparked some controversy among Latinos who felt it portrayed Hispanic women as loose. Someone did not do his or her homework.

Difficulties often relate to faulty concept or language translations such as these. After launching a promotional campaign, an Italian food company's efforts to reach Latino audiences met with amusement. In their haste to sell their folded over pizza called calzone, company executives neglected to find out *calzones* means underwear in Spanish. In another blunder, a native speaker with good intentions translated the Air Force slogan "United We Stand" to the English equivalent of "United We Stand on Our Feet" or "United We Are Stopped" using the words *"Unido Estamos Parados"*.

A Denver zoo marketer reached out to Latino audiences with the same tools she focused on the general market audience, a touching visual with animals and a single mother with children. To her surprise, she later realized that conservative Catholic Latinos did not appreciate the campaign's single mother lifestyle.

A beer manufacturer using the slogan "The King of Beers" had trouble converting it into Spanish since the word for beer in Spanish, *(la) cerveza*, is feminine. A candy campaign with a celebrity spokesperson resulted in a "misunderstanding" due to the use of a product name, *cajeta*, which is considered objectionable by some Hispanics.

In contrast, Taco Bell encountered success with its marketing and advertising campaign centered around a Mexican themed chihuahua. Marketers for the "Got Milk?" campaign realized a literal translation would be equivalent to asking Spanish-speaking consumers if they were lactating. They adapted the slogan to *"Más Leche, Más Logro"* which in English means "More Milk, More Achievement," an effective idea when approaching Latino moms.

Often the company spokesperson will have to respond to public concerns and media interviews resulting from a campaign or mishap; although the launch, acts or issues of concern may have resulted from somone else's inappropriate positioning or lack of sensitivity to market needs and characteristics.

As these examples illustrate, to be effective and avoid frustrating and costly mistakes, public relations professionals and interviewees should do their homework before addressing the public. There are often cultural, political, socio-demographic, historical, and linguistic issues worth considering. In the same way, Hispanic media training must take into account Latino market nuances to be effective.

This chapter describes the three most important media interview issues and how they relate to each other, the basic elements of a Latino market oriented media training program (including an interview benefit explanation), a brief discussion on crisis management and a summary.

Media and Language

Hispanic oriented media have come a long way in the past two decades. Even industry skeptics have realized the significance and increasing buying power of Latino markets. Latino oriented media now come in many flavors, sizes, competencies and one or two languages. These specialized media outlets are available in English, Spanish or in both. Examples include Spanish language versions of well known magazines such as: *People en Español, Cosmopolitan en Español, Harper's Bazaar en Español;* magazines such as *Vanidades* and *TV y Novelas;* newspapers like *El Nuevo Herald* and *La Opinion;* online websites such as Terra.com, Yahoo *en Español;* television networks such as Telemundo and Univision; and radio networks like Radio Caracol and Spanish Broadcasting System. In English, there are publications including *Vista, Hispanic*, and *Hispanic Business* magazines, online bilingual websites like QuePasa.com; and television programming.

There are many issues relative to Latinos and language. For purposes of this discussion, there are three Hispanic subgroups: Spanish Dominant, English Dominant and Bilingual. Spanish is the preferred language for media for Spanish Dominant Latinos. Given a choice, they will select television, radio, online and print media in Spanish. These Latinos likely are recent immigrants or immigrants who arrived in the U.S. as adults. They cannot, or will not, learn English easily, or they simply prefer Spanish media, its content or style.

English dominant Hispanics will select English language media over Spanish language media, even when the topic is Latino oriented. They immigrated to America as children or are U.S. born. Their Spanish language proficiency is likely poor or weaker than their English language skills. Bilingual Latinos have the ability and alternative of selecting English or Spanish language media options. They are first or second generation Hispanics who have maintained their bilingual skills and enjoy the opportunities and diversity that having access to two languages and cultures provides.

Although there are some bilingual media outlets, most U.S. media broadcast or publish English or Spanish language programs and articles. Latino oriented media outlets target Hispanics in English or Spanish. A small segment of the Latino oriented media reach out in both languages. Mainstream media broadcast and publish, implicitly, in English. A spokesperson conducting an interview in Spanish reaches a Latino audience. Though there are non-Latinos fluent in Spanish who watch, read and listen to Spanish language media, Hispanic media target Hispanics. English language interviews may reach Hispanic or mainstream audiences. Even when reaching a mainstream audience in English, the spokesperson is reaching the English dominant portion of the Latino market that is part of the mainstream audience watching, reading or listening to the interview.

Language alone is no longer enough to identify the audience. Spanish speakers interested in Latino issues, wishing to market to Hispanics or simply to improve their language skills may watch, read or listen to a story in Spanish. English dominant Hispanics are an integral part of the English language mainstream, which means any mainstream interview or story will reach them.

As a result, spokespersons preparing for interviews, whether or not they set out to reach Latino audiences, must be aware that they will inevitably reach a segment of the Hispanic audience. Likewise, they must realize that they may reach a non-Hispanic audience even when the interview is in Spanish. This means any communication, regardless of language, has the potential of reaching a broader audience than may be expected at first glance. Communications professionals and marketers at the forefront of their fields realize the importance of these changes, and encourage their clients to understand and prepare to take advantage of them.

The days of collateral and news release translations as the sole elements of a Latino marketing and communications plan are over. Perceptive professionals are aware of the Latino market and media diversity and cater to it whenever possible. At a minimum, they realize the significance of Hispanic oriented media and its effect on their communications strategies. As a result, they prepare and encourage their spokespersons to be sensitive to the cultural and linguistic nuances of the market and to position their brand, product or service favorably by taking advantage of this knowledge and fine-tuning their interviewing skills.

At the same time, they understand that the interview process requires Hispanic marketing coordination and support. The spokesperson's efforts must be language appropriate and culturally sensitive. Examples of marketing tools supportive of Latino oriented strategies include bilingual and bicultural telemarketing, research, customer service and sales staff; as well as bilingual and bicultural promotional mate-· rials, brochures, sales flyers, instructional manuals and website content.

Three Sides of the Interview Triangle

Though media training sessions vary depending on time, budget, available resources, organization or company policy and goals, past experience and style, to name a few, there are three issues a communicator must always take into account to develop effective Hispanic media training.

- Target audience
- Media outlet
- Spokesperson or expert

A successful interview approach will incorporate a message relevant to how these three elements relate to each other. The speaker and/or communications professional should have an understanding of the target audience, media outlet and spokesperson to define an appropriate audience specific message.

Target Audience

For purposes of this discussion, we divide the audience into a large English speaking mainstream audience and a small Spanish speaking audience. Then we subdivide the mainstream audience into four seg-ments: English speaking (or understanding) Hispanics, General Main-stream, Hispanic Aware Mainstream and Highly Acculturated Hispanics. English speaking Latinos understand or speak English and can read, listen or watch a program or story in English. Mainstream is the middle section representing the general market in English. Hispanic Aware audiences are non-Hispanics with an interest in Hispanic market issues, and may or may not speak Spanish. Highly Acculturated His-panics are English fluent Latinos who are fully integrated into the main-stream (with or without interest in Hispanic market issues).

The Spanish speaking audience is divided into three segments: Spanish Dominant Hispanics, Bilingual Hispanics and Bilingual non-Hispanics. Spanish Dominant Latinos main language is Spanish and they possess limited English skills. The Bilingual Hispanics are fluent enough to listen, read or watch media stories in English or Spanish. Bi-lingual non-Hispanics are individuals who for business or personal rea-sons have an interest in Latino markets and issues, and typically learned Spanish as an additional language. They may watch, read or listen to Latino oriented media.

A well-defined message fits the target audience. This was the case at a major pork association whose executives wanted to target Latino con-sumers with a national campaign. Instead of just launching a translation of their English language materials, the pork association representa-tives learned that Latinos, unlike their mainstream counterparts, were concerned about health related issues. Because they learned in their countries of origin that eating pork that was not fully cooked was dan-gerous and unhealthy, many Latinos were hesitant to cook pork at home. "The other white meat" slogan was irrelevant to Latino women.

The communicators realized that to reach the Hispanic community effectively, in whatever language, the campaign would have to address Latinos' pork related health concerns. The slogan used by the National Pork Board was "El Cerdo es Bueno," Spanish for "pork is good."

It is important to know as much as possible about the target audi-ence. A mainstream audience might consider an interviewee dressed in solid black stylish. Older Latinos may perceive him or her to be in

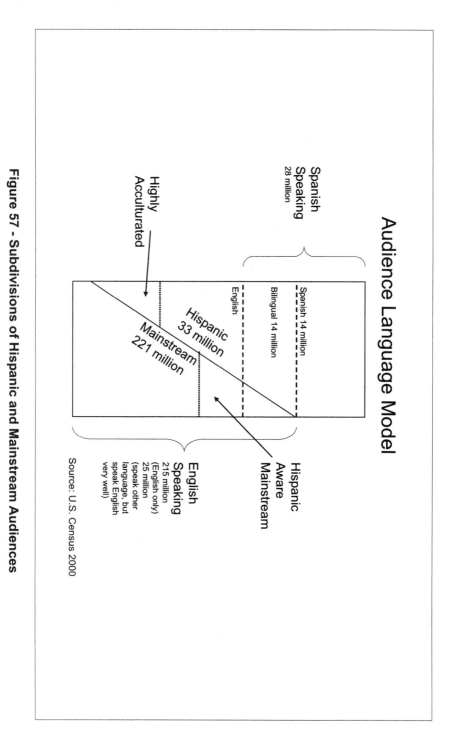

Figure 57 - Subdivisions of Hispanic and Mainstream Audiences

mourning or *luto*. Younger bicultural and bilingual Latinos may have a different perspective.

In Figure 57, we examine the audience for a media campaign involving Hispanic and non-Hispanic or mainstream audiences. This division is somewhat arbitrary, based upon the personal perceptions and cultural background of the audience, and not on any racial boundaries, (i.e. an audience member is Hispanic if they perceive themselves to be Hispanic). Within the audience group, there are also language capability boundaries.

Highly Acculturated Hispanics and Hispanic Aware members of the mainstream audience form the final subdivisions relevant to the audience model. Though the Highly Acculturated Hispanic audience members may consider themselves part of the Hispanic audience, they may not actively follow Hispanic media. The Hispanic Aware members of the mainstream audience monitor the Hispanic market as potential clients, or pay attention to Hispanic issues that might affect a friend or loved one.

According to the U.S. Census, there were 221 million non-Hispanics and 33 million Hispanics in the U.S as of 2000. Of these, 215 million speak English only and 25 million speak another language though they speak English very well. About 28 million Latinos speak Spanish. Of those 14 million speak Spanish only and 14 million are bilingual.

The approximate sizes of several of the key groups in the populations are shown in the figure, based upon the 2000 census. As discussed elsewhere in the book, projections show that the Hispanic population is growing more rapidly than the general population, and the numbers of acculturated and English speaking Hispanics are increasing. The numbers shown in Figure 57 are for the entire U.S.; there are also metropolitan areas where the population ratios are quite different.

Se Habla English

In some instances (for example, breast cancer prevention), targeting Spanish dominant Hispanics is most effective in English. Health care studies of Latino women's attitudes toward family, health and their children indicate many women are willing to overwork themselves to take care of their families. As caretakers, they are likely to forego luxuries and even health care check-ups for themselves, in favor of their family members. Across the country, breast cancer prevention programs encounter enormous challenges. Latinas are not participating in screening programs. There seemed to be no way to convince them to have a regular breast cancer screening.

One breast cancer prevention program approached Latino children through an English language campaign at school. The children went home and asked their mothers to have a breast cancer screening so that they would be around to see them grow up. The campaign was a success.

As this example illustrates, reaching Latinos effectively is about much more than language. A media trained spokesperson will be aware of the importance of cultural understanding in reaching Hispanic audiences. A key to success during an interview depends on the communicator's ability to take the pulse of the community he or she is addressing in order to fine tune the message and delivery. In the long term, a thoughtful, insightful spokesperson who understands his or her audience will garner good will and credibility for the company he or she represents.

Media Outlet

Hispanic media outlets reflect much more than just language. Some Latino programs and publications, for example, are produced and published in English or are bilingual. This does not mean the interviews will be the same as mainstream media interviews or that the interview procedure will be the same as with mainstream or other minority media.

Understanding the media outlet is a first step. Knowing how to deal with and approach the producers and reporters is another.

Figure 58 describes how Spanish language dominant media such as Univision (television, website, radio and cable), Telemundo (website and cable), *El Nuevo Herald* and *La Opinion,* enjoy a significant audience within the U.S. market and abroad. Total audience figures for some of their more popular programs such as *Sabado Gigante,* are

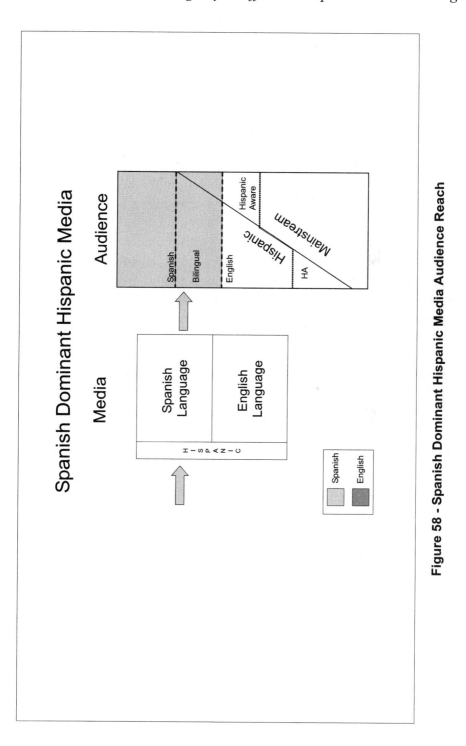

Figure 58 - Spanish Dominant Hispanic Media Audience Reach

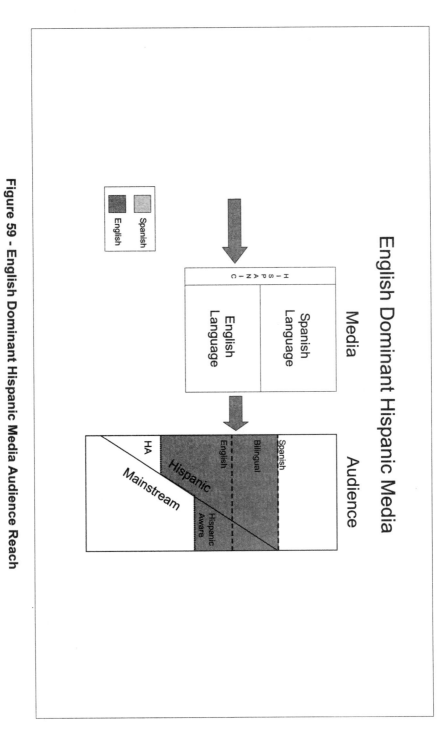

Figure 59 - English Dominant Hispanic Media Audience Reach

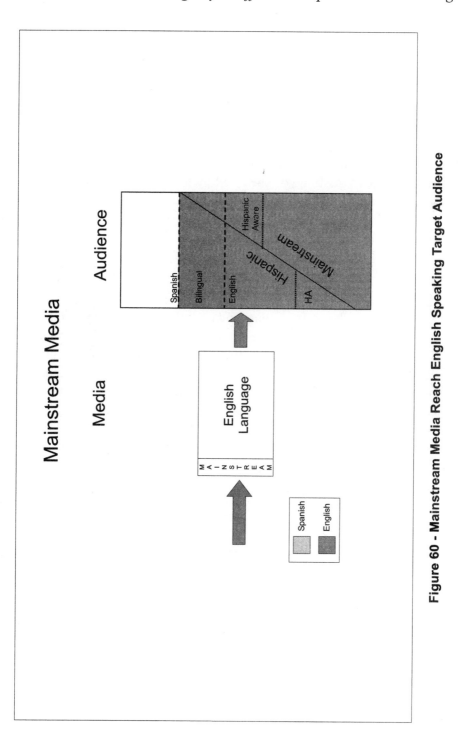

Figure 60 - Mainstream Media Reach English Speaking Target Audience

larger than those of major U.S. mainstream networks (due in part to their large international audience). Working with these outlets requires the communications professional to treat the media representatives as equals to the mainstream outlets; and to develop a cultural understanding and sensitivity appropriate for their programming and production style.

For example, although a reporter for a Spanish dominant media outlet may speak English, he or she is likely to prefer to do interviews in Spanish and receive media releases in Spanish. A reputable and experienced translator with knowledge of universal or generic Spanish should translate these releases; they should be Spanish appropriate for the specific media outlet targeted. In the same way, interviews should respond to the format and needs of the media outlet where they are conducted.

Figure 59 describes English dominant Hispanic media such as *Hispanic*, *Hispanic Business, Latina Style* and *Vista* magazines, who produce their product in print and online. This is likely to change as Hispanic audiences grow and become more acculturated. These outlets produce stories of interest to the Hispanic target audience in English. For the Hispanic Aware mainstream target audience (who often do not speak Spanish), they play a vital role in the flow of information. For public relations professionals trying to expand their markets, these media outlets provide a way to reach a concentrated Hispanic target audience with few language issues.

Traditional mainstream media (Figure 60) reach a significant portion of the Hispanic audience, including the Highly Acculturated who may seldom pay attention to traditional Hispanic media outlets. It behooves the spokesperson to remember that mainstream media interviews also reach a segment of English speaking Latinos. This becomes relevant when preparing a message and interview approach.

Spokesperson

A spokesperson's motivations (or lack of them) to participate in an interview vary depending on the circumstances and the spokesperson. People find themselves in the role of a spokesperson for a variety of reasons. They may be the most qualified experts on the subject in their or-

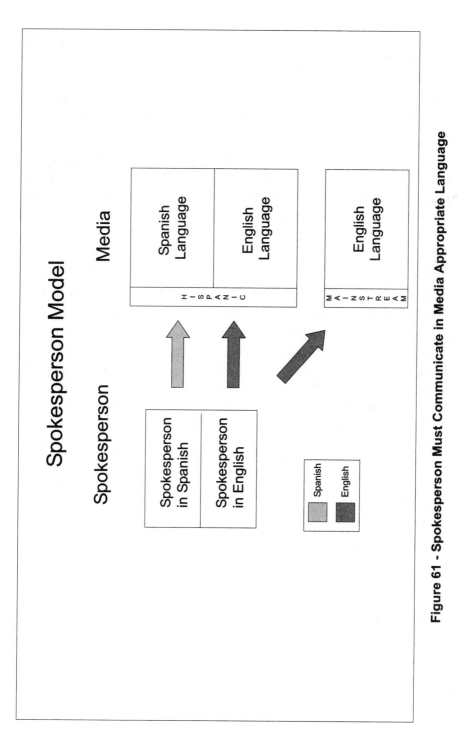

Figure 61 - Spokesperson Must Communicate in Media Appropriate Language

ganization, company or geographic area; they may have the least seniority, which lands them the least desirable task; or they may enjoy being in the spotlight, for example. Whatever an expert's motivation, they will be better off understanding media basics and practicing interviews before they face an actual interview.

Only a relatively small percentage of the overall Latino population is fluent in English and Spanish. Few of those are completely bilingual and bicultural. This means most media-training trainees will strongly favor one language over the other. If they are required to conduct interviews in both languages, they will likely be over anxious about some interviews and their language skills.

In addition to language, Latinos share a common heritage and a number of socio-demographic characteristics. At the same time, Latinos may also be significantly different from each other depending on a number of factors such as age, educational and economic background, location, heritage, profession, and political and religious views. These differences become relevant when attempting to affect their opinions or behavior through media interviews.

A spokesperson or speaker's own background, experiences, heritage, language abilities, knowledge of the topic, familiarity with the company and message points, and familiarity with the media outlet and the audience may affect his or her interview. For example, a Hispanic spokesperson may have cultural insights not held by a non-Hispanic one. Alternatively, a non-Hispanic speaker may be objective and perceived as unbiased. Taking into account the spokesperson's interview "assets" and "liabilities" relative to the topic, media outlet and audience may go a long way toward optimizing the opportunity or crisis.

Composing the Message

When composing the message, consider the spokesperson, the media outlet and the audience, before integrating the individual or company goals and message points. An experienced marketing and communications professional knows the message may vary depending on the spokesperson, the media and target audience. This is particularly true when reaching out to Latino audiences because of cultural, social and ethnic nuances.

Different combinations of these three criteria affect the message, emphasis and possible outcome of an interview. In order to prepare a spokesperson adequately for an interview, it is important for the spokesperson and/or the communications professional to develop an understanding of the possible influencing factors and results. For example, a Hispanic interviewed on a Latino radio station (in Spanish) addressing a Hispanic audience may approach the interview differently than if he or she was being interviewed by a mainstream radio station (in English) and addressing a Latino audience. At the same time, the topic should influence the approach.

To be effective, the speaker and the message should match the audience and media outlet or vehicle through which they convey the message. For example, it is not enough to translate a message and have someone read it on camera. If they do, chances are high that the audience will find the spokesperson emotionally inappropriate, not credible, not knowledgeable or all of the above.

This is true regardless of the spokesperson's background and occupation. Latinos are perfectly capable, unwittingly at times, of offending fellow Latinos. Celebrities can become confused, be unprepared or unwilling to position the product or brand appropriately in the absence of well constructed media training, message point awareness and rehearsals.

In other words, a well-prepared message ill conveyed can have less than desirable consequences. On the other hand, a weak message presented in the most becoming manner can be quite effective. A substantive message well conveyed . . . can move mountains!

Media Models

What does that mean in practical terms? Different experts, media outlets and target audience combinations require different approaches. There are eight main scenarios, which vary depending on three basic factors: Person interviewed, media interviewing them, and the audience's characteristics. The first four involve Hispanic speakers and the last four involve non-Hispanic speakers.

1. Pass Through: a Hispanic expert interviewed by mainstream media with a message targeting a Hispanic audience

2. Acculturated: a Hispanic expert interviewed by mainstream media with a message targeting a general audience

3. Traditional: a Hispanic expert interviewed by Hispanic media with a message targeting a Hispanic audience

4. High Profile Hispanic: a Hispanic expert interviewed by Hispanic media with a message targeting a mainstream audience

5. Expanding Audience: a non-Hispanic or mainstream expert interviewed by mainstream media with a message targeting a Hispanic audience

6. Cultural Sensitivity: a non-Hispanic or mainstream expert interviewed by mainstream media with a message targeting a general audience

7. Public Interest: a non-Hispanic or mainstream expert interviewed by Hispanic media with a message targeting a Hispanic audience

8. High Profile Non-Hispanic or Crisis: a non-Hispanic high profile or celebrity expert interviewed by Hispanic media with a message targeting a mainstream audience

Communications professionals should consider the eight Media Models, the media outlet, the spokesperson and the target audience when drafting, or integrating, message points and preparing the spokesperson's message.

Although the models apply to all media types, visual and auditory impressions are strongest in broadcast media (radio and television). At the same time, broadcast media interviews are by their very nature in one language (there are a few exceptions) while print and online media can be more flexible in this respect. Bilingual or multilingual print and

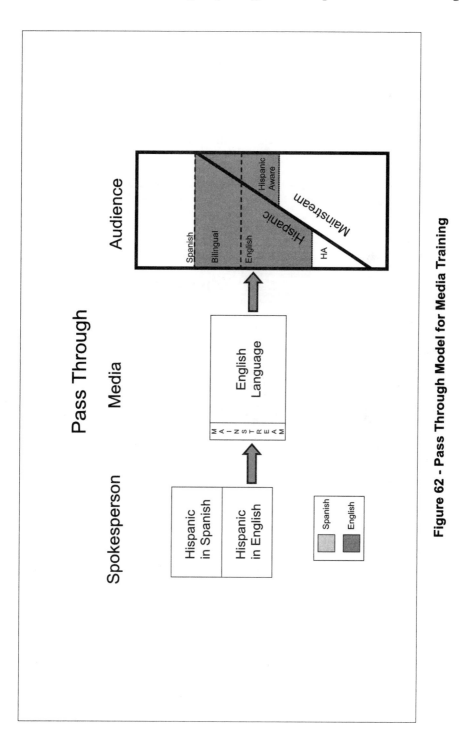

Figure 62 - Pass Through Model for Media Training

online media reporters have the option of interviewing the spokesperson in one or more languages and writing the article in one language.

The audience's visual and auditory impressions of the expert spring from their physical appearance including their race, the way they dress, their make up, hairstyle, and mannerisms. Other features include the way they sound, their voice, their ability to speak the language of the interview, their speech patterns including pronunciation, enunciation and any accent; the way they communicate including body language and the way they emphasize or reject an idea; and how they address the audience and the interviewer or make a point. For all of these reasons, emphasis is on broadcast media in the examples and during the media training sessions. Similar principles apply to print and online media. The interviewee should be aware of and cater to the interviewer's style and the interview requirements whenever possible.

Pass Through

Whenever a Latino expert reaches out to Hispanic communities during a mainstream media interview with a Latino audience message, he or she must convey the message in an effective way without alienating the general audience. The model is depicted in Figure 62.

A Latino physician (endocrinologist) interviewed on a major network about diabetes could mention the risk factors of that disease. One of the risk factors of diabetes is belonging to certain ethnic groups including Latinos. He could briefly draw the attention of Latinos in the general audience and urge them to have diabetes screening, seek a physician or take other relevant measures once they know they are part of a high-risk group. The general audience benefits from the diabetes-oriented interview while the Latino specific message also reaches the Hispanic portion of the general audience watching the interview.

Acculturated

The speaker's demeanor can affect the public's perception. A Hispanic expert interviewed by mainstream media with a general audience message would want to come across in a way compatible with and sensitive to the general population. For example, when addressing a main-

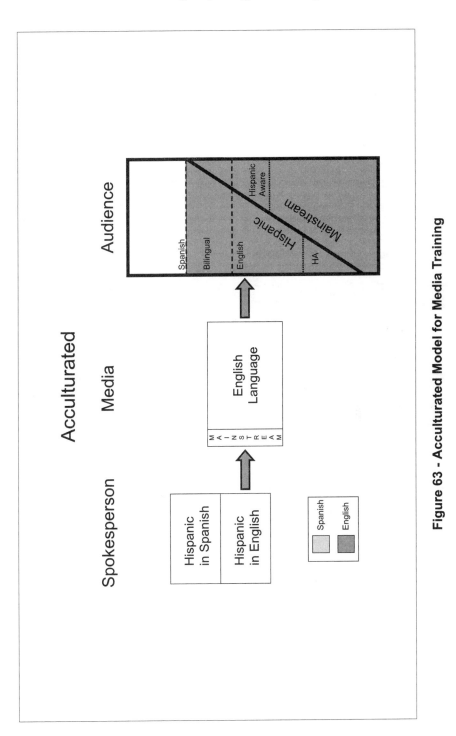

Figure 63 - Acculturated Model for Media Training

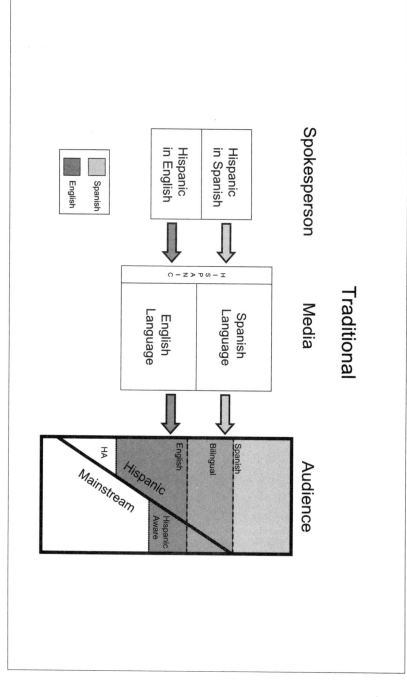

Figure 64 - Traditional Model for Media Training

stream audience with a mainstream message, a speaker would do well to keep use of his or her hands to a minimum. At the same time, facial expressions and emotions should be discreet. Latinos, especially during an interview in Spanish, might perceive this lack of expression as cold and unfeeling. The model is depicted in Figure 63.

A Hispanic corporate executive interviewed in a mainstream program about the initial public offering of his company and its success would likely wish to appeal to the broadest possible audience. He would maximize his chances of achieving that goal if he were culturally sensitive in his message and the way he conveyed it. This would include being sensitive to minority markets including Latinos. Ways to acknowledge market segments could include an item of clothing (e.g. guayabera, lapel pin) or a discreet culturally relevant comment.

Traditional

Most people think of this model when they discuss Hispanic media training. This may also be the easiest model for a Spanish dominant speaker interviewed by Latino media conveying a Hispanic audience message. The larger and more diverse the audience, the more complex the interview becomes. Ideally, the spokesperson will have some knowledge of the media reach and audience characteristics prior to the interview. Effective strategies may include speaking as a member of the group, avoiding slang words whose meaning may vary from one group of Latinos to another, being aware of sensitive cultural issues, and building on commonalities. The model is depicted in Figure 64.

An example of such an interview would be an entertainer supporting a public service campaign (e.g. drunk driving or AIDS) on one of the national Spanish language networks. She may discuss her experiences with the issue and invite the audience to contact the public service agency.

High Profile Hispanic

This model, shown in Figure 65, applies whenever a Latino becomes part of the mainstream by virtue of his or her standing in the overall community. When she communicates with the community, it is with all

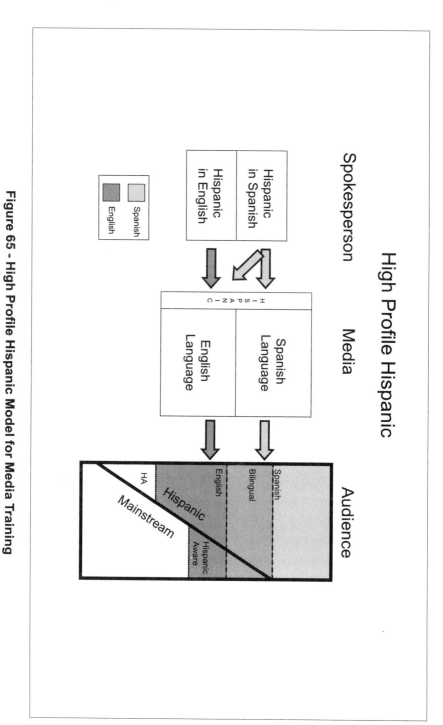

Figure 65 - High Profile Hispanic Model for Media Training

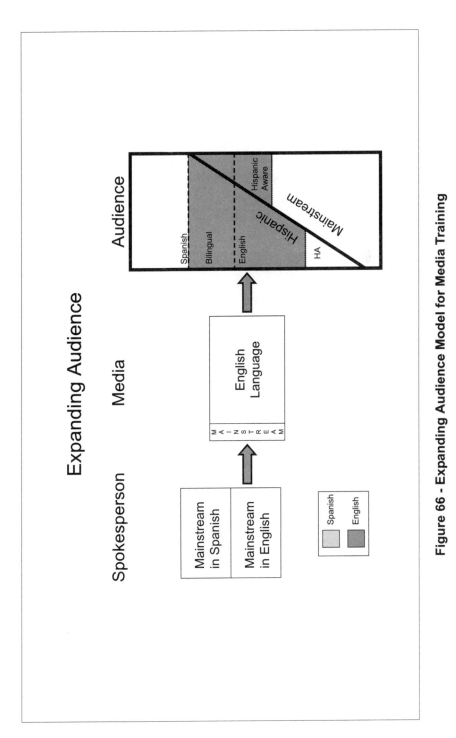

Figure 66 - Expanding Audience Model for Media Training

the members of the community including Latinos. Even during an interview on a Hispanic media outlet, the Latino leader should take into account the issues from the perspective of the general population.

A good example is an elected official such as a mayor or senator. More than one elected official in Hispanic dominant Miami has gotten into political hot water for saying one thing during English language interviews and another on Spanish language ones, especially when the issues affected everyone. A particularity of this model is that if the spokesperson is high profile, but does not speak English, the English dominant Hispanic media are still likely to pick up the story, and add voice-overs or translate the message. This is often the case with politicians, sports figures, actors, singers or other international celebrities.

Expanding Audience

This model, depicted in Figure 66, involves a non-Hispanic expert interviewed by a mainstream media outlet conveying a Hispanic audience message. An example of that might be an education system representative conducting a mainstream interview to discuss high school drop out rates. Historically, Latinos are one of the ethnic groups with the highest drop out rates. The expert could discuss positive measures to reduce Hispanic dropout rates, such as hiring a Spanish language counselor to encourage children to remain in school to increase their overall earning potential instead of leaving to help support the family.

During hurricanes Frances and Jeanne in Florida, some network stations in Palm Beach County broadcast the most critical data in English and then again in Spanish. Normally, Spanish dominant viewers would not tune into these network channels. On this occasion, the around-the-clock coverage was only available through the local English language stations. As a result of their bilingual broadcasting efforts, the networks may have expanded their audience reach and standing in the Hispanic community.

Cultural Sensitivity

Improbable as it may seem, it is possible for a non-Latino expert to bungle, from a Hispanic market perspective, a general market media opportunity while addressing a general audience. A non-Hispanic expert addressing a general audience with a general message can end up on the wrong side of an issue without meaning to if he or she is insensitive to Latino hot buttons. (Note from the model in Figure 67 that a significant portion of the Hispanic audience is tuning into mainstream media).

Such was the case of a *Vanity Fair* columnist who responded to a reader's letter in a way that some Latino readers deemed offensive. Though she was non-Hispanic, writing in a mainstream magazine to a general market audience, there were Latino readers in her audience who found her comments insulting. Because of her remarks, several Latino leaders called for a boycott of the magazine, which in the end may have lost credibility and Hispanic readers.

Public Interest

In this model, shown in Figure 68, Hispanic media interview a non-Hispanic expert on a Latino sensitive or Hispanic oriented topic. This situation often requires the most preparation. The spokesperson would do well to identify his or her audience in advance. It would be good for him or her to know as clearly as possible whom they are addressing including the audience's perspectives on the topic they will discuss. The expert should tailor the message and its delivery around the audience and the speaker's style.

A culturally aware non-Latino spokesperson addressing crime, for example, during a Latino media interview would be aware that public perception of Latinos and crime statistics are challenging subjects among Hispanics. In terms of audience reach, it would be a bonus if the spokesperson were capable of delivering his or her message in Spanish. In terms of impact, ideally the spokesperson would discuss the topic with sensitivity to the issue of Latinos and crime. Advance research, including outreach to community leaders would likely enhance the interview.

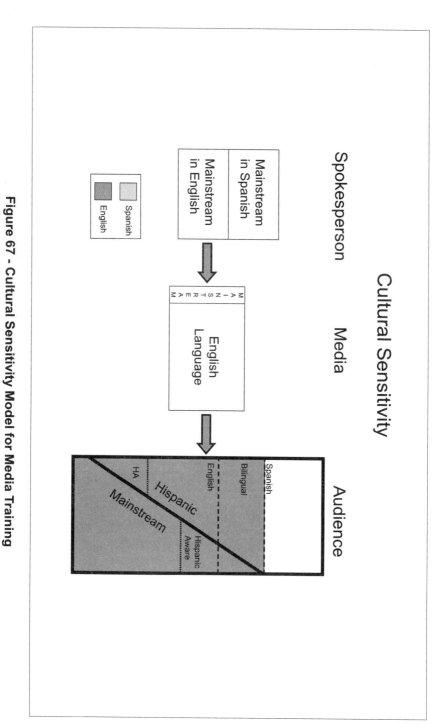

Figure 67 - Cultural Sensitivity Model for Media Training

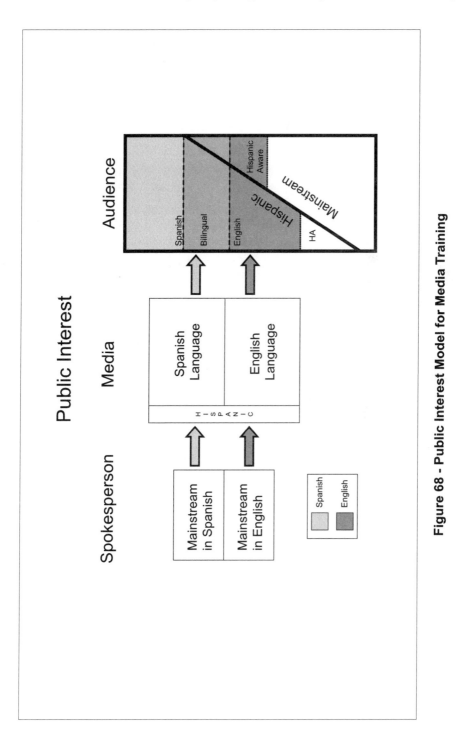

Figure 68 - Public Interest Model for Media Training

High Profile Non-Hispanic or Crisis

Whenever Hispanic media interview a high profile non-Hispanic, he or she needs to be sensitive to market specific issues even if the message is generic. Although the message may be the same for all audience segments, to be effective and credible, the speaker must consider how, when, where and in what way to convey it.

Anti-smoking, diabetes, AIDS, spousal abuse, and accident prevention are examples of topics a high profile non-Hispanic spokesperson may address under this model as depicted in Figure 69. Crisis management cases could involve terrorism alerts, evacuation orders, health warnings, and strike prevention efforts. Any of these scenarios could require a high profile non-Hispanic to address a Latino audience on Hispanic media.

In Florida, for example, Governor Jeb Bush attended press conferences and briefings during the 2004 hurricanes. On more than one occasion, he spoke to the audience in English, and then repeated the same message in Spanish. This gave the Hispanic media the opportunity to broadcast interviews of the governor speaking directly to their audience without a voiceover or translation. These efforts are likely to have long-term benefits when the governor seeks political office in the future. This is another case where the spokesperson or issue is prominent enough that the Spanish language media would consider broadcasting translated versions of an English language message in order to cater to their audience.

Media Training

Thorough media training provides the spokesperson with an understanding of how and why media interviews can be worth their time, describes basic media types, outlines possible interview formats, and conveys the importance of matching the messenger, the medium and the target audience using a well designed and culturally sensitive message.

Although it may seem obvious to the communications professional, the first issue worth considering is the relevance and benefits of a media

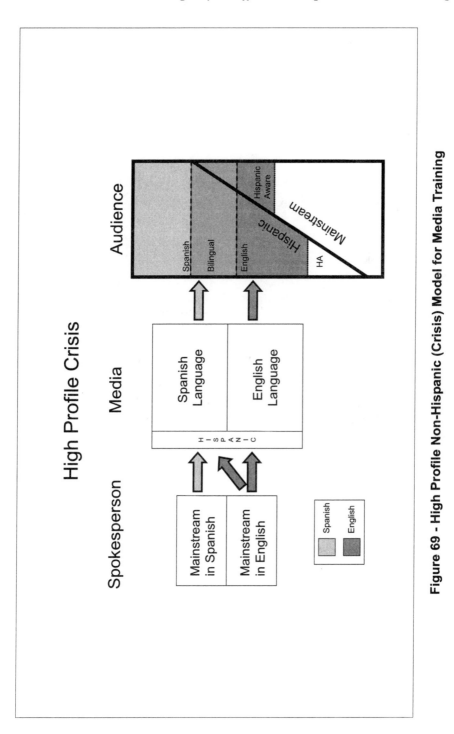

Figure 69 - High Profile Non-Hispanic (Crisis) Model for Media Training

opportunity for the person interviewed. Consider how the interview benefits the spokesperson or expert, and the organization he or she represents. Begin the media training by conveying the possible benefits of accepting an interview. Depending on the circumstances, it may also be worthwhile to explain the possible drawbacks of declining an interview.

This explanation is appropriate in standard or mainstream media training. It is particularly relevant in Hispanic media training. Assume the expert you are training knows little to nothing about marketing, public and media relations and media. Most of the time, a spokesperson will know anywhere from a little to a great deal about these topics. Sometimes he or she will know enough to get into trouble without your guidance.

Just about everyone, regardless of his or her occupation, can benefit from a media training session, especially from the opportunity to practice and rehearse interview tactics. This is particularly the case when addressing Latino audiences which are inherently diverse.

You may ask yourself, "Why explain the obvious?" What may appear obvious to you may be unfamiliar or confusing to someone else. For example, how many times have you heard someone refer to an ad, infomercial or advertorial (ad that looks like editorial copy) as editorial content? Many people think of marketing, public relations and advertising as identical or similar disciplines. At best, they are unclear on the differences between them. At worst, they believe these fields to be the same.

Designated spokespersons may be ambiguous about attending media training and about media interviews in general. Most people, including experienced speakers, are afraid of public speaking. At the same time, media interviews, a new and unfamiliar assignment, may provoke anxiety. Sometimes a company assigns spokesperson duties indiscriminately or to an employee unable to reject them. It is also possible that the individual selected is the best qualified from an expert point of view, although he or she is a poor or mediocre speaker. They may consider media interviews an inconvenience or waste of time. It is also possible that they feel overconfident. This occurs too often when an expert is familiar with the topic though unfamiliar with media training principles and the specific characteristics and expectations of the audience he or she is addressing. These experts tend to rely on their knowledge of the topic and do not prepare or rehearse their presentation and responses. Usually this leads to a weak interview and may affect the expert's (and their company's) image and credibility.

This belief that media training, practicing, reviewing and rehearsing interview techniques is a waste of time is often seen among senior executives, celebrities and media insiders. They mistakenly think that because they are familiar with the material that it will be simple to formulate answers and project a positive image in the high pressure environment of a media interview.

Participants in a Latino oriented training may be self conscious about their communication and language skills, and of how the audience may perceive them, especially if they are noticeably different from the audience they plan to address. Language skills anxiety may be more common than you think.

Monolingual speakers will usually be limited to interviews in one language. An exception is when they are one of few or the sole expert on a topic. A second exception is possible when the reporter is bilingual. The reporter's linguistic ability allows him or her to conduct the interview in the speaker's language and translate it into the audience's language. This is most likely to occur with print or online interviews. Broadcast media only feature a voiceover (translation) or subtitled version of an interview as a last resort.

Spanish speaking non-Latino experts may be self-conscious facing a Latino audience, especially if they have an accent when speaking Spanish. Hispanic speakers may face language issues as well. Second or third generation Latinos will likely be English dominant. They may be self-conscious facing a Latino audience in Spanish, especially if their Spanish is poor or if they have an accent when speaking Spanish.

Recently arrived Latinos are often Spanish dominant. In some cases, their primary language may be a Latin American native tongue. According to the Archive of the indigenous Languages of Latin America of the University of Texas, hundreds of indigenous languages are spoken in Latin America. Examples include various kinds of Quetchuan, Otomanguean and Mayan languages. They may also speak Spanish and some English. English speaking Latino experts may be self-conscious facing an English speaking audience, especially if their English is weak or if they have an accent when speaking English.

In addition to the content of their presentation or the possible responses they may offer during an interview, experts may have other concerns. They may be apprehensive about their appearance, clothing, hair, make-up, weight and countless other issues. At the same time, if the speaker is shy, all of the interview, communication and language skills and anxieties may be aggravated.

Explaining the benefits of media interviews at a professional and corporate level can go a long way in boosting your trainee's enthusiasm, attention and cooperation during the media training. If the spokesperson perceives the interview as an opportunity, rather than a chore, you can often deal effectively with many of the challenges or disadvantages.

Benefits

Benefits vary depending on the speaker, situation, individuals, organization or company, audience and media outlet involved. Most companies are at least somewhat aware of the value of positive public exposure resulting from media stories. Even companies that are only minimally familiar with public relations recognize the potential impact of a media interview and know that editorial coverage can provide or enhance brand awareness, and sometimes stimulate sales.

On the personal and professional level, the speaker usually benefits from the broad exposure of an article, story feature, interview or passing mention. This includes enhanced visibility within the company, and among the spokesperson's colleagues and superiors. This exposure can also provide the expert an opportunity for industry leaders to see him or her in a positive light. If the experts are interested in promotion or advancement opportunities, being able to conduct themselves well during a media interview will usually enhance their marketability. A Spanish speaking non-Hispanic health care professional recently trained in a new medical procedure agreed to be interviewed in Spanish. As a result of the Spanish language interviews, his reputation and desirability for media interviews increased, and his practice attracted new patients.

The media training should convey the potential benefits an interview may offer and how to prepare to increase the likelihood of attaining those benefits. It should also illustrate the potential consequences of ignoring the training guidelines. These can include wasting an opportunity for positive branding and exposure, offending some or all of the audience, and damaging their company's image.

Such was the case of a professional who felt overconfident in his knowledge and skills and refused to participate in available media training. Following his first appearance on a highly rated Spanish language television program, the producers rejected similar appearances because of his poor performance during the original interview.

Setting the Stage

Most public relations professionals would agree: media interviews are about much more than what happens during the interview. The interview process includes several preparatory steps before the interview and some follow-up steps after it. Although the typical media training session lacks the time for a complete discussion on the entire interview process, it behooves the media trainer, and to some extent the spokesperson, to grasp the importance of the pre- and post- interview steps. This is especially true in Latino markets where personal relationships often play a pivotal role in the process.

It is important to explain how producers, reporters, editors and other media representatives behave and what they want from a spokesperson. Once experts learn about media from the interview perspective and what the producer or reporter expects of them, they are better able to decide if a particular media opportunity is appropriate for them or if they are willing to dedicate the time to it. This is especially relevant when the trainees are doctors, middle and executive level professionals or celebrities, an hour of whose time may be worth hundreds of dollars or more.

Often, spokespersons are accustomed to special treatment from their staff, clients, patients and/or the community in general. Although media representatives may address them as experts during an interview, they usually treat them like regular guests when they interview them or when they arrive at a television or radio station. If the interview relates to a sensitive issue, the experts may find themselves in a defensive position, or they may have to dedicate more of their time than they anticipated to the interview process. The better their understanding of the media outlet, interview process and their role as spokespersons or experts in the process, the more likely they are to perform well and feel satisfied with the process and results at the conclusion of the interview. Whenever possible, public relations practitioners should accompany their clients to media interviews to maximize the likelihood of a positive experience and outcome. This is especially the case with Latino oriented media.

Another way to make the spokesperson aware of what to expect is to examine media types including online, broadcast, and print media. Describing interview formats (e.g. news, entertainment, and talk show), and their characteristics, expands the expert's understanding and equips him or her to respond appropriately to the situation.

"What makes Hispanic media training different?" you ask. In some cases, everything. How can Hispanic media training support your efforts to create a successful Hispanic market campaign? By understanding the unique aspects of language, culture and economic issues of this valuable target market, your Hispanic market spokesperson will be more effective and your campaign will likely be more successful.

Think Global, Act Local

Each interview requires an understanding of the particular characteristics of the audience. As the diversification of America continues, it becomes increasingly difficult to create one message to reach everyone effectively. Among U.S. Latinos, this diversification is also a factor. The challenge is that because the market is made up of a number of small groups rather than one single Latino group, there is no one approach or cookie cutter formula. An identical approach could have opposite effects in two different Latino groups. For example, a speaker reaching out to New York Latinos would not necessarily use the same language, media outlet or message as a speaker addressing Los Angeles, El Paso, Chicago or Miami Hispanics. This holds true for a variety of issues from public service announcements to telecommunications, food and beverage, travel and politics.

No single media training, regardless of the language, can address all potential situations and solve all possible problems. It can convey some of the essential issues and challenges to the spokesperson making him or her more effective and sensitive to Hispanic market nuances. It can help him or her avoid the pitfalls of cultural misunderstandings and improve the chances of success of their company's Hispanic market campaign. It can help pave the way for fruitful and beneficial relationship building and many positive interviews in the future.

Crisis Management

For purposes of this discussion, remember that just as regular interviews are categorized taking into account the spokesperson, media outlet and audience, crisis management requires a similar analysis and much closer inspection.

Set aside resources for your crisis management plans. These should be separate from other public relations, marketing, communications and advertising resources. Include time and funds to identify, train, meet with, prepare and maintain materials, rehearse, video and audio record and playback these materials with multiple teams. Make sure your budget includes funds for third party experts and post crisis analysis and damage control.

If possible, make sure each authorized spokesperson has undergone extensive media training. Be sensitive to cultural, community and linguistic issues. As with other communications crises, it is best to prepare in advance. Identify designated spokespersons and a specific communications procedure in advance. That way, even if the precise issue is unexpected, the organization and individuals responsible will be prepared and equipped to respond.

Maintain Hispanic market sensitive general organization, corporate or individual message points available in English and Spanish on an on-going basis. Review and revise these at least once a year, more often if possible and necessary. Make sure everyone authorized as a spokesperson and decision makers in the crisis management process have current copies of the message points in both languages, even if they are monolingual. In the event of a crisis or unanticipated event, the spokesperson or decision maker will be able to provide culturally sensitive "in language" information in writing to a newly designated spokesperson and/or to media representatives in a timely fashion. Facilitating information access to media can go a long way toward diffusing a charged situation. Facilitating information "in language" can help establish goodwill and open lines of communication.

In advance of the crisis, develop a process to prepare appropriate message points in response to the relevant issues when they arise. Include a step to consider the implications of the issues to Hispanic audiences and to the specific Latino audiences the crisis is likely to affect, especially those in your target audience and client base. Identify potential in-house and external sources and experts to consult. Include one or more Latino market experts on your list. They will be in touch with the wants, needs and concerns of the communities you may know little or nothing about and wish to reach effectively. Make sure they are included in your outreach and response efforts if appropriate.

Whenever possible and appropriate, make a bicultural and bilingual spokesperson available for interviews. Make sure that spokesperson is Hispanic media trained and understands the issues and their relevance to the Latino audience. It is important that the chosen spokesperson be senior enough and topic appropriate to address the crisis. You want the Latino audience to perceive that they are deserving of the same attention by senior management via the spokesperson as the mainstream market. Offering a spokesperson who is too junior or not knowledgeable enough about the issues could be insulting and have the opposite effect of the one desired. Having a bicultural and bilingual spokesperson available at the same time as the mainstream spokesperson is important. Usually the deadlines and time lines for English and Spanish language media are similar or identical, especially during a crisis. The Spanish language or Hispanic oriented media representatives will be prompted by similar time constraints as everyone else, yet there will probably be fewer spokespersons available. Making someone from your company available may position you well; depending on the circumstances, this may assist you in converting a challenging situation into a favorable one.

If time allows, conduct a bilingual and bicultural practice or mock interview session. Include built-in internal and external feedback features whenever possible. These sessions will provide the experts an opportunity to practice in a realistic setting. The feedback will provide the communications crisis team an idea of the likely public response and reaction to the message points and interviews.

Identify Latino market opportunities within the crisis. Dealing with, and overcoming, difficult situations often provides relationship building and strengthening opportunities with colleagues, competitors, media representatives, stockholders, clients and the public. Being aware of the potential of those opportunities and encouraging them may benefit the participants in the future.

Anticipate specific Hispanic market weaknesses in your program or ability to respond, as well as organizations and individuals likely to oppose you and your issues. It is much easier to identify ways to counter their arguments with the cold head of advance planning than during the crisis. Identify the key concerns relevant to opposite points of view and ways to respond effectively to their concerns in a culturally sensitive and substantive manner.

Once the crisis has passed, obtain copies of interviews, request feedback from all the participants and analyze the results. Recognize positive aspects and commend those who excelled in their roles and duties. Identify negative aspects or areas needing improvement and develop a plan and time line to follow up. Translate and analyze Latino market stories in both languages in order to minimize damages while learning from, and capitalizing on successes.

A New York public relations practitioner reached out to Hispanic Market experts across the country during a crisis. After explaining the situation, she requested their unbiased opinions and asked if they would be willing to respond to media queries on the topic. This immediate response satisfied her client. The crisis dissipated before any interviews were necessary.

Chapter Summary

- There are three key aspects of Hispanic media training especially worth dwelling on: the spokesperson or expert, the media outlet and the audience.
- A successful interview approach incorporates a message relevant to how these three elements relate to each other.
- The message varies depending on the messenger, the media and the target audience.
- Similarities and differences become relevant when attempting to affect audience member's opinions or behavior through media interviews.
- The speaker and the message should be sensitive to the audience and the vehicle through which they convey the message.
- It behooves the media trainer and the spokesperson to grasp the importance of the pre- and post- interview process.
- Understanding Hispanic media means realizing it is about much more than Spanish.
- It is important to know as much as possible about the media outlet and target audience.
- Different experts, media outlets and target audience combinations require different approaches.
- There are eight main scenarios, which vary depending on three basic factors: spokesperson interviewed, media where they are interviewed, and the audience's characteristics.
- Media training provides the spokesperson with an understanding of how and why media interviews are worthwhile; describes basic media types; outlines interview formats; and conveys the importance of matching the messenger, the medium and the target audience.
- Assume the expert you are training knows little about marketing, public and media relations, and media.
- Designated spokespersons may be ambiguous about attending media training and media interviews.

- Language skills anxiety is common.
- Experts are often concerned about their appearance.
- Explaining media training benefits improves your trainee's enthusiasm, attention and cooperation during the media training.
- Editorial coverage can provide or enhance brand awareness, and stimulate sales.
- The speaker usually benefits from the broad exposure of an article, story feature, or interview.
- During a crisis, consider the spokesperson, the audience and the media involved.
- Define a separate budget and strategy for crisis management in advance of a crisis.
- Maintain bilingual and culturally sensitive crisis materials up to date and available year round.
- Develop crisis management procedures in advance of a crisis.
- Make sure you include Latino leader input before, during and after a crisis develops.
- If possible, include a Hispanic spokesperson in your crisis team.
- Look for opportunities to reverse a challenging or difficult situation.
- After a crisis, make sure to assess results and learn from the experience.

About the Author

Elena del Valle, M.B.A., J.D., President, LNA World Communications

Elena del Valle, who has 20 years of experience in Hispanic marketing and public relations, is president of LNA World Communications, where she is responsible for media training, strategic planning and client relations. She is a graduate of the University of Miami with a Master in Business Administration and a Juris Doctor.

Bibliography

Chapter 2 Sources

Acuna, R. (1988). *Occupied America: A history of Chicanos, 3rd ed.* NY: Harper and Row.

Anzaldua, G. (1987). *Borderlands: The new mestiza.* San Francisco, CA: Spinsters/Aunt Lute.

Bonilla, Melendez, Morales, Torres (1998). *Borderless Borders: U.S. Latinos, Latin Americans, and the paradox of interdependence.* Philadelphia, PA: Temple.

Chideya, F. (1999). *The color of our future.* NY: William Morrow.

Cortese, A. (1999). *Provocateur: Images of women and minorities in advertising.* NY: Rowman and Littlefield.

Fernandez, C. A. (1992). *La raza and the melting pot: A comparative look at multiethnicity.* In Root, M. P. (Ed.), *Racially mixed people in America* (pp.126-143). Thousand Oaks, CA: Sage.

Gutierrez, D.G. (1995). *Walls and mirrors: Mexican Americans, Mexican Immigrants, and the politics of ethnicity.* Berkeley, CA: University of California.

Halter, M. (2000). *Shopping for identity: The marketing of ethnicity.* NY: Schocken.

Hero, R. E. (1992). *Latinos and the U.S. political system: Two-tiered pluralism.* Philadelphia, PA: Temple

Morales, R. and Bonilla, F. (1993). *Latinos in a changing U.S. economy.* Thousand Oaks: Sage.

Marin, G. and Marin, B.V. (1991). *Research with Hispanic Populations*. Newbury Park, CA: Sage.

Oboler, S. (1995). *Ethnic labels, Latino lives: Identity and the politics of (re)presentation in the United States*. MN: University of Minnesota.

Parillo, V. (1995). *Diversity in America*. Thousand Oaks, CA: Pine Forge Press.

Portes, A. and Bach, R.L. (1985). *Latin journey: Cuban and Mexican Immigrants in the United States*. Berkeley: University of California.

Rios, D. I. & Gaines, S. O. (1998). Latino media use for cultural maintenance. *Journalism and Mass Communication Quarterly*, 5, 4, 746-761.

Rios, D. I. & Gaines, S. O. (1997). Impact of gender and ethnic subgroup membership on Mexican Americans' purposive media use for cultural maintenance. *Howard Journal of Communications*, 8, 2, 197-216.

Rios, D. and Mohamed, A. (Eds.) (2003). Brown and Black communication. Latino and African American conflict and convergence in mass media. Westport, CT: Praeger.

Rodriguez, C. E. and Sanchez-Korrol, V. (1980). *Historical perspectives on Puerto Rican survival in the United States*. Princeton, NJ: Markus Weiner.

Schreiber, A. L. (2001). *Multicultural marketing: Selling to the new America*. Chicago: NCT.

Subervi-Vélez, F.A. (1986). The mass media and ethnic assimilation and pluralism: A review and research proposal with special focus on Hispanics. *Communication Research*, *13*(1), 71-96.

Suro, R. (1998). *Strangers among us: Latino lives in a changing America*. NY: Vintage.

Tharp, M.C. (2001) *Marketing and consumer identity in multicultural America*. Thousand Oaks, CA: Sage.

Thernstrom, S. (Ed.) (1980) *Harvard encyclopedia of American ethnic groups*. Cambridge, MA: Harvard.

U.S. Census Bureau. (March 2000, Internet Release). Population profile of the United States. Our diverse population: Race and Hispanic origin, 2000.

Vargas, J. A. G. (1996). A case study of Hollywood's constructed Puertorriqueña identity. *Studies in Latin American Popular Culture*, 15, 2-19.

Wilson, C., Gutierrez, F., and Chao, L. (2003). *Racism, sexism, and the media: The rise of class communication in multicultural America*. Thousand Oaks, CA: Sage.

Woods, G. B. (1995). *Advertising and marketing to the new majority*. Belmont, CA: Wadsworth.

Chapter 5 Sources

Campbell, Paul R., 1996, *Population Projections for States by Age, Sex, Race and Hispanic Origin: 1995 to 2025*, U.S. Bureau of the Census, Population Division, PPL-47.

United States Bureau of the Census. *Population Projections by age, sex, race, and Hispanic origin: 1995 to 2050; 1999 to 2100*.

The Rise of the Second Generation: Changing Patterns in Hispanic Population Growth [Study; October 14, 2003; Suro (PHC) and Passel (Urban Institute)]

Latino Growth in Metropolitan America: Changing Patterns, New Locations [Report; July 30, 2002; Suro (PHC) and Singer (Brookings Institution Center on Urban and Metropolitan Policy)]

U.S. Born Hispanics Increasingly Drive Population Developments [Fact Sheet; PHC; January 2002)]

Humphreys, Jeffrey M. *"The multicultural economy 2003: America's minority buying power,"* Selig Center for Economic Growth, Terry College of Business, The University of Georgia (2003).

Ramos, Jorge. *The Other Face of America.* HarperCollins: 2002.

Barone, Michael. *The New Americans.* Regnery Publishing: 2001.

Emerging Communities: A Snapshot of a Growing Hispanic America. 2003: League of United Latin American Citizens (LULAC).

LatinWorks newsletter (Austin, TX).

Growth Strategies newsletter (Santa Monica, CA).

Chapter 15 Sources

Anders, Gigi (September 2004). American Idol Why Are Latinos Hooked. *Hispanic.*

Ayala, Nancy (December 2004). How Many Is Too Many? New Titles Ready for 2005. *Marketing y Medios.*

Baier, Angela (October 2003). Reaching the Hispanic Market. *American Zoological Association Publications.* http://www.aza.org/Publications/2003/10/Oct03Hisp.pdf

Brass, Kevin (December 2004). Turning up the Volume. *Hispanic Business.*

Cox, John and Limon, Anthony (November 2004). Captivating Their Audience. *Hispanic Business.*

Butler, Sana (March 2005). Finding The Right Word Is Key To Your Message. *Marketing y Medios.*

Coombes, Andrea (February 2, 2004). Foreign-language fluency increasingly important. CBS MarketWatch/*The Miami Herald*.

Crowe Deborah (December 2004).Tuning In. *Hispanic Business*.

Erichsen, Gerald (March 9, 2005). Hershey ad wasn't intended to be risqué. Spanish.about.com. http://spanish.about.com/b/a/152378.htm

Erichsen, Gerald. The Chevy Nova That Didn't Go. (March 2005). Spanish.about.com. http://spanish.about.com/cs/culture/a/chevy_nova.htm?once=true&

ElCerdoesBueno.com http://www.elcerdoesbueno.com

Fonseca, Felicia (May 6, 2004). Ads cause groups temperature to rise. *Daily Lobo University of New Mexico*.

Herbig, Paul. International Marketing Lecture Series Session 2: Culture. (March 2004). http://www.geocities.com/Athens/Delphi/9158/kwuintlmktg2.html

Hessekiel, David (Winter 2004). Hispanic Cause Marketing: Poised for Growth. *InterAccion*. http://www.hmca.org/ia011005.htm

HispanicMedia100.org http://www.hispanicmedia100.org/

Hoag, Christina (May 7, 2003). Luring viewers en español. *The Miami Herald*.

Goodstein, Anastasia. (January 3, 2005). Teens Take on Tecate. Ypulse.com. http://ypulse.com/archives/2005/01/teens_take_on_t.php

Jordan, Miriam (March 7, 2004). Ads surge in Hispanic magazines. *The Wall Street Journal*/*The Palm Beach Post*.

Lee-St. John, Jeninne (March 28, 2005) Selling in Spanglish. Time.com http://www.time.com/time/business/article/0,8599,1042547,00.html

MSN Groups Liberal Arts Business Fiascos
http://groups.msn.com/liberalarts/businessfiascoes.msnw

National Pork Board http://www.porkboard.org

Navarro, Mireya (May 22, 2003). Media Business Advertising. The
New York Times. *Urban Latino.*
http://www.urbanlatino.com/press/nyt_052203.html

Norma Niurka (April 21, 2003). Why Hispanics are called Latinos,
albeit incorrectly. *The Miami Herald.*

Patsuris, Penelope (June 12, 2002). Hispanic Media Soars.
Forbes.com. http://www.forbes.com/2002/06/12/0612univision.html

Pretter, Yitzie. (Spring 2002). Culture and Ethnicity in Consumer Decision Making. *The Tabs Journal* Touro College Accounting and
Business Society. http://www.touro.edu/tabs/journal02/tabs18c.pdf

Russell, Joel. (December 2004). The Press in Print. *Hispanic Business.*

Russell, Joel. (July/August 2004). Cable: The New Frontier. *Hispanic
Business.*

U.S. Census Bureau, http://www.census.gov/

Webmaster (February 19, 2005). Heard and overheard III 2005 Best
of Newspaper Design Society for News Design, Judging Journal
http://snd.org/competitions/2005/2005/02/heard-and-over-
heard-iii.html

(April/May 2005). Spanish-language ads and publications, vehicles of
choice for blue-chip advertisers *Portada.*

(April/May 2005). Does minority ownership matter? *Portada.*

(March 13, 2005). Will Hershey Cajeta Elegancita 'dulce de leche' Succeed? Ahorre.com. http://www.ahorre.com/blog/archives/2005/03/will_hershey_ca_2.html

(March 2005). Allied Media Corp. Ethnic Publications. Allied-Media.com http://www.allied-media.com/Publications/hispanic-publications.htm

(December 31, 2004). About The Latino Market A Changing America: How Three Companies Are Catering to Latino Market. Ahorre.com. http://www.ahorre.com/archives/2005/12/about_the_latin.html

(August 9, 2004). Spanish radio plays evolving role in politics.*The Miami Herald/The Palm Beach Post.*

(July 2004). Newspaper giants set off the race to reach Hispanics. *Portada.*

(December 2003). A House Divided. *Hispanic Business.*

(December 2003). Language of the Middle Class. *Hispanic Business.*

(September 19, 2003). Lost In Translation: Language Blunders Can Sully Ad Efforts. *The Wall Street Journal Europe.* TransPerfect Translations http://www.transperfect.com/tp/eng/wsj.europe0919.html

Index

A

abuelas 369

accents 36, 149, 176 - 177, 179

acculturated 22, 42 - 44, 143, 145, 155, 162, 164 - 165, 310, 312, 376, 383, 388, 394

Acculturated 8, 310, 392

acculturation 1, 7 - 8, 10, 21 - 22, 26, 42 - 44, 85, 147, 150 - 151, 153 - 167, 199, 230, 246, 248

Acculturation 19, 153, 155 - 157, 159, 161, 163, 165, 167

acculturation issues 41

acculturation segments 21

actuality 345

Adapters 86, 95, 100 - 102, 107

AdTrack 71

advertising agencies 71, 172, 197, 204, 230, 244, 250 - 253, 265 - 266, 269, 276, 280 - 281

Advertising agencies 203

agriculture 14

Aguilera, Cristina 67, 352

AHAA 126 - 127, 133, 223, 225, 244 - 245, 248, 265, 279, 281, 314 - 315

airings 339

AJ Lamas 68

ajiaco 56

Al Día 302, 304

Alazraqui, Carlos 70

Alertanet.org 58

Allen, Derene 85, 114

Allied Business Intelligence 189

ALMA 68

American Family 68

American Latino TV 313

American Multicultural Marketing 260

Amigo Broadcasting 295

ancorman 135

animation 338 - 339

ANR 335, 344 - 346, 349

antibaby 135

AOL/RoperASW Hispanic CyberStudy 207

Arboleda, Maria Eugenia 59

Architectural Digest en español 307

arepa 56, 72

Argentines 57

Arizona 132

Arnaz, Desi 51

Ashton, Jonathan R. 1, 27

Asian Diaspora 58

assimilation 7 - 8, 42 - 44, 135 - 136, 138, 153 - 158

Association of Hispanic Advertising Agencies 126, 179, 199, 234, 244, 265, 278 - 279, 314

Athens Banner-Herald 179

audience figure 339, 348, 384

audio feed 343

audio news release 360, 363

Audio News Release 335, 344

Audit Bureau of Circulation 300 - 301

ayacas 56

Azocar, Patricio Aylwin 80

Azteca America 297, 331

B

Babalu 51

Babies'R'Us 125

backtranslation 186 - 187

Balearic Islands 60

Ball, Lucille 51

Banderas, Antonio 50

Bank of America 132 - 133, 227

banking 131 - 132, 184, 187, 221, 223 - 224, 227, 352

Banzer, Hugo 80

Barr, Roseanne 68

barrios 73

Basque 60

425

427

429

431

 Poyeen Publishing

www.poyeen.com

To obtain additional copies of *Hispanic Marketing & Public Relations* , visit your local retailer or order direct from the publisher.

 Fax and ✆ telephone orders: 1 (561) 892-0494

📠 Email orders: sales@poyeen.com

✉ Postal Orders:

Poyeen Publishing Sales, 2901 Clint Moore Road #265, Boca Raton, Florida, 33496 U.S.A.

Please include the following information with your order:

- Name
- Address
- City
- State (if appropriate)
- Postal Code
- Country
- Email address
- Method of payment (checks and all major credit cards accepted)

Indicate if you would like additional information on any of the following topics:

● Book updates   ● Other Titles   ● Seminars/Presentations

The retail price for each book is $49.95. (Florida residents, please include 6% sales tax). Include shipping costs as shown below:

Air Mail	Media Mail
U.S.: Add $6.00 for one book, $4.00 for each additional book	**U.S.:** Add $3 for one book, $2 for each additional book
International: Contact us	**International:** $10 per book

Call us or visit our website for further details. Remember to order copies for your friends and associates!